AN UNCOMMON HANGMAN

RACHEL FRANKS holds PhDs in Australian crime fiction from Central Queensland University and true crime texts from the University of Sydney. A qualified educator and librarian, her work on crime fiction, true crime, popular culture and information science has been presented at numerous conferences as well as on radio and television. She is an award-winning writer whose research can be found in a wide variety of books, journals, magazines and online resourc[illegible]

'Riveting, startling and brimming with powerful insights. With meticulous research and an unflinching eye, Rachel Franks brilliantly recovers the story of the most unpopular man in NSW, and the stories of the condemned people he hanged. Through this deeply human story of Robert 'Nosey Bob' Howard, and the Faustian pact he made with the authorities to make a living, she lays bare the grotesque hypocrisies of judicial hanging. "The act of hanging is an act of brutality" writes Franks. I defy anyone who reads this book to disagree.'

Emeritus Professor Grace Karskens, author of *The Colony: A History of Early Sydney*

'Franks displays wit, writerly sensitivity and a scholar's rigour, methodically revealing modes of crime and punishment, and entire ways of living and dying, in colonial Australia. She does this via an examination of the life of a plain, simple, everyday hangman. Who happens to be without a nose. What's not to like?'

Dr Peter Doyle, author of *Crooks Like Us*

'A bold and brutal biography of NSW's longest-serving executioner. Franks weaves a compelling and compassionate narrative of one man's life, told through the deaths of condemned criminals. Fearless in its detail, Franks' prose has a light touch on this dark subject matter. Through the man we contemplate the history of capital punishment, law and order, and colonial social mores, making this a vital contribution to death studies in Australia.'

Dr Lisa Murray, author of *Sydney Cemeteries: A Field Guide*

'Rachel Franks' account is lively and humane, and her narrative unfolds with warmth and curiosity. Rich with gruesome detail and resonant with Franks' noir humour, she has a keen ear for colonial administration's little bureaucratic absurdities. She lays out a colony awash with violent crime, and with scant evidence of mercy. Despite its brutal realities, her book is never grim nor prurient. Her exhaustive research, relying on fragmentary records, is apparent throughout this deft and tightly written narrative, which also illuminates the slow and bloody process by which the death penalty was finally abolished.'

Professor Katherine Biber, author of *In Crime's Archive: The Cultural Afterlife of Evidence*

'A gruesome story told in unsparing words. Someone had to be a hangman in colonial NSW. Rachel Franks reveals the real and living person who sent the condemned to their deaths.'

Rodney Cavalier AO, author of *Power Crisis: The Self-Destruction of a State Labor Party*

'Utilising an average 8-foot drop and a well-oiled manila rope knotted so as to fracture the second cervical vertebra, Bob Howard executed sixty-two people in NSW between 1876 and 1904. In fast-paced forensic detail leavened with gallows humour, Rachel Franks casts a fascinating and sympathetic light on this so-called "finisher of the law" and his "patients".'

Andrew Tink AM, author of *William Charles Wentworth: Australia's Greatest Native Son*

'A gripping, forensic history of one man, his "clients" and the bureaucracy of punishment that he served. Tautly written and humane, *An Uncommon Hangman* exposes the contradictions in the machinery of state morality by asking: what kind of person kills for a living, and how does society treat them for doing its dirty work?'

Dr Alexandra Roginski, author of *The Hanged Man and the Body Thief: Finding Lives in a Museum Mystery*

AN
UNCOMMON
HANGMAN

THE LIFE AND DEATHS OF
ROBERT 'NOSEY BOB' HOWARD

RACHEL FRANKS

NEWSOUTH

A NewSouth book

Published by
NewSouth Publishing
University of New South Wales Press Ltd
University of New South Wales
Sydney NSW 2052
AUSTRALIA
https://unsw.press/

A catalogue record for this book is available from the National Library of Australia

ISBN   9781742237343 (paperback)
          9781742238401 (ebook)
          9781742239309 (ePDF)

Cover design Philip Campbell Design
Cover image Nosey Bob, as featured in *Truth*, 20 January 1901, p. 5. Paper background from Darlinghurst Gaol Ground Plan, 1890, WL Vernon, Government Printing Office, State Library of NSW, 89/457
Internal design Josephine Pajor-Markus

CONTENTS

LIST OF ILLUSTRATIONS

CONVERSIONS

1 mile ≈ 1.61 kilometres
1 foot ≈ 0.30 metres
1 inch ≈ 2.54 centimetres
1 foot pound ≈ 1.36 newton metres
1 stone ≈ 6.35 kilograms
1 pound ≈ 0.45 kilogram

Currency conversions from 1901 to 2020
£1 (pound) ≈ $157.10
1s (shilling) ≈ $7.85
1d (pence) ≈ 0.65¢

ABBREVIATIONS

CSNSW	Corrective Services New South Wales (Cooma & Sydney)
GROEW	General Register Office, England and Wales (London)
NAA	National Archives of Australia (Canberra)
NSWBDM	New South Wales Births, Deaths and Marriages (Sydney)
NSWSA	New South Wales State Archives (Sydney)
PROV	Public Record Office Victoria (Melbourne)
QSA	Queensland State Archives (Brisbane)
RBDB	Register of Births in the District of Brisbane (Brisbane)
SCV	Supreme Court of Victoria (Melbourne)
SLNSW	State Library of New South Wales (Sydney)
SLV	State Library of Victoria (Melbourne)
TNA	The National Archives of the United Kingdom (Kew)
WLLSC	Waverley Library Local Studies Collection (Sydney)

THE COMMON HANGMAN

FIGURE 1 The common hangman

SOURCE *Bulletin*, 31 January 1880, p. 4

Some terms for being executed: cast off, hanged, danced on air, dispatched, executed, operated on, passed into eternity, put through, putting 'em off, scragged, seen off, send off, sent into eternity, sent off, suffered the final act of the law, swing off, turned off, worked off.

Some terms for the executee: client, condemned, criminal, culprit, felon, patient, prisoner, unfortunate man or woman, unhappy man or woman, victim of the law.

Some terms for the executioner: Bull (after a 16th-century English executioner), William Calcraft (after an 18th-century English executioner), chief executive officer, choker, common hangman, doomsman, dropper, finisher of the law, hangman, Jack Ketch (after a 17th-century English executioner), man finisher, neck stretcher, public executioner, rope-and-trap artist, scragger, scragman, sheriff's journeyman.

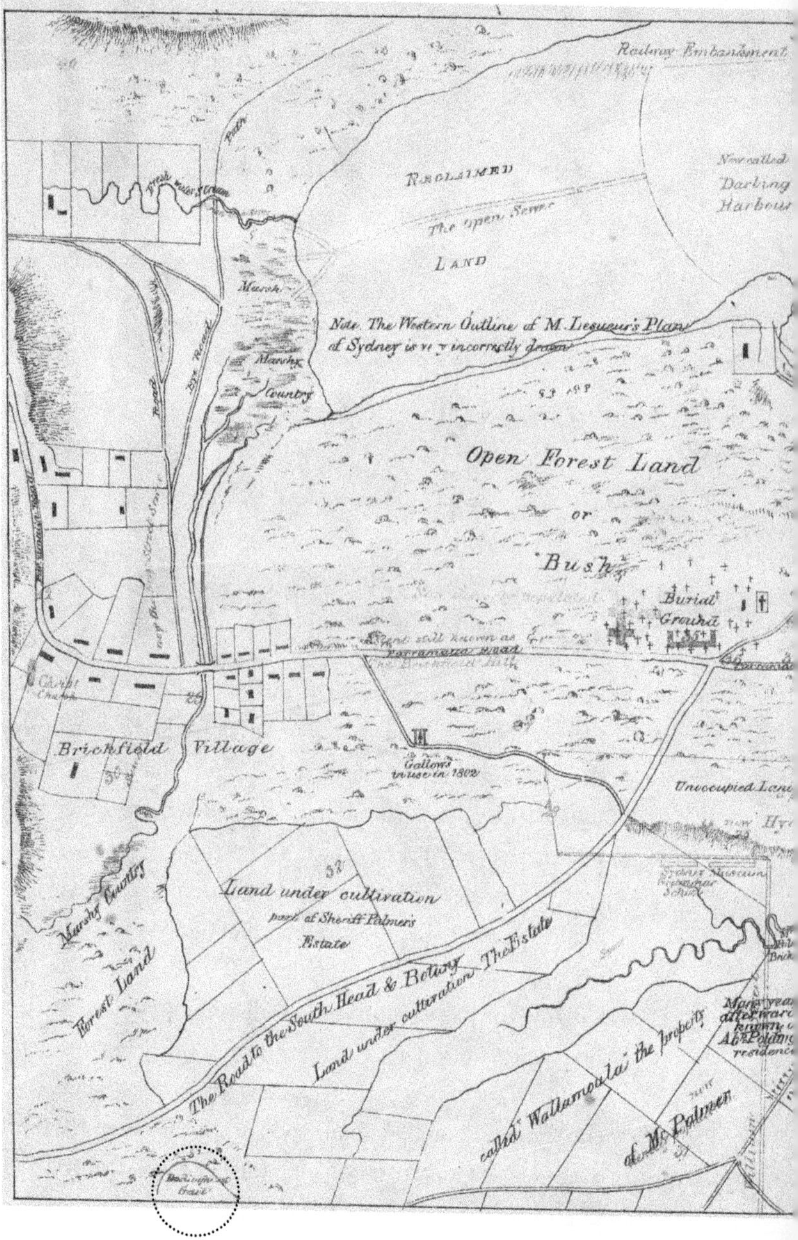
Railway Embankment
Now called
Darling
Harbour
Reclaimed
The open Sewer
Land
Fresh water Stream
Path
Marsh
Marshy
Country
Note. The Western Outline of M. Lesueur's Plan of Sydney is very incorrectly drawn
Open Forest Land
or
Bush
Burial
Ground
Parramatta Road
Brickfield Village
Gallows
in use in 1802
Unoccupied Land
Land under cultivation
part of Sheriff Palmer's
Estate
Marshy Country
Forest Land
The Road to the South Head & Botany
Land under cultivation The Estate
called Wallamoula the property
of Mr. Palmer

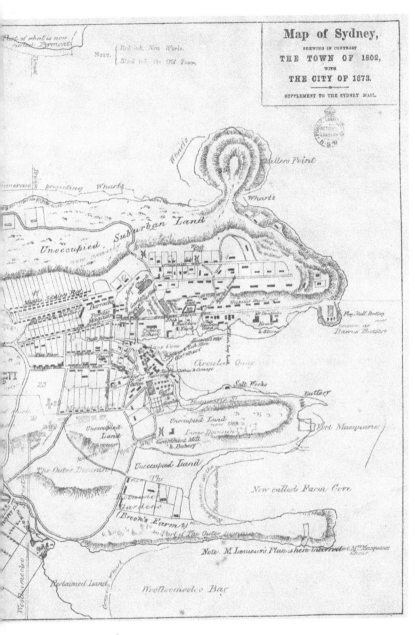

FIGURE 2 Map of Sydney in 1802,
updated in 1873 [with Darlinghurst Gaol]

As, for a capital felony, it is written opposite to the prisoner's name, 'hanged by the neck'; formerly, in the days of Latin and abbreviation, '*sus. per coll.*' for '*suspendatur per collum*'. And this is the only warrant that the sheriff has, for so material an act as taking away the life of another.

William Blackstone,
Commentaries on the Laws of England,
vol. IV, chapter 32

Special Care Notice:
First Nations men and women were inevitably
caught up in the legal system enforced by colonial
authorities as perpetrators and, more obviously,
as victims of crime and injustice. Readers are advised
that this book tells some of the colonial-era crime
stories that centre First Nations people.

Note:
Some of the felons discussed in this book had names
with multiple spellings, with some operating under
numerous aliases. The spellings used here are taken
from the Medical Officer Statements, confirming
an execution was carried out, published in the
New South Wales Government Gazette. The names
of Chinese people are also reproduced here as
they were published in the *Gazette*.

LOOKING FOR A NOSELESS HANGMAN

ROPED IN

Executioners were once a critical component of the justice system in New South Wales. In an era when judges handed down death sentences as easily as they toasted the good health of the monarch, someone had to do the dirty work of the authorities.

The role of executioner was, literally, a dead-end job, and nobody who had something to live for wanted anything to do with carrying out a judicial hanging. It is one thing to sit in a sanitised courtroom and talk about the ultimate act of the law. It is quite another to fit a noose around a condemned criminal's neck and feel their sweat on your hand. To hear their laboured breathing. To smell their fear. When it came to holding fast to the policy of the death penalty in Australia, the gulf between theory and practice was enormous. This meant that the supervisors of the colony's early, makeshift gallows had to reconcile themselves to employing hangmen who were prepared to trade their conscience for their freedom.

Soon after the European settlement of Sydney Cove, the first executioners were selected from shortlists made up of crooks who were facing their own death sentences. These men – robbers and thieves, but not killers – certainly did not embrace the task at hand. The noose was a symbol of the most extreme punishment available in England and its outposts, but for men with limited options the fatal cord was also a tool to escape the horrors of their own predicaments. Shrouded in the language of administration and law, the recruitment of the first hangmen essentially came down to forcing convicts to make a choice: kill or be killed.

Most of the men who took up the rope regretted the pact that they had made. Sure, their own necks did not feel the force of hemp so strong they could not gasp for air. Their stomachs did not flip as they fell to their deaths. But those who agreed to hang instead of being hanged, or to hang in exchange for being reprieved from a long period of incarceration in a cruel penal settlement, still died. They just died very, very slowly. Being a hangman in Sydney usually resulted in a life of poverty, social ostracism, alcoholism and insanity.

These men, having agreed to become murderers in the name of the law, did as they were told, but they were routinely discarded as soon as they were no longer considered useful. Nobody in the colony's emerging bureaucracy cared very much. A few more unpleasant ends, here and there, in the great war on crime, were of little consequence to those who knew they were able to make a new bargain with a new man. If there was somebody who needed to be hanged, there was always someone who could be coerced into doing the hanging.

Not everyone supported the carousel of executioners and their assistants. As the late 18th century folded into the 19th century, the various leaderships of the government and church held fast to the idea that the death penalty was the greatest deterrent to those who dared to disrupt the society spreading out from Sydney by breaking its rules. More and more people disagreed with the death penalty. As the decades went by, and as concerted efforts were made to distinguish an advanced colony from its penal past, quiet disapproval of capital punishment became a thunderous rage. Progress, however, was slow. Hangings became less frequent as appointments with the executioner were reserved for criminals of the very worst type, but judicial murder remained an option to keep the citizenry in check. Even after convicts had been replaced by free settlers, there was still a requirement for colonial administrators to have someone on the personnel books who was reasonably confident with a rope.

The debates around the death penalty, its effectiveness and its inhumanity, continued. The arguments of the abolitionists were at their loudest when the role of executioner for the colony of New South Wales was held by a man known, disparagingly, as 'Nosey Bob'. A successful cab driver until he lost his nose, Robert Rice Howard was avoided by once-loyal customers and struggled to find new trade. Then, as a noseless executioner, he was cast to represent everything that was wrong with law, order and the worst punishment in the government's arsenal to fight crime.

FINDING THE MANY MYTHS OF NOSEY BOB

Robert Howard was different to all the hangmen who went before him. The longest-serving executioner for Australia's oldest colony did not take up his role for the sheriff to save his own skin; he became the finisher of the law to save his family. Howard, disfigured and desperate, needed a job after his cabbing career collapsed, and he took the only one on offer to him that had a decent salary and employment security.

I first met Howard when I was reading newspaper articles that had been published in early 1889, just after he had executed Louisa Collins, for murder, in Darlinghurst Gaol. It was 2014, and I was researching how women – as victims and villains at the centre of criminal cases – were treated by journalists working in 19th-century Sydney. Entwined with the story of Collins and her punishment is the story of Howard. When I came across Collins, who was accused of murdering not one but two husbands, I came across the man who executed her. At the time Nosey Bob sent off Collins, he had been on and around scaffolds for about thirteen years. Unfortunately, despite a lot of practice, Howard's dispatch of Collins was brutal and ugly.

Hanging has a formula and clear outcomes. Hangings should be quick (with no loud and drawn-out strangulations), and they should be clean (with the body remaining in one piece). Howard nearly decapitated the last woman hanged in New South Wales, which did not make much sense. How could an experienced executioner botch such a seemingly straightforward process? Many of the contributors to the major papers of the day claimed to have the explanation for Howard's error: he was careless and incompetent. I believed the members of the press corps. I was wrong. Intrigued by a man who was able to retain his position in defiance of so much strident criticism, I decided to go beyond the headlines and soon came to know someone who was much more complicated than a bloke who had good, and not-so-good, days at work.

This book is about how the executioner who was routinely presented in print media as an affront to civilisation was one of the best finishers of the law that a New South Wales sheriff ever engaged. Howard's record in rope is not flawless, but the idea that he routinely bungled when he took care of a felon is a myth. It is not the only myth about Nosey Bob. Indeed, so much of what is commonly accepted about the history of this important Sydney identity is confused and contradictory, demonstrating how easily myths can, over time, be accepted as truths. Myths suit us and our instinctive preference for dramatic narratives. Maybe, in this instance, myths make it easier to understand why someone would serve as a hangman.

In separating fact from fiction, I have examined archival evidence and, where possible, the executioner's own words, to build a profile of the man who was, from the late 1870s through to the early 1900s, the most infamous public servant in New South Wales. Over this period, people were introduced to the common hangman through accounts of hangings, botched and routine, that were published in broadsheets and tabloids. When comparing these execution reports to the official records and to interviews with Howard, I discovered a man unlike any of his predecessors. Nosey Bob was, in fact, a most *un*common hangman.

In contrast to quite a few biographical subjects, Howard does not offer a rich archive to raid. There are no shelves of boxes dedicated to the memory of his life and work. He was, after all, only an executioner. To give this biography of Nosey Bob structure and substance, I have told his story through the stories of the sixty-one men and the one woman that he hanged, across New South Wales, between his appointment in 1876 and his retirement in 1904. Here, the hangman's successes and failures as an employee for the Department of Justice are laid bare, while sketches of Howard at home reveal a man who would not, who *could* not, conform to the stereotype of the evil executioner.

A book about an executioner is, inevitably, a book about capital punishment. The story about Nosey Bob is, therefore, also a history of hanging in New South Wales that delves into the logistics and mechanics of how to kill someone in the name of the law. On paper, hanging is a science. On the gallows, it is a combination of science, art and luck.

This book is also an account of some of those who fought for the abolition of the ultimate punishment and those who wanted to keep it. For all the people who protested passionately for more humane consequences for wrongdoers, there were others who believed that the death penalty was the only way to deal with the monsters who lived among us. At the centre of the political scrum was Nosey

Bob. The noseless hangman was scrutinised and leveraged for arguments that judicial execution was good and right on one side (when hangings were neat and tidy), and a hideous stain on our moral fibre on the other (when hangings were long or bloody).

Nosey Bob passed away in 1906. When a short obituary on him appeared in *Freeman's Journal*, two weeks after his death, it included a suggestion that the 'stories told of Robert Rice Howard, the retired executioner of New South Wales, who died at Bondi the other day, would make an interesting book'.[1] Here, over a century after Howard's death, is a book that tells the tale of a once-prominent and now largely forgotten hangman.

CHAPTER 1

LEARNING ON THE JOB

'A LICENSE TO SLAUGHTER'

On 15 August 1894, a bearded man with bluish-grey eyes in his early 60s asked for a licence to slaughter pigs at his home in North Bondi. The mayor of Waverley, William T Ball, presented himself at the Paddington Police Court, where the application was being heard, and objected strongly. The court promptly ruled in favour of the good citizens living, working and playing in Sydney's eastern suburbs.[1] There would be no pork production a short stroll from one of the city's favourite beaches. Perhaps it was the risk, however slight, of blood and entrails staining the area's most beautiful strip of sand that had revolted Mr Ball and his constituents. It could have been the sounds and smells of slaughter that sparked the concern of the small community of locals. The protest might have been out of consideration to visitors. This was, after all, the year the steam tramway to south Bondi, opened in 1884, was extended to take passengers all the way to Bondi Beach in an early effort to bolster tourism. The extension was a success and it coaxed even more daytrippers to sit on a golden shore and enjoy the coastline.

A License to Slaughter.

FIGURE 3 **A license to slaughter**

SOURCE *Bulletin*, 25 August 1894, p. 13

The most likely explanation for the objection to this small-scale abattoir is that, quite simply, people were tired of the almost-tangible haze of death that surrounded an unassuming cottage on Brighton Boulevard, off modern-day Campbell Parade. The home was ordinary enough. A single-storeyed structure with a corrugated iron roof, a picket fence and two imposing Norfolk Island pines in the front yard.[2] The occupant, though, was not so ordinary, for he was the colony's senior hangman. At the time of the application for a pig slaughtering licence, the man colloquially known as 'Nosey Bob' had, as a principal executioner, fitted nooses around the necks of forty-three men and one woman for the crimes of murder, attempted murder and rape. The man who killed felons at work would not be allowed to kill swine at home.

Some of those who took the time and trouble to know Nosey Bob found him an obliging and quiet man with a dry sense of humour, someone more concerned about his garden and keeping a neat home than about the goings-on in court houses and gaols across the colony. They found a family man who was proud of his children and determined to see them complete at least a basic education. A recreational fisherman who liked his beer, the occasional gin and his pipe. An average bloke who lived and worked and had a pet dog. Some found a hardened civil servant, a man weighed down by the revulsion and scorn attached to his occupation. Yet, Nosey Bob had not always been known by this sobriquet alone and he had not always been a hangman. Allow me to introduce you to Robert Rice Howard, an Englishman who could never have predicted he would hold down the most unpopular job in New South Wales.

Robert Howard was born in early 1832 in the small village of Marham in Norfolk, England to Henry Howard and Mary Ann Howard, née Rice. Details of Howard's first years do not survive, but it is known that on Tuesday 26 October 1858, the young Howard, who was working as a coachman like his father, married Jane Townsend at St Luke's Church in Charlton, a south-east suburb of London. The newlyweds quickly welcomed their first three children: Mary Ann in 1859, Emily Jane in 1862 and Edward Charles in 1864. The Howards then immigrated to Australia, arriving in Brisbane's Moreton Bay on Tuesday 27 February 1866, the anniversary of the first judicial execution under British law in the Antipodes. The Howards were just five souls out of hundreds of thousands of people who moved to Australia in the 1850s and '60s looking for gold, land, work or simply hoping for a better quality of life. Fanny was born in 1867, before the family of six left Queensland for New South Wales and grew again with the births of sons Sydney in 1869 and William George in 1872.[3]

The Howards lived in western Sydney in the late 1860s before establishing themselves and a cab business in the inner city, occupying several different properties not far from Darlinghurst Gaol during the 1870s and '80s. In the late 19th century, this area on the edge of what is now the city's central business district was a chaotic mix of grand villas and tightly packed terraces. People and livestock jostled for space as pressure on the area saw the subdivision of large parcels of land, sparking the construction of a maze of laneways, while a swell of boarding houses accommodated a growing population of itinerant workers and the poor. Howard, who was, according to many reports, a tall and good-looking man who 'passed for an Adonis amongst the horsey crowd', embraced the area and thrived.[4] As a cabbie, he enjoyed the hustle and bustle of city life. As a hangman, however, he sought solitude, and in the late 1880s he gave up the hectic metropolis and moved to the sparsely populated sandhills of Bondi.

Numerous newspaper articles, written after his ascendancy to the position of hangman, attribute Howard's cabbing success to his popularity with female passengers who resided in exclusive, waterfront suburbs. Several articles indicate he was the preferred coachman for Government House. Some pieces claim Howard was such a good cab driver, and so discreet, that he was called upon to drive for Queen Victoria's son Prince Alfred, Duke of Edinburgh, during the first royal tour of Australia that began in 1867. A tour that included a spectacular attempt to assassinate the Duke, at Clontarf, on 12 March 1868.[5]

Howard was a cabman in Sydney, but there is little evidence to substantiate the stories of his fabulous accomplishments. He was obviously good at what he did as he was a cab proprietor and not just a driver. Able to cope with the everyday dangers of driving in Sydney, he was always polite and well presented, despite long hours and the physical demands of keeping a cab and horse. That Howard was a driver for royalty is stretching the story. He was in Brisbane in 1867 and either still in Brisbane or in Prospect in 1868, during the Duke's royal tour.[6] His Royal Highness was in Australia again, unofficially, in 1869 and 1870–71, so it is possible Howard undertook princely driving duties when the Duke returned to Sydney. These tales of success became more elaborate as Howard's decades on the scaffold passed by. They also became more entrenched. Like most good myths, there are morsels of fact and fiction.

In July 1873, Governor Hercules Robinson and his family were going for a night out at the circus when, on Elizabeth Street near Liverpool Street, the pole-chain of their carriage gave way and frightened the two horses pulling the vehicle. The animals bolted and the driver was thrown. It was only the bravery and quick thinking of an orderly, who was riding along with the group, who galloped forward and seized the runaway horses that brought the coach to a stop and saved the day. The Robinsons were startled but unhurt. It was reported in what was and continues to be Australia's longest-running newspaper, the *Sydney Morning Herald*, that 'the coachman, named Howard, to whom no blame is attributed, received some injuries to his knees on falling from the box; and had to be conveyed home in a cab'.[7]

The most commonly told story about Howard is the tale of another accident. Almost every published account of Howard's life includes a statement that he lost his nose when he suffered a horse's kick to the face, with his terrible disfigurement extreme and instant. The typical Australian response was to rename the respectable businessman 'Nosey Bob': a moniker firmly entrenched by 1880.

The verification for this life-changing event is elusive. The story of Howard's assault by a horse has been told, over and over, but never with any details. There is no date. There are no particulars. There is some consistency in that the equine villain in this tale has been cast as a distinctly vicious horse, and one account specifies the horse kicked Howard in a livery stable on Bligh Street.[8] Cab and coach incidents were big news in Sydney and across the colonies, with episodes of horses biting, kicking, throwing and trampling people recounted regularly by the press. A horse's kick causing such dreadful injuries should have received widespread coverage.

In Howard's own lifetime, explanations for the loss of his nose were varied. A weekly sports rag, *Bird O'Freedom*, speculated that 'a festive horse bit it off', that it was lost 'in the "execution" of his duty' as a hangman or that Nosey Bob's plight was from smoking a pipe, with cancer the cause of 'Howard's well-known mutilation'. Although a man with cancer in the 1870s would not have lived, as Howard did, to see the 1900s. A reporter for the Sydney-based *Sunday Times* interviewed the hangman in January 1896. Howard refers to an accident with a horse in this piece, but he does not clarify what happened. Instead, he merely repeats the most frequently published description of how he lost his nose 'through an accident with a horse'. Also in 1896, the *Bulletin*, a publication that had a long-running fascination with Nosey Bob, asserted that Howard 'lost his proboscis through an accident, nature unspecified'.[9]

The most extensive account of Nosey Bob appears scattered across the pages of *Truth*, a newspaper founded in Sydney in 1890 with subsidiaries established around Australia from 1900. A scandal sheet specialising in colourful but influential stories over the late 19th and early 20th centuries, *Truth* published some stand-alone pieces on the hangman. These articles were supplemented by a long-running series started by 'Old Chum', a pen name of JM Forde. An Irishman who relocated to Australia in 1857 as a teenager, Forde was a much-liked historian who wrote extensively about Sydney.

Like tabloids today, the material published in *Truth* cannot always be certified as entirely accurate, even if content comes from a reliable contributor. Out of belief or out of habit, Old Chum wrote that Howard, in an accident with a horse, 'secured an injury to his nose which destroyed his sense of smell'. Another writer for *Truth* went further and declared Howard 'was kicked by a horse, and his nose so badly smashed as to almost obliterate all semblance of even a snout'.[10] The newspaper adds to the mythology of Nosey Bob, but it does not include any information to substantiate the claims about Howard and an altercation with a horse.

CONTEMPLATING A CAREER CHANGE

Running parallel with the story of how Howard lost his nose is the story of how he lost his livelihood. With severe facial injuries, Howard's cab business allegedly went into a steep decline as passengers, particularly women, no longer wanted to ride with him. A man who made no effort to hide his disfigurement would not have been an accessory of choice for ladies wanting to keep up appearances as they shopped or socialised. In the mid-1870s, the small business owner was at 159 Darlinghurst Road, Potts Point, just off William Street and close to where Sydney's famous Coca-Cola illuminated billboard is today.[11] This might have been a good place to pick up trade, with or without a nose, but Howard was staring down a changing city. Horse-drawn public transport services began in Sydney in 1861 and the first steam trams arrived in 1879. Cab drivers were still very popular but they had some serious competition.

Financial problems could explain Howard's court appearances in 1874. In May, he was 'fined 20s, and 2s 6d costs of Court, for furious driving'. He was also 'charged with using obscene language' and ordered to pay an additional penalty and another set of court costs. In August, he was fined for 'using obscene language', with any failure to pay resulting in a gaol term of four days.[12] A stint in a lock-up is a hefty penalty, but Howard was a repeat offender. Even with scant detail, it is clear Nosey Bob was under pressure. He had a large family to take care of at this time; his youngest child was only 2 years old.

The timing of Howard's solution to his immediate financial issues is not certain, but his next major decision must have shocked everyone he knew. Robert Rice 'Nosey Bob' Howard became an executioner. Some accounts of Howard's life state he started as a casual hangman to compensate for the plummeting revenue of his cab business. Taking on a second job in tough times is not unusual. When Howard started doing extra work as a labourer, nobody said anything, but taking on the job of executioner was shocking. Hangings might have been acceptable to large swathes of society, but nobody thought highly of the hangman. It has been assumed that doing disgusting work for the sheriff saw Howard shunned by other cabbies, resulting in a further loss of revenue. The damaged and desperate driver supposedly had no choice but to take on the role of executioner full time.

There was no standard career path to the position of hangman. There were no institutes of hanging. As time passed, the occasional how-to manual was released. In the early days of the colony, it was a reluctant acceptance of the job, not previous experience or any relevant skills, that was sufficient to be considered for the role. There is some consensus that Nosey Bob began by learning on the job as an assistant executioner in 1875 or 1876. This initial step to the position of senior executioner, or 'scragger', as the hangman was often called, makes sense and mirrors how some other Sydney-based hangmen undertook an informal apprenticeship.

Alexander Green was one of the colony's early floggers, the man who set the lash to the backs of men and women, before he was given the role of hangman in 1834. John Franks put his hand up to assist hangman Joseph Bull in 1871 and was promoted to principal in time for a job in early 1873. Howard's predecessor and first supervisor on a scaffold, William Tucker, was the assistant executioner before taking on the top spot in mid-1876, while it was assumed Howard's own assistant from 1894, Samuel Godkin, would eventually become the senior scragger.[13]

The lack of information around Howard is not a surprise as there are gaps in the historical record when it comes to the documentation of law and order. Details about hangmen are particularly vague as these men did not belong. Cloaked in the same horror as the condemned felon, the government hangman, though comparatively well paid and a professional tradesman in his own way, was neither a terrible felon nor a member of polite society.[14] Even enthusiastic supporters of the death penalty thought the act of hanging was grotesque. Some of Sydney's early executioners could not hide and became reluctant celebrities of the macabre. Others managed to fade into obscurity over time, and the anonymity they craved in life was finally awarded in death.

Also keeping some hangmen out of the historical spotlight were the social sensibilities of the 19th century. It was considered bad form to publish the executioner's name. There was no need to draw unnecessary attention to the man doing the work most people were not prepared to do. Shortly after Howard was made a finisher of the law in the mid-1870s, an open plea calling for the hangman's privacy appeared in the press. It was argued that, since we had abandoned public executions in the 1850s, we should also 'keep out of sight the details of the domestic life and personal characteristics of the public executioner'.[15] Not all journalists agreed.

The colony's senior executioner in 1875 was Franks. This was a year that saw two men hanged: one was a rapist and the other a murderer. The first of these executions, on 14 September in Darlinghurst Gaol, was of an Aboriginal man. The jury took forty-five minutes to declare Johnny McGrath guilty of raping Sarah Murphin near Bega, south of Sydney. The judge, in 'evident pain', handed down a death sentence, while the prisoner regretted his actions and 'died calmly, admitting his guilt, and expressing his sorrow, and attributing his position to drink'.[16] McGrath could have also blamed racism. First Nations peoples were more likely to feel the full force of the legal system transplanted to Australia from England than their colonisers who broke the same laws.

The next person hanged by Franks was the unfortunately named George Rope on 7 December. The first felon executed at Mudgee, west of Sydney, Rope had shot and killed his sister-in-law Hannah Jane Rope in an argument over alcohol the previous April.[17]

Some executions were festive events, crowds outside a gaol's walls gathered for a morning out. A hanging was an opportunity to see justice done while teaching children about the dangers of doing the wrong thing. In an era before modern-day distractions, executions were also diversions from routine; a chance to see official witnesses arrive or to hear the trapdoors give way, but there was no sense of celebration at Rope's passing. The press reported that those present left the scene 'sadder if not wiser' and commented on the excellent efforts of the deputy-sheriff who had 'taken every precaution to divest that sensationalism which too often accompanies the last act of the law'.[18]

The final engagement undertaken by Franks was for a Chinese man hanged the following year. The 'patient', as those doomed to meet the executioner were sometimes called, was Ah Chong, who had murdered Po Tie when both men were incarcerated in Parramatta Gaol.[19] Reports on the execution, on 18 April 1876 in Darlinghurst Gaol, include detailed descriptions of the hangmen:

> One was white-faced and nervous, and dressed like a labourer in his best clothes, the other was cool and collected, and dressed like a gentleman. He was mistaken by many for the chaplain. He wore a well-fitting black cloth suit, with black silk hat and kid boots, white shirt with studs, white collar, and white necktie, white wristbands, and cambric pocket handkerchief peeping out of one of his coat pockets.[20]

The *Evening News*, the first penny paper in New South Wales, published an account of the hanging that identified the dishevelled 'labourer' as the drunkard Franks. Readers were told the chief hangman looked 'nervous and depressed' and 'was leaden pale, and ill at ease', while the 'gentleman' who was deliberately avoiding his supervisor was referred to as 'Mr Tucker'. Another reporter was content with noting one executioner was 'dainty', with his hair 'oiled and brushed, his beard and moustache well arranged'.[21]

Some hangmen, understandably, worked to keep their identities a secret by adopting disguises or false names. The members of the press corps usually supported these efforts by only referring to the 'common hangman' or 'the executioner' in reports on judicial hangings. It is feasible there were no journalistic qualms in mentioning Franks, as his name had appeared in print before. In contrast, it is unusual that Tucker, the comparatively new man on the scaffold, who would not engage with his alcoholic manager, was not uniformly afforded some professional courtesy.

Accounts of Howard's career, stating he began on the scaffold in 1875, are based on gossip and descriptions of the tall, stylish man described in reportage on executions printed around the time that Tucker started working with Franks. There are numerous articles and illustrations of Howard that present him as dressed in a 'black frockcoat and white necktie', earning him a reputation as a 'gentleman hangman'.[22] Yet 'Tucker' was not an alias for 'Howard'. In another example of mythmaking, Nosey Bob was not at the gallows for McGrath, Rope or Chong. Tucker, the dandy, was Nosey Bob's immediate predecessor. Howard was, though, nearby and he was very close to holding a rope.

The days of Franks, a man struggling to stand up, were coming to an end. The American, who found himself in Australia and became an executioner, drank heavily as a tonic against a life of violence. It was heartless but logical that Tucker, watching Franks kill himself with grog, would have worked hard to secure the upcoming vacancy of senior man on the gallows. Tucker was part of a growing trend that saw men from all walks of life willing to do the work of death. Indeed, the fashionista was so keen to carry out the ultimate act of the law, that he had applied for a hangman's position in 1873 despite no billet being available.[23]

Charles Cowper, appointed New South Wales sheriff in 1874, complained in 1876 that the executioners were slovenly and that he 'had to pay in advance for their clothes in order that they might appear respectable'.[24] Early law enforcers had to be satisfied with convicts prepared to kill their mates in exchange for a commutation of their own sentence or with men willing to do anything for a regular income. The new sheriff wanted more; Cowper wanted a hangman of quality.

'NO ONE REGRETS THIS MORE THAN I DO'

Sometimes, those who did the hanging died in as much disgrace as those who had been hanged. John Franks, a deserter from the United States Navy, who signed on for the sheriff's dark work while an inmate in Darlinghurst Gaol, was discovered at death's door in Sydney's Hyde Park on 27 April 1876. A policeman took Franks, 'an almost lifeless carcass', to the Sydney Infirmary where he passed away from 'fever and debility' due to 'habits of drunkenness'. One obituary declared the regular lawbreaker 'lived and died like a dog' and that the bottle brought about death as effectively as the hangman's 'wretched machinery' of noose and trapdoors.[25] He was 26 years old.

Samuel Knapp, lawbreaker, put his name forward to fill the opening. Knapp's application features a fervent, if unusual, endorsement in the margin: 'I think this man would make a first rate executioner – he would hang anybody'. Good references cannot always compete with on-the-job experience, and William Tucker, the fashionable assistant hangman, was promoted to lead executioner, leaving the offsider's position vacant. The cabbie was ready. In June 1876, a year after being fined 40s 'for having by furious driving endangered public safety' and the same month his youngest child turned 4, Nosey Bob was employed by the colony's Department of Justice.[26]

Hanging already had a long and infamous local history when Howard first stood on a scaffold. The place referred to as 'Noose South Wales' had been busy dispatching criminals for almost a century. Nobody lists all the men and women executed in Australia's earliest years, but it is known that close to 2000 lives were cut short on scaffolds scattered over the continent and some of its closest islands between colonisation and the final abolition of capital punishment in 1985.[27]

Vilification of the hangman had a long history too. In echoes of the British class system, a social hierarchy emerged early in the life of the colony. Nobody, not even convicts, wanted to be on the bottom rung of society's ladder. The best candidate for the lowest of the low was the man who carried out the most dreaded sentence of the law: the executioner. So lowly was this task, just calling someone a hangman in Australia was an insult that could find you in court.[28] Held in open disdain, based purely on his profession, the hangman was barely tolerated. The only opportunity for redemption was to ensure each dispatch was quick. Mistakes were not acceptable. The hangman, as the physical embodiment of a brutal state, had to answer to his employer and to the public.

One of Howard's most famous forerunners was Alexander Green. Born in Holland and a circus tumbler by profession, Green found himself in England and in trouble. He was done for stealing fabric and sentenced to transportation, with a life term reduced to seven years, and he arrived in New South Wales in 1824 at the age of 22.[29] Green's time as an executioner, from 1834 through to 1855, pre-dates Howard's arrival in Australia, but his bunglings were vividly recalled by many colonists, with his errors easily recounted in the corridors and the yards of Darlinghurst Gaol. Nosey Bob would have quickly learned all about those men who had fitted nooses before him.

Green's sloppiness with a rope was seen when he hanged Patrick Bryan for the murder of Eliza Neilson on 20 October 1848 in Newcastle Gaol, north of Sydney. Bryan, a labourer, was a former employee of the victim's husband Arthur Neilson. The case against Bryan was unconvincing. There was only circumstantial evidence, some innuendo of impropriety between the prisoner and the victim and no witnesses for the defence.[30] Found guilty, Bryan maintained his innocence but still took his place on the scaffold. Green adjusted the rope. Bryan shifted his head. The knot of the rope slipped under his chin. His neck did not snap:

> The unfortunate man thus remained hanging in the greatest of agony for thirteen minutes, beating his breast with his hands, and ejaculating 'Oh! my God!' Mr Prout [the under-sheriff] sent the executioner up, who jammed the knot under the chin and also laid hold of the end of the rope with his weight upon Bryan.[31]

It was declared that the error was the victim's fault. Bryan moved. The point here is that those presented for judicial murder should stand obedient and perfectly still. Cold but sensible advice. The basic concept of hanging seems straightforward. A rope is set around the neck of a felon and then they are dropped. By Howard's day, slow and terrifying strangulations were no longer tolerated, and the hangman's goal was to achieve an instantaneous death by breaking a person's neck.

Initially, patients were dropped a generic 3 feet, and protracted chokings were standard. Innovations in the trade over the 1860s and '70s demonstrated that patients should drop between at least 7 and 10 feet, with even longer drops suggested. It was then confirmed, in the 1880s, that prisoners should drop a specific distance according to their weight.[32] Even when the science of hanging was better understood, hangmen still had to hope for instant deaths. A slip of the rope could result in slow suffocation, complete with painful groans and gruesome twitching of the body. A rope too short could also bring about a drawn-out process of strangulation. A rope too long might cause an ugly decapitation. A poorly chosen rope, one too hard or too thin, could also cut someone's head off.

The botched hanging of Bryan at Newcastle in 1848 was not Green's first or last error. Green, like Franks, turned to drink when his services were called upon, increasing the likelihood of a bad day at work. This also reinforced the colonial stereotype of the drunkard executioner. The hangmen of Sydney, including Howard, were renowned for seeking solace from their profession in alcohol.

Across Howard's career as an assistant and then principal hangman, hanging became more sophisticated while the sets of gallows available, permanent and temporary, became more substantial. The job was, theoretically at least, easier. Though the trade was considered repellent by most people, Howard took his work seriously. He wore a good black coat. He offered a few solemn words. He did his best. Yet, mistakes were made. Blood was spilt. Men kicked and thrashed, like ghoulish marionettes, as they struggled to breathe after being sent through the trapdoors. These types of blunders energised the abolition movement and served to garner widespread support for the eventual phasing out of capital punishment in Australia. No argument, no matter how convincing or eloquent, could compete with the visceral reminders that hanged men and women were human. The sights, sounds and smells of a bungled hanging only ever forced reactions of disgust and shock.

Howard's early mishaps were viewed as revelations of the risks of judicial hangings. Though an ancient and common method of execution, it was, like all methods of dispatch, known to be imperfect. Considering alternatives – like burning, boiling, drowning, shooting, stoning, quartering or chopping people's heads off – would force a confrontation with the abhorrent nature of all types of executions and so threaten the policy of the death penalty.[33]

During Nosey Bob's tenure, from the mid-1870s through to the early 1900s, the increasing popularity of abolitionist ideals began to leave little room to show any generosity towards the hangman. Rebukes for mistakes, from slight mishaps to catastrophic bunglings, were often issued without remorse. A noseless hangman was easy to cast as a monster representing a system seen by many as inhuman. A piece from *Truth*, published in the late 1890s, ignores all efforts to maintain a hangman's anonymity:

> His real name is ROBERT HOWARD, and he seems to owe his position to the fact that during the stay of the Duke of Edinburgh among us, some thirty years ago, ROBERT HOWARD, then a handsome, comely, stalwart fellow, acted as coachman to that right royal but very dubious Duke. It is impossible to account for his degradation to the position of official scragger of his fellow creatures on any other ground than that he, having done dirty work for a dirty Duke, was degraded to do still dirtier work for the victims of the Law.[34]

Regularly criticised, Howard still added some dignity to the process of hanging. He crafted a speech for his first victim, one he repeated for all the men and the one woman who stood before him in the course of his duties. Without fail, he walked up to the condemned and said in his distinctive, snuffly voice: 'My poor man (or woman) no one regrets this more than I do'.[35]

Undoubtedly, Howard's very first patient was George Pitt, who was hanged on 21 June 1876 in Mudgee Gaol. The widowed Ann Mary Martin had been in a relationship with Pitt, but, upon Martin 'transferring her affections elsewhere', Pitt decided it was reasonable to cut his former flame's throat. The regrets Nosey Bob offered that day, on a gallows about 16 feet high, were probably his most sincere. For, once the bolt was drawn, allowing the trapdoors to give way, there was no turning back for the convicted man or the men who supervised his fall. The bolt was the key to death. The sound of the mechanism being drawn meant that feet, without the trapdoors to stand on, would be forced to dance on air. Energetic steps gave way to shuffling moves as death overcame the prisoner. The only thing the hangman could do at that point was watch. As Howard said twenty years later, 'once in the business I had to stick to it'.[36]

Howard was not alone in Mudgee; Tucker was with him. The dandy was described as the principal 'promoted from former position of assistant' and wearing 'a handsome suit of black, which he afterwards changed for a grey tweed'. Tucker was followed by his offsider, 'a new hand' who 'was recognised as having once been in good circumstances in Sydney'.[37] This simple statement is more telling than any of the elaborate claims about Nosey Bob's death debut. It is a pity there is no mention of a nose absent, elegant or otherwise worthy of comment, but this report fits neatly with the known facts of Howard's life and accommodates the story of a successful cabman who fell on hard times.

Hanging a human being is not something that reasonable people can gloat about to family and friends, but Tucker and Howard would have been pleased with the review on their work in the *Evening News*: 'Death was apparently painless'.[38] It was done, and the executioners were able to go home. There was, though, no opportunity for respite. The newly paired workmates needed to head north and deal with a convicted wife killer.

CHRISTMAS EVE

Six months before Nosey Bob began his education as an executioner under William Tucker, a farmer in the colony's north-east committed a crime that booked him an appointment with the most feared officers of the law. On Christmas Eve 1875, the lifeless body of Mary Connolly was discovered in the home of her estranged husband. The marriage of Michael and Mary Connolly had begun happily enough, then something shifted. Newspaper coverage of Michael's trial for the murder of Mary described the results of this shift:

> He became accustomed frequently to strike her with a heavy stick, and with a spade knock her down, kick her, and absolutely, in the words of a witness, 'to dance upon her'. This kind of thing lasted till [the] prisoner's inhuman treatment of his wife drove the poor creature from her home, and in consequence of the fearful beatings she had received she became partially demented, and eventually found herself in the Gladesville lunatic asylum.[39]

After a year in an institution, Mary Connolly, like many women who endured a world with limited options, went back to the Peel River, near Tamworth in the colony's north. Her husband 'repulsed her with morose savagery' and she was taken in by the Bratten family who lived and worked on land that was close to what had been her own farm. On 23 December 1875, Michael visited the neighbours where Mary was living. When he left for home, his wife 'followed him with some bread, tea, sugar, and a billy of water'. On 24 December, Connolly was out walking when he came upon two locals, Lavers and Chapman, and announced: 'My wife is dead'. Chapman's immediate reaction was to ask: 'Did you kill her?' When pushed, Connolly continued: 'About sunrise I went down to the stack to get some straw for the pigs, and was away about fifteen minutes, and when I went back I found my wife dead on the floor, with a hole in her head'.[40] The neighbours rushed to the Connolly hut.

Upon arrival, the door to the home was tied closed, but it opened easily. There, on the floor, was the body of Mary Connolly. Her head had been beaten in. More neighbours arrived, crowding together in the small hut that was now a crime scene. The group noticed blood-like stains on Michael Connolly's clothing. In another statement, one about as authoritative as his alibi given earlier in the day, Connolly explained the blood by saying that he had moved 'the body of his wife from where he found it lying, in front of the fireplace, to the corner of the hut'. It would have been easy for Connolly's neighbours, knowing how he had abused his wife for years, to assume that the blood on his clothing was from killing her, not because he had, inexplicably, decided to drag her dead body across the floor of what had once been their marital home. Another piece of circumstantial, but gripping, evidence was a spade found close to the victim 'upon which were stains that looked very like blood, and part of the spade had been brightened recently'. The farmer had bashed his wife with a spade before. The visitors to the hut took things into their own hands; they chained Connolly under a dray and sent for police.[41]

The case was controversial. Nobody denied Connolly was a man of bad character, but character evidence cannot prove that someone committed a crime. There were witnesses, including close neighbours who had taken the Connolly children, a son and a few daughters, into their own homes to keep them safe, who knew of the domestic violence inflicted upon Mary Connolly. Such testimony certainly spoke to Connolly's attitudes towards his wife, but it did not show he had murdered her. Connolly pleaded not guilty, but he offered no information that could compel an exoneration or at least generate reasonable doubt. The matter was complicated when Connolly refused to engage with legal representation. Counsel had been assigned, 'but no assistance could be got from the prisoner, and his legal representatives could not come to a conclusion that any line of defence was practicable'.[42]

The trial, in the absence of a defence, was perfunctory. Connolly's bloodstained clothing and the spade found near his wife were strong arguments for the prosecution. No alibi was confirmed. No other suspects were put forward. Such violence, and such strange circumstances, made this crime news across the continent. The South Australian–based *Naracoorte Herald* noted it was proven at trial 'by medical evidence that Connolly was perfectly sane both before and after the murder'. Sometimes, just saying 'not guilty' is not enough. Even the *Evening News*, a newspaper known for offering views that were vehemently against the death penalty, carefully pointed out how the case against the prisoner was circumstantial before reporting on sentencing without any emotion: 'Verdict, guilty; sentence, death'.[43]

The hanging day arrived on 28 June 1876, and the first judicial execution in Tamworth Gaol was facilitated by Tucker and his assistant Howard. Religious counsel, from the Roman Catholic church, tried desperately to have Connolly repent, but the prisoner refused to confess or to even ask, as was generally expected, for mercy on his soul. Instead, the convicted man maintained his not guilty plea and repeated several times: 'I have nothing to say – I have no business to be here'.[44]

In an era before the investigative techniques that are taken for granted today became standard and without the benefits of forensic science, confessions (though not always reliable) made for a neat ending to any criminal trial. A confession could ease the conscience of those charged with seeing the law take its course, like the police, the lawyers, the witnesses, the judge, the jury and the executioner. Private views on the death penalty may have differed between men and women, they may have evolved over time, but at least there was some reassurance, from the lips of the condemned, that the right person was being punished for the right crime. Even the most staunch supporters of capital punishment were reluctant to kill people for no reason. Confessions also reiterated the right to punish, and so ensured that hanging was, effectively, seen as just another normalised result of a legal process.

The colonies, as outposts of the British Empire, were considered Christian and had built up justice systems based on the words of St Paul who had advocated that the ruler 'bears the sword' as 'God's servant, an agent of wrath to bring punishment on the wrongdoer'.[45] This saw the idea of the sword, so often depicted in imagery of Paul the Apostle, modified to accommodate a noose, but the basic concept was the same. The death penalty represented civil rule as well as a restoration of the moral order, and so the workers of Christ were essential in endorsing secular power at a hanging. It was, though, a delicate balancing act. Fear of the ultimate punishment was good, but complete terror could be hard for authorities to control.

For those representatives, from various religions, who were assigned to attend to the spiritual needs of those who found themselves residing in a condemned cell, a confession also brought the added benefit of saving a soul before it was cast into eternity. Another advantage to a confession was that a 'criminal with a soul properly prepared to meet the afterlife often delivered the executioner a body of little resistance' and was appreciated by all involved in a hanging.[46] Admissions of guilt could come before a trial, after a guilty verdict was delivered or while in gaol awaiting execution. Some confessions came on the scaffold, offered in a panic as the noose was fitted. There were those who, out of recalcitrance or out of a firm belief in their own innocence, never confessed.

Connolly kept his composure when his time came, and he showed no obvious signs of apprehension. When he ascended the ladder, he did so 'without assistance; and when he gained the platform he stood on it firmly, and apparently unmoved'. A white cap was placed over his head by the principal executioner, the noose was fitted and slowly tightened around Connolly's neck. The bolt was pulled, and the trapdoors opened. The man held responsible for the murder of Mary Connolly fell 7 feet. 'Although death was instantaneous, the usual convulsive twitches followed some four or five minutes after the drop'. After the body had been suspended for about twenty minutes, it was lowered into a cheap coffin, the rope was cut away and the lid was screwed down.[47] The execution ceremony was over. Everything had gone smoothly. Tucker and Howard could relax.

For this execution, the focus was firmly on the felon. There were no long descriptions of the executioners and their sartorial choices. No names were listed. The executioner and his assistant were, in hanging Connolly, quiet agents of justice. The incongruous pair, the dandy whose fashionable appearances had attracted thorough observations and his much less glamorous assistant, had heard or read some criticism of capital punishment. Comment could be particularly vocal in relation to those cases in which there was no confession from the condemned. Yet, no fault was found in their application of the death penalty. They did their work well.

After Connolly's dispatch, more details on the murderer's past emerged. It is one thing to report on the testimony given at a trial, it is quite another to publish non-relevant material that might influence that trial. The penalties for interfering in justice in this way, known as sub judice contempt, can be severe. Nearly a week after the hanging, when there was no possibility of a reprieve for Connolly, the *Evening News* printed a piece looking at the murderer's lurid background. Connolly had committed a murder in Galway, in the mid-1850s, and before he married Mary Connolly, he had been in a relationship with a woman in Tasmania 'whose end cannot be accounted for'.[48] Connolly claimed he had no business being on a scaffold, but his multiple victims may have disagreed.

It could be speculated that the dispatches of George Pitt and Michael Connolly, in June 1876, affected Howard deeply and shored up his resolve to follow through on his new line of work. Nosey Bob, the uncommon hangman, revelled in domesticity. He would have had no time for the man who ruthlessly murdered his lover, or the man who had brutalised his wife and children for years. This is not to suggest that the recently appointed executioner enjoyed his role, but these early experiences as a finisher of the law likely helped Howard to justify his position. The law said that bad people who did bad things had to die. The church agreed, and Howard, as a Christian, believed that evildoers on Earth had 'better prospects in the next world'.[49] Besides, the executioner had no say in who was sentenced to death, and if there was no sympathy for the felon, a hangman might, with only a little bit of effort, convince himself that he was just another worker earning a living.

CHAPTER 2

ALLOWING THE LAW
TO TAKE ITS COURSE

HOPING FOR MERCY

In October 1826, the first attorney-general for New South Wales, Saxe Bannister, called Robert Wardell 'the scum of London'. Sledging a fellow barrister rarely ends well, and Wardell, who was also co-owner with William Charles Wentworth of the colony's first independent newspaper, the *Australian*, was enraged. If nothing else, Wardell was a Yorkshireman and not a Londoner. He challenged Bannister to a duel. The pair at the centre of the conflict took the matter seriously, while most thought it was foolish. Fortunately, the insult did not morph into a serious criminal case as nobody was hurt. Bannister went on to accuse Wardell of libel as he was accused in the press of 'highly indecent and ungentlemanly' behaviour, but the men soon formed a frosty truce and went their separate ways.[1]

This incident is an example of hot tempers in colonial Sydney, and it also shows how one person's unruffled response to a wrongdoing is another person's fury. This conflict is, in part, because justice is a legal construction as much as it is a personal one. Over time, we build systems of right and wrong. We craft standards of what is fair and what is not fair. Sometimes the law cohabits nicely with our own beliefs and values, but not always. An obvious point of friction is how social attitudes can change faster than legal statutes. A bridge between cultural expectations and legal requirements is the concept of mercy.

Mercy ensured the end of a criminal trial was not necessarily the end of the criminal. Judges could recommend mercy in handing down a death sentence. The *Judgment of Death Act 1823* (UK) allowed judges in the United Kingdom and by extension in New South Wales, except in cases of treason or murder, to issue sentences as 'death passed', resulting in a quick trip to the scaffold, or as 'death recorded', saving the neck of an offender considered worthy of another chance. A sentence of death recorded allowed a man or woman to live and breathe but subjected them to what is known as felony attaint, which meant they were dead according to the law; they could not hold property and were unable to give evidence in court, act for another person or sue.[2]

A jury could recommend mercy when delivering their decision. The prisoner, their family or friends might make a claim for mercy. On rare occasions, victims pleaded for mercy. Members of the public petitioned for mercy by gathering signatures, writing letters and holding protests or public meetings. Those concerned with the plight of a particular prisoner knew that the end only came when the governor signed the death warrant.

The power to offer mercy has been invested in the governor of New South Wales since the commissioning of Arthur Phillip, the colony's first governor, who was authorised 'to grant pardons for all offences except treason and wilful murder' (he could, though, offer reprieves to treasonous and murderous felons while awaiting the monarch's advice). Phillip was not an ardent supporter of the death penalty. While he knew executions were 'quick, effective, economical', he also knew they were not merciful.[3] Mercy had been exercised in different ways when capital punishment was law in New South Wales, and it had attracted complaints that those able to offer mercy were too lenient or not lenient enough. For those with the most to lose, mercy was like buying a raffle ticket. You might win, but there were no guarantees.

The *New South Wales Act 1823* (UK) established the colony's first executive council of at least five but no more than seven men to advise the governor. Over time, the size of the council grew while those who were appointed were systematically replaced by those who had been elected by registered voters (the council – now comprising the governor and cabinet ministers – still operates today). The next major development came when the governor was given the power to pardon all crimes, including treason and wilful murder, in 1842. Responsible government, under the *Constitution [Conferral] Act 1855* (UK), gave the colony a legislative council and a new legislative assembly to represent the people. This meant the government, not the governor, held the bulk of power and influence in New South Wales.

Parliamentarians had to engage with constituents on matters of mercy, increasing pressure on the governor to make just and politically palatable decisions. Today, the governor only exercises mercy on advice from the executive council or a pertinent minister.[4]

In the mid-1870s, giving mercy to bushranger Frank Gardiner generated a scandal. Gardiner and his gang robbed the Eugowra gold escort, in the colony's central west, in 1862, making off with around £14,000 of cash and gold. Many gang members were tried with various crimes, including John Bow, Alexander Fordyce, John McGuire and Henry Manns, who faced charges of robbery and firing on police. All four men entered pleas of not guilty, but Manns admitted his guilt when in the dock. McGuire was acquitted while Bow and Fordyce had their death sentences commuted, but there was no reprieve for Manns. The bushranger, who was just 24 years of age, was hanged on 26 March 1863 in Darlinghurst Gaol.[5]

Manns was well dressed for his last day alive. The hangman, Robert Elliott, though careful and sober, botched the job. He then made matters worse when he tried, unsuccessfully, to take a new pair of boots from his freshly made corpse. Despite some support, Elliott would be demoted to assistant executioner after the bungling and what was, for the sheriff, a public relations nightmare. *Freeman's Journal*, founded to promote Roman Catholic interests in the colony, declared that 'never has so much sympathy been manifested in the fate of a misguided man, who in the flower of his age' was forced to face 'the degrading death of a common malefactor'.[6]

Gardiner was found in Queensland in 1864 and brought to Sydney where, after being tried for multiple offences, he was sentenced to thirty-two years of hard labour. A decade later, not long before Nosey Bob changed careers, Gardiner was granted mercy and released on the condition that he go into exile. The outcry was loud and relentless. That a young man was hanged and his gang leader went free was unacceptable. Crisis ensued, and Henry Parkes resigned as premier of New South Wales in the opening days of 1875.[7] Mercy might be gracious, but it was also risky.

When Johnny McGrath's death sentence for rape was reviewed in 1875, in pre-empting any potential calls for mercy the public was reminded that 'since sentence was passed upon the unhappy criminal', the executive council had considered the case 'but found nothing in the circumstances connected with the crime which would at all justify a commutation'. It was also 'decided that the extreme penalty of the law shall be carried out upon George Rope for the murder of his brother's wife at Lawson's Creek, near Mudgee'.[8]

Sometimes, specifics were included in a statement on mercy. Newspaper readers were told in April 1876 that the murderer Ah Chong's 'insanity has been investigated', and it had been decided not to interfere with the law taking its course. Similarly, short, sharp words were printed for the murderer George Pitt in June that year. Again, the executive council chose 'to let the law take its course'. Michael Connolly was also denied mercy in 1876, and he was hanged the same month as Pitt. Not everyone thought his case was one of coincidences; many believed he 'knew what he was doing' when he killed his wife.[9]

About three weeks after Connolly's end, Daniel Boon, of Wagga Wagga in the colony's south, sat and waited and hoped for mercy. None was on offer, even after his wife and seven children obtained an audience with Chief Justice James Martin before the scheduled hanging. The charge that Boon had taken a double-barrelled gun to Alexander McMullen's place of work on 10 January 1876 and shot him in the left shoulder was not in doubt. There were two witnesses. Boon also confessed, saying to police just after the shooting took place: 'That is right; I intended to murder him; he had called me a scoundrel and a great many names; he has annoyed me a great deal, and would not pay me what he owed me'. When McMullen succumbed to his wounds a week later, Boon was charged with murder. The prisoner was devastated and cried: 'I have had good advice and have not taken it; and I may blame the drink for it all'.[10]

Leniency was requested for Boon, who was now sober and sorry. The shooter's legal defence argued the crime was manslaughter and not murder, for 'the prisoner could not be held to be accountable for his acts at the time the fearful crime was committed, as he was suffering from drink'. The jurors recommended mercy, but the jurists had other ideas. The judge, Martin, 'held out no hope that the course of the law would be interfered with', and he reiterated this belief when he said that drunkenness 'is no excuse for crime: and in no case has it been ever held a ground to alleviate or excuse murder into the less crime of manslaughter'.[11]

Many crimes were committed while drunk, with drunkenness also a crime. Often disreputable rather than dangerous, many a man and woman sobered up in New South Wales police cells across the 19th century. Heavy drinkers were usually fined according to how drunk they were, if they had been disorderly and whether they were habitual offenders. In defiance of the sheriff's expectations around the behaviour of staff representing the Department of Justice, William Tucker appeared drunk in public while on official business. The smartly dressed and, to all appearances, self-assured hangman, was charged with being drunk and disorderly in Gundagai on his way to see Boon. Again, the tension of being a public servant while dealing with the derision and pressure that came with holding the worst position on the government's books was made plain. Alcohol was a quick but ineffective and temporary remedy. Tucker appeared in court where he pleaded guilty and was given a choice of a 40s fine or sixteen hours in gaol. As his presence was required elsewhere, he made arrangements to pay the fine and was on his way. The hangman asserted that 'Gundagai was the last place the Almighty had created' before arriving at his destination, where he was locked within the gaol walls.[12]

Executions were not common in Wagga Wagga. The end of Boon meant that a scaffold had to be erected in the gaol yard, and as the 'scaffolding was not high enough to enable the execution to be sufficiently private, a deep well was dug underneath the drop'.[13]

Boon was hanged on 19 July 1876. The work was done

well, and it was 'a sufficient drop'. His death was, all things considered, neat and tidy. After a few convulsions, the doomed man was dead. One of the most remarkable points in the coverage of Boon's dispatch is the description of the hangman and his assistant. The chief executioner, despite his recent humiliation, had 'consulted appearances. He was dressed in black clothes, the very *minutiae*, of his toilette having received scrupulous care. His assistant whose naturally repulsive appearance was heightened by the absence of any nose, proved a very fitting foil'.[14]

On Tucker's and Howard's return to Sydney, Tucker was arrested in Gundagai for his own protection. A drunk hangman who had raised the ire of a whole town, albeit a small one, was safer behind bars. He claimed he was overwhelmed by 'the worry and anxiety attending his position' and spoke of how his profession, and trying to keep it a secret, 'would drive him mad'. He was, simply, not equal to the task, and 'he intended to give up his appointment'.[15] The dandy, after three jobs as the principal hangman, parted ways with the sheriff.

STRONG AND CIRCUMSTANTIAL CASES FOR MURDER

Angus McGregor, a well-to-do farmer, held a large property in the colony's central west, not far from Coonabarabran on the Castlereagh River. When his daughter, Mary Ann McGregor, was raped, killed and abandoned at the foot of a yellow box tree near a sheep paddock, the community was stunned.

Mary, 'an intelligent, pleasing girl, of twelve years', went missing as she walked home, after visiting a neighbour, on 18 February 1877. Her body was found, after an extensive search, the next day. Thomas Newman, a recent arrival in the region, was tending his flock on the edges of the search area when he pointed out Mary's corpse to her brother David. She was horribly bruised, had a broken arm and her nose had been bitten off. Newman was questioned by police and, suspicions raised, a search was made of his property, where a ribbon from the victim's hair was found under his pillow. Investigators also discovered the girl's brooch and a pair of her earrings in Newman's possession.[16]

Not yet tried for the crimes he stood accused of, there were absolutely no feelings of mercy for Newman, and the press readily took to the practice of framing crimes committed against the prettiest or the most vulnerable victims as crimes of the worst type. As reported by the *Sydney Mail*, a weekly edition of the *Sydney Morning Herald* in magazine format, there was a general mood of horror with the local people so 'intensely incensed against Newman' that the police had to provide the accused with protection. Adding to the trauma of the girl's family, her body had to be 'preserved in spirits, pending the arrival of a qualified medical man from Gulgong', about 120 miles away.[17]

The trial was held at the Dubbo Circuit Court, west of Sydney, the charge being that the prisoner had 'wilfully, feloniously, and of malice aforethought, killed and murdered one Mary Ann McGregor, a little girl'. The prisoner pleaded not guilty and assumed a 'stolid, nonchalant air', and so 'seemed the most unconcerned person in the crowded court'.[18] Newman should have taken the situation seriously; the case against him was substantial.

Evidence included a piece of bloodstained rope found with the girl's body, matching the marks around her neck. The court was told there was rope at Newman's place used to lead his dog. When asked where the remainder of the rope was, he said he used it for the sheep. The court was also advised of blood on the prisoner's clothes, though the defendant stated this was from killing a sheep and not a child. Rips in the fabric of the prisoner's shirt and coat were also offered to the jurors. It was claimed the shirt had been ripped deliberately to mend the coat. The prisoner had also told police that, despite making the repair just after McGregor's murder, he had torn the coat some time before his arrest.[19]

The court also received witness testimony, including from Catherine McGregor, the victim's sister. She swore that the ribbons and jewellery found in Newman's sleeping quarters had belonged to Mary. There was testimony, too, from the victim's brother. David McGregor described the scene standing over his sister's body. He saw bite marks on her face and, in an era before crime scenes were preserved to aid investigators, he explained how difficult it had been to remove the rope from around her neck. He also swore that a pair of earrings, found in the prisoner's personal effects, had been his sister's. They were a gift, from him to her; there could be no mistake as there was an easily recognisable flaw in one of the stones. A neighbour said he had seen Newman follow the victim just before she disappeared but had not been suspicious enough at the time to make sure Mary was safe, even though 'she seemed frightened'.[20]

The accused had also tried to cover his tracks, literally. The *Sydney Morning Herald* reported how it was shown by an exceptional tracker that the 'prisoner had rushed his sheep round the body, apparently to remove all footprints or other marks'.[21]

Newman was sentenced to death without any hope of mercy. After the trial, Newman confessed to a long career of crime. He also confessed to the murder of Mary McGregor but not to rape, despite irrefutable medical evidence showing the child had been sexually assaulted. Upon hearing that there would be no commutation of a death sentence, prisoners often sighed in resignation or collapsed in shock. Newman's first reaction to such news was calm. Then, when his time came on the morning of 29 May 1877, he cried with 'tears as big as peas rolling down his cheeks' before meeting the executioner and his assistant. Facing the execution party, he whispered, 'don't let them hurt me'. The under-sheriff, JG Thurlow, was unmoved by the prisoner's sudden anxiety. The last words of the first man hanged in Dubbo Gaol were uttered as the noose was arranged around his neck: 'Don't put it on too tight', he said. Death was 'instantaneous – not a limb moved, and in a second after the bolt was drawn, he swung in the cold morning air a lifeless corpse'.[22]

The hangmen are largely overlooked in reports on Newman's end, although it is specified the 'principal executioner stepped aside' and allowed his assistant to handle the bolt. This confirmed that Nosey Bob, who, unlike other hangmen, did not like to draw the bolt himself, had replaced the disgraced William Tucker. In a modern workplace, Tucker might have been offered some counselling. In the 1870s he was left to disappear. The press, temporarily enamoured of the dandy, moved on without pause, and *Freeman's Journal*, never afraid of an adjective, went straight to business by stating that Newman's 'scaffold had received its unhallowed baptism of blood' and that 'death was wonderfully instantaneous'.[23]

Nosey Bob would not have read this coverage as his literacy skills were quite poor. John Feltham Archibald, a Sydney-based journalist and Francophile, also known as Jules François or JF Archibald, would recall, long after the hangman's death, that Howard could not read or write. He could, though, sign his name and he claimed to make lists.[24] Howard engaged with current affairs. He was aware of the crimes that brought his patients to him, including details of their victims, and while he might not have read the newspapers, he certainly had family and friends who did. It is easy to imagine that Howard, as he stood on the scaffold with Newman and offered his regrets, thought of a little girl who shared the name of his mother and his oldest child. A girl who had also lost her nose.

Five months after Howard's trip to Dubbo, Peter Murdick was tried for the murder of Henry Ford. The case against Murdick, made in October 1877, was not as strong as the case against Newman for the murder of McGregor earlier in the year. For this reason, it was thought Murdick, also known as Peter Higgins, might be the beneficiary of mercy.

After he was sentenced, it was reported that the crime 'may be quoted as one of the clearest, yet most elaborate cases of circumstantial evidence that ever came before any court, and of necessity it involved a very large amount of labor', undertaken by the police, to complete the chain of evidence 'which eventually surrounded the murderer'.[25]

Not everyone was sceptical and Murdick was found guilty of killing Ford and dumping him in the Murrumbidgee River, near Wagga Wagga, startling a local gardener who had gone to do some fishing. Murdick was also accused of stealing a cheque and personal items from his victim. One reporter noted that 'after an arduous sitting' – the trial had lasted an entire day and into the middle of the night – 'the guilt of the prisoner was clearly established'. A short trial by today's standards. Still, it was much longer than the average of half an hour, including a jury's deliberations, seen in England prior to the *Prisoners' Counsel Act 1836* (UK), which guaranteed accused men and women the right to legal representation at a trial. Prisoners in New South Wales had to wait a bit longer for such rights and the passing of the *Defence on Trials for Felony Act 1840* (NSW).[26]

Murdick had a fair hearing, according to the expectations of the time, but it was not enough. He was found guilty. When the prisoner was informed there would be no reprieve, 'he completely gave way, falling in a fit on the floor of his cell, and writhing most frightfully'.[27]

New South Wales hangmen often operated in pairs. Not all felons gave up without a fight, and there is safety in numbers. Curiously, reports on Murdick's send-off in Wagga

Wagga talk about a lone scragger. First, the reports covered the stigma attached to being an executioner. The local press advised residents that on 'Saturday, the hangman arrived from Sydney, and much anxiety was manifested by the local hotel-keepers to inspect him, as it was feared he would want board and accommodation, and none were inclined to give it to him'. Denied local hospitality, the hangman stayed in the gaol.[28]

Second, the reports on Murdick's end offer no details of an assistant. It appears that when Howard went to work on the morning of 18 December 1877, he went alone. Murdick never confessed to murdering Ford, but at this point it was irrelevant. The trapdoors gave way, and 'Murdick seems to have made a clutch at the rope, but it passed through his hand and he dropped about eight feet with the usual telling thud'. Howard, working alone, might not have tied the prisoner's arms down correctly. A lack of good strapping, or pinioning, would have allowed Murdick to interfere with the process. Something certainly went wrong that morning and death was not instant. The body gave 'two spasmodic jumps' and took fifteen minutes to relax 'into silent death'.[29] Howard was obviously at ease with his own work because 8 feet became his preferred drop. It would usually break a neck quickly but not generate so much force that a head would come off.

Not much was made of the drawn-out strangulation, and it was reported that Murdick 'was hanged in the ordinary way'.[30] Howard's employment was noxious, but there were sporadic public admissions that the work was not easy.

'MR HOWARD JOINS THE CIVIL SERVICE'

The hanging of In or Ing Chee on 28 May 1878 is the only execution not listed in the overview of Nosey Bob's career started by Old Chum, the go-to historian for *Truth*. John Norton, who owned and edited *Truth* from 1896, oversaw some of the headlines for the 'Howard's Holocaust' series that began in August 1897, with instalments documenting the career of the 'Champion Choker' appearing until July 1903. A few headlines are in 'grotesque bad taste', but the articles are 'a useful record of some executions during the Howard period'.[31] Apart from some gaudy word choices, there are only a few faults with Old Chum's accounts of who was hanged where, when and why.

The series for *Truth* begins with stories of hangings predating Howard's career. By the ninth instalment, in October 1897, Nosey Bob is front and centre of the 'Death-Doings at Darlinghurst' with the headline: 'Mr Howard Joins the Civil Service as Assistant Executioner, and as such operates on Johnny McGrath'. Another history of Howard in the *Mudgee Guardian and North-Western Advertiser*, founded in 1890, states that George Rope's hanging at Mudgee was Howard's first publicly acknowledged experience as an executioner.[32] Linking the name of the felon to the most recognisable tool of the hangman's trade might have been too good a story to pass up.

Old Chum claims Nosey Bob joined 'the New South Wales Civil Service in 1875 as Assistant Hangman with the promise of the chief position when it became vacant'. Or, as he conceded, at 'least such is the legend in the office, as prior to 1880 the records appear to have been kept most indifferently'. In 1876, Sheriff Charles Cowper made a similar complaint about poor recordkeeping.[33]

The government did not openly recognise Howard until the mid-1890s. There is a first, basic gazetting of Howard in 1896 in the *New South Wales Government Gazette*. A more detailed listing appears in the 1897 *Public Service List* or 'Blue Book'. This entry specifies Howard's appointment was made in June 1876, that he was employed by the Department of Justice under 'Messengers, Court Keepers, &c' and paid an annual salary of £156. No allowances are listed, although executioners were paid travel and forage allowances as required. Howard was baptised in March 1832, but the *Public Service List* notes his date of birth is unknown. His name does, however, appear on a report on sheriff employees over the age of 60 in 1897, when he would have been 65. This information also highlights a mercantile point of difference between Howard and more common hangmen. Some executioners squabbled about rates of remuneration, but Nosey Bob never received a pay rise. These official acknowledgments are also anomalies. After Howard's retirement, the *Public Service List* includes the position of executioner but does not identify position holders. The last mention of an executioner or an assistant in the Blue Book appeared in 1917.[34]

Old Chum was correct when he stated that Howard began as an assistant executioner, but he is one year out. The historian-turned-journalist put Howard's start date as 1875, with McGrath being Howard's initiation, but it was not until 1876 that Nosey Bob stepped up on a scaffold to help hang George Pitt. When Howard was first publicly listed as a civil servant in the 1890s, he had been the principal hangman for almost two decades. An appointment in June 1876 as a lead executioner leaves scope for earlier work in 1875 as an assistant. Yet, the *Public Service List* does not detail Howard's promotion and the 1876 date indicates Howard's first job as William Tucker's offsider. Another writer for *Truth*, identified only as 'One of the Unhanged', put together a summary of the career of 'Sydney's Scragman' when Howard retired. This piece also questions an 1875 start date but asserts 'there is no doubt' Howard stood on a scaffold with Pitt.[35]

The research serialised in *Truth* counts sixty-four persons hanged by Nosey Bob; including In Chee's death brings the toll to sixty-five. Removing the three men dispatched before Pitt and mistakenly allocated to Howard's service – McGrath, Rope and Ah Chong – from Old Chum's biographical work brings Nosey Bob's damage down to sixty-two. A few reports speculate wildly about the number of men and women attended to by the noseless hangman. The *Bulletin*, in campaigns against the death penalty in general and Howard in particular, asserted in 1896 that he had 'made as many corpses as would reach to the top of Sydney Post-office tower [239 feet high] and half-way down the other side'.[36] There were also rumours that in addition to travelling across New South Wales to do his duty, he also went to other colonies and as far as New Zealand to ply his trade.

Howard had a love-hate relationship with the press.

Eager to accept the praise of reporters, he dreaded harsh reviews of his work. This might explain why Howard was evasive about the number of patients he served when asked. This could have also been because of a head injury. If it is true Nosey Bob was kicked in the face by a horse, then the force of that impact and of landing after being struck would have generated more than the visible damage that made him so recognisable. Another theory is that Howard played with the press, small acts of revenge for printing nasty accounts of him and the way he executed his duties.[37]

In an 1896 piece in the *Bulletin*, Howard denied making a tally of those he met on the gallows, saying he 'never reckoned the total'. When talking with another representative from the press a few years later, he said: 'I have hanged a good few. The number I forget, but if I was at home I could give them to you, for I keep a list'. A hangman's reputation is important, and Howard was clear that no matter the number of send-offs, he 'had very few bungles'.[38]

Keeping count of executions is a bureaucratic process, but it is also a chilling activity. It is, conceivably, a reluctance for such a loathsome chore that keeps the exact number of executions a little hazy. It is also possible that, especially in the earliest days of the colony, life was so cheap it did not really matter if the hanged were counted or not. In practical terms, a felon dispatched was not one more hanging, it was just one less problem. Frightening numbers also served an often-cited goal of the death penalty: deterrence.

For example, it is estimated that Alexander Green was involved in delivering three million lashes to the backs of men and women, while it is regularly stated that he hanged 490 murderers, thieves and other types of offenders. The belief that capital punishment discourages a life of crime is clung to by some, so Green's record is a questionable, but potentially useful, figure for those in favour of the ultimate penalty. Today, Green is still famous for impressive statistics. He is also known for prominent facial scarring inflicted on him by a convict who flew into a rage when he recognised the hangman, attacking him with an axe. Like Howard's missing nose, the details around Green's injury are muddled.[39]

Returning to the case of In Chee, Nosey Bob needed to pay attention to the man who had, on 18 December 1877, the same day Peter Murdick was taken care of, murdered another Chinese man, Li Hock, in Goulburn, south-west of Sydney. In's trial in April 1878 was a fraught affair. There were attempts to move the trial to another location and issues when selecting jurors. The defence team and the judge kept things professional but frosty, while the witnesses were almost unanimous in their condemnation of the prisoner. For In, the complexities of a criminal trial were exacerbated as he relied upon a countryman, Charley Ship, to serve as an interpreter.[40]

In Chee was seen running from Li Hock's house 'without coat or hat' shortly after the sounds of screaming. In was found covered in blood and he confessed, three times, to murdering Li. In initially claimed Li had cheated him when they were gambling. Later, he stated Li Hock sexually assaulted him, and it was this crime that had driven him to commit murder. In Chee told police he had used a butcher's knife, but a medical examination revealed the weapon was a chopper. This was followed up at trial with testimony that unpacked each cut inflicted upon the victim in detail. The defence pleaded with the jury for mercy, arguing that provocation was central to the consideration of declaring the prisoner guilty or not guilty. If In Chee's motive was 'sufficient to justify the killing, they must acquit the prisoner; but if they thought it insufficient justification they could find him guilty of manslaughter'. The jury retired at 7:30 pm to deliberate, returning at 10:00 pm 'with a verdict of guilty'. The judge, through the interpreter, passed the sentence of death.[41]

In Chee was hanged without fuss. 'Death must have been instantaneous as there was no movement of the body beyond that caused by the sway of the rope consequent upon the fall'. After the execution, the gallows for Goulburn Gaol were 'taken down and stowed away'. Key members of the execution team, including the sheriff and the executioners, then took the train back to Sydney.[42]

Howard oversaw one more death that year, but not one of his own doing. His wife of almost twenty years died at home, aged 42, on Thursday 22 August 1878. Another myth surrounding Nosey Bob is how Jane had died of shame, that being married to a hangman who was constantly insulted and taunted was more than she could cope with. Her death was not quite so theatrical, with the cause being 'Disease of lungs' and 'Pleuritic effusion' or water on the lungs.[43]

RAPE, RACISM AND A MAN NAMED ALFRED

That Howard's wife died of a broken heart slips in neatly with another myth about Nosey Bob. It has been said that his 'three beautiful daughters were condemned to lives of lonely spinsterhood because, as the story goes, no suitor was willing to suffer the ignominy of having a hangman as father-in-law'.[44] Yet, two of Howard's daughters married during his tenure as an executioner and one died when she was a teenager.

On Tuesday 20 May 1879, almost nine months after his wife's death, Howard watched his oldest daughter marry. It was not an elaborate ceremony. Aged 19, Mary married a 22-year-old New Zealander, Edward Hawkins, at a registry office. Her siblings Emily and Edward served as witnesses. Howard approved of the marriage between a housemaid and a carpenter, and he was listed on the official documentation as a labourer. This was a title John Franks also used on publicly available documents in unsuccessful efforts to avoid being labelled an executioner.[45] Identifying as a judicial hangman would have felt a little awkward at a family celebration, so listing Howard's side hustle as a labourer was a sensitive choice.

Howard may have preferred the title of labourer, yet he was an executioner the very next month. There are no comprehensive descriptions of the hangmen in reports on the send-offs for Thomas Newman and Peter Murdick in 1877 or In Chee in 1878. Howard was certainly the senior man on the scaffold following William Tucker's hasty resignation in 1876, but it was not until mid-1879 that he was described in detail and, though not named, positioned as the colony's lead executioner.

In April 1879, an Aboriginal man known as Alfred, who was living in Mudgee, was convicted of having sexually assaulted Jane Dowd, a woman in her mid-60s, the previous February. Like many First Nations men and women in the colonial era, Alfred was only referred to by a common first name, and no surname, by his colonisers. In the oppressor's toolkit, this was just one more way to belittle and disempower the continent's rightful owners. Claims for mercy for Alfred were based upon the obnoxious idea of 'extreme ignorance'.[46] Unfortunately, Alfred's case was not about the benefits of a Christian upbringing. This was an example of black and white justice.

The abolitionist movement in Australia was gaining traction and making some noise, but the voices of retentionists were louder, even though executions were, comparatively, rare events by the late 1870s. Society, and most of its institutions, had become more civilised since the colony's staggering spike in hanging men and women over the 1820s and through to the early '40s, which saw up to fifty-two people hanged a year.[47] The number of death sentences carried out under the watches of Governors Thomas Brisbane, Ralph Darling, Richard Bourke and George Gipps looks like a disturbing last hurrah for a penal settlement that had formally rejected the transportation of convicts in 1840, with the last transportees arriving in Sydney in 1850. There was, however, an acute awareness that an easing in the application of the death penalty was not an eradication of this punishment. Arguments about hanging rapists were always heated and often racist.

In a *Sydney Morning Herald* piece covering the rape of Dowd, the widow was described as a true victim, one 'leading a lonely and industrious life' and found 'to be a uniformly well-conducted, respectable woman, the mother of a family'. This piece also detailed the January 1879 rape of 13-year-old Amelia Smith, attacked near Lithgow on the western foot of the Blue Mountains by two teenaged farmhands: Alexander Medcalf, or Metcalf, and Charles Wilkinson. Smith was also positioned as blameless, her innocence 'proved beyond room for doubt, not alone by the evidence, but by the result of subsequent inquiries, cautiously made in the interests of justice'. It was also stated that her 'master says that he never heard of any familiarity between her and the two criminals'.[48] Then, as now, female casualties of assault had to go through legal and public processes of being declared a victim. Then, as now, it was often thought easier to blame those who had been wronged.

The death sentence for rape was mandatory in the colony at the time. The *Sydney Gazette and New South Wales Advertiser*, the colony's first newspaper, which ran from 1803 until 1842, asserted in 1840 that 'rape and murder are the only crimes which we think worthy of [the death] penalty'.[49] Many agreed that the conditions of the colony, with women vulnerable in a sparsely populated landscape, necessitated the greatest deterrent. Hanging was, however, increasingly considered by many to be an unreasonable response to the crime of rape.

The case against Alfred was not as strong as the case against Medcalf and Wilkinson, but both juries returned verdicts of guilty and death sentences were automatically issued. A petition on behalf of the three prisoners held so many signatures the final scroll was 203 feet long; almost as impressive as the Garden Palace that was built for the 1879 International Exhibition and, at 223 feet high, was Sydney's tallest building at the time. The petition was augmented by a large-scale rally outside Parliament House in Sydney, one with thousands of protestors, a band, torches and placards. Mercy was expected for all three, but the reality was that Aboriginal men were more likely to be executed for the crime of rape than white men. The racism was obvious, and it was publicised that, in addition to other pleas for mercy, all the 'coloured men that can in the time be got together in Sydney will form [a] deputation [to Government House], and they will present a very strong petition for mercy'. The acting governor at the time, Alfred Stephen, facilitated reprieves for Medcalf and Wilkinson, who were told they would face life imprisonment instead of the gallows. Stephen, a supporter of capital punishment for murder and rape, did not offer mercy to the Aboriginal man.[50] Alfred was scheduled to meet the executioner on 10 June 1879.

One of the people who stood and watched Alfred's last moments that cold morning in June was newsman JF Archibald, who represented the *Evening News* where he had been employed by John Haynes. This was the year before Archibald, with Haynes, founded the *Bulletin* in Sydney. Published weekly from January 1880, the *Bulletin* became known as a fiercely pro-Australian publication that often saw the world through Archibald's misogynist and racist lenses. It was also a publication known for taking on the colony's hangman, an extension of Haynes' commitment to abolishing the death penalty.

When the two were at the *Evening News*, they contributed to the coverage of these cases of rape with relentless vigour, with content on the 'proposed judicial murders' occupying approximately 'ten times the space it found on any other newspaper'. Reportage intensified after the white teenagers were reprieved. Even the career politician Henry Parkes, probably contemplating the bushranger Frank Gardiner and the political cost of mercy, said he was forced to wonder, 'why should not the blackfellow get the benefit of some of this sentimentality?'[51]

Expecting the worst, Archibald went to Mudgee. He caught the same train, then coach, as the execution team, and in a 'passionate symbolic protest', he stole the hangman's 'mortal coil' and flung the rope needed for the noose into the bush. The issue of the rope was resolved, but the episode gave Archibald more material for his article. Meanwhile, at the Mudgee Gaol, while Christians debated the right to punish and the responsibility to forgive, Alfred was baptised into the Church of England. There was hope until the end with the telegraph office kept open all night in anticipation of receiving word of a reprieve, but there would be no mercy in Mudgee.[52]

Archibald's final report of over 4100 words was savage. He highlighted, albeit paternalistically, the blatant racism in the justice system. He railed against the awful cruelty of capital punishment. He saved most of his venom for the executioner:

> Words fail to express the horror of the scene witnessed by those who, from the workshop door, saw the procession wending its fatal way. The wretched blackfellow was borne along between the frowsy executioners, who gripped his arms as though they liked their work of blood. The hangman, 6ft 2in in height, broad shouldered, spider-legged, with arms like a gorilla, a flat face without a nose, and huge feet, presented a spectacle to be seen nowhere else out of Hades. Men, whom experience of criminals had rendered familiar with the most detestable sights shuddered at the monster who dragged with him the man he was about to slaughter.[53]

According to the press, Alfred's death by hanging 'was almost instantaneous, all the arrangements being well carried out' for the only execution that year.[54] That did not matter. Archibald's campaign against Howard had begun. In a draft of his article for the *Evening News*, Archibald also referred to Howard's assistant in Mudgee. The executioner's offsider is identified as Risby and described as 'a hideous fat little spider with the cobbler's waxy beard'. Interestingly, the journalist cut this line in his notebook from the final published piece.[55] Archibald had decided that concentrating on Howard would be more effective because, in making Nosey Bob monstrous, in positioning the senior hangman as an animal or as something evil, it was easier for people to focus their opinions on capital punishment. There was no need to stare down an entire legal system. Attention only had to be directed at the one man who was responsible for carrying out the ultimate sentence of the law.

A few weeks after hanging Alfred, Nosey Bob was in trouble again. On 7 July 1879, Howard was charged for drunkenness and using obscene language. 'Robert Howard', it was reported, 'seems to find time hang heavily on him during vacation, and consequently indulges in deep potations to pass his leisure hours away'. He asked to be forgiven 'this little once' and he was fined just 10s.[56] The sheriff had found a reliable and respectable hangman, but he still had an executioner who drank too much between shifts. The anguish that came with holding the position of colonial scragger was inescapable.

Then, on 31 August 1879, one of Howard's forerunners died at the Parramatta Lunatic Asylum. Alexander Green passed away aged 86, although he looked 'about 500'. The former hangman, who 'used to amuse himself by hanging a number of dolls all day', had been declared insane in 1855 and so had been institutionalised longer than his twenty-one years as a scragger. Green outlived his replacement Robert Elliott, who was recommended to an asylum but died at home aged 80 in 'a filthy and neglected condition' on 24 May 1871. Green also outlived Elliott's successor, Joseph Bull, an executioner remembered for the 'exceeding stiffness of his cravats'. He died aged 67 while a resident at the Benevolent Asylum in Liverpool on 9 May 1873.[57]

CHAPTER 3

IN THE SWING OF THINGS

TWO BUSHRANGERS AND A JOURNALIST

In January 1880, Nosey Bob had two problems: the logistics of his first double hanging and JF Archibald.

For people in eastern Australia, the beginning of 1880 was all about Thomas Rogan and Andrew George Scott, better known as Captain Moonlite. The pair had been members of a gang of six roaming felons who, in November 1879, at Wantabadgery, east of Wagga Wagga, went on a violent rampage that culminated in a shootout with law enforcement officers. Bushrangers James Nesbitt and Gus Wernicke were killed, as was constable Edward Webb-Bowen. Rogan and Scott, alongside fellow gang members Graham Bennett and Thomas Williams, were tried for murder. On 11 December 1879, all four men were sentenced to death by the eminent, if occasionally controversial, William Charles Windeyer.[1]

The criminals waited in their cells, hoping for a reprieve, but not everyone was in a forgiving mood. Barrister and legislator David Buchanan, in a lengthy letter to the *Sydney Morning Herald*, criticised the weakness of the executive council. 'If any mercy is called for', he raged, 'it should be shown to the unprotected settlers in the interior of this country, and not to the marauders who carry terror and crime with them wherever they go, and who should be struck down, ruthlessly, as the plagues and pests of society'. Buchanan was half right. After considering the four cases, the executive council decided the younger men, Bennett and Williams, would have their sentences commuted to life in prison, with the first three years in irons. Rogan and Scott, on the other hand, would hang in a yard of Darlinghurst Gaol on 20 January 1880.[2] The story of the first execution in a new decade would be told in publications across the Australian colonies, including in an article written by Archibald.

Archibald had, as many people knew, met Howard as he travelled with him to Mudgee when Alfred was hanged about six months earlier. The journalist felt that he had an advantage as the hangman had a 'bad memory for faces', and he did 'not recollect voices at all', and so he comfortably assumed he was not recognised when he called on the hangman at home shortly before Rogan and Scott were scheduled to swing. The obliging Howard invited Archibald in, the journalist observing a carefully maintained garden, a tidy home and two young boys who read a passage from the Bible to their father every night. There were others who lived in the Howard household in Paddington, but they were out that evening to see a play.[3] Archibald offered a small token of honesty; he told Howard he was a newspaper man. He gave no indication he was the same newspaper man who had written so extensively, and so scathingly, about Howard in his coverage of Alfred's execution for the *Evening News*.

The pair quickly settled into their roles as interviewer and interviewee. The first matter on Archibald's agenda was gaining access to the gaol yards on the morning the two bushrangers were to be executed. He was writing for the first issue of the *Bulletin*, his new publishing venture with John Haynes. He wanted that story. Howard was courteous but firm. He also gave an indication that he did not know who his new companion was:

> Can't give you any information without permission from the sheriff. You know, sir, I've been very badly treated by the newspapers. THE EVENING NEWS was too severe on me. In fact, I was thinking of taking a libel action against the NEWS, which is largely circulated among my friends. Sir Alfred Stephen and Sir Henry Parkes offered to back me up in it, but I let the matter drop. I thought it was best to do so. Their article did me a lot of harm in my business. I used to work for a great many people who now don't employ me. However, I'll tell you what I'll do. If I ask for a couple of admission tickets they'll be given to me and even if the sheriff's not able to spare you a ticket, you may come in as a friend of mine.[4]

This passage can be read as a simple response. The hangman, a bloke with few opportunities to enjoy the company of others, suddenly had a chance to chat and to complain. Howard does not bother to offer a segue. He talks about the article penned by Archibald that had labelled him a gorilla.

He tells his guest, quite firmly, that he had considered legal action. He indulges in some impressive namedropping and gives a short summary of the personal and professional costs attached to such libellous words being printed before sliding into an offer of assistance – with the sheriff's permission, of course.

The loss of business Howard refers to could have been the end of his cab driving years or his work as a labourer. Though employed on a gallows in 1876, Howard was listed in the *Sands Sydney, Suburban and Country Commercial Directory* as a cab proprietor up until 1877 and, with no directory issued in 1878, as a bricklayer in 1879. In this way, Howard reversed his father's career trajectory. Henry Howard started as a labourer and became a coachman, while his son was a coachman who was forced into a labourer's job. This decline in social standing continued. A one-line reference to a noseless hangman in the *Burrangong Argus*, a small regional newspaper in Young, south-west of Sydney, in July 1876 for a report on the hanging of Daniel Boon might not have attracted too much attention. Two and a half columns in the *Evening News*, one of Sydney's more popular papers, covering the hanging of Alfred in July 1879, would have made it to all Nosey Bob's employers and potential employers. It had 'oozed out in the cab ranks' that Howard 'had attended the sheriff on certain official occasions', making paying passengers harder to find while bricklaying work would have also been harder to obtain.[5]

Howard makes his point, but then he quickly cycles back to the topic of admission tickets and calls the journalist a friend. This puts Archibald in Howard's debt, for a little while at least. Howard is either as simple as he is assumed to be, or he knows exactly who he is talking to and is only feigning ignorance in a masterclass on manipulation.

Later, the reporter says: 'People have formed an altogether false impression as to your character. But you'll perhaps be kind enough to explain how it was that you came to take your present billet'. Howard shrugs. 'Well, sir, the truth was that I was liquoring a little too much at the time, and I took the situation without thinking, like'. Howard explains he is a comfortable man who can support clean, well-read and well-mannered children. He also has 'as good a garden as there is anywhere'. The journalist is, surprisingly, respectful. Archibald mocks the way that Howard talks when he puts the conversation into print, emphasising his clipped English accent and his speech impediment due to his missing nose, but he does convey the points that were obviously of most importance to Nosey Bob. A good home. A good family.[6] This might not have been the absolute win that Howard had hoped for, but it at least made the encounters between the two men a draw.

Archibald was startled, even mildly impressed, by the hangman's domestic affairs and wanted to talk about business. He asks Howard if he believes Scott and Rogan will hang. The executioner thinks Moonlite will swing, but he hopes Rogan is reprieved. Shocked, Archibald pushes the point: 'Then you don't particularly want to hang them both?' This was not the story of the bloodthirsty executioner he had come for. 'No, indeed', Howard exclaims, 'would you?

I don't get any more for doing the work. It's a lot of trouble to me, I can tell you'. Howard talks about all the time he spends 'in preparations, for if anything goes wrong, here's the man as gets the blame. I've never had a mishap yet and I hope I never will have'. Archibald cannot help himself: 'What do you mean by a mishap?' Howard gives some detail, but he stops short of describing a worst-case scenario.[7] Instead, he tells his interviewer about how much effort he goes to for each execution:

> The night before, I fixes all the things as I remember,
> and then I takes my pipe in my mouth and I walks up
> and down and says to myself – 'Is there anything more'
> – and if there's anything more I thinks of it. It doesn't
> do to get flurried, for the day you gets flurried that's the
> day as you makes the mistake. And then when I sees the
> people walking in I thinks again and makes sure that
> everything's as nice and ready as a kid glove.[8]

Howard was not flurried for his first job at home, and the hangings were as smooth as could be expected. The *Evening News* recorded that: 'The hangman, known as "Nosey Bob," appeared to have made his arrangements well'. It was also noted that Howard had an assistant on the day (Risby was with him), and that Scott died instantly. 'Rogan quivered for about four minutes, and his mouth twitched convulsively'. The medical officer in attendance explained that 'what was noticed by the spectators was merely involuntary muscular action'. The Darlinghurst Gaol Death Register, kept from

1867 until 1914, records that Scott suffered a fracture of the neck while Rogan died of asphyxia.[9]

Archibald's story in the *Bulletin* is long, melodramatic and at times confused. Howard is pictured as dignified and professional, with Archibald's three-page rant finding little fault with Nosey Bob. There is some speculation about the horror of the fall for the condemned men who fell 6 or 7 feet, or what, according to Archibald, felt like 10 000 feet, with the work concluding that the 'hand of Death is laid upon him and he wakes – in the other world'.[10] Howard, with the worst job in the colony, comes across as just another man doing what he was paid to do.

Nosey Bob would have felt relieved, and probably quite satisfied with himself, going home that day in January. A double hanging was a lot of work as it required a significant amount of preparation. If nothing else, it was a lot of rope to set up. A double dispatch also meant twice as much worry that something might go wrong. While hardly an everyday occurrence – Howard would only do four double send-offs across all his years at the gallows – they were not considered unusual. After all, the scaffold for the Darlinghurst Gaol had been purpose-built to accommodate two condemned criminals at the same time. For authorities, a double hanging was a strong display of state power. It was also good time management and easier for administrators to arrange.

FIGURE 4 The last scene

SOURCE *Bulletin*, 31 January 1880, p. 5

HOMICIDE, HOMICIDE

Albert, another Aboriginal man known only by a first name, was hanged on 26 May 1880 in Dubbo Gaol for the murder of a fellow Aboriginal man, Nugal Jack. It was suggested that white men should not interfere as it 'was a blackfellow's row, and we cannot understand their motives and their customs'.[11] The colonisers had, however, claimed a right to rule over First Nations peoples.

One of the longer articles printed about this case presented a critique of law enforcement instead of the usual condemnation of the lawbreaker, as there was a serious issue with Albert's confession. The prisoner had been cautioned, but the constable conducting the interview added: 'You need not be frightened'. It was argued that these words, 'uttered in a soothing or persuasive tone, would undoubtedly have the effect upon most offenders of making them loquacious and heedless of caution'. The police were warned not to add such a reassurance in future 'as the evidence thus obtained would not be admissible'.[12]

Some reports stated Albert shot a woman, out of jealousy, and the 'bullet struck her ribs, passed around them, and entered the abdomen of the man'. Most reports claimed Albert had acted in self-defence and that the victim was a known murderer. Despite the facts of the case, a guilty verdict was given and a death sentence was delivered. The *Sydney Morning Herald*, a usually animated advocate of capital punishment, was vocal in observing 'much surprise' at the decision of the executive council to withhold mercy and stated that scragging Albert is 'a great mistake'.[13]

The hanging day came and the report on the ceremony took the near-standard format. There was an observation about the weather, a description of last-minute religious consolation and instruction, as well as a review of the mental and physical states of the condemned. On this occasion, the prisoner's bravery was apparent. He 'showed no signs of fear' and he was described as walking to the scaffold 'more unconcernedly than the hangmen, Nosey Bob and his aide-de-camp'. There was, though, some criticism of the crowds. Despite restrictions around witnesses at executions, large groups of people gathered in Dubbo hoping to catch a glimpse of the hanging.[14] As it turned out, there was not much to see that morning. Albert's death was quick. Nosey Bob's work was not done, though. He had another murderer to attend to that year.

Elizabeth Harris, of Maitland in the Lower Hunter Valley, married a Chinese man known as James Hart in 1872. Mrs Hart lived with her husband in Bathurst, west of Sydney, before he took her to live on the tin mines at Inverell, just south of the Queensland border. Hart then sold his wife to Dan King for £7. It was reported Hart was sold several times before she was re-purchased by King. Then, in late 1879, King decided to sell Hart again. The latest purchaser was Charley Hung Yung of Tamworth. A receipt, produced in evidence in this case of human trafficking and murder, showed that a £5 down payment on Hart had been paid only days before she was stabbed to death.[15]

It was suggested that Elizabeth Hart's experiences were

not out of the ordinary within Chinese communities, and that if a man went back to China, he might sell his Australian wife instead of taking her home with him. Exact figures are not known, but it is clear that 'unmarried men or married bachelors (married men with wives remaining in China) formed the majority of the early Chinese population in Australia'. It made perfect sense for Chinese men to form relationships with local women, including the building of families, in New South Wales and other colonies. It was, though, frowned upon by conservatives worried about 'racial mixing'.[16]

Importantly, the treatment of women and girls as property was not the exclusive purview of any one society. Wife selling was, sadly, much more universal than implied by the press at the time of Hart's murder. In 1811, Ralph Malkin tied a rope around his wife's neck and took her to Windsor, west of Sydney, and put her on sale. She was purchased 'on the spot' by Thomas Quire for £16 and a few yards of cloth. As it turned out, Mrs Malkin, now Mrs Quire, had no objection to the arrangement, perhaps agreeing that a simple sales transaction was much easier than a divorce. Before the establishment of the no-fault divorce, legally ending a marriage required resources that were often well beyond the means of the average person. The *Sydney Morning Herald* presented their readers with a long history of wife selling in England in the 1860s. Indeed, some women were not just sold, they were auctioned. The *Herald* went on to offer some follow-up commentary, which noted that the selling of spouses was an ongoing issue in the mother country into the early 1880s, quoting prices as diverse as '25 guineas to a pint or half-a-pint of beer, or a penny and a dinner'.[17]

Elizabeth Hart was found dead behind Tamworth's Town and Country Hotel. King, who was known to have a history of threatening Hart, was an obvious person of interest. Some witnesses testified they had seen King where Hart's body had been discovered, while it was alleged King was disappointed with Hung Yung's payment plan for Hart.[18] Matters of slavery were sidelined as King was charged with and tried for murder. The prisoner proclaimed his innocence, but he was found guilty at the Tamworth Circuit Court and sentenced to death. He would meet Nosey Bob, just over a fortnight after the executioner had attended to Albert at Dubbo.

On 11 June 1880, within the yard of the Tamworth Gaol, King paid the ultimate price for murder. The *Armidale Express and New England General Advertiser*, first published in 1856, set the scene with a weather report: 'The air was frosty and calm under a cloudless sky of brilliant blue, and the dazzling rays of the sun lit up the upper portion of the framework of the engine of death just as the officer of the law demanded the body of the condemned man'. At least there were no public spectators. Crowds had gathered outside the gaol, but the area had been boarded up to ensure that only official witnesses, a few representatives of the press and those tasked with carrying out the execution were able to view proceedings. Again, there was not much to see as Howard had operated at his cool and efficient best. 'Apparently the spinal vertebrae were severed instantly', followed by some slight twitching of the body. 'The whole of the horrible business was conducted with the utmost decorum, and the fearful work of the executioners was done with all the satisfaction possible under the painful circumstances attendant on their duties'.[19]

By mid-1880, Howard had been a finisher of the law for four years. The former cab driver and labourer had, despite a run-in with JF Archibald, enjoyed a good run with the rope. This was because, as he had told the co-founder of the *Bulletin* at the beginning of that year, he always attended to every detail. He always 'gets their height and their weight', to determine the length of each rope, and he is careful not to 'go near 'em till their time comes'.[20] Nosey Bob knew how important it was to treat the rope carefully, and that a soft rope allowed the noose to draw tight quickly while being gentle on the skin.

This was the type of information that Nosey Bob had access to as he unpacked the mechanics of judicial execution by hanging. He was certainly in the swing of things after a few years on the sheriff's books. In 1880, Howard was also offered some professional development. The Secretary of State for the Colonies, based in London, distributed two circulars across the Empire. The material was, essentially, an executioner's how-to manual. It was also an attempt at 'bureaucratic concealment'.[21] A shameless shirking of responsibility that would see all blame for any errors on a scaffold put on the executioner rather than on the system he worked for. Policymakers could cry it was not their fault. It was the hangman. We told him what to do.

Howard's reputation was largely intact at this time, but not all hangmen were as careful as the noseless one. It had been considered necessary to issue instructions because 'through mismanagement or an adherence to barbarous usages, the execution of criminals has been attended with revolting circumstances, the recurrence of which it is necessary, in the interest both of humanity and decency, to prevent by every possible means'.[22]

A bungled hanging was bad for everyone. For the administrators and witnesses of an execution, for those who wanted neat and straightforward events that flawlessly demonstrated the ultimate punishment, and for the patient whose suffering was compounded with every error made by the man doing the send-off. Even abolitionists, who routinely leveraged botched executions to argue for the abandonment of capital punishment, did not want a dispatch to go wrong.

The first document from the Secretary, two tightly typed pages, outlines the best way to hang a human being. Every necessary specific is given. The interval between sentencing and the carrying out of the execution, how the prisoner is to be advised of the date of their execution and the hour of execution (mornings were always preferred as they helped prevent the gathering of large crowds). Also listed are the finer points on the role of the executioner, including how 'a trustworthy and intelligent person' is required. There is, too, an explanation on how the apparatus is to be tested, as well as information on the gallows and the rope, with a 'normal drop' quantified as being 8 feet. Helpfully, the circular describes how the new style of noose with a metal eye, instead of the old-style hangman's noose, is very efficient and that supplies 'can be obtained from Newgate through the Crown Agents'.[23]

In addition, the pinioning of the prisoner and the procession to the scaffold are all explained. The role of the chaplain is detailed, and the duties of the executioner are listed in point form, including the best way to take the body down after the hanging. For those with any doubts about what to do, a set of illustrations makes the more difficult aspects of a hanging perfectly clear. The second document addressed requests for information on the construction of an executioner's device. It included lithographs of the plans and sections of the gallows at Newgate Gaol.[24]

For Nosey Bob, there was death at work, but death also lingered around his home that year. In early March he met his first grandchild, but Charles Edward, son to Mary and her husband Edward Hawkins, did not live out the month. The first of the couple's six children died of debility and marasmus, or what would be diagnosed today as malnutrition, when he was 25 days old.[25]

Later in the year, on Monday 20 December 1880, Howard's second child, Emily, died. The 18-year-old had suffered from heart disease for nine years and had developed dropsy. It was not Howard's first loss of a child.[26] At some point, Robert and Jane Howard had another son who was listed as 'male deceased', under previous issue, on the birth registrations of their three children born in Australia. It is unclear where and when this child was born or what happened to him, as he quickly became a memory no longer acknowledged. He is not listed on the death certificates, alongside his siblings, of his mother or father.

DIAGRAMS.

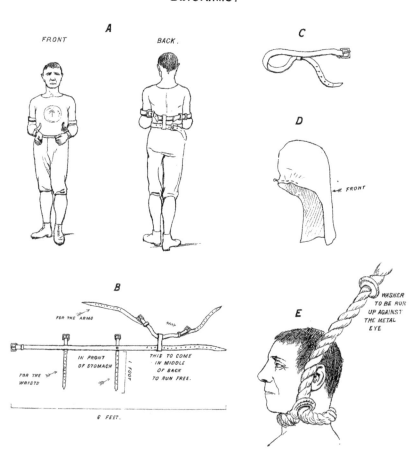

FIGURE 5 Circulars on capital punishment

SOURCE Queensland State Archives, 1880, ITM17282

THE UNIQUE CONDITIONS
OF A PENAL SETTLEMENT

A system of common law (the law of precedent, of judges basing their decisions on other decisions made in similar matters, established in the Middle Ages) and a set of statutes (laws enacted, by parliaments, through legislation) accompanied the first major export of criminals to New South Wales in the late 1780s. The goal was for England's colonies, be they settled, conquered or ceded, to mirror the heart of Empire. The reality was more complicated. Sydney Town was not just another English county. It was a prison. The immediate challenge for David Collins, the colony's first judge advocate, was to tailor the laws of England to the specific conditions of a penal settlement. Simplicity was the order of the day and it resulted in an astonishing concentration of power. The local court would, as Collins wrote, have the 'power to inquire of, hear, determine, and punish all treasons, misprisions of treasons, murders, felonies, forgeries, perjuries, trespasses, and other crimes whatsoever that may be committed in the colony'.[27]

With military know-how but no legal training, Collins had his hands full ruling on civil law and criminal law. Serious challenges, in a town with more felons than free persons, included locating twelve men able to pass the character test for jury service. The right to trial by jury would eventually be secured by those who also fought for a free press and responsible government. In the interim, military tribunals had to suffice. New South Wales also had to wait, but not as long, for solicitors, barristers, magistrates, judges and professional police. Another hindrance in replicating a recognisable legal system was finding reliable witnesses to testify. In an example of making do with what you have, John Johnson, one of the early Sydney-based hangmen, testified when Isaac Nichols was tried on a matter of stolen goods in February 1799. It was the 'first instance ever known of the common executioner' giving evidence (Nichols was found guilty but pardoned after the trial was deemed unfair).[28]

Deciding who to punish had its issues, but the delivery of punishment was much easier. The infrastructure of iconic institutions such as the Old Bailey, Newgate Gaol and others were noticeably absent in Sydney Town. Still, only basic equipment was needed to hang, gibbet, chain, flog, exile or send a crook to an even more distant site to serve a sentence of incarceration. Punishment would, Collins specified, be 'inflicted according to the laws of England as nearly as may be, considering and allowing for the circumstances and situation of the settlement and its inhabitants'.[29] These circumstances were, in some respects, specific to Port Jackson. It was not impossible to erect primitive sets of gallows and enforce the ultimate sentence of the law, but on the far side of the world, killing off a workforce desperately needed for agricultural and construction efforts was not good strategic planning. Mercy could be focused on benevolence towards an individual, but it could also be about the immediate and self-serving labour needs of authorities.

Unique conditions would see the colony, across the 19th century, make a couple of radical departures from English rules on punishment. The first move was progressive and redefined who could and could not watch someone hang. The second was a recalcitrant refusal to acknowledge the idea of over-punishment, a stubbornness that set up a decades-long debate about protecting women from sexual assault.

In many parts of the world, over the 18th and 19th centuries, public executions fell out of favour 'with the authorities and with the audience. It seemed at once disorderly and dangerous, garish and cruel' and 'audiences were perceiving the spectacle of torture and punishment as horrifying and barbaric, an affront to standards of decency'. This was part of a global trend that saw 'a general increase in sensibilities toward violence, which extended to state violence exemplified by the scaffold. Almost everywhere, executions were removed indoors between 1850 and 1870'. A ritual that had been referred to as the 'theatre of death' was being reduced to private performances.[30] In New South Wales, the reformers were driven by claims of dignity and a desire to civilise the colony. This was not just about process; this was a symbolic gesture to the world that the days of convictism were over.

Henry Grattan Douglass, a medical practitioner who served as a member of the legislative council of New South Wales for ten years from 1851, initiated a piece of legislation that would become known as the *Act to Regulate the Execution of Criminals 1855* (NSW). First introduced in 1853, the law stipulated the end of public displays of state-sanctioned violence.[31]

The scaffold was no longer open access; instead, reading accounts of executions in newspapers became 'the dominant medium through which the death of a criminal could be understood by the public.'[32] More importantly, though, this legislation was a major step forward in improving the system of punishment in Australia and predated the banning of public executions in England, in 1868, by fifteen years.

As keen as many men and women were to emphasise progressive attitudes and to further distinguish the modern colony from the settlement's dubious beginnings, there was a lot of resistance to some reforms. When it came to the death penalty and rapists, lofty ideals of social improvement were abandoned in favour of arguments that centred on protecting those on the frontier: a paternalistic state assuming the role of guardian. Britain removed rape from the list of capital crimes in 1841, but New South Wales retained this crime as a capital offence throughout the 19th century.[33] Even as the colony became a state in 1901, discarding its penal origins, rape was still punishable by death.

The 'gender imbalance within the colonies, an isolated frontier, the presence of convicts and a desire to safeguard the "purity" of women and children were all invoked' to argue it was necessary to keep rape as a capital offence, long after England had instituted alternative punishments for this crime. It was even claimed in parliament that the 'temptations' to perpetrate this type of assault 'were greater here than in England, because people were more isolated.'[34] But women and girls were at risk of sexual assault regardless of where they lived. This could be seen through the offences committed by another type of criminal, a predator rarely invoked in debates on rape and punishment, and one for whom setting, metropolitan or regional, was irrelevant: the incestuous assailant.

The *Sydney Morning Herald* and the *Evening News* printed statements that, though different in tone, revealed a shared opinion on the execution of a paedophile on 29 March 1881 in Darlinghurst Gaol. The paper that routinely supported the enforcement of capital punishment, the *Herald*, went straight to the point: 'After a very mature deliberation it was resolved that the sentence of the law should be carried into effect. The criminal will therefore be executed this morning'. The *Evening News*, having lost its greatest abolitionist, John Haynes, to the *Bulletin*, calmly advised readers that: 'The right the law gives one man to take away the life of another was exercised at Darlinghurst this morning, when William Brown was executed for criminally assaulting his own daughter', who was just 12 years old. The *Evening News* continued: 'His crime or series of crimes – for others of his family had suffered in a similar way to the child he maltreated – were such as to alienate from him all human sympathy, and no one doubted the justice of the sentence or the refusal to remit it'.[35]

The case was so repellent that many of its details were considered too dreadful for publication. It was revealed that Brown's defence focused on the claim that his daughter Ann had consented. This line was maintained even though the victim was not old enough to consent and had suffered substantial injuries. There were also statements from two of Brown's other children, William and Bridget, who witnessed Ann's trauma, which proved their father's crimes beyond doubt. The man in the dock said his children had simply 'conspired together to take his life'. It was further argued that Brown had been separated from his wife for six years, as though this, somehow, served as justification to sexually assault a minor. Little else is known of Brown's life, and it is difficult to substantiate rumours that the rapist had also killed a man who worked for him.[36]

Brown wanted an illustration of his dispatch done for the press. He also made multiple requests for his children, including Ann, to stand with him on the scaffold when he was hanged. The requests were repulsive. They were also illegal. The legislation dictating the administration of executions prohibited any child from being a witness to a hanging. Brown's end was a straightforward, 6-foot drop. There was no incident. No struggle. Howard sent him off with detached precision. A period of twenty minutes 'was allowed to elapse, and then the rope was slackened, and the suspended figure, which had been gently swaying in the cool morning breeze', was cut down and lowered into a coffin.[37]

Later the same year, Howard was back dealing with the type of felon that he most often encountered on a scaffold: a murderer. On 1 June 1881, Nosey Bob attended to Henry Wilkinson at Albury, on the New South Wales border with Victoria. Just over six months earlier, Wilkinson had gone into the home of Martin Mentz and shot him twice in the head before shooting his daughter, Mary Pumpa, in the chest and head. The body of Mentz was consumed by fire after Wilkinson set his property alight. Pumpa, 'drenched in blood', escaped the blaze. She was able to identify Wilkinson as the man who had shot her and stolen a few shillings from the home she shared with her father before she succumbed to her wounds and died a week after the attack. Her statement was corroborated when the bullets extracted from her body and her father's were identified as a match to the rounds that remained in Wilkinson's revolver.[38]

One newspaper offered readers a pantomime of the murderer's end that described the finisher of the law as bearded and noseless, with an offsider 'who, not nearly so large in stature, was almost as villainous looking'. Another paper wrote, more seriously, that: 'We are informed that the hangman's name was Robert Howard, and his assistant's name Reed. The expeditious manner in which they carried out the just sentence of the law shows that they are not novices at their calling'.[39]

LIBEL, ASSAULT AND MURDER

Libel cases were common in colonial Sydney. Newspaper men of all political, religious and social leanings were vulnerable to accusations of publishing libellous material.

In early 1881, William Henry Traill was working at the recently founded *Bulletin*. A savvy journalist, Traill wrote up a story about the outrageous behaviour of the crowds at Sydney's Clontarf Picnic Gardens on Boxing Day. The front-page article published on 8 January did not hold back in describing Clontarf's patrons, with young women attracting special scorn: 'Drink and excitement, inherited impulse, and above all, example and evil associations were doing their work and breaking down the last barriers of modesty'. The women, in their enthusiasm for debasement, 'flew wild-beast fashion at one another, boxed like men, and anon scratched and bit like cats'.[40]

Brothers William and Thomas Moore, who owned the site where the debauchery was said to have taken place and where, in March 1868, Henry James O'Farrell had attempted to assassinate the Duke of Edinburgh, took great offence and denied all impropriety. The *Bulletin* published a follow-up story on 15 January. It was then, in the language of the keen litigant, 'game on'. The Moore brothers sued the *Bulletin*. In an era where a trial for a capital crime typically unfolded over just one or two days, the Clontarf libel action consumed over a week of a courtroom's time and featured accounts from fifty witnesses. In May 1881, the jury, after an hour of careful consideration, awarded the Moores a single farthing in damages.[41] This insult, of one small coin, in compensation to the plaintiffs and their bruised business and egos, would not be the last of the matter.

The parties were back in court in December the same year. The Moores were refused a new trial, but the matter of costs was reserved. In March 1882, the *Australian Town and Country Journal*, known for publishing news and essays, suggested that the 'public will, perhaps, be surprised – and doubtless indignant – to learn that Mr John Haynes and Mr John F Archibald, two of the proprietors of the "Bulletin", were last Monday arrested'. The issue was around the legal costs incurred by the plaintiffs, which stood at about £1,000. Many thought the pair from the *Bulletin* had helped render a public service in their reporting on Clontarf and a subscription raised around £800. A momentous sum, but this amount barely covered the legal costs of the defendants.[42] In lieu of fiscal compensation for the Moore brothers, Haynes and Archibald were ordered to spend the next twelve months in Darlinghurst Gaol, the main workplace of Nosey Bob.

In Howard's day, the colony's gallows did not see the same levels of frenetic activity generated by the court system in the early to mid-1800s. This gave the hangman some free time. As a salaried civil servant, Howard was required to attend work like any other sheriff's officer, and so he was 'employed as "general utility" about the court house grounds at Darlinghurst, with the "supreme duty" when the necessity arose'. Nosey Bob's tasks included looking after the sheriff's buggy and horse, a role for which he was eminently qualified. Also, when he was 'not engaged obeying that law which decrees that certain people are to be hanged by the neck till they are dead, Howard puts in a good deal of his time attending the garden at Darlinghurst'. Another job he had was to make sure the turkeys on the grounds were fat.[43] Humans were not the only ones whose necks were at risk.

In other duties as required, Howard had helped Mary Cowper, the wife of Sheriff Charles Cowper, prepare for a dinner party, but the event became a disaster 'when guests learned that the cutlery they were using had been polished by the same fingers that adjusted the noose around local murderers' throats'. Not everyone was so particular, and there were no complaints when Nosey Bob did the washing up for the restaurant attached to the court house.[44]

Archibald and Howard must have seen each other in this strange twist of events that saw the journalist a guest of a gaol's governor instead of a guest in Howard's home. There would have been little time for socialising in the yards, though; the hangman had his own problems.

In 1882, Howard was in court again under a charge of 'unlawfully and maliciously inflicting grievous bodily harm upon one Charles McLean'. The assault had occurred late on the night of 13 March in Paddington, where both men lived. McLean testified that as he walked past Howard's house, the hangman's dog, 'which was lying on the door step, rushed at him', and he was forced to defend himself. It was claimed that Howard opened his door, dressed only in a night-shirt, and struck McLean over the head with a life preserver. The *Daily Telegraph*, published as a Sydney-based broadsheet before becoming a tabloid, described McLean's wounds as serious. Nosey Bob was released on bail of £80. The defendant also had to arrange two sureties, people who were willing to pay £40 each to guarantee he would turn up in court as ordered.[45]

The matter went to trial at the Court of Quarter Sessions at Darlinghurst on 4 April. McLean repeated his story, while Mrs McLean corroborated her husband's testimony. Howard gave his own version of events and stated McLean had yelled abuse at him from the street while he threw a stone at his dog. McLean then grabbed Nosey Bob's legs and Howard, afraid of falling, struck his attacker with the leg of a chair. Mary Brady, who lived across the road from Howard, testified that McLean was 'falling about in a drunken state' and that she had told him to go home. Brady's next-door neighbour, Margaret Toohey, said that McLean had 'threatened to flatten the defendant's face as well as his nose'. Toohey went on to say that she knew 'as a fact' that Howard's nose was already flattened, and that she regarded the hangman as 'a quiet, inoffensive man'. Another witness, Mary Johnson, heard McLean threaten Howard and then saw the carpenter try to pull the hangman down his front steps. More witnesses testified to McLean's 'quarrelsome disposition'.[46]

The medical evidence given at trial described the injuries to McLean's head as well as his intoxicated state on the night in question. It was observed that the 'wounds might have been caused by a fall'. The jury agreed that there was reasonable doubt and, 'after a short deliberation, returned a verdict of not guilty, upon which the accused was discharged'.[47]

The sheriff might have been embarrassed by his man's day in court, but Cowper did not suffer the indignity forced upon his predecessor, Harold MacLean, almost a decade before. On 28 November 1873, the senior scragger John Franks was at the Central Police Court, where he was done for common assault. At the very same session, the assistant hangman, Ernest Henry Dowling, appeared for failure to pay his wife maintenance.[48] Howard would have generated some gossip in gaol tea rooms, but he was free to go home and, more importantly, he was free to go back to work. This was just as well. November and December 1882 saw Nosey Bob with a full calendar as he made business trips to Armidale, Goulburn and Deniliquin.

Soon after Howard's appearance in front of a judge and jury, Haynes and Archibald were also back at work, having been released from Darlinghurst Gaol on 21 April 1882 after members of the public raised enough funds to cover the costs that they owed in connection to their libel case.[49]

Howard might have been relieved to see off the journalists, but he was also busy preparing for hangings. Nosey Bob's first job that year was John McGuan, for murder, on 22 November 1882 at Armidale, north of Sydney. In 1880, McGuan was accused of murdering Thomas Smith, an elderly shoemaker who lived alone in Inverell. When first arraigned, McGuan complained that he had no counsel and so his case was deferred. When tried, the jury failed to reach a decision. A second trial, in which more proof was presented by the prosecution, saw a verdict of guilty returned and the sentence of death read out. A bloodstained hammer found in McGuan's cart was a match for the damage done to Smith's skull, though McGuan said the blood on the hammer was his own. Smith's throat had also been cut, with a medical doctor stating that he could have died from either the head or neck wounds. It was asserted that the motive for murder was money, with the prisoner frequently talking about how much cash Smith kept at home.[50]

Some prisoners exhibit stoicism when a judge reads out the fatal words. Not McGuan. 'During the sentence and after, the prisoner was most violent, blaspheming, cursing the judge, jury, and witnesses in an awful manner'.[51]

Howard's heart must have skipped a beat on the scaffold when his assistant, on the first attempt, was unable to dislodge the bolt that would release the trapdoors on the gallows. Another push and the bolt moved. McGuan, a heavy and well-built man, was sent off with a drop of 8 or 9 feet. Death seemed to be almost instantaneous, a common variation on the theme of the instant death that everyone on and around the platform hoped for, but some signs of life remained. After 'hanging a few moments, the knees were slightly and slowly raised, as by some muscular contraction and then sank again, after which, beyond a tremulous motion, no movement was visible'.[52]

McGuan never confessed. It was fervently hoped he would admit to the crime and facilitate the recovery of Smith's money and property, which had not been located by police. McGuan did, however, offer a sincere retraction of the curses he issued at his trial.[53] Howard had no time to consider the circumstances surrounding McGuan's drawn-out case. He was off to Goulburn to hang someone for attempted murder.

CHAPTER 4

KEEPING COUNT

GOING 'ON WITH THE JOB'

Howard was asked, numerous times over his career, about how many patients he had seen off. Some newspapers proposed outrageous figures, while others tried to downplay the damage. One account said that he only 'executed thirty-four persons', including Captain Moonlite 'and his mate Rogan'.[1]

A fellow known as a gentleman hangman should not come across as boastful or, worse, as a man aiming to be a top-ten executioner. On one occasion Howard said he kept a list. If this is true, and the man who could not write much more than his name had someone to do his recordkeeping for him, then like many records from Nosey Bob's time the list has not survived. Howard's usual and probably more honest response was that he did not keep count. When talking about having worked twenty years as a hangman in 1896, Howard reiterated that he did not run a tally and said: 'I have not kept a record'. He did, though, have a rough idea of the number of appearances he had made on a scaffold.

'In a couple of years before the last year there was an average of six a year', he told a reporter. 'But, on the whole', he said, 'the average would be perhaps four. That is for Sydney and throughout the colony'.[2]

Nosey Bob's estimation of the score on his dispatch card is not quite right. Four hangings a year for twenty years, between sending off George Pitt in 1876 and his twentieth-anniversary interview in 1896, would bring Nosey Bob's tally to around eighty. A more accurate total in the mid-1890s, which was about two-thirds of the way through Howard's career as an executioner, is that he had dispatched around fifty felons.

In one respect, for Nosey Bob at least, the number of people he executed was irrelevant because the hangman claimed he had never *actually* hanged anyone. Shortly before the hanging of two of the Wantabadgery bushrangers in January 1880, Howard told the *Bulletin*'s JF Archibald, that he had never fixed a rope and he had never pulled a bolt. It was not him. It was not his fault:

> Do you know, sir, that I never put a rope round a man's neck in my life! I never pulled a bolt either. I've a man to do it for me. I stand there, d'ye see, and I pulls his cap over his face and I walks round him to see that the knot's nice and comfortable. Then I looks at the sheriff to catch the wink of his eye, and then I tips the wink to my mate, and he pulls the bolt and lets the man down. It's not a fact that I ever hung a man – never, sir; never![3]

This is Howard at his most disingenuous. He may have been trying to unsettle Archibald, or he could have been deflecting blame to cope with how he earned his salary. A balm to make life a little easier.

Several reports that outline Howard's early work with William Tucker identify Tucker as the one who attended to all the finer details and who drew the bolt. This was certainly the case for Pitt in June 1876, with Nosey Bob, who was serving as the assistant executioner, only charged with taking Pitt's 'handkerchief, which he had previously requested the gaoler to hand to his mother'. When Michael Connolly was hanged, just a week after Pitt's dispatch, the assistant executioner stood to the side while 'his confrere, the principal, took hold of the handle connected with the fatal bolt, received the signal, and with a movement of the hand the trap opened with a dull sound'. Accounts of Daniel Boon's execution, in July 1876, are not very specific and little information on what the principal executioner and his assistant did on the scaffold is presented to readers. When Thomas Newman was hanged in May 1877, after Tucker had vanished from view, it is the principal executioner who steps aside, allowing the assistant to approach the steps and deal with the bolt.[4]

Contradicting Howard's claim that he never pulled a bolt is that he appeared to be on his own when he carried out the final sentence of the law upon Peter Murdick in 1877.[5] The duties of pinioning the prisoner, escorting him from his cell to the scaffold, fitting the noose, adjusting the cap and drawing the bolt could not be delegated that day in Wagga

Wagga. Howard routinely fitted the cap and noose, and while he did not like handling the bolt, there was nobody for Howard to outsource to at Murdick's dispatch. There were not going to be any local volunteers on standby to help the visiting sheriff's officer, no one to share the shame. Howard, surely, drew the bolt and it was not the last time he did so.

Howard may have allocated key tasks to others when he could, but he was, as his position title indicated, an executioner. A man who participated in sixty-two hangings, between 1876 and giving up the rope in 1904, cannot honestly say that he never hanged a fellow human being. If Howard was seeking absolution through distancing himself from his work, he did not need to make this bold and, frankly, unbelievable claim. Despite the disgust with which many people held the hangman, it was acknowledged that he only acted as the law demanded. Permission to carry out the hated task could also come from the felon as Nosey Bob discovered on 29 November 1882 in Goulburn, when he stepped up to meet his fifteenth patient.

Charles Cunningham, also known as John Smith, had a rap sheet and a few aliases. His first sentence, for horse stealing, was a term of three years with hard labour. His second sentence, for a bank robbery committed in the small village of Cannonbar in the colony's north, saw him allocated seven years of room and board in Darlinghurst Gaol. He was then sentenced, a third time, to another nine years for attempted murder, committed in Darlinghurst, when he stabbed another prisoner. Upon being moved to Berrima Gaol, in the southern highlands, he attacked the gaoler and continued to exhibit behaviours that entrenched the idea he was a 'human bear' who, though not declared insane, was treated with the utmost caution.[6]

On 2 September 1882, Cunningham crossed another line when he tried to kill an officer of the law. Warder John Izard had fetched Cunningham and was leading him through a narrow passage so that he could exercise in the gaol yard. Unfortunately for Izard, someone had carelessly left an axe in the passageway. Cunningham saw an opportunity; he grabbed the axe and swung at the warder. Unable to attack with a full swing due to the restricted space, he still managed to slice 'a small piece of flesh off the cheek bone' in addition to 'cutting the neck and breast' of Izard. Another prisoner, Moses Bendon, saw the assault and rushed forward to grapple the axe from Cunningham. Reinforcements arrived on the scene, but Cunningham was not done. He injured the gaoler and the chief warder. Even when he was restrained, he managed to tear through strong leather muffs using his teeth and then take his handcuffs off. Finally, Cunningham was brought under control and order was restored at Berrima. When Cunningham was transferred to Goulburn to answer for his latest crime, authorities took no chances and he was accompanied by a heavy escort.[7]

The trial was almost a non-event as it only took two hours from start to sentencing. The spectators in attendance were still excited, 'owing to the outrageous conduct of the man in the dock, who used profane language to the witnesses, the barristers, and the judge'. The trial could have been even shorter, but Cunningham dismissed the defence counsel offered to him and he took control of his own case. Thus, 'all the witnesses were subjected to an annoying examination by the prisoner, who called them by the foulest names'. The jury found Cunningham guilty and the judge sentenced him to death. The prisoner revealed that he had only claimed he was innocent so that he could have his day in court and air his grievances about the colony's criminal justice system.[8]

The fatal day arrived and Cunningham blamed Her Majesty Queen Victoria for his plight. He yelled out from the scaffold: 'I curse the Queen of England. May God strike her dead with leprosy'. A local newspaper, the *Goulburn Herald*, reported that the 'hangman, Robert Howard, then drew the white cap over the convict's head, and the assistant hangman drew the bolt'. Death was reported as being instantaneous, with only slight muscular twitches being discernible by the small crowd of witnesses.[9]

Howard would declare, when reminiscing years later, that Cunningham was one of the worst men he ever faced on a scaffold. 'He was terrible', Howard said when talking about his time out at Goulburn:

> He would have no one to see him, and he cursed and fumed terribly while in the condemned cell. I thought I would have a task, but as soon as I got into the cell he said: 'Hello! I know who you are. Come on Bob, it's all right'. When he stood on the scaffold and looked round at the few people he cursed them all, and committed them to perdition. He cursed all in authority, high and low; then, turning to me and holding out his head,

he said: 'Now then, old man, go on with the job; I'm ready'.[10]

When Cunningham left the courtroom after his trial, despite his behaviour throughout the short process, he told the judge that he hoped 'the sentence would be carried out as passed'.[11] When the time came, he held onto that hope, and while not exactly endorsing Howard's role in his demise, he politely acknowledged what Nosey Bob had to do.

AN INSANE PRACTICE?

On 12 July 1882, three of the five children of William and Elizabeth Preston were walking to school in Moira, near Deniliquin in the colony's far south. At a house along the route, the oldest child in the group, 9-year-old Mary, threw a stick against the front wall. Henry Tester, a man who was 25 or 26 years of age, who had been working for Mr Preston for a few weeks, came out in a rage. In a reaction out of all proportion to a child's silliness, he smashed the skull of Mary's sister, Louisa, aged 7, with an axe. Mary testified at the coronial inquiry on 19 July that when she threw the stick, it was only in fun. She said: 'I had no idea it would make him angry'. After the hideous assault, a terrified Mary grabbed her brother, who was about 5 years old, and ran for home.[12]

The inquiry heard that Tester confessed once he was taken into custody. He told police: 'I struck the girl twice on the head because her father told me a lie'. He then identified the weapon when it was shown to him, saying yes: 'This is the axe I done it with'. The victim's parents were called to testify before the coroner. Mrs Preston was only able to say that she was the wife of Mr Preston before she 'became so hysterical that her evidence could not be taken'. Mr Preston testified that he and his wife, upon the alarm being raised, ran to the house of the prisoner and found Louisa. He carried her home, then took her to the Echuca Hospital where she died early in the morning of 18 July. Tester's employer said that the axe was his, but he had never seen 'anything about the prisoner to lead him to suppose he had a violent temper'. He also stated that, apart from asking the prisoner why he had slept very late one morning even though he was on wages, he had not had any trouble with him.[13]

When Tester, also known as Searey, was arraigned in late October, he was incoherent and refused to engage with the essential processes of the court. On being asked a second time if he was declaring himself guilty or not guilty, he told the judge: 'Oh, anything you like'. He then brashly insisted that his honour should: 'Go ahead, I'll take my chance: hang me up to the wall if you like'. The gaoler intervened and advised that 'when the prisoner was first admitted he spoke rationally, but had latterly become moody and refused to speak'. In response to Tester's perplexing behaviour, a jury was empanelled a few days later to see if he was sane and so fit to be tried for his crime. Three medical professionals and the local gaoler all 'swore that in their opinion the prisoner was feigning insanity, and the jury found accordingly'.[14] Tester would be made to answer for his actions.

The trial in October was a reasonably straightforward

affair. It was shown that Tester had wasted no time in running off after his homicidal rage, and that he had stabbed a constable while resisting arrest. These actions, combined with Tester's confession and other evidence presented to the court, proved beyond doubt that he had murdered little Preston.

There was some publicity around his supposed insanity, but the jury was comfortable 'that he was shamming' and a guilty verdict followed. He was 'sentenced to death in the usual manner'.[15]

The executive council was in a merciful mood when it met in early November 1882. Ah Hing's death sentence, for assault with intent to murder, handed down in Deniliquin in October, was commuted to fifteen years in prison. A death sentence given to Jimmy Hing or Hong for rape, issued in Armidale in the same month, was commuted to life imprisonment. The executive council was not, however, feeling merciful enough to offer Tester a reprieve. He would hang as ordered by the court. It was then reported that, as he was awaiting execution, he had 'commenced to talk rationally to his gaolers' and so showed that his insanity was a pretence.[16]

Tester's behaviour in prison after his sentencing confirmed the opinions of the medical professionals and those who served the court at his trial. In answering 'questions from the gaoler and warders, the unfortunate and misguided man returns rational replies, betokening that his insanity was only feigned during his trial for the purpose of frustrating justice'. He also ate and slept well in prison, asked for tobacco but refused religious instruction. When Tester was offered a Bible to help him to prepare for his meeting with Nosey Bob, he just said: 'I don't want it, I won't have it, I don't believe in it'. The gaoler offered to read passages to him, but Tester could not be swayed.[17]

When clemency was denied by the executive council, nobody was surprised. One of the oft-cited arguments for capital punishment is that there is no other option when it comes to the most odious criminals: 'It was an atrocious and bloodthirsty occurrence, and the hanging of such a monster is a relief to society'.[18] Confronted by what was now the inevitable, Tester took some of the religious consolations that were offered to him in Deniliquin Gaol.

On 7 December 1882, the day of his execution, Tester woke up early to go and inspect the gallows before he sat down to a hearty breakfast. When he was collected from his cell, he was found on his knees praying with the reverend who had been assigned to him. The man of the cloth could only achieve so much. Fervent prayers and an escort to the gallows were not sufficient to see Tester ask for forgiveness. There was the usual removing of irons and pinioning. The procession took place, a few more prayers were said, and 'the hangman proceeded with the horrible details of his work'. There was some impatience at the gallows that morning. It was felt everything was taking too long and so 'the white cap was thrust hurriedly over the doomed man's head'. The bolt was drawn and the criminal fell. In at least one report, which might have annoyed Nosey Bob, it was specified that the hangman and not an assistant drew the bolt.[19]

Henry Tester became Robert Howard's first major bungle on a scaffold. Peter Murdick's strangulation at Wagga Wagga in 1877 was very low-key. When Thomas Rogan was hanged in Darlinghurst Gaol in 1880, his neck was not broken, but Nosey Bob's error was not obvious with the strangulation easily defended by the medical officer supervising the execution. When Howard offered his standard statement of goodbye to Tester as the pair faced each other on the scaffold, he was an experienced executioner. On the job for over six years, Tester was his sixteenth send-off. It was the sixteenth time Nosey Bob had said: 'My poor man no one regrets this more than I do'.[20]

The act of hanging is an act of brutality.

In a clean hanging, the neck dislocates or snaps. There are seven neck bones, or cervical vertebrae, immediately beneath the skull. The second of these bones, situated behind the teeth of a closed mouth, is known as the axis and forms the pivot that allows the vertebra above, the atlas, to rotate. It is the axis that is the focus of the executioner's attention. The demolition of this small bone, along with causing irreversible injury to the spinal cord, renders the condemned unconscious.[21] This damage is often referred to as a hangman's fracture.

The noose contracts, compressing the neck, preferably without tearing it, and because the brain is denied oxygen, it dies in approximately eight minutes. While this is happening, the rest of the body is also deprived of oxygen and starts to shut down. Muscles will twitch, making for a traumatic display for witnesses. Males will have erections and ejaculations are not uncommon. Waste products are to be expected. Bladders and bowels loosen. Blood and other fluids might leak from the eyes as well as the ears, nose and mouth. The hood placed over the head of the prisoner offers a grim transition to complete darkness for those about to die, but it also offers some protection to those lined up to watch a hanging. As the body fails, the 'heart keeps beating until its own supply of oxygen runs out and after a short period of quivering it finally stops'.[22]

Phrases such as 'death was instantaneous' or 'death was almost instant' are pacifiers for those wanting to quibble about the rights and wrongs of the death penalty and assert its deployment. In an absence of mercy, death itself, at the very least, should be merciful. Justice could be claimed as just. The idea of death as instant is, more accurately, merely a death of which the man or woman dying is completely unaware. If a neck is broken, then unconsciousness acts as a primitive form of anaesthetic. There is hardly any pain, hardly any suffering. There is terror, but once the bolt is drawn, there should be not much else. The body falls; it hangs from the beam above the gallows and life just quietly seeps out. Unless, of course, there is no hangman's fracture. If the neck is not broken, or the head is not completely taken off, then the criminal remains conscious while they experience an agonising and lingering death. When Tester was hanged by Nosey Bob, he knew exactly what was going on:

For two or three minutes after the bolt had been drawn
Tester struggled violently, it being evident that the
neck was not broken, but that he was suffering death
by strangulation. His body showed signs of life for
twenty minutes, and he was observed to breathe for a
quarter of an hour after the fall took place. It was indeed
a ghastly sight, and the few civilians present expressed
their opinion that the hanging was a bungling piece of
business.[23]

The exact drop is not known, but it was widely reported
that it 'was not sufficiently great'. One journalist argued that
the rope should take some of the blame for the botched
execution; it was too thick, while the prisoner was too
light. This writer was also clear about 'some bungling on
the part of the executioner' and explained that 'the painful
proceedings were disgustingly prolonged'. Another account
specified it was a full thirty-five minutes before the medical
officer in attendance at the gaol declared that Tester was,
finally, dead.[24]

The executioner's good run of reasonably clean deaths
was over. Howard was not allowed to forget, with reports
on his errors often published in list form after Tester's elim-
ination. It was not an accident; it was a pattern. Tester's crime
was vile, but so was his death. The prisoner's insanity was
not real, but the insanity of the death penalty was apparent
to many. Unnecessary cruelty was not justice, it was only
another episode of violence.

HAVING SOMEONE TO BLAME

On 17 March 1883, the *Evening News* reported on a murder that had been committed in the north of New South Wales. Two articles on the same page told the story of how the victim, James or Jimmy Young, was a popular and respected Chinese doctor. Young was described as being a very decent fellow, a man who did not engage in antisocial or disreputable activities like heavy drinking or gambling, and so locals were flummoxed when he was found on the bank of the Armidale Creek having been 'foully murdered'. A first assessment of the corpse revealed that the weapon used was an American axe, the same type of long-handled axe that had been wielded by Charles Cunningham when he tried to kill John Izard at Berrima in 1882. In the Armidale case, 'the muscles of the neck were completely severed' and there was 'another severe wound on the right temple, where a blow enough to produce death had been given'. There were also deep cuts upon the face and shoulders that looked to have been made by a much smaller weapon than the axe, probably a tomahawk.[25]

The articles speculated on some of the clues that had been left behind by the killer, noting how the body had obviously been dragged a great distance. A timeframe for the murder was outlined, based on how the victim had been found on a busy walking track but was cold to the touch. There was also some speculation that the doctor was in that part of town to visit a patient at the local tannery. It was pointed out that there was 'a Chinese gambling hell' located close to the crime scene, but the victim was found with £16 and a gold watch still on him, so robbery, a common motive for murder, was ruled out. There were no suspects. Readers were told that 'great excitement and indignation' prevailed.[26]

Within days, a trail of blood had been followed 'from the creek where the body was discovered, to a house some distance away'. The four occupants of the property were arrested. It was soon believed that a robbery had still taken place, even though Young was found with some cash and his watch. A deposit receipt for £182 was missing, and there was evidence that someone had tried to cash the receipt at Uralla, south-west of Armidale.[27]

There was quite a lot of confusion around the number of culprits connected to this crime. One report claimed police had arrested a Chinese man and a European boy named George. Another stated that the police had six Chinese men and a woman in custody for the murder. And yet another claimed that three Chinese men and a white woman had been arrested on suspicion of murder.[28]

Finally, most of those who had been detained were released, but police kept a Maltese man, George Rugsborne, under arrest when they discovered he had cashed a cheque by forging the signature of the murder victim. A young boy, George Scarr, who was reported to be just 12 years old, was also arrested. Scarr told authorities that he had been recruited by Rugsborne to aid in committing the crime and that it was his role to go and fetch the doctor. This allowed Rugsborne, lying in wait near the creek, to launch an attack. Evidence at the coronial inquiry, which also identified Rugsborne as Japanese, revealed that this was the third attempt the assailant had made to take the doctor's life.[29] The jury serving the inquest decided it was wilful murder, and Rugsborne would go on trial.

The trial went for two days. Rugsborne's barrister, who had been assigned to him by the government, made every effort to save his client from the gallows and even 'made a powerful speech to the jury, which occupied about four hours'.[30] The jury did not need that length of time to reach an agreement, deciding that the accused was culpable after only fifteen minutes of deliberation. The death sentence was issued. It was the second death sentence read out at the Armidale Circuit Court that April.

The judge held out no hope for mercy for Rugsborne, but he said he hoped that 'a wise and merciful executive' council would remit the sentence of an 18-year-old girl.[31] As women who were young and pretty could be cast as ideal victims, they could also be presented as offenders who had, themselves, been wronged and were deserving of public sympathy. The judge's instincts on who should be offered mercy were correct:

> The Executive Council of New South Wales having considered the case of Milbra Nott, the young girl who was found guilty of the murder of her lover, Robert Mitchell, [at Armidale], have commuted the death sentence to one of five years' imprisonment. Public sympathy had expressed itself strongly in favor of the prisoner, who had been greatly provoked and exasperated by the refusal of Mitchell to marry her after

promising to do so. It was decided that the sentence of death passed on George Rugsborne, for the murder of a Chinese doctor, should be carried into effect.[32]

The date for Rugsborne's execution was set for 23 May 1883. He would hang in Armidale Gaol. Howard's preferred rope for a hanging was a manila rope, made from the leaves of the abaca plant. Manila rope, sometimes referred to erroneously as manila hemp, is the strongest natural fibre rope available and a good choice when a rope's integrity is the difference between a good job and a tragic one. The numerous ropes that were deployed by Nosey Bob were about 3 inches in circumference or just under 1 inch in diameter (with hangmen across the Empire using ropes between ¾ of an inch and 1¼ inches thick).[33]

Manila is a rope of excellent quality, but it does pose a conundrum for the executioner as the shock load absorption is poor. This is an undesirable trait in a noose, as the full force of the fall must be felt at the patient's neck. Nobody wants a rope to break or unravel, but a rope that stretches or coils too much absorbs a lot of force and reduces the impact upon the neck, which increases the odds of an untidy death.

To overcome this problem and make the rope pliable, Howard would treat manila by boiling it in water and linseed oil. The longer you boil a rope, the softer it becomes, which has the added benefit of sliding more easily through the knot or the eye of the noose. Greasing and stretching the rope after boiling also helped achieve a smooth action on hanging day. In addition, softening the fibres removed the coarseness of

FIGURE 6 Stretching the rope

SOURCE *Bulletin*, 31 January 1880, p. 4

the rope and reduced the risk of tearing the skin of a person's neck. Nosey Bob would then test each piece of rope 'with sand-bags up to the weight of the man to be hanged'.[34]

Howard claimed that he would never go out of his way to see the condemned prisoner before the day of their execution. He did not want them to make their introductions earlier than necessary. Instead, he relied on the gaol authorities to supply him 'with a document, giving the weight, height, and age of the prisoner'.[35] Nosey Bob would then make his drop calculations accordingly. It is almost incomprehensible that a hangman would not engage, directly, with this component of the job. Nosey Bob's literacy skills were not good enough to process paperwork, and he knew how important it was to assess the condition of a person's neck when it came to setting the drop.

Howard was usually neutral in his commentary on judicial policies. He was just a man doing his part to keep the dual systems of law and punishment functioning smoothly. In an atypical statement on his employer, he once openly whined that prisoners were 'treated too kindly and kept too long. They get flabby. The muscles of the neck soften, and the neck gets as tender as a chicken', he said. 'No man should be kept longer than a week or a fortnight if you want good work and a first-class execution.'[36] Avoiding prisoners might have come as a blessing to the condemned, but it was also an example of how Nosey Bob could be cunning. As the Secretary of State for the Colonies outsourced responsibility of botched hangings to the executioners, Howard, in the event of a catastrophe, also had someone he could blame an incident on. He could claim it was not him; it was the information.

There are different versions of Rugsborne's death, with reports that he died instantly contradicted by statements that the patient struggled after being dropped. The claim that Rugsborne was strangled is impertinent; Howard had set the drop to 10 feet and the struggles seen by witnesses were more likely standard muscular contractions. Adding credibility to reports of an instantaneous death, the medical officer in attendance said that the neck was broken.[37] Howard may have set a long drop to avoid a scene of strangulation, but he is lucky he did not take Rugsborne's head off.

This speculation does add to some of the uncertainties around this murderer, a prisoner who gave different stories about his own life and whose ethnicity was in doubt. He did confess to committing murder, and his behaviour at his trial and on the scaffold was dignified. He even bowed to those present in the courtroom and then to those in the gaol yard. There were no final speeches, but there were prayers on his last morning as he had been baptised, into the Anglican faith, just a few days before his death.[38]

Rugsborne was also an indicator of how the law in the colony, despite so many crimes remaining capital, was regularly tempered by mercy. Of the nine death sentences issued in 1883, Rugsborne's was the only one carried out. After the bungling of Henry Tester's execution in 1882, Howard must have been relieved that his workload had eased.

AN UNCIVILISED PROGRESS

In Sydney, gallows have ranged from the crude to the elaborate. The earliest gallows were ladders put up against trees judged suitable for the task at hand. Felons would climb up and balance themselves before nooses were fitted around their necks and the ladder pulled out from underneath them. Slow strangulations ensued.

Another inefficient type of gallows was the cart. Men and women would be strung up while standing on the back of a cart that would then be pulled away. Again, death was slow as without a sudden drop the condemned died because they were strangled. The cart did, however, accommodate mass hangings. Carts also offered authorities and spectators convenience as they made it easy to transport felons to the scenes of their crimes. This enacted a highly visible lesson of cause and effect. Do the wrong thing and punishment will be swift and ugly. Executions at crime scenes also gave those most impacted by a crime or set of crimes, a chance to watch the ultimate judicial closure to a criminal case without the annoyance of making a trip into town. Ladders and carts were easy to deploy but they were diabolically ineffective. There were few opportunities for quick deaths with such primitive equipment so achieving a 'scientific jerk', and its associated instant death, was rare.[39]

What Sydney needed was progress. Specifically, the uncivilised progress of custom-built gallows. In 1804, new gallows were built at the corner of Park and Castlereagh Streets, just a block from where the western edge of Hyde Park is today. These were moved a few times. At one point they were situated on the site of the old Barker's Mills near the intersection of Sussex and Bathurst Streets, not far from Darling Harbour. The gallows were then near the old Devonshire Street Cemeteries, a block of land known today as Central Station. In 1820, the gallows were moved again, this time to the old gaol in Lower George Street, near Essex Street. This offered a neat nod to history as it placed the hanging platform very close to where Sydney's first judicial hanging, of Thomas Barrett for theft, took place in 1788. The old gaol also accommodated mass hangings. On 20 October 1828, to demonstrate an intolerance of property crimes, nine people were dispatched at once: Joseph Bradley and Patrick Troy for forgery; John Nuyley and Samuel Clark for burglary; John Welch for highway robbery; Patrick Rigney, Joseph Spicer and James Tomlins for stealing in a dwelling house; and James Henry for cattle stealing.[40]

The gallows then went to Darlinghurst Gaol when it opened in 1841. An early set of gallows faced Forbes Street, but with the abandonment of public executions, gallows were built inside a gaol yard. Even this improvement was up for debate in the 1850s, with objections to the idea of a permanent gallows and the proposed cost of £500. Most Sydneysiders were not troubled by the instrument of judicial death. Some people found it an almost benign contraption. One visitor, who had lived not far from the colony's largest prison when he was a young boy, said: 'I have now seen the gallows itself, and have found it a much more cheerful locality, viewed apart from its melancholy associations.'[41]

For prisoners in Darlinghurst, from petty criminals through to sadistic murderers, it was a constant reminder of what could happen to someone on the wrong side of the law. For the condemned, there was something worse than the sight of the gallows: the noise. The writer of the short-lived 'Behind the Bars' series that appeared in the *Arrow*, a once-a-week broadsheet, described the hangman's work. Identified only as an 'Ex-Warder', the man writing about his time at Darlinghurst Gaol, for a publication focusing on sport, detailed how Nosey Bob and his assistant treated the rope and prepared the gallows. The 'scaffold is not far from the condemned cells, and in the night the gruesome work of the hangman can be heard proceeding'. There would be an ominous 'tap, tap, tap as the knots of the rope were fixed to the beam'. Then, 'bang! the hangman is trying the lever, and the drop falls'. The sound of the trapdoors could not be mistaken for anything but the sound of death. 'The poor wretch in the cell hears all these preparations for his judicial murder, and his heart leaps to his mouth as he hears the bang of the trap opening and knows that in a few hours he will be banged off the same way'.[42]

Some regional centres, including Bathurst, Dubbo and Maitland, had their own gallows. Some gaols erected gallows as required. When a hanging platform for two was needed for Tamworth in 1894, it was a major story:

> Last week workmen were engaged in Tamworth Gaol in constructing the gallows for the execution of the two men on Friday next. The structure, which will permit of two men being hanged at the same time, is a very substantial one, and is built upon plans prepared at the Colonial Architect's office. The principal part of the work has been done in the yard adjoining the Courthouse, and the various parts will be taken to the gaol where they will simply require bolting together.[43]

In the late 19th century, Darlinghurst's gallows were busy with almost half of all Nosey Bob's dispatches completed in the colony's capital. In 1884, the Darlinghurst gallows saw the end of William Rice of Surry Hills, who shot and killed James Griffin in a jealous rage. Sophia Holmes, the focus of

Rice's affections, and an Aboriginal man known as Jumble, were present in the Phelps Street home when Rice pulled out a revolver. Griffin and Holmes sought shelter at a neighbour's house while Jumble ran towards Moore Park. When Griffin and Holmes returned to their own property, Rice was still there. Without any hesitation, Rice fired several shots, with two rounds finding their target. When neighbours arrived, they 'discovered Griffin lying on his back with his head on the hearthstone, quite dead'. Meanwhile, Jumble had alerted a constable while the 'shrill screams of murder caused great sensation', with 'hundreds of people turning out' and completely blocking traffic in the street.[44]

Rice's guilt was obvious and so his defence team pursued an argument of insanity, 'but the jury, no doubt believing that he could discriminate between right and wrong, returned a verdict of guilty'. Rice was sentenced to death, and a public petition for mercy was raised that collected 1200 signatures. The petition to the executive council was based on Rice being of unsound mind, that he was just a youth, that he had an upbringing that was 'wholly without good, motherly, home influences' and had suffered an injury that left him blind in one eye. The members of the executive council were cognisant of public opinion but also aware that Rice, despite being only 21 years of age, had been incarcerated on thirteen previous occasions.[45] The execution would proceed.

On 23 April 1884, Rice was led from his cell to the scaffold of the Darlinghurst Gaol. He was followed by 'the executioner, Robert Howard, his assistant (Charles Begg) and one or two gaolers'. An article on the hanging describes how the executioner prepared the rope, but after the white cap had been placed over the patient's head, the rope was adjusted by Howard's assistant, 'who looked paler than anyone present'. Howard had set a long drop. Rice fell 10 feet. After 'a slight convulsive jerk not the slightest symptom of vitality was observed'. It was a relief to all who were present. The increasingly prosperous *Evening News* thought the work was so fine and so painless that it 'would have removed many of the scruples of those who are in favour of abolishing capital punishment'.[46]

The same month that Rice was dispatched, Joseph Gordon, a Frenchman also known as Cordini, was convicted of murdering George Mizon, a hawker on the Hay Road not far from Deniliquin, on 10 October 1883. The case was largely circumstantial. There were also issues around the late allocation of counsel for the defence and the fact that there was no interpreter for Gordon at his trial. It was also thought that he was merely a victim of anti-French sentiment common at the time.[47]

At trial, the jury agreed there was enough evidence to declare the defendant guilty. The standard sentence for murder was issued. In May, the executive council 'saw no reason to interfere with the execution of the sentence, which will therefore be carried out in due course'. The request for a reprieve was debated in both houses of parliament while, as a French subject, the French consul lobbied on Gordon's behalf. A direct appeal was also made by Gordon's lawyer to the governor.[48] The efforts exerted to save Gordon's neck were all in vain. After a few extensions of time, it was confirmed that he would hang on 13 June 1884 in Deniliquin Gaol.

On the scaffold, Gordon was closely attended by religious counsel. As soon as he was aligned on the drop, the hangman placed the cap over his head but, in an unusual challenge to the standard procedure, Gordon asked for it to be removed. Pious advisors normally discouraged any last-minute statements and tried to focus the felon on penitence and prayer. On this occasion, it was clear the condemned had something to say: 'I did not hurt anyone in my life, and did not know anything of the murder as you can all see. That is all I know about it'. The statement calmed the prisoner and he submitted to having the cap replaced and the rope adjusted. The bolt was drawn, and an 8-foot drop produced a death that 'was almost instantaneous'. In a potentially devastating postscript, Gordon might have been telling the truth. In 1889, William Harrison stood on a gallows in Victoria for murder and said he knew that the Frenchman was innocent, but it was too late.[49]

Nosey Bob had strung up and dropped Gordon in 1884, nearly five years before Harrison supported the Frenchman's claim of innocence. Nothing could be done. You can release a wrongly incarcerated man, but a hanged man could only stay dead.

CHAPTER 5

THE HORROR OF
BOTCHED HANGINGS

CAUSE OF DEATH

On Saturday 4 April 1885, Howard's youngest daughter, 17-year-old Fanny, took the hand of Harry Bullenthorpe, an Englishman in his mid-20s, at St Peter's Anglican Church, near Darlinghurst Gaol. Fanny declares no occupation and states she is 18, while her new husband, the son of a detective, is identified as a mariner. The father of the bride is listed as a bricklayer's labourer. It was a bitter start to married life. The couple's only daughter, Maria Frances, was not yet two weeks old that Easter Saturday, and she died of severe malnutrition just nine days after the wedding.[1]

On 14 April 1885, the day a notice was published in the *Sydney Morning Herald* inviting mourners of his grandchild to gather that afternoon, Nosey Bob hanged Charles Watson in the yard of Darlinghurst Gaol's 'E' Wing, near Darlinghurst Road. Watson, described as an elderly man, had been found guilty of the 1884 murder of William Matthews near the Cowl Cowl station in the Hay district of central New South Wales. Watson was in court for three days, where it was shown he had bashed in the skull of Matthews before tying his ankles up with fencing wire and disposing of him in the Lachlan River. Before the development of technologies that facilitated the presentation of complex visual information to jurors, it was considered appropriate to bring human remains into courtrooms. For this trial, the 'skull of the murdered man was produced in court and examined by the jurymen'. The leg bones of the victim were also passed around to show Matthews had been lame. This affliction saw him vulnerable to an attacker, including an assailant who was advanced in years. Watson admitted taking possession of Matthews' property, but he denied committing murder.[2]

Appearing in Watson's defence were a couple of witnesses who spoke of his good character, but this was not enough to secure an announcement of not guilty. The judge, in his final comments, said that the prisoner's statement on how he came to possess the victim's 'waggonette and horses was simply incredible' and pointed out 'that no mercy could be extended' on this occasion.[3] The executive council allowed the law to take its course.

Newspapers were consistent in their descriptions of Watson's death and how it was, or how it at least appeared to be, a neat scragging. There was some disagreement on the drop, with one report stating it was about 11 feet and another that it was 12 feet long. One journalist specified that: 'The execution was admirably carried through by Howard and his assistant. Not a single hitch occurred, and death must have resulted almost instantaneously', though the assistant 'appeared to be visibly agitated'. Another reporter noted how the 'executioner', not the assistant, 'pulled back the lever, the drop fell, and all was over'.[4]

The body was then the subject of a coronial inquest, a type of inquiry that investigates the cause of a death. Coroners have a long history within the English legal system, with the office of the coroner only predated by the office of the sheriff. Inquests were occasionally held for hanged bodies, but there was nothing in the *Act to Regulate the Execution of Criminals 1855* (NSW) to indicate an inquiry was needed as there was, technically, no mystery to solve. The cause of death was execution by hanging. To modernise judicial dispatches and make executions more transparent, as well as bring New South Wales in line with other colonies, the *Criminal Law Amendment Act 1883* (NSW) dictated that coroners would, as soon as practical, 'hold an inquest upon the body of the executed person and the jury on such inquest shall inquire and find whether the sentence was duly carried into execution'.[5]

The first hanged bodies subjected to the new legislation were the murderers William Rice and Joseph Gordon in 1884. As this was a formality, instead of a true inquiry, the process was formulaic. For Watson's inquest in 1885, a gaol warder told those present he had witnessed the hanging. The under-sheriff had also witnessed the proceedings and he produced the prisoner's death warrant. The gaol's surgeon, Maurice O'Connor, had completed a post-mortem and he revealed 'the cause of death was strangulation by hanging'. The jury, 'after having heard the evidence, returned a verdict to the effect that death had resulted from strangulation from hanging by the neck' in accordance with a death sentence issued and carried out.[6] Howard may not have overtly bungled the execution, but without a broken or dislocated neck, the dispatch was not as clean as it could have been.

The next hanging in Darlinghurst Gaol saw the send-off of Thomas Williams on 14 July 1885. Coverage of the trial was nothing short of nefarious colonial melodrama, complete with a story of unrequited love:

> An inexpressibly sad scene was witnessed at the Central Criminal Court, Darlinghurst, on Friday. In the dock there stood a prisoner over whom but 23 years had passed, of slight build, with intelligent countenance, marred with the traces of early and acute suffering. From a pale, attenuated face gleamed eyes large and restless, the mouth and chin were feminine in their outline and power, and the face intellectual but weak. He nervously clutched the bars of his cage, or paced with measured tread up and down the confined area, or thrilled the listeners with some passionate appeal. Whether acted or real, the scene was vivid and touching.[7]

Public interest in Williams, better known as Frank Johns, was insatiable. Williams was one of the Wantabadgery bushrangers who had his death sentence commuted with fellow gang member Graham Bennett, while Thomas Rogan and Andrew Scott famously swung in Darlinghurst Gaol in January 1880. Williams and Bennett were sent to prison for life, but Williams was unable to stay out of trouble. The young man, who had turned to bushranging when he was a teenager, decided to steal a knife from the dining room at the Parramatta Gaol. Williams had fallen in love with a woman who visited the gaol and he had decided to kill himself. Once out in the yard, he thought two other prisoners were gossiping about him and, abandoning suicide, he instead launched a sudden attack. 'After an exciting chase, the knife was knocked from [his] hand, and he was overpowered and secured.'[8] His victim survived a deep stab wound to the chest, and Williams was charged with wounding with intent to murder. He faced Judge William C Windeyer in May 1885, the same man who had issued a death sentence to him in December 1879.

Williams went for a defence of temporary insanity and refused counsel. The jury found him guilty, but they also recommended mercy. Windeyer read out the death sentence and said that he held no hope for a second commutation. The executive council considered the court proceedings and the mass of public opinion in a meeting that lasted around two and a half hours. There was, too, a vocal gathering of about 8000 people pleading for mercy for Williams.[9] The council members could not be swayed and advised that the ultimate penalty of the law would be carried out.

Williams gave an extended speech on the scaffold. He forgave the woman he had fallen in love with, along with everyone else he blamed for his downfall. He spoke about his mother. He prayed aloud that he hoped he would 'be the last man who will be legally murdered in New South Wales'.

Howard and his assistant worked quickly. The execution was finalised and, although the Darlinghurst Gaol Death Register lists Williams as dying of asphyxia, the press focused on his long speech rather than any perceptible struggles after the drop. There were some concerns that a protest would break out and 'police and detective arrangements had been made to cope with any action', but the day passed without incident and rain saw the small crowds disperse and go home.[10]

Another man was hanged just before Christmas. Howard was told to dispatch Matthew Friske on 10 December 1885 at Grafton, the same year that the town in northern New South Wales was proclaimed a city. Little is known of Friske, aged about 67, or his victim, friend Mathew Matson, aged about 26, except that they were both Russian Finns. Friske's confession was graphic and shocking. He waited until his companion was leaning over to tend their campfire before striking him on the spine with an axe as hard as he could. The blow knocked Matson into the small blaze. Friske tried to push the entire body into the flames, but he was struggling to force one of Matson's legs into the pyre. He eventually settled for chopping the leg off and throwing it away. The motive given for the murder was that Matson had passed Friske a bad cheque.[11]

A public meeting was held in Grafton, days before Friske was due to be hanged, 'to consider the steps to be taken to obtain a commutation of the sentence of the condemned man'. It was agreed that there was no fault with the verdict or the sentence, but a reprieve was required to prevent the barbarity of an execution. The motion to petition for the prerogative of mercy had 49 votes in favour, but 54 against.[12] There was little support for Friske from the executive council, either. The hanging would go ahead.

Grafton's first judicial execution was unexceptional. Gallows were erected in the gaol yard based on the colonial architect's plans, but as reported by the *Evening News*, modifications were made at the direction of the under-sheriff, who thought the device was unsatisfactory. Friske continued to claim Matson's murder was not premeditated, but he made no speech from the scaffold. The procession was a generic one of gaol officers and religious support. 'Death was instantaneous, there not being the slightest movement beyond the oscillation of the body visible after the drop.'[13] It was an incident-free day for Nosey Bob.

OFF WITH HIS HEAD

The personal presentation of the executioners for New South Wales often determined how they were perceived by their employers, their colleagues in the justice system, the men of the ever-growing print media industry and the public. Howard, though never as fashionably dressed as his immediate predecessor William Tucker, was always neat and respectable in his attire. Matching his good black coat, his behaviour on the scaffold was consistently dignified. Nosey Bob might have spoken the odd harsh word to his assistants over the years, but he always treated his clients with respect. Not all the colony's hangmen could have made such a claim. Alexander Green, for example, was known for being a drunkard and trying to do his work while he slowly went insane.

In 1853, Green was tasked with a double hanging at Bathurst. The first man was Patrick McCarthy, who was being dispatched for the murder of Henry Williamson. The second was an Aboriginal man known as Paddy, who was being sent off for the rape of Catherine Schmitt. McCarthy pled his innocence, but it took a jury only ten minutes to find him guilty. There was little media commentary on the case, with broad acceptance, at the time, for applying the death penalty to wilful murderers. Paddy argued that his case was one of mistaken identity, that another man had committed the crime, but he, too, was found guilty.[14]

There was support for a commutation for Paddy, even though 'the unfortunate woman who was advanced in pregnancy, subsequently miscarried from the effects of the outrage'. The tragedy was acknowledged, but it was also asserted that 'we must, as we have ever done, decry the infliction of capital punishment in all cases wherein the *intention to take life* be not clearly established'.[15]

The execution process, for Green's only appearance that year, was an unmitigated disaster. An alcoholic after almost twenty years as the principal public executioner, Green had been denied a drink in the lead-up to the hangings. The *Bathurst Free Press and Mining Journal*, known for its detailed articles on hangmen and its contemptuous commentary on crowds that celebrated executions, informed readers that 'the executioner was suffering so severely from *delirium tremens* that it was considered unsafe to trust him for any length of time upon the fatal platform'.[16] The symptoms of alcohol withdrawal include shaking, confusion, hallucinations and an irregular heart rate. The dangers of having someone suffering these symptoms on a scaffold was soon plain for all to see.

To reduce the hazards created by a hangman recently put through an enforced detoxification process, the order of proceedings was changed. Usually, final prayers were read on the platform. On the morning of 8 April 1853, the 'prisoners said their prayers at the foot of the ladder inside the gaol wall'. The procession to the scaffold commenced with the patients being attended to by their religious counsellors, when the 'ghastly and pallid countenance of the hangman finally made its appearance, and the sickening details of an execution were commenced'. This is when things went horribly wrong. The nooses were fitted, but the rope for McCarthy 'was left so slack' that the criminal fell through it and was 'precipitated a distance of about 20 feet to the ground'. The bolt had not been drawn, but one of the prisoners had already been flung from the platform. It had to be pointed out to Green that he was missing a felon. The hangman tried to recover the situation by bringing the man back up, and he 'commenced pulling and hauling the rope as if he had been handling the carcase of a dead bullock'.[17]

After several attempts by Green, a horrified turnkey of the gaol went and tightened the rope around McCarthy's neck, allowing Green to bring him back onto the scaffold and line him up with Paddy. Then, without waiting for the signal, Green rushed to pull back the bolt. Another official had to make a desperate lunge for Green, otherwise one of the attending reverends 'would have been thrown off the platform along with the culprits'. Green, when permission was given, then struggled to pull the bolt but, finally, both men were cast off. Paddy 'appeared to die almost instantly, but the sufferings of McCarthy were more protracted no doubt in consequence of the rope being improperly placed'.[18]

The story in Bathurst was reprinted for Sydney-based readers on page three of *Freeman's Journal*, a twelve-page weekly newspaper. Green was dismissed after the bungle, and although he was soon reinstated, it was clear that his days as the colony's executioner were numbered. Two years later, on 4 May 1855, an order was approved to commit Green to the Tarban Creek Lunatic Asylum.[19]

Nosey Bob also drank to distract himself from his work, but he never let a few beers or a gin interfere with his public appearances. Howard was solemn, and sober, when he was back in Grafton just over six months after hanging Matthew Friske in December 1885. Nosey Bob's task, in June 1886, was to see off William Liddiard for murder. In an unusual example of press corps solidarity, Howard's bungling of Liddiard's execution was a universally underreported event.

Liddiard was sentenced to death at the Grafton Circuit Court for murdering Patrick Noonan in the town of Wardell on the Richmond River in the colony's north. Liddiard maintained, right until the end, that he was only an accessory to Noonan's murder and that the real killer was William James Hirlsford. The 17-year-old Hirlsford turned crown evidence, sharing information with authorities in exchange for a reduction of his own punishment, and he testified that Liddiard was the killer while he had only helped hide Noonan's body.[20]

Liddiard's wife, Elizabeth Liddiard, was also accused of being involved. The charge against her was later withdrawn, and she did not have to face trial. Another accusation directed at Mrs Liddiard was that she had been having an affair with Noonan, a relationship that was utilised to offer a compelling motive for her husband to commit murder.[21]

There were different versions of events given to authorities, with police having to carefully untangle all the testimony and match what they could with proof of the crime. The competing narratives agreed that the three men – Liddiard, Hirlsford and Noonan – were walking along the river, but diverged when it came to who assaulted and killed Noonan and who, out of fear, just helped to hide the body. In the end, the judge declared that Liddiard had been given 'a most patient and fair trial'. The jury went to deliberate and 'had very little trouble, in coming to a decision' delivering a unanimous declaration of guilt.[22]

On 8 June 1886, Howard's continued gambling with an extra-long drop failed to pay off. Nosey Bob had not attracted much attention when the hangings of Peter Murdick in 1877 and Thomas Rogan in 1880 did not go exactly as planned. He was criticised, and rightly so, for bungling the execution of Henry Tester in 1882, and he received mixed write-ups on George Rugsborne's instant death in 1883, while his work on Charles Watson and Thomas Williams in 1885 was largely overlooked. When a prisoner is slowly strangled to death, it is a dreadful and drawn-out process that highlights the true nature of an execution. A long drop, much longer than the standard of 8 feet for an average-sized person, reduced the risk of strangulation. Nosey Bob liked an 8-foot drop, but he had started using long drops of 9, 10, 11 and even 12 feet. This approach reduced the likelihood of strangulation, but it did bring another risk into play: decapitation.

Sometimes referred to as a tracheal fracture or rupture, a decapitation or near-decapitation is an appalling way to die. For the victim, death is at least fast. For the witnesses, death is a truly visceral outcome of a judicial execution replete with blood splatter and the sound of tearing flesh. It is a death that is also a big story. It is, therefore, almost inconceivable that the botched hanging of Liddiard did not inspire bold headlines across all the major newspapers that covered the execution. There are no descriptions of the hangman and his assistant. No details about the length of the drop. There were statements that death was instant, or instantaneous. This is, scientifically, correct. In an era of ever-increasing awareness of the issues around capital punishment and the fundamental inhumanity of state-approved murder, it is odd that dozens of articles do not mention what went wrong at Grafton. Instead, most reports offer a summary of Liddiard's last speech and his continued assertion that Hirlsford had perjured himself at the trial.

On this occasion, Howard's bungling was glossed over by most reporters. One article, in the *Northern Star*, a Lismore-based newspaper, described the outcome but downplayed the grotesqueness of a partial decapitation: 'Death must have been instantaneous, for the head was almost severed from the body by the rope, and no signs of life were visible after the bolt was drawn'. At the inquest, the foreman of the jury 'asked the doctor if he ever knew a case in which a man's head had been almost severed from his body by hanging as in this case'. The coroner advised that 'he had heard of cases in which the body had been completely severed'.[23] An undesirable, but not unheard-of, outcome. Nosey Bob may have felt forlorn on the return trip to Sydney, but at least he did not have to face the wrath of angry protestors.

In an administrative curiosity, newspaper readers were informed that 'the jurors at the inquest on William Liddiard are not entitled to fees, the verdict being "suicide by hanging". Fees are only awarded in cases of attendance at fire, murder, or manslaughter inquiries'.[24] For some people, crime really did not pay.

THE SCAFFOLD AS A STAGE

The Nichols family achieved two important firsts for New South Wales. Isaac Nichols, an ex-convict who had been sentenced to transportation for stealing, was the colony's first postmaster, while his son, George Robert Nichols, was the first Australian-born man to be admitted as a solicitor in New South Wales. 'Bob' Nichols became, despite battles with illness, a productive member of the colonial parliament from his first election to the legislative council in 1848 through to his election to the legislative assembly in 1856, where he held a seat until he died the following year.

In one of the debates leading to the *Act to Regulate the Execution of Criminals 1855* (NSW), first presented when the colony was on the cusp of responsible government, Nichols summarised some of the anxieties around the crowds that gathered to watch an execution. He argued that witnessing 'the execution of criminals condemned to death, by crowds of persons of both sexes and all ages, has a demoralising and hardening influence', and so executions should, if possible, be conducted 'within the prison walls'. As summarised by the *South Australian Advertiser*, soon after it was founded in 1858, the powerful visual of state-endorsed violence could generate crime for 'no one was ever brought to repentance at the foot of the gallows' and there was no faith 'in the hangman as an Evangelist'.[25]

These remarks also de-gendered an issue that, too often, focused on the number of females that gathered to watch hangings across the colony. The *Australian*, founded by lawyers and progressive in many respects, revealed a deep conservatism when reporting on the hanging of John Knatchbull. The ex-naval officer's dispatch on 13 February 1844 outside Darlinghurst Gaol, for killing a widowed mother of two with a tomahawk, attracted a crowd of about 10 000 people. The murderer of Ellen Jamieson faced a biddable gathering, but the *Australian* suggested the number of females present to witness the execution 'was incredible' and asked if 'the mind of woman, which we have hitherto admired for its gentleness, purity, and innocence', has become 'so utterly lost and debased as to delight in gazing upon the dying agonies of the condemned?' Another complaint in

Bell's Life in Sydney and Sporting Reviewer, a weekly paper, was that 'the proportion of females to the sterner sex' at an execution could be 'nearly three to one'.[26] Such derision directed at women was unfair. When these grumbles were published, executions were public events and, as hangings took place on weekdays, most men would have been at work and not available to partake of the sheriff's productions.

Though nobody was immune to criticism, women were routinely called out in descriptions of a hangman's crowds. Throngs that included well-dressed persons jostling for a position with 'mechanics, labourers, vagrants, thieves, prostitutes, and (worst of all!!) mothers with infants in their arms and young ones by their sides'.[27] There was an outrageous hypocrisy in the endorsement of public executions. Authorities wanted to be able to utilise the spectacle of punishment as a tool of deterrence, but on very specific terms. There were no published orders that detailed the preferred profiles of who should and should not turn up to watch a hanging, but the organisers and recorders of these events generally believed that such gatherings should be small, sombre, middle class or above, adult, male and white. When hangings became private affairs, who could be an official witness was clearly stipulated in legislation.

Part of the problem was the conflict between needing to educate society about crimes and their predictable punishments and the idea that the most extreme punishment available was a symbol of convictism that interrupted conversations around progress. The impetus for change came from 'a culturally loaded desire to appear civilised to the outside world and distance the Australian colonies from their often chequered beginnings'.[28] The scaffold was a stage, that was acknowledged, but it was a stage for the presentation of serious legal lessons, not raw entertainment. Unable to control the configuration of large audiences at public executions in New South Wales, with crowds often in their thousands, it was decided that the curation of small sets of onlookers for private executions was an essential judicial reform.

One of the regularly cited concerns in debates on the matter of private or public executions was transparency. There was a chance, highlighted by the *Sydney Morning Herald*, that an execution behind gaol walls allowed for corruption and deception. Even the usually sensible attorney-general of the day, John Hubert Plunkett, famous for prosecuting those who perpetrated the Myall Creek Massacre of 1838, was concerned the integrity of a hanging could be called into question.[29]

Plunkett had handled the biggest case of the 1830s when he prosecuted a group of men for a set of crimes committed at Myall Creek, west of Inverell. On 10 June 1838, 'about 30 Wirrayaraay men, women and children' were massacred by twelve colonists. Of the twelve, eleven were tried but found not guilty. Of those men, seven were tried a second time, with all seven found guilty and hanged. The attorney-general was clearly not afraid to see the gallows put to use, but he also believed that 'public executions were extremely demoralising'. At the same time, he felt that 'the greatest caution must be exercised in making any change' to the established processes for executions 'so as not to allow the slightest doubt as to the identity of the criminal'. The *Freeman's Journal* advised other commentators, editors and journalists to 'discard all such old womanish apprehensions' and 'frightful nursery maids' tales'.[30]

At the conclusion of this dispute, civilisation came first and conspiracy theories came second. The new legislation specified that whenever the 'judgment of death shall have been passed upon any person, and a day be fixed for the execution of such judgment', that the execution would be conducted 'within the walls of the Prison of the County, City, Town, or District, in which the conviction was had, or within the enclosed yard of such Prison' and that the sheriff, under-sheriff, or deputy shall be present with the gaoler, 'and proper Officers of the Gaol, including the Physician or Surgeon, together with all Magistrates who shall think fit, and such Constables, Military Guard, and adult spectators as the said Sheriff, Under Sheriff, or Deputy as aforesaid, may think fit'.[31] For those worried that executions would be carried out on the wrong person or not carried out at all, medical certificates and witness statements became standard for all executions conducted across the colony. There were penalties for making false declarations:

> Any person who shall subscribe any such certificate or declaration knowing the same to be false or to contain any false statement shall be deemed guilty of felony and being thereof lawfully convicted shall be liable to be transported for any period not exceeding fifteen years

or to imprisonment with or without hard labor for any period not exceeding three years.[32]

The practice of hanging in cloistered settings also 'bolstered the notion of this being a state-sanctioned act, and built upon it the symbolic weight of the prison as a site of punishment and correction'.[33] Despite the invigilation of executions being exclusive events in the second half of the 19th century, people still turned up to watch.

When In Chee was hanged for murder at Goulburn in 1878, a large crowd of people had assembled, hoping to view the action, but 'as the authorities had taken the precaution to enclose the upper part of the scaffold with tarpaulins, it was impossible for them to see anything beyond the crossbeam to which the rope was attached'. When Albert was hanged for murder at Dubbo in 1880, many locals climbed trees around the gaol or scrambled up onto the roof of the nearby Masonic Hall to view the proceedings.[34] No tarps or other types of temporary barriers were needed in the colony's biggest city. It was not easy to peer over the intimidating sandstone walls of Sydney's gaol, a complex that was spread out over nearly five acres. To watch an execution in the New South Wales capital, you needed a ticket.

On 8 October 1886, in Darlinghurst Gaol, Nosey Bob took care of Alfred Reynolds for the murder of his wife Rhoda Caroline Reynolds. Mr Reynolds had forced Mrs Reynolds to write a suicide note and then ordered her to drink a cup of liquid, a concoction of 'a quantity of opium with cold water'. If she failed to comply, he would cut her throat with a knife.

In summing up the case at trial, the judge said that: 'From the inquiries we have been able to make, and from the statements of the unhappy mother of your victim, it would almost seem that there is only one ray of comfort about this inexpressibly distressing case, which is that the poor woman is at rest'.[35]

In covering the crime, trial and punishment, the *Evening News* highlighted the heinous nature of the murder rather than the savagery of the death penalty. Readers were reminded of Thomas Williams, bushranger-turned-attempted-murderer, hanged the previous year, and how his case 'caused much excitement', with public meetings leading to efforts focused on seeking clemency for him. In contrast, the Reynolds case generated no sympathy, with nothing 'done to interfere with the course of justice'. The felon did not plead for mercy. The day of reckoning came, and no kind words were offered:

> The morning broke dull and heavily, the sky was overcast with leaden grey clouds, the hum of traffic sounded less cheerfully, and a spirit of gloom pervaded the atmosphere. It was a fitting day for the expiation of a dark and dreadful crime. A few people, attracted by idle and morbid curiosity, were assembled without the walls of the building, and numerous applications were made to the officer in charge for admittance. Some persons in their desire to gratify a purposeless curiosity offered to pay for the privilege of seeing the last scene in the terrible drama about to be enacted; but, as is needless to say, their efforts to obtain admission were unavailing.[36]

There was no turmoil on the scaffold. The white cap was drawn over the felon's face, 'the rope placed about his neck, and turning quickly to the lever, Howard drew the bolt'. Death, specifically attributed to Nosey Bob, was reported as being instantaneous, with the inquest revealing two breaks in the neck of Reynolds, who had fallen 6 feet on a 1½-inch manila cord.[37]

The noseless one's next appearance at Darlinghurst would see an overt generosity in the issuing of tickets. The number of people pressed up against each other in front of the gallows would draw loud complaints and recall the days of public hangings. The crowd was the largest audience Howard ever faced, a great mass to view one of his most controversial pieces of work.

'THE DROP WAS AT LEAST A FOOT TOO SHORT'

Nosey Bob had one job in 1887.

Mary Jane Hicks was pack-raped for six straight hours on 9 September 1886 at Mount Rennie in Sydney's Moore Park. Hicks, a 16-year-old orphan with a convent-school education, had come to the city from Bathurst. She was making her way to an employment registry when she was deceived by a cab driver, Charles Sweetman, who took her to the park where she was assaulted. The cabbie and another fifteen men, all around the age of 20, were arrested. Eleven were tried for rape, with nine found guilty and only two, Michael Mangan and Thomas Oscroft, acquitted and set free. After a meeting of the executive council that lasted several hours, it was decided that six prisoners would hang while three – Michael Donnellan, Hugh Miller and George Keegan – would spend life in prison. The granting of reprieves for two of the men sentenced to death, William Hill and William Newman, meant that only four would meet Nosey Bob. George Duffy, aged 17, Joseph Martin, also aged 17, would hang alongside two of their slightly older friends, William Boyce and Robert Read, both aged 19.[38]

The first complaint was about the need for a mass execution. Hanging felons in pairs was not unheard of, but four men swinging together was considered unnecessarily hideous. Similar scenes had not played out in the colony for decades, not since Edward Davis and five of the bushrangers that he worked with were hanged simultaneously on 16 March 1841 at the old Sydney Gaol.[39]

Another complaint was directed at Sheriff Charles Cowper. As the move in New South Wales to make executions private affairs was being formalised in the mid-1850s, gaols in the colony began pre-empting the illegality of public hangings. Francis Thomas Green, a murderer, was the last man hanged on the old gallows outside the walls of Darlinghurst Gaol on 21 September 1852, but the morning of 7 January 1887 resembled a hanging as public as the dispatch of Green almost thirty-five years earlier. In addition to thirty-two official witnesses, Cowper had given access to between 120 and 150 spectators.[40]

The *Sydney Morning Herald* regarded the ultimate sentence of the law as public performance 'as most undesirable', with a regional newspaper suggesting the sheriff could have just 'conducted the hanging over the front gate of the prison'. Cowper was defended by the *Goulburn Evening Penny Post*, a masthead that covered most major crimes in detail, which stated that the crowd, though rowdy, was mostly made up of 'old chums of the unfortunate men who were to expiate their crime', though 'they certainly did not conduct themselves as if they possessed any great depth of feeling for them'.[41]

The lengthiest, and fiercest, complaints were reserved for the executioner. Howard had received mixed support from the media, with outrage at some of his botchings, while a few of his errors attracted little, if any, commentary. For this mass hanging, it was declared that the way 'in which the hangman performed his duties was a disgrace to civilisation', and that New South Wales was the most barbarous of the supposedly advanced 'communities in carrying out capital punishment'. There were even accusations that Howard was deliberately cruel, and in 'adjusting the ropes he knocked the criminals as if they were swine, and he pulled the canvas caps so roughly over their faces that he must have inflicted upon them severe pain'.[42]

The job description of executioner is inherently hard-hearted, but Howard did not seek to magnify the savagery of the death penalty. Part of the problem on this occasion was that there were 'far too many persons on the scaffold at the last moment, whose presence interfered considerably with the hangman and the performance of the work'. The felons were lined up with 'Boyce to the extreme left, then Martin, Duffy, and Read'. There were no fewer 'than seven clergymen

FIGURE 7 **Entrance to Darlinghurst Gaol**

SOURCE State Library of NSW, 1887, SPF/169

on the scaffold, all of them remaining there while the men were being hanged'.[43] The jostling on the gallows upset the executioner greatly.

It was, without doubt, a poorly managed event. That three out of the four 'criminals were strangled to death shows how shockingly the hangman bungled in connection with the final act of his duty', while the 'ropes used were two inches in diameter' and 'large enough to hang oxen'. Such a heavy rope is far too thick, but this assertion was unsubstantiated and is in sharp contrast to all the evidence that shows Howard's care with the rope. It was also reported how the 'knots of the nooses did not, in at least two cases, appear to have been drawn sufficiently tight'.[44]

There was, too, an issue with the drop. Duffy bit his own tongue off when he fell, but he was the only one who had a spinal fracture. Just one instant death out of four is an indicator that the fall might not have been long enough. Martin suffered the most. The rope was caught on one of his pinioned arms, which checked his fall. It took Martin around ten minutes to die. It was a terrible display and at least one reporter fainted.[45]

The colonial architect had ordered new gallows to be 'specially erected for the purpose of this execution close to the condemned cells, the old gallows not being large enough to admit of the simultaneous execution of more than two persons'.[46] Like any structure, gallows were subject to design flaws as seen with the gallows built for Matthew Friske's dispatch at Grafton in 1885. It appears that this bespoke device, with accommodation for four, might not have been quite right for the task at hand.

The equipment was constructed at the foundry of Hudson Brothers and delivered to the gaol in sections. The pieces were then fitted together with the 'massive structure, bolted and stayed to prevent any possible spring or unsteadiness', finished off with a piece of '12 by 8 ironbark', a hardy type of eucalyptus. The beam, 'weighing nearly three quarters of a ton', would easily take on a group of teenagers.[47]

Unfortunately, the drop of 8 feet 6 inches 'was at least a foot too short'. Like the gallows at Newgate Gaol, the plans of which had been distributed to the colonies several years earlier, it is possible that the contraption was simply not high enough. The lithograph documenting Newgate's gallows came with the advice that in 'adapting the drawings for Colonial use, a longer drop than that attainable at Newgate might be had by raising the Gallows ... or by hollowing out the ground immediately under the drop' to give the executioner an extra 2 feet to work with. Nosey Bob had, as was his practice, tested the gallows before the event.[48] If Howard did realise that the frame was too short, it was too late to do anything about it and he went with lengths of rope just over his usual drop of 8 feet.

It did not matter how many factors contributed to the slow and terrible deaths witnessed that day, the blame for the botching was laid at Howard's feet. The abolitionists and those wavering on their support for the eradication of the death penalty now had, or so they thought, the evidence they needed to force a policy change and the favouring of incarceration over execution.

Nosey Bob blamed his assistant. He talked about how some of his helpers on the scaffold 'were very bad, and altogether unsuitable'. 'A young man is no good', he said. 'He may boast about his nerve, but unless he has had some experience of life, or has naturally a strong nerve, he fails at the critical moment'. The crowd in January 1887 was also an issue for Howard. 'It is a great mistake to allow anyone but the executioner and his assistant on to the scaffold', he complained, 'it only hinders the work and tends to make the unfortunate person break down'.[49]

In November that year, Howard was the victim of violence. The man who had abandoned the streets of Paddington and Potts Point to build a cottage at North Bondi to escape the crowds still needed to deal with people on the commute to and from work. Not nearly as densely populated as inner Sydney (Bondi did not boom until most of the sand dunes were cleared around 1920), the area in the late 19th century still offered access to public transport, an array of local businesses and a few neighbours. The executioner would have enjoyed plenty of space while still feeling safe. Until, that is, he was set upon by a gang of boys not too different from the group of youths he had hanged in January. Even the *Evening News*, a publication quick to vilify the hangman, was sympathetic and reported on the 'disgraceful exhibition of ruffianism' and how 'the public executioner, who lives at Bondi, in close proximity to the beach, was set upon and maltreated by a number of young men who appear to have a prejudice against Howard's profession.'[50] Nosey Bob's statement, on the beating he took as he walked past a pub on the way home, conveyed how frightening the ordeal was:

> Another young man then came behind me and struck me in the right ear; and another one, who wore a white waistcoat and a gold watchchain, also struck me and knocked me. They then said they would hang me; and three of them got hold of me and tried to shove me in Brown's back premises. I clung to the counter, and while holding, one of them kicked me in a dangerous place

and again struck me in the ear. I managed to get loose
from them, and ran out of the house into the street.
I ran towards Sydney, but could see no one about to
assist me. After a while I ventured back past Brown's
public-house. The four young men were then out on the
verandah. They came after me and assaulted me again,
and tore my coat and parcel. They tried to throw me
over the embankment on the road and then commenced
to stone me with blue metal. They swore they would
settle me some day, and burn my place down.[51]

There were no follow-up stories. No charges laid. No trials
held. Nosey Bob was left to go about his business. It did take
some time for the hangman to recover; nearly five months
after the attack, the *Bulletin* reported his health was 'in such
a condition as to give great anxiety to his friends'. Years
later, Howard recanted to a man from the *Sunday Times*
and said the lads were just persistent in wanting to drink
with him. The hangman did, though, avoid public houses
and he famously trained a horse to carry a billy on errands
to a local establishment. The billy carried a sixpence to the
pub and beer on the way back to Howard's Bondi cottage.
Anyone who approached the horse 'during his pilgrimage'
was 'promptly threatened with its hind hoofs'.[52]

CHAPTER 6

A CRUEL EQUALITY

PROGRESS, BUT NO MOVEMENT

In February 1888, Nosey Bob might have still been feeling the effects of the assault he had suffered the previous November as he missed a banquet in honour of Judge William C Windeyer. At least one gossip column observed that the 'sheriff appropriately took the vice-chair in honor of the hanging Judge who had thrown so much work into his department'. The obvious question was then asked: 'But where was Nosey Bob, the public executioner?' The hangman's vacant chair that February was 'an insult to the occasion.'[1] Howard was, though, fit enough to go to work in May and was on a scaffold the same month John Haynes, known for his work on the *Evening News* and the *Bulletin*, celebrated the first anniversary of his election to the colony's legislative assembly. The member for Mudgee, then Wellington and then Willoughby, spent nearly thirty years in parliament where he was an outspoken advocate for the abolition of the death penalty.

Frederick Lee, another abolitionist, focused on how the death penalty was not in sync with ideas of civilisation and progress. Lee, a successful merchant and mercantile broker, spent much of his life supporting various charitable organisations and lobbying for the total abolition of capital punishment. A man who gave regular public presentations on how the ultimate sentence failed society, he was a preacher seeking conversions to his cause who wrote that 'it is only by the exertions of the many that prejudices can be overcome and truth prevail'.[2]

One of Lee's early achievements was writing the *Abolition of Capital Punishment* (1864), a pamphlet that rehearsed the reasons for abolition presented in his numerous public talks and other efforts lobbying against the death penalty. He wrote of the crowds, though public hangings were a practice of the past in New South Wales. He wrote, too, of the chance of a bungled hanging. He also made a strong rebuttal of the religious arguments that supported the right to punish men and women with death. Lee did this by reading the Bible as a merciful rather than vengeful guide for the treatment of wrongdoers, citing how Cain was merely marked for the murder of his brother Abel.[3]

Lee repeatedly looked at how the death penalty was not a deterrent. He sent statistics to the press on convictions for rape immediately before and after this crime was removed from the list of capital offences in the mother country in 1841. He cited statistics that showed how the 'number of persons committed in England and Wales for capital assaults on females, were for 3 years immediately preceding the repeal of the death penalty 174, and for the 3 years immediately subsequent to the repeal 185'. These figures revealed a hesitancy to issue punishments out of proportion to the crime. Some victims, for example, would think twice about making a complaint for fear of seeing someone hanged, while juries were often reluctant to return a guilty verdict for a capital crime. In these instances, felons avoided death, but they also avoided any other type of punishment. Sometimes, juries would manipulate the punishment that was on the table and commit pious perjury. This reduced an offence to a lesser crime so a felon avoided the scaffold.[4]

Lee's pamphlet claimed that the gallows did not address the causes of crime. There was, too, in his pleas for progress, the standard and universal argument against the death penalty: the possibility of hanging an innocent person.[5] If you hang the wrong person, there is no redress. No correction.

As many Australians noted the centenary of Sydney in 1888, there had been progress in abandoning a policy of routine capital punishment but no real movement to see the ultimate act of the law eradicated. Hangings became private and increasingly infrequent affairs in the mid-19th century. The continued civilising of the justice system in New South Wales was, though, slow work. This is partly because the focus for abolitionists, despite the oft-stated goal for complete abolition of the ultimate sentence of the law, was often on individual cases and therefore more reliant upon leveraging the prerogative of mercy than on sweeping, legislative reform.

Short-lived organisations like the Society for the Abolition of Capital Punishment concentrated on the urgent action required to prevent specific executions from going ahead. The Society was conceived in late 1867, formalised in February 1868, and active until the early 1870s. First chaired by Terence Aubrey Murray, a politician who was appalled by capital punishment and an advocate of non-denominational education, the Society benefited from Lee's services as secretary. One of the challenges the Society faced was that not all felons sentenced to the scaffold were able to inspire public sympathy, and so support for a prisoner's commutation of a death sentence was not guaranteed. A large cohort of high-profile people was involved in the Society, with the *Sydney Morning Herald* cynically observing in 1868 that even John Plunkett was one of the 'victims of a craze'.[6] This Society, or fad, was so fleeting it was over before Nosey Bob signed on to work with the sheriff in 1876.

The execution of John Creighan, also known as John Grace, on 29 May 1888 was seen by some to represent progress. 'Happily, we have done away with the barbarous customs of earlier centuries', one journalist reported, 'and the privacy which surrounds the last scene at the gallows is certainly preferable to the old-time executions'. Creighan had been tried for the murder of John Stapleton at the Hillgrove Mines. The *Armidale Express and New England General Advertiser*, a newspaper keen on merging execution and weather reports, informed readers that the morning 'broke clear and frosty, rendering great coats and wraps an indispensable addition at the early hour of 8.15 a.m.'. The evidence against the prisoner about to be hanged at Armidale had been circumstantial, but nobody was holding out for a commutation for the man found guilty of cutting the throat of a workmate in the mines as part of a violent robbery.[7] Those in attendance did not have to suffer the cold air for long:

> Crash! With a sickening thud the [7 foot] drop fell, and those who cared to look saw the body move convulsively for a few seconds, the legs being drawn up once, and then one shoulder was slightly elevated, and one hand clenched, and all was over. It is satisfactory to think that the sufferings of the wretched man were of very short duration, and the hangman and his assistant also appeared relieved that their dreadful work was over.[8]

Creighan may not have benefited from the work of the abolitionists, but the men and women who protested the death penalty were undeterred. Though no longer part of a formal organisation, Lee still ran interference with Howard's schedule of customers into the 1880s and '90s. He was a member of a deputation petitioning for mercy for William Rice in 1884, leveraging claims that Rice was insane. Lee was also involved in efforts to try and save the nine members of the Mount Rennie gang scheduled to hang in January 1887, resulting in five felons escaping the noose and leaving just four to swing in front of Nosey Bob.[9]

As Howard continued to have the odd issue at work, he also faced a few personal problems. Howard made it clear that he wanted his children to be happy. He wanted them to have a good education and a stable home life. Unfortunately, stability must have seemed like an out-of-reach goal for his youngest daughter. Fanny had separated from her husband, Harry Bullenthorpe, shortly after the death of their only child in 1885. On Tuesday 31 July 1888, Fanny married again. She wed, probably bigamously and definitely pregnant, drayman James Pamment. The ceremony, for the self-identified bachelor and spinster, was held at the Roman Catholic Presbytery in Leichhardt. There are no details of the groom's or bride's parents on the marriage certificate, nor are places of birth listed.[10]

A couple of months after the wedding, the *Sydney Morning Herald* reported on how Lee helped organise a petition to try and save Robert Hewart, one that included the signatures of nine of the twelve men who had found him guilty (with three jurors unable to be located). There was some conjecture around Hewart's state of mind when, on 25 May 1888, he mutilated Thomas Park, with a knife, 'in one of the cells of the Central Police Court'. Park, a hairdresser, was being held for drunkenness, and Hewart, a ship's fireman, had been detained for 'having maliciously injured a screen valued at 35s' at the Silver King Hotel on Kent and King Streets in Sydney.[11]

Hewart was, at least according to some, 'insane with drink'. Lee talked about moral insanity, a concept first tested in New South Wales when the brilliant barrister Robert Lowe tried to save John Knatchbull from the noose for the murder of Ellen Jamieson in 1844. Like Lowe, Lee's efforts were not enough. No reprieve was forthcoming for Hewart. The executive council considered the case and advised that the law should be carried into effect. The execution was scheduled for 11 September 1888.[12]

On the eve of his execution, Hewart wrote a statement, maintaining his innocence, and that while he had made mistakes, murder was not one of them. Hewart was, thankfully, stoic on the scaffold as Howard's composure broke. The prisoner stood perfectly still while the assistant hangman, who was described as a new hand, stood by the Darlinghurst Gaol bolt but failed to draw it. According to at least one newspaper report, Nosey Bob 'cried, "Let go!" in a loud voice. Still the assistant hesitated, and had the prisoner struggled or fainted a scene of horror might have resulted'. Howard, who denied ever letting anyone go through the trapdoors despite numerous reports to the contrary, 'rushed to the lever with an oath' to pull the bolt. Hewart plunged 8 feet. Death was quick.[13]

In the late 1870s, Howard continued to indulge in the occasional alcoholic beverage. By the mid-1880s, it was widely acknowledged that his drinking was heavier than it had been: 'It has to be admitted, Robert usually gives way to drink, and may often be seen, clad in the strictest black, helplessly clasping a lamp-post'.[14] Howard was in a strange space; executions were not the regular events they had been, but he was still a hangman. Public sentiment towards hangings was also changing. Haynes, Lee, Murray, Plunkett and their contemporaries were sparking real, if excruciatingly slow, change. The long-reviled role of executioner was increasingly out of place in an evolving society.

Howard was also facing a changing world on his own. In between dispatching Creighan in May and Hewart in September, he marked ten years without his beloved wife.

Surely nobody could deny the widower a moment of escapism every now and then.

A SINGLE WOMAN

Usually, Nosey Bob gave his regrets to men. Only once did he stand on a scaffold and say: 'My poor woman no one regrets this more than I do'.[15] On this occasion, his regrets would have come *before* and *after* the trapdoors were released; he regretted taking a life, and he also regretted making a mess of the job. When Howard hanged Mrs Collins on 8 January 1889, things went wrong, and though her death was immediate, it was incredibly bloody.

In 1888, Collins stood accused in four separate trials for murder. These trials were sideshows for what was really at stake. If women wanted equal rights, equality could not be selective. Sure, women would eventually be allowed to vote, but they would also hang for murder.

The case had enough sordid details to fascinate and scandalise colonial Sydney, even without charges of murder. The story began when Louisa Hall married Charles Andrews, a butcher by trade, who was employed as a wool washer in the mid-1880s. To support a large family of nine children, the couple took boarders into their Botany home, which was a reasonably profitable, if crowded, arrangement. It worked well until Mrs Andrews had an affair with a lodger by the name of Michael Peter Collins. Mr Andrews evicted Collins in December 1886. The very next month, Mr Andrews fell ill and, unable to recover from bouts of diarrhoea and vomiting, died in February 1887. By April, the widowed Mrs Andrews had collected on her first husband's life insurance policy and had become Mrs Collins. When she walked down the aisle on her wedding day, she was pregnant with her tenth child.[16]

Death kept knocking at Mrs Collins' door. Her baby with her second husband, a boy, died when he was just over 4 months old. Then, on 8 July 1888, her second husband died after a short illness in which he presented with the same symptoms that her first husband had suffered from just before his own death nearly eighteen months earlier.[17] The shadow of suspicion was cast, and it was unshakable.

Traces of arsenic had been discovered 'in the vomited matter of the deceased', and 'in some milk that had been given him by his wife'. The discovery was shared with the city coroner, Henry Shiell, who 'instructed the police at No. 3 Station to place the wife of the deceased man, Louisa Collins, under arrest'. The coroner, in an aggressive search for answers, demanded exhumations of the body of her first husband, Charles Andrews, and the body of the infant that she had carried on her wedding day, John Collins. The coroner was looking for traces of arsenic and if there was, as some suspected, a pattern of poisoning by the woman dubbed the Borgia of Botany. Nobody was stepping forward as an 'admirer of "Lucretia Borgias" and poisoning', but there was general agreement that the matter should 'be proven beyond all reasonable doubt'.[18]

Collins' first trial, for the murder of her second husband, was held over 6–9 August. The second trial, also for the murder of her second husband, was held over 4–8 November. Collins was tried for the third time, for the murder of her first husband, over 19–22 November. After three juries were unable to return a verdict, a fourth trial was held, again for the murder of her second husband, over 5–8 December 1888.[19]

Finally, the prosecutors heard the word 'guilty'. The judge in Collins' last trial characterised the crime as of 'peculiar atrocity'. The *Evening News* published a piece assuming the general feeling of satisfaction and public relief, coupled with an endorsement of the death penalty. 'While no spirit of unreasoning vengeance was entertained towards the woman', it was reported, 'a wide-spread fear prevailed that through the disagreements of juries the perpetrator of two deliberate and atrocious murders might ultimately escape the punishment her crimes deserve'.[20]

Everyone, it seemed, had a view on Collins and her punishment. There was a meeting at the Sydney Town Hall demanding mercy. The *Australian Star*, a Sydney-based daily edited by William Traill, who had left the *Bulletin* in 1886, recorded 'not the slightest sympathy' for the prisoner. 'We have no doubt whatever that she committed the crime of which she was found guilty, and, after making the fullest allowance for the provocation she received, we unhesitatingly say that the crime was cruel and atrocious. In the interests of society', it was declared, 'the woman should be severely punished'. Traill, who was about to leave journalism to take up a position in the New South Wales legislative assembly as the member for South Sydney, maintained, in principle, an 'objection to the carrying out of the capital sentence in this instance' as it was 'felt by a very large number of people that in this age no female should be hanged'.[21]

Hope was placed in Henry Parkes, back in the coveted role of premier, who was not afflicted with 'gallows mania' and might advise the governor 'to commute the sentence'. The premier, however, refused to intervene, suggesting interference with a decision of the executive council would be 'utterly and wholly inexcusable'. Even the usually conservative *Sydney Morning Herald* editorialised that 'since protests have arisen against the decision of the Executive to carry out the death-sentence in the case of the criminal LOUISA COLLINS, it is only right that the opinions of the community generally should be heard'.[22]

Protests against hanging a woman in general, and Collins in particular, were widespread. The abolitionist Frederick Lee was at the forefront, organising meetings and circulating petitions. Lee complained that the glass of milk taken in evidence from the Collins household 'was not immediately sealed up in the presence of two responsible witnesses' and then delivered sealed to the government analyst. He claimed that there had been a clear failure to offer a motive for murder, while the prosecution could not prove that poison had been procured by Collins.[23] Indeed, arsenic was a common product in the 1800s. Arsenic was, for example, found in rat poison, including the rat poison found in the prisoner's home at Botany. In addition, Andrews and Collins had both worked as wool washers and would have been exposed to arsenic daily.

Lee also led a deputation to the governor, delivering a petition signed by 584 women that set forth 'that it was abhorrent to every feeling of humanity and a shock to the sentiments in this 19th century that a woman should suffer death at the hands of a hangman so long as imprisonment could be substituted'. It was also pointed out to the governor that there was 'no positive proof of the prisoner's guilt'. Collins also submitted her own claim for mercy, written on 6 January 1889. Marked 'urgent', the claim is on a prisoner's application or statement form, a business-like document printed on dull grey paper. The request, completed in scrappy handwriting, includes a gut-wrenching plea to 'have mercy and pity on me and spare my life'. She asked for mercy, not just for herself, but for her 'poor children' too.[24] Public support proved ineffective against a system that was, it appeared, determined to achieve a cruel equality.

The hanging took place in Darlinghurst Gaol. It was reported by the *Sydney Morning Herald* that of the two women warders who escorted her to the scaffold, 'one was weeping'. The *Australian Star* explained that Howard had, on account of Collins being a woman, made sure that a chair was ready 'in case she shouldn't bear up'.[25] Howard had also, apparently, crafted Collins a poem, which he recited to her as she was led from the condemned cell to the gallows:

My pretty Louise
Step on the trapeze
And I'll let you down
With the greatest of ease.[26]

For Howard's assistant, it was his first day on the payroll as an executioner. The regular incumbent had 'refused to have anything to do with the execution of a woman'.[27] This last-minute change on the dispatch team would be disastrous.

A small group attended the execution. Some witnesses were officials and others were men who had told the 41-year-old woman's story to newspaper readers across the colony. The dignity of Collins was recorded by a journalist who wrote that only 'a slight twitch of the hands was noticeable' and explained that the chair procured by the executioner was not required. This level of calm was quite an achievement as the lever designed to send the convicted to their doom was stuck. Several attempts were made to force it until, with frantic whispers, a mallet was called for. It was written that the bungling 'sent a thrill of pain through all who heard the strokes of the mallet doing their deadly task'.[28] This would add to the horror that unfolded after the trapdoors gave way. One witness report held no detail back:

> We who look, and are muttering in our throats everlasting torment to the bunglers, see, as the rope stretches to its fullest, first an abrasion, then a spout of blood, which trickles over her chest and down her prison garb, and on to the floor of the pit beneath, and then we see bloody and ghastly the top of the severed windpipe, and a great wide opening in the neck, which is closed by the knotted cord. Not a movement of any kind; the hands turn blueish, but there is no quiver of the muscles; nothing to indicate pain or suffering.[29]

Howard blamed his assistant for the mess. Years after her hanging, Howard said he was holding her up as she stood on the trapdoors, and that without him she would have fallen. 'I could not leave her', he said. The assistant was unable 'in his nervous condition' to do anything and it fell to one of the gaol warders to attend to the bolt and 'to knock it away with a mallet'. When it was all over, Collins was alone. There was nobody to claim her corpse from the small morgue at Darlinghurst Gaol. In an afterword, she was offered a single kindness from the system that had been so determined to destroy her; she was buried by the government contractor for funerals at Rookwood Necropolis.[30]

WORKPLACE HEALTH AND SAFETY

Gaols can be dangerous places, and not just for the prisoners. A few years before Nosey Bob became a hangman, Thomas Kelly was sent off on 2 January 1872 in Darlinghurst Gaol. Kelly, who was doing time in Parramatta Gaol for a robbery committed in Deniliquin in 1869, was working in the stonemason's yard when the superintendent, William McLaren, asked him to cut the stone into smaller pieces. Kelly took offence. He then took a hammer and bashed McLaren, and he was soon convicted of attempted murder and sentenced to death.[31]

After Kelly's devotions on the scaffold, and in opposition to the preferences of authorities, Kelly made a statement, published in the *Evening News*, that he was about to 'die as innocent of the crime of attempted murder as the child unborn'. The executioner at the time, Joseph Bull, who according to *Truth* was 'old, fat and frowsy', approached the prisoner. In contrast, Bull's assistant, John Franks, was, at least in his early years on scaffolds, an able-bodied man.[32] That Franks could pass a basic fitness test that day was fortunate, because Kelly had decided he was not going to cooperate:

> The condemned man turned sharply round and raising his right foot planted a terrific kick in the part of Bull's anatomy which must not be mentioned to ears polite. Suffice it that the kick delivered straight *in front* completely doubled up the hangman, who straightway retired and could not be induced to re-appear.[33]

Franks sprang into action and tried to subdue the prisoner, who in turn attacked the clergyman. 'I'll not be hung; I do not deserve it', Kelly cried out. At one point, all three men nearly toppled off the edge of the newly built scaffold. At last, Kelly was pinned down. The noose was placed around his neck and his religious counsel, 'greatly overcome with emotion', withdrew leaving his spiritual charge alone. The bolt was pulled and Kelly plummeted as he continued to thrash. 'The knot twisting to the front, the noose not closing, but being several inches above the windpipe. For ten or twelve minutes the doomed man struggled, kicked and breathed convulsively. Twice the assistant executioner adjusted the rope, and attempted to pull the noose tighter, which was at length accomplished'.[34] Most felons accepted the inevitable once they were standing beneath the beam and prayers were being read. Some protested their innocence, some quivered in fear, but very few prisoners put up a fight. The scaffold was, after all, as dangerous a workplace as any other within the criminal justice system.

Bull never recovered from Kelly's kick in January 1872. The man who shared his surname with a famous hangman of London saw off three more murderers. The hanging of John Conn was bungled on 4 June 1872, with the 'head wrenched

FIGURE 8 **Gallows at Darlinghurst Gaol**

SOURCE State Library of NSW, before 1914, SSV1/Gao/Darh/2

from the body' and remaining 'in the rope until taken down'. He then saw off George Nichols and Alfred Lester a fortnight later. After these appearances, Bull was institutionalised before he died from his injuries in May 1873.[35]

Such danger presented a risk to the life and limb of those who carried out the final sentence of the law, as well as to anyone else who happened to have cause to be on a scaffold. It also jeopardised the legitimacy of the entire procession. The 'careful management of the execution ceremonies was essential to ensure that the use of violence by the state was seen as the culmination and fulfilment of the ordinary legal process'.[36]

In the days of public hangings, displays were less effective if the authority of the colonial government was challenged in any way. Everyone had to play their part as scripted. The sheriff, or his delegate, alongside the gaol warders and the executioners, took care of the business at hand. Representatives of the colony's religious factions offered consolation to the condemned and an open endorsement of judicial hangings. The prisoner, preferably penitent and certainly powerless in the face of the ultimate punishment, was to accept, bravely or not, their fate as a just response to their own iniquity. The medical officer was required, after an appropriate pause, to declare that the deed had been done. The audience should, but did not always, behave in a suitably sombre manner that reiterated the seriousness of the crime and its consequences. Journalists should report on the gravity of the occasion to those unable to attend a hanging.

In the early to mid-1800s, the colonial press was generally on the side of the governor and his administration, with the *Sydney Gazette and New South Wales Advertiser* just one masthead that supported hangings. Even when censorship was lifted in 1824, the newspaper continued to promote the position of the death penalty as not only right but necessary. A few of the *Sydney Gazette*'s earliest competitors also supported capital punishment. As the number of newspapers printed in New South Wales increased, so too did the number of editors and owners. Some of these men voiced opinions, either out of a desire to increase circulation or in a genuine effort to challenge the status quo, that had rarely been voiced openly before. As executions had moved behind gaol walls, the role of newspapermen in advocating for, or at least acknowledging the value of, capital punishment became more and more important to authorities keen on communicating displays of justice.

Sometimes, journalists obliged. When Kelly broke protocol and attacked Bull, several reports sanitised the event. There was a low-level fracas, but nothing too serious. Bull had been kicked and was replaced by his assistant. At least one account censored the fight and stated Bull had been kicked 'violently in the stomach.'[37] Any assault on the executioner is an unwanted challenge to state power. There is the imperative to tell readers a good story, but some journalists were prepared to downplay an execution to privilege a larger, more straightforward, narrative of crime and punishment. This was most obvious when the hangman botched his work. Howard had been offered some support by journalists over the years. A few editors understood the pressure on the hangman and the imperfect art of hanging. Other newsmen supported the death penalty and held a belief that there was no point alarming people about the odd bungling here and there. There was, too, the notion that newsmen, despite being known for their toughness, had been so personally horrified by a crime that there was no need to dwell on a mistake that, at the end of the day, was not nearly as terrible as the offence being punished.

Community sentiments were shifting, and the tone of many newspapers was shifting as well. For some, this was about changing the world, or at least a small corner of it. For others, this was about the less noble pursuit of economic survival. Regardless of editorial motivation, full coverage of executions in newspapers had become standard. The short articles advising readers of a dispatched prisoner were increasingly being replaced by multi-column coverage that recounted crimes, trials, appeals and hangings in minute detail. The mix of facts and opinions often coalesced into ferocious critiques of the judiciary and legislators. Such pieces had been appearing with greater frequency since the middle of the century. As Nosey Bob's error rate increased, even the more conservative papers were prepared to criticise the death penalty, the failure to offer mercy, and the skills, or lack thereof, of the hangman. Since the bungling at the execution of four of the Mount Rennie rapists, the idea of protecting the hangman's reputation was almost unthinkable.

After the terribly botched hanging of Louisa Collins, Nosey Bob might have wanted some time off and an opportunity to move on. There would be a few months of inactivity, but on 20 August 1889, Howard was back on the gallows at Darlinghurst Gaol to hang James Morrison.

Nobody had forgotten the blood spilt at the execution earlier in the year. Journalists made sure of that. 'This was the gallows', readers were reminded in a report on Morrison's dispatch, on which Collins, 'condemned to die for murdering her husband, was the last to suffer'. Nobody, especially not Howard or his assistant, wanted another decapitation or anything close to one. It is not clear how far Howard's first near-decapitation, William Liddiard at Grafton in 1886, was dropped, as the very few reports that did comment on Nosey Bob's error kept things simple with brief statements on how the rope caused 'a clean cut from ear to ear'. In the case of Collins, a woman who had obsessed the colony, it was specified that in early 1889 she weighed 11 stone 3 pounds, and that her drop had been set at 5 feet 6 inches. This was much shorter than the 8 feet 2 inches that was recommended, at the time, for someone who was around 157 pounds. Nosey Bob had adjusted her fall, just not enough. For Morrison's dispatch, just over seven months after Collins was sent off, Howard set a drop that was a lavish 12 feet.[38]

Thankfully, Morrison's exit was much cleaner than some of Howard's previous send-offs. Morrison, unsatisfied with making an honest living, was working as a burglar in Potts Point when he shot and killed Constable David Sutherland. Tried and found guilty, when his time came, Nosey Bob sent him off without error:

The lifeless body of James Morrison was hanging a few feet above the cavity which had been prepared. It would be difficult to conceive how an execution of this character could be carried out with less suffering. For two minutes there were certain reactionary movements of the muscles: but death, which was due to fracture of the cervical vertebrae, was to all intents and purposes instantaneous.[39]

In the chapel at Darlinghurst Gaol, Morrison was confirmed into the Roman Catholic faith and celebrated mass in his cell shortly before his execution. Nosey Bob might have been pleased by this. Though scenes like the one Kelly created in 1872 were rare, Howard 'once confided to an official that he preferred to hang Catholics to persons of any other denomination, not that he had any prejudice against Catholics, but because their religion taught them how to die with resignation, and they gave him the least trouble'.[40] Well, Howard was in luck. He only had one more hanging that year, and the victim was a Roman Catholic.

A PERFECT PRISONER

Confessions in the colonial era were given in primitive conditions. There were no tape recorders or video cameras. Nobody was forced to sweat it out under harsh lights. In gathering evidence, great weight was given to confessions and extorting statements was a serious issue. To prevent the extraction of coerced confessions, England enacted a law in the 1780s stipulating that a confession 'forced from the mind by flattery of hope, or by the pressure of fear' was legally inadmissible. This principle was then applied in New South Wales in the 1820s and remains law today.[41]

The consequences of giving a confession, then and now, are usually dire. When a young man confessed to murder in 1889, he did so fully expecting that his statement would result in a noose being fitted around his neck: 'I, Thomas Reilly, charged with the murder of Christian Eppel, wish to make a full statement and confession'. Reilly told police that Eppel, also spelt Epple, had employed him at Bourke, in the colony's west, to help drive cattle to Wodonga in Victoria, just over the southern border of New South Wales. He stipulated that he did not murder and rob Epple because of 'any evil spirit or any ill-will', but because he wanted to urgently raise funds so he could marry the woman he loved.[42]

After a missed opportunity to shoot his quarry near where the team of drovers had set up camp in the Wagga Wagga area, Reilly found Epple in his tent on the morning of 15 September 1889. His victim saw him at the door of his sleeping accommodation with the rifle in his hands. Reilly, aged 20, shot Epple who was aged 45. The newly minted murderer stole his victim's purse, watch and chain before he took off, but the young felon did not resist arrest when he was caught by authorities soon after the crime was discovered.[43] The coronial inquiry and the criminal trial were uncontested processes. Reilly freely admitted his guilt.

Alfred Reynolds, who murdered his wife in 1886, requested that he meet Nosey Bob without any interference. The man, who had forced the mother of his children to overdose on opium, made no defence at his trial and advised 'that he was tired of life, that he had done the deed with which he stood charged, deserved the punishment which the law would inflict, and was desirous that his crime might be expiated as soon as possible'. Reilly made a similar, though more genuinely remorseful, request when he made it known that 'he richly deserved his fate, and desired that no effort should be made to obtain a remission of the death penalty'. Frederick Lee, in his pamphlet arguing against capital punishment, went further than these feelings of resignation and asserted that occasionally murderers expected, even anticipated, a meeting with the executioner. In some cases, murder was 'in fact indirect suicide', with felons not needing to gather the courage to end their own lives; they just needed to commit a crime that was a capital offence and then simply submit themselves to the ruthlessness of a government's policy on punishment.[44]

Reilly lived in his condemned cell in the Wagga Wagga Gaol until his hanging day on 6 November 1889. He was, by all accounts, 'thoroughly contrite, reading his prayer-book daily', from early in the morning until late at night, 'and he is said to recognise the justice of his punishment which he is anxious to get over'. Even his gaoler was glad to host him, for he had 'given no trouble of any kind since he entered the gaol, showing a ready disposition to comply with all regulations, and never indulging in any grumbling'. Reilly did not even complain about the food.[45] In another symbol of remorse, the murderer wrote an open letter to his victim's widow and her four children:

I must ask you now, Mrs. Epple, to forgive me for my
unmanliness of forethought in giving way to the vile
temptations of the devil. I told my brother to see you
as soon as he could and to help you in your trouble.
He will do so and remain a good friend to you. I hope
you won't refuse his assistance, as it would be a great
consolation for me to know that you were not altogether
deserted or forsaken, and may the Almighty God pour
his blessing on you and protect you and help you and
your family in your trouble through life, and I hope He
will repair the injury I have done to you.[46]

Reilly had accepted his slot on the gallows, but not everyone
in Wagga Wagga was pleased about a hanging. Howard's
treatment at the station, on his arrival in the town, was so
bad that it made international news. Nosey Bob is presented
in an English newspaper as the object of the first boycott
in Australia because the cabbies at the railway station 'one
and all, refused to take him, and a long and dusty walk was
the result. But "Nosey Bob" cherishes a forgiving spirit,
and declares that whenever any of these ill-natured Jehus
require his professional assistance he will give it with the
greatest good will'.[47] The story was wrong on two counts.
First, Howard would not have been so offended by a cold
shoulder that he would have enjoyed his work if one of those
cab drivers presented to him as a patient. Second, this was
not the first time that Nosey Bob had felt the abrasiveness
of a boycott.

Howard 'had the coach to Uralla all to himself' when he

headed north to hang John McGuan in 1882, as 'the other passengers refused to travel with him'. A couple of years later, when Howard and his assistant arrived in the town of Hay in 1884, having just taken care of Joseph Gordon at Deniliquin, they ate at the Tattersall's Hotel but had to dine alone as nobody would share their table. In another blow, they 'could get no beds', and the police accommodated them in the court house. Howard had been through this before and, to go home after dealing with Gordon, he 'started to trudge through the mud to the railway station'. His assistant was more hopeful and waited for a cab, but he was also refused a ride and had to follow his supervisor on foot. The news in Hay made it all the way to Darwin, with the *North Australian* suggesting that the bad treatment of the men could give rise to thoughts of revenge, and that should the services of the executioners be required in the area, they 'wouldn't guarantee safe and comfortable' dispatch for residents of those parts. Indeed, it was assumed that a 'great deal of ill feeling has been aroused in Sydney at the unfriendly treatment, by the Hay people, of the hangman and his assistant'.[48]

This was, regrettably, not unusual and it was something Howard had to tolerate, especially when on business trips. The sheriff had to order local gaolers to provide a room in the gaol 'with fire-place accommodation, and necessary fuel' for visiting executioners. Nosey Bob did complain about being neglected while travelling and believed 'that as a public official a conveyance should [always be] provided for him'. Any other man, for any other purpose, may not have suffered from a walk into town. For the hangman, the emotional and physical loads were heavier. Even if Nosey Bob was preparing for a short drop, a length of hangman's cord should be 'capable of bearing a strain of at least a ton and a half'. That was a lot of rope to have to carry. Maybe, just maybe, he was able to take pride in his family history in times like these. There was 'something in a name after all', said Howard, when reminiscing one day, sharing with a small group that he 'was related (in a very distant way) to the Duke of Norfolk, and had running in his veins "all the blood of the Howards"'.[49] A bold claim for a hangman, even one who did like a Norfolk Island pine. Or simply a form of consolation for a man tired of being slighted just because he was handy with a rope.

Despite issues at the station, it was reported in the press that, as always, the executioner had arrived in plenty of time. After the issues with the custom-made gallows for the quadruple hanging in Darlinghurst Gaol nearly three years earlier, Howard personally supervised the erection of the gallows at the Wagga Wagga Gaol, located in the exercise yard for male prisoners. Great care was taken to ensure the privacy of the patient.[50] There would only be official witnesses to Reilly's last moments.

So much attention was paid to the penitence of the prisoner that there was minimal coverage of the actual killing. The *Sydney Morning Herald* mustered a single sentence: 'THOMAS REILLY was executed at Wagga yesterday morning', but did offer a short report, nested with country news, a couple of pages later. The *Australian Star*, which had printed an illustrated biography of Reilly the day before, tried harder, but not by much: 'The usual official telegram has been received from Wagga Wagga that Thomas Reilly was executed this morning, and that he died instantaneously'.[51]

In contrast, the *Goulburn Evening Penny Post* gave a fulsome report on proceedings. Erasmus Wren, the medical officer, was tardy, so the hanging did not take place at the scheduled time of 9:00 am. There were fifteen official witnesses and a small gathering outside the walls of the Wagga Wagga Gaol. Reilly, in trying circumstances, managed to maintain his profile as the perfectly penitent prisoner. 'He was firm and bore up remarkably well. He did not evince the least sign of fear'. He acknowledged those who had come to watch, he looked over the gaol walls and up at the sky, but he focused his attention on the two priests accompanying him in his last moments. Howard was as efficient as usual. He did not like to spend more time on the scaffold than he had to, but when he gave the signal to his assistant with a nod of his head, the assistant 'seemed unprepared'. Howard had to nod again before his offsider drew the bolt 'and Reilly disappeared down the drop' of 9 feet.[52]

This time, Howard used a rope around 3½ inches in circumference or just over 1 inch in diameter, a little thicker than his usual cord. The long drop, and the heavyweight manila, did not disadvantage Reilly, who was a cousin of notorious bushrangers Dan and Ned Kelly (his mother was the sister of Ellen Kelly). Death was as ideal as it could be under the circumstances, although it was observed that a groan was heard and that some blood from the nose of the prisoner had stained the white cap.[53] Reilly was gone.

CHAPTER 7

SHORT AND LONG DROPS

'IT WAS ENOUGH TO DIE
FOR THE ONE MAN'

For hangmen looking to earn extra cash, the spoils of the executioner's trade offered a significant source of additional income. Some finishers of the law sold the clothing of their victims. Considering the mess made at executions, this was hard work. On occasion, other personal items could be stripped from the body if there was something worth taking. The easiest opportunity for profit was the rope. For Sydney-based hangmen, a good length of rope was a useful product in a busy port city, even if it came second hand.

Disconcertingly, rope was also the foundation of a lucrative souvenir industry. Robert Elliott, a man who was 'about the middle stature, with a very slight irregularity in his eyes, and projecting white eyelashes', was another New South Wales executioner who had a problem with alcohol. Charged with drunkenness in 1857, Elliott had been going to pubs and, in exchange for a few drinks, gleefully showing off lengths of rope deployed at a double hanging. It was quipped in *Empire*, a masthead started by Henry Parkes, that 'if the gallows is a "great moral teacher," Elliott is certainly a dull scholar'.[1]

When Elliott was demoted to the position of assistant executioner in 1863, after bungling the hanging of Henry Manns, his replacement and new boss was Joseph Bull. Another entrepreneur, Bull cut up, and then started selling off, the rope that he had used to hang the aspiring assassin Henry O'Farrell on 21 April 1868 in Darlinghurst Gaol. O'Farrell had shot Prince Alfred at a public event almost six weeks earlier. The royal guest to Australia was seriously wounded, but he survived. The government of New South Wales was outraged by the crime, as well as by the international embarrassment it generated, and refused to recommend the Irishman for mercy. The rope, which had taken care of the would-be murderer of the Duke of Edinburgh, was quite the money maker, with Bull achieving prices as high as £5 for a 6-inch length. The scam was discovered after Bull found that he had run out of genuine O'Farrell Rope. Not wanting to lose a valuable income stream, the part-time salesman had turned to generic rope stock, which he sold off as O'Farrell Original.[2]

By personal inclination, and by order from his employer, Howard never engaged in these types of schemes. With only his children and his work to live for, he usually lit a fire in the gaol yard and burnt the rope he had carefully prepared and used for an execution. In some instances, the rope used in a hanging was buried with the victim. Nosey Bob avoided capitalising on the industry of punishment, but tourism at Darlinghurst Gaol was a major activity. Unprofitable and a nuisance to officials, there were those who could not deny themselves a visit to the place dubbed, due to the meagre food rations for prisoners, 'Starvinghurst Gaol'[3]:

> In the first place these visits do incalculable harm to the prisoners themselves, and in the second there is no object attained by such visits, except satisfying idle curiosity. The class of visitors who come are recruited from all grades of society, but particularly from country visitors and theatrical shows. It will hardly be credited when I say that often 200 to 300 visits are paid in a week to Darlinghurst Gaol. Warders have to accompany the sight-seers, and a lot of time is taken up by these officials in escorting the visitors round. The visiting days are Tuesdays and Fridays.[4]

In writing for the *Arrow*, an Ex-Warder of Darlinghurst Gaol divulged that the 'morbid curiosity of these people who have come to gloat over the surroundings of crime and criminals is often disgusting.'[5] Ex-Warder's articles, wedged in between the more generic sports commentary the *Arrow* was known for, offered pieces on how a society founded on punishments had managed to turn the penalties inflicted upon their fellow citizens for various wrongdoings into amusements. Not as socially acceptable as cricket or rugby, or even horse racing, but still an entertainment based on stamina and strength. Indeed, the survival of prisoners in a colonial facility for felons, even for those not living under the shadow of a death sentence, was not guaranteed. In a morbid twist, it was those players for whom the final score was predetermined – executioner one, condemned criminal nil – who attracted the most animated spectators.

Most of those touring Darlinghurst Gaol wanted to see a condemned man. This was routinely refused, 'for under no circumstances will the feelings of the wretched man be hurt' by allowing just anyone to see him. Only visitors approved by the condemned saw the cells that nobody wanted to occupy. Undeterred, those seeking proximity to death pleaded: 'Oh, do let us see the gallows!'[6]

This was no trend, no passing interest piqued by a celebrity crook. This was an unfettered desire by many to see the death penalty. When Darlinghurst Gaol closed in 1914, a decade after Nosey Bob's retirement, huge crowds swamped the site when it opened to the public. A staggering 14 000 people visited on the first day the gates were unlocked. By the end of the week, it was estimated 100 000 had been through the cell blocks, work areas and yards, while 'hundreds of curious citizens flocked to the condemned cell and stood on the gallows where many noted criminals had stood before them'.[7]

Some tourists might just have wanted to acknowledge that for the first time since European settlement, the city of Sydney had 'no gaol within its borders'. Some may have wanted to contribute to the Prisoners' Aid Association collection, which raised £350. A few were shameful souvenir hunters who took the opportunity to pick a small piece of timber off the trapdoors on the gallows. The sight of hordes of pleasure-seekers distressed David Hall, the attorney-general and minister for justice, who complained about the crowds that had descended on the site and was 'disagreeably surprised at the popularity of [his] decision to throw open the gaol', a move that demonstrated an obvious 'morbid sentiment which it is desirable to suppress rather than encourage'.[8]

There were no great crowds present when Albert, or Allesender, Smidt was hanged for the murder of John Young Taylor on 18 November 1890 in Wagga Wagga Gaol. Smidt's confession, a chaotic narrative about an argument between friends that turned tragic on a rural road, was given to an inspector of police and a minister of religion. Smidt said he was from Potsdam in Prussia, and that he had been in Australia for eight or nine years when he and Taylor were driving in the Wagga Wagga area. According to Smidt, Taylor had criticised his skills with a horse and told him he was a bad driver. 'He hit me several times', Smidt said, he 'called me a liar and said I was no good'. Smidt tried to fight back, but Taylor landed another blow before Smidt could make contact. Then, in a fit of rage, Smidt 'got a tomahawk and hit him on the head'. It took Smidt a few minutes to realise what he had done, and he 'stood, not knowing what to do and wondering if he was dead'. Taylor was dead, although Smidt was sure that he had only struck him once with the tomahawk.[9]

After an anxious night driving around with the body of Taylor in the waggonette the men had once shared, Smidt bought a shovel from a store in Old Junee, north of Wagga Wagga. Another night of anxiety and Smidt was forced into action because Taylor began to smell. Smidt then decided to cut Taylor's head off, and he buried the head and the body of his victim separately so that, should the body be found, nobody would recognise the corpse in its shallow grave. Smidt then burnt Taylor's clothing and tried to wash his equipment and vehicle, which were covered in blood. Having gone to all this trouble, the stressed felon's plan was to confess to a clergyman and then kill himself. Before committing suicide, he would write in his pocketbook that he was taking his own life because he had killed his friend in a silly spat. Smidt did not make it to a church. Tip-offs to police about a trail of blood led to him being pulled over by constables on the road to Junee, with questions about the bloodstains they could see on the rear of the wagonette.[10]

Skipping the part of the plan that involved a confession, Smidt attempted suicide after being placed in handcuffs. When a stop was made to let the horses drink, he tried cutting his own throat. The constables stripped him of his knife and razor, but they did not search him for other weapons. Smidt, on his own in the back of the waggonette, contorted his body to fetch a revolver from his pocket. Grasping the weapon, he lifted it to his head and pulled the trigger. It did not go off. He put the small muzzle in his mouth and fired again. This time, the weapon discharged.[11]

The murderer survived his self-inflicted wound and was committed to stand trial in September 1890. Smidt was only tried for one murder, even though it was believed he had murdered an unidentified man on the Murrumbidgee River in 1888 (his body was headless) and Jacob Rick near Wagga

Wagga in 1889 (his body was never found). The prisoner only cryptically said that 'it was enough to die for the one man'.[12] With so much evidence, a lengthy confession and directions to where Taylor's head and body could be found, a guilty verdict was the only conclusion a jury could come to. The consequent sentence of death was just a piece of paperwork in the process of seeing Smidt executed.

When Smidt's time on the scaffold came, he was reasonably firm, although he shuddered visibly at several points in his execution ceremony. Seeing Smidt off was, in the end, a simple affair. 'At a given signal the hangman's assistant drew the bolt, and Smidt was shot quickly through the trapdoor'. The drop was 6 feet 6 inches. Death was instantaneous. After some bad publicity, Howard would have felt some relief when he heard about his report card for that morning: 'The execution was carried out in a highly satisfactory manner'. Then, at 11:00 am, an inquest was held, 'at which the usual statutory verdict was returned'.[13]

2:1

Nosey Bob stepped up on a scaffold three times in 1891, twice in Dubbo and once in Sydney. All his clients were murderers.

Despite a few accidents over fifteen years, Nosey Bob usually met his key performance indicator as a hangman. The idea of a Hangman of the Year sounds vulgar, but if such a title had existed in the colonial era, Howard would have been a frontrunner for the prize. It was even argued he had introduced several innovations, with one reporter pronouncing, 'it is now almost a pleasure to fall into the hands of the genial Mr. Howard, whose consideration for his patients amounts almost to paternal fondness'.[14] Those that Howard offered his regrets to might have thought differently. Howard did not relish his work, and he was not deliberately clumsy. He was, in contrast to many others, sober when he stepped up to perform. The goal of an instantaneous death was not, however, guaranteed and Nosey Bob's success rate in 1891 was only 2:1.

One of the innovations Howard is given credit for is the introduction of straps, to replace ropes, for pinioning prisoners. Pinioning, or restraining, a person in their condemned cell before leading them to the gallows was a standard safety measure. In the late 1890s, it was suggested that 'straps are an idea of Howard's own, and supersede the brutal cords which used to pinch the arms of the condemned'. This was such an excellent idea, *Truth* informed their readers, that 'Bartholomew Binns, the English hangman, hearing of the "comfort" of these straps, wrote to Bob for specifications, and the "noseless one" accommodated his British confrere with the straps complete'.[15] This is a great story, and it fits in well with what we know of Howard and his personality: a chap always pleased to help.

Unfortunately, the dates do not align. Binns was an especially incompetent hangman who only held his position as an executioner for a few months from late 1883. Straps can also be seen in the diagrams on hanging sent out by the Secretary of State for the Colonies in 1880. It is possible that

Howard had been of some assistance to Binns' predecessor William Marwood, who was a hangman from the mid-1870s for almost a decade, but as the cobbler-turned-executioner was known for initiating his own improvements on the scaffold, this is improbable. It is certain that Marwood, a well-known and well-regarded English hangman, was using straps during his tenure, as per the 1880 instructions, because when he died suddenly in 1883 it was publicised that 'twenty-one ropes and nine sets of straps have been obtained from his wife and sent to London for sale'.[16]

Howard was even credited with lodging a patent 'for an improvement in the hanging business'. It was also claimed, though the design was not directly attributed to Nosey Bob, that the 'double-barrelled gallows' used for the Mount Rennie rapists in 1887 was patented. Another rumour around Howard's inventiveness, that he was lodging a patent for a new gallows, surfaced in 1902.[17] These attempts to perfect the execution process were of immediate benefit to some prisoners, but they sat uncomfortably with notions of a sophisticated society and were considered appalling to those advocating an abandonment of the death penalty. For most prisoners, such refinements were luxuries. What those who were about to die really wanted as they stood on the trapdoors, and they had their cap and noose fitted, was to be next to a hangman who knew what he was doing.

Lars Peter Hansen, a Danish man, was Nosey Bob's thirty-fifth job when he was hanged for the murder of Charles Duncker, or Dunke, on 2 June 1891 in Dubbo Gaol. Upon the scaffold, Hansen said: 'Did not murder him. I die as a Christian in the hope of being forgiven'. This generated some confusion among the official witnesses, a group of about twenty men, as Hansen had confessed to killing his German friend in self-defence. Newspaper reports at the time observed that, with limited English, the felon was attempting to distinguish between murdering with intent and the lesser crime of killing to protect himself. After the sentence of death had been passed at his trial a couple of months earlier, the condemned man said to the judge: 'I no guilty. I kill him to save myself'.[18]

This claim was made despite the belief that Duncker, who, like Hansen, was an itinerant worker trying his luck on the goldfields, was asleep in his hammock when he was killed with a tomahawk. His body was then burnt, and his possessions were plundered in late September 1890 with many of Duncker's effects found on Hansen.[19] Duncker's wounds were savage, and his corpse would have been an unspeakable sight when it was discovered.

Having been tracked down and arrested for murder in October, 'the prisoner was taken to deceased's grave, with deceased's mates, and the body was exhumed. The prisoner admitted that he recognized the little German's body. The deceased's mates also recognized the prisoner'.[20]

In a reflection of the reduced appetite for executions, only a few people gathered at the rear of Dubbo Gaol, on a piece of rising ground, to try and take advantage of a view that revealed the very top of the gallows. These would-be spectators were in the minority as a 'general feeling of regret and horror at the execution prevail[ed] in the town'. The 'white cap having been drawn over his face by the executioner', the trapdoors gave way and Hansen fell about 8 feet. He 'died without the slightest struggle'. In an indication of the neat work done by the hangman and his offsider, the patient was pronounced dead five minutes and ten seconds 'after the bolt was drawn'.[21]

Howard's next job was the dispatch of Maurice Dalton on 17 November 1891 in Darlinghurst Gaol. It was not Nosey Bob's best effort, but not everyone was complaining. The *National Advocate*, a daily newspaper based in Bathurst, told readers that the 'rope burst the flesh, causing a stream of blood to gush from the neck. Notwithstanding, he deserved it. His manner of murdering the woman he had sworn to love and cherish was cruel in the extreme, and his was a case deserving of no mercy whatever'. Despite some of the known difficulties around confessions, there was still a prevalent public desire for wrongdoers to openly admit their misdeeds, even if admissions of guilt came after a guilty verdict was announced and a death sentence was issued. Dalton was stubborn, and 'he made no confession of his guilt, but, on the other hand, he has not, since his trial, thought fit to deny it'.[22]

Catherine Dalton had complained about her husband's failure to try to earn any money, and she had decided to follow through on her threat to sell the furniture and to break up the family home in Foveaux Street, Surry Hills. The burden on a woman of 50, who had taken in boarders and turned to dressmaking to keep the household functioning, was too much. In reflecting on the murder, the *Wagga Wagga Advertiser*, which was a tri-weekly paper at the time, noted how, on 14 April 1891, 'there was a desperate quarrel, out of which only one participant emerged alive'. Mr Dalton bashed Mrs Dalton over the head with a branding iron. The tool, which was kept in the shed at the back of the house, was covered in blood and hair and found hanging in its usual place.[23] The man accused of not wanting to work could not even be bothered to clean incriminating evidence off the murder weapon.

Dalton, admittedly 'an old man' of 71, was found guilty of murder in a case that 'lasted all day', and was sentenced to death. The killer maintained an icy demeanour in prison; he seemed to accept his fate, so he slept well and ate well. On the outside of the prison walls, there was no sympathy with no attempt made, 'at any rate publicly, to obtain a reprieve for him'.[24] Dalton would hang as scheduled.

Nosey Bob had set an unusually short drop of 6 feet, on account of the prisoner's age, but it was still too long. 'The rope cut through the flesh, severing the jugular vein. The blood gushed out in torrents, down the clothing and hands of the dead man' with 'Dalton's head being almost severed from his body'. An examination of the deceased 'proved that a drop of even a few more inches would have been sufficient to complete the work of decapitation'.[25]

The open disgust for the prisoner offered some protection to Howard. There was no hiding how the neck of the victim 'was severely mutilated', but 'apart from this unpleasant incident the execution was conducted with due decorum and with dispatch'.[26] The end was ugly, but at least it was quick.

Howard's last job that year saw him back out at Dubbo. Harold Dutton Mallalieu's real name was Harold Massey, and he also went by the name of Michael Black. Mallalieu was hanged on 26 November 1891 for murdering Jerome Carey, also known as John Wilson. Accounts of Mallalieu's life, before his conviction, are split. Some reports outline that he was almost 20 and had been born in Cheshire, England. Other reports, including Mallalieu's confession, state he was 22 and had been born in California, America.[27]

The narratives of murder were much more consistent. The murderer and his victim had met near Condobolin, in central New South Wales, where Carey had offered Mallalieu his spare horse. They travelled together for a few days, but they bickered over unionism, with Carey criticising unionists and saying he might offer himself as scab labour. One argument, near Nyngan, north of Condobolin, turned violent. Carey cut Mallalieu with a knife. Mallalieu wrested the weapon from his attacker and stabbed Carey in the chest. Realising his companion was dead, the young man tried to burn the body before taking the horses and riding away. The murderer sold one of Carey's horses and was found by police with the other horse, in addition to having all of Carey's clothes, razors and his shearers' union ticket. Mallalieu had nowhere to go. He confessed.[28]

There would have been some relief when Mallalieu was dropped 9 feet. His end was not as neat as Hansen's hanging, but it was much cleaner than Dalton's. Howard 'adjusted the white cap, fixed the rope, and drew the bolt. Death appeared to be instantaneous, there having been only a few twitchings of the muscles'.[29]

'NO DROP SHOULD EXCEED 8 FEET'

Nosey Bob nearly decapitated Maurice Dalton in 1891. It was his third throat cut open. The noseless one's work was, though, in line with the best-practice recommendations of the day. In England, an investigation into the 'Existing Practice as to carrying out Sentences of Death, and the Causes which in several recent Cases have led either to failure or unseemly occurrences' began in January 1886.[30] Known as the Aberdare Report, after Henry Austin Bruce, 1st Baron Aberdare, who led the inquiry, the Report of the Capital Sentences Committee was published in 1888. The most confronting recommendation was that hangmen should commit a decapitation over any other type of error:

> We are desirous, however, of recording our opinion with respect of 'decapitations,' that if the condition of the culprit is such as to suggest the risk on the one hand of decapitation, or, on the other, of death by strangulation, *i.e.* of pain needlessly prolonged, we have no hesitation in saying that the risk of decapitation should be incurred.[31]

It is a nauseating concept, but in deliberately setting longer drops to reduce the risk of strangulation, Howard was exhibiting his professionalism and his capacity to put his patient first. For, as the Aberdare Report pointed out, it is unconsciousness that needs to be instantaneous. It is imperative that capital punishment not be harsher than necessary, and while decapitation is traumatic for everyone in attendance at an execution, including the hangman, the client is oblivious to their own condition. Aberdare and his co-authors were prepared to sound callous and cruel to reduce the rate of suffering among condemned criminals. Hanging was hardly a compassionate choice of punishment, but it did not have to be overtly vindictive.

The Aberdare Report also attempted to consolidate drop lengths, publishing a table suggesting how far felons should fall according to their weight. The origin of the long drop is uncertain. It might have been theorised, or it might have been the outcome of watching the effects of unintentionally long drops. It is known that long drops, as well as drops tailored to the weight of the prisoner being hanged, were promoted by Samuel Haughton, an Irish scholar with wide-ranging interests and skills, in the 1860s. The long drop was then introduced by English hangman William Marwood, after some lobbying, in the 1870s. One of the men who followed Marwood into the trade, James Berry, refined the drop in the 1880s 'aided by suggestions from the doctors'. Berry's 1892 memoir included a Ready Reckoner for Hangmen and a statement that his calculations had resulted from a gradual growth of knowledge and were not 'the invention of any one man'.[32]

Tailoring drops and determining how much force was required to facilitate a neat death is the most striking advancement in the art of judicial hanging. The tables were guides that took much of the guesswork out of sending someone off and were essential when many hangmen had little education. In 1866, Haughton advocated 2240 foot pounds (a foot pound being the torque or force required to produce an instant result) to allow for elasticity in the rope. Stretching the rope was essential, but some give was required to ensure the cord would not snap. The 1888 drops presented in the Aberdare Report as a 'provisional standard for future executions' favoured 1260 foot pounds, with some variations. A person of 7 stone or 98 pounds needed to fall 11 feet 5 inches, while a larger person of 20 stone or 280 pounds only had to fall 4 feet 5 inches. When Charles Watson was cast off for murder in 1885, his fall of 11 or 12 feet sounds exaggerated but was in line with popular thinking about hangings in the 1880s.[33]

In April 1892, Nosey Bob had access to a new table of drops. In this official guide, issued by the Prison Commission and Home Office of the United Kingdom and closer to the Aberdare table than the Berry table, drops were 'calculated by dividing 840 foot pounds by the weight of the culprit and his clothing in pounds, which will give the length for the drop in feet'. In a significant departure from Nosey Bob's practice, it was specified that 'no drop should exceed 8 feet'. The new table insisted criminals 105 pounds should fall 8 feet, while those weighing 210 pounds should fall just 4 feet. Any deviations, such as a change in rope length based on the 'diseased condition of the neck of the culprit', needed to be approved by the gaol's governor and the medical officer rostered to attend the execution. In October 1913, the table

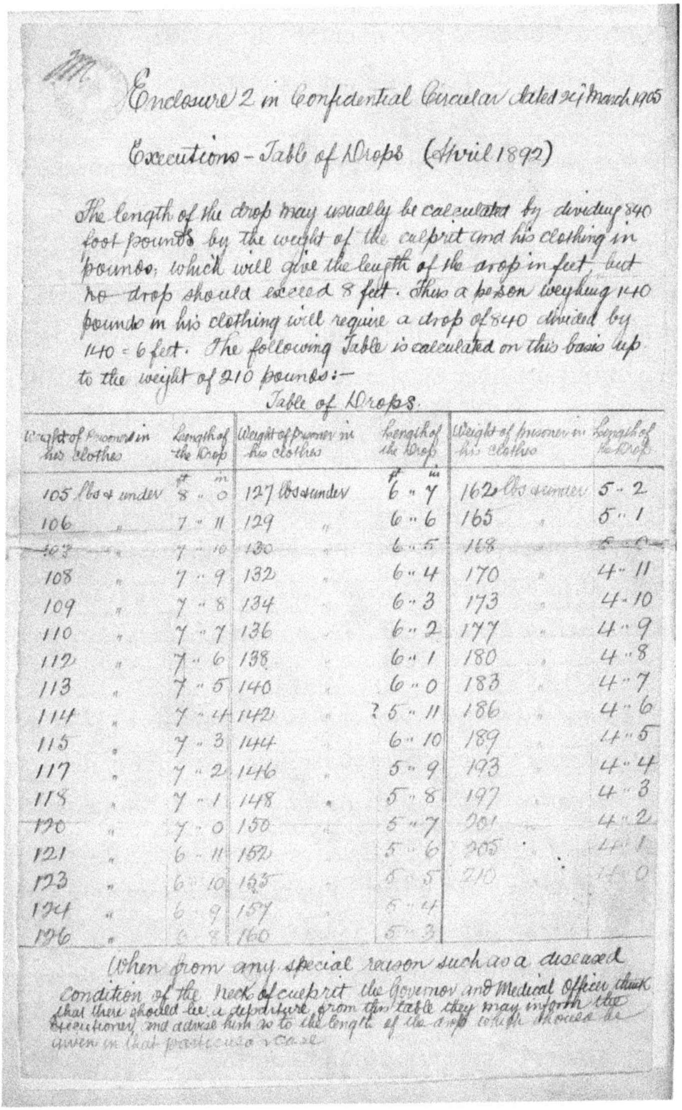

Enclosure 2 in Confidential Circular dated 24 March 1905

Executions – Table of Drops (April 1892)

The length of the drop may usually be calculated by dividing 840 foot pounds by the weight of the culprit and his clothing in pounds; which will give the length of the drop in feet, but no drop should exceed 8 feet. Thus a person weighing 140 pounds in his clothing will require a drop of 840 divided by 140 = 6 feet. The following Table is calculated on this basis up to the weight of 210 pounds:—

Table of Drops.

Weight of Prisoner in his clothes	Length of the Drop	Weight of Prisoner in his clothes	Length of the Drop	Weight of Prisoner in his clothes	Length of the Drop
	ft in		ft in		
105 lbs & under	8 " 0	127 lbs & under	6 " 7	162 lbs & under	5 " 2
106 "	7 " 11	129 "	6 " 6	165 "	5 " 1
~~107 "~~	~~7 " 10~~	~~130 "~~	~~6 " 5~~	~~168 "~~	~~5 " 0~~
108 "	7 " 9	132 "	6 " 4	170 "	4 " 11
109 "	7 " 8	134 "	6 " 3	173 "	4 " 10
110 "	7 " 7	136 "	6 " 2	177 "	4 " 9
112 "	7 " 6	138 "	6 " 1	180 "	4 " 8
113 "	7 " 5	140 "	6 " 0	183 "	4 " 7
114 "	7 " 4	142 "	? 5 " 11	186 "	4 " 6
115 "	7 " 3	144 "	6 " 10	189 "	4 " 5
117 "	7 " 2	146 "	5 " 9	193 "	4 " 4
118 "	7 " 1	148 "	5 " 8	197 "	4 " 3
120 "	7 " 0	150 "	5 " 7	201 "	4 " 2
121 "	6 " 11	152 "	5 " 6	205 "	4 " 1
123 "	6 " 10	155 "	5 " 5	210 "	4 " 0
124 "	6 " 9	157 "	5 " 4		
126 "	6 " 8	160 "	5 " 3		

When from any special reason such as a diseased condition of the neck of culprit the Governor and Medical Officer think that there should be a departure from this table they may inform the executioner and advise him as to the length of the drop which should be given in that particular case

FIGURE 9 Table of drops

SOURCE Sheriff's Office, Supreme Court of Victoria, Public Record Office Victoria, 1892, VPRS 14526 was revised to 1000 foot pounds with the recommendation of a minimum drop of 5 feet and a maximum drop of 8 feet 6 inches.[34]

For Nosey Bob and his peers, the 1892 table meant that felons across Australia were supposed to dangle on lengths of rope that had been carefully predetermined. Drops were not to be calculated by executioners struggling with concepts of force and the careful division of 840 foot pounds by the weight of a prisoner or, worse, set by the random availability of rope in a gaol's stockroom. These tables, though often disregarded by hangmen, exemplify how bureaucracies can sanitise violence, how bureaucrats can distance themselves from the tough policies that they set and then enforce. It was, on the surface at least, all about the convicted felon and a well-intentioned desire to facilitate a comfortable passage from this world to the next.

Concern for the prisoner was not new. In 1837, in New South Wales, the practice of sending a body for dissection after execution was abolished. As was the medieval practice of gibbeting, where prisoners, once hanged, were put on open display in chains in a ghoulish public service announcement that bad things happened to bad people. Gibbeting had also enabled rotting flesh to taint a place, generating 'unease and fear' while imprinting 'the terror of the law in people's minds'.[35]

Another change was around how long a body would stay strung up after being hanged. The usual time was an hour.[36] This makes a lot of sense. If a man or woman was strangled, it could take quite some time for life to be safely assumed as extinct. It would be very unfortunate if a prisoner was cut down after a hanging, only to gasp for air and then go through the process of being executed all over again. Without public audiences, and not wanting to extend private displays of violence for no reason, hanging a body for twenty minutes after a send-off became more common.

A qualified medical officer had to be present in a gaol yard before an execution could take place. When Erasmus Wren was late for Thomas Reilly's execution for murder in 1889, everyone had to restlessly wait for him to arrive as a doctor was required to declare that the right person had been hanged on the right date. In cases of decapitation, death was evident even to those without any formal training in health care. In other cases, the doctor declared the prisoner deceased and ordered that the body be cut down. A standard statement had to be made and published in the *New South Wales Government Gazette*. When Jimmy Tong was hanged for murder in 1892, just over a year after Harold Mallalieu was sent off at Dubbo, he was the subject of one of these notices:

> I, GEORGE WIGAN, being the Medical Officer of the Gaol at Armidale, hereby certify that I have this day witnessed the execution of Jimmy Tong, lately sentenced to death in the Circuit Court holden at Armidale on the twelfth day of October last, which said Jimmy Tong was, in pursuance of such sentence, hanged by the neck until his body was dead. – Witness my hand, this twenty-ninth day of November, A.D. 1892.
>
> GEO. WIGAN, M.R.C.S., Eng.[37]

Tong was arrested on suspicion of murder in Walcha, in northern New South Wales, in late 1891. 'Harry Hing, a Chinese fruiterer, was found murdered in his bed, his head having been severely cut by a tomahawk'. Tong was taken into custody after he was found with blood on his body and his clothing. The *Australian Star* confirmed it was not an accidental death, with the victim subjected to fourteen head wounds. Tong was found guilty of wilful murder at a coroner's inquest soon after the crime, but he had to wait until the following April to stand trial at the Circuit Court at Armidale.[38]

Tong's day in court finally came. There were numerous witnesses for the crown, including the constable who had arrested Tong. The court was also told about how approximately £18 had been located by police after Tong told a fellow prisoner where he had buried the cash he had stolen from Hing. Tong's gaolhouse friend, doing time for horse stealing, did not hesitate to turn informant. The prosecution may have been confident, but the jury was not convinced. The men deciding Tong's fate retired for deliberations just after 11:00 pm, and at 1:00 am it was reported that they could not agree. Having deliberated for not quite two hours, they were locked up in the courtroom overnight. The next day, 'at half-past 11 the jury was called into court, and the foreman stated they had not agreed upon a verdict'. The jury was discharged, but Tong was kept in custody.[39]

In October 1892, nearly a year after the crime, Tong's case was heard again. After day one of the second round of court proceedings, Tong 'made an un-successful attempt to escape'. The instinct to make a break for it was a good one. The *Daily Telegraph* reported that the jury retired at 8:30 pm, returning less than an hour later to say 'guilty'. The sentence of death was delivered. Tong, who was 'happy and quite content to die', was hanged on 29 November 1892 at Armidale. The murderer made a full confession before he was hanged, freely admitting that he killed Hing for money. The gallows were 8 feet high and straddled a pit that was 8 feet deep, to allow the body 'to fall the required distance'. The execution was uneventful and the cook's death so quick it was as if he 'had been struck by lightning'.[40]

'STRANGULATION EXECUTED'

Howard's social fortunes were mixed. Boycotted by cabmen, hoteliers and fellow citizens when he travelled for work, he normally received better treatment in Sydney. There were insults and snubs, the rare exchange of blows, but Howard at home was an accepted member of the community. Some people still avoided him, but this might have been a combination of his day job and his noseless state. Facial deformities in Howard's day were not unusual – disfigurements could be present at birth or the result of accidents, brawls, diseases or wars – but many had not trained themselves to cover their shock, or not to stare.

For those who saw Nosey Bob regularly, he was just another man making his way about the city. Yes, he was the finisher of the law, but he was also Robert Howard. He was a civil servant and a gardener. A widower with children.

He was generous and kind. These small repairs made to Howard's social standing were fragile. It could take a lot of effort to mentally accumulate all the ordinary aspects of the hangman's life when a barrage of press coverage cast him as a villain.

The first half of 1893 was not a good time at work for Howard as he struggled with, or disregarded, the new table of drops. Howard was, however, on-trend. The table appears to have been almost universally ignored by those who had access to it.[41] Besides, Howard had years of experience. He knew 8 feet was a good drop. The new rules might have been due to how the tolerance for decapitations had abated. It could still be argued that this was the most humane option for the prisoner, but having someone's head come off in front of a small, if carefully curated, crowd does bring a certain media management challenge. There were no issues when Jimmy Tong was sent off at Armidale in 1892, but there were problems on Howard's own gallows the following year. There was little comment when Edward Smedley was hanged on 13 June 1893 at Darlinghurst, but when George Martin Walter Archer stood on the same scaffold weeks later, the press coverage of the hanging was extensive.

Smedley had butchered his wife at the Volunteer Artillery Hotel in Quirindi, north-west of Sydney, where they both worked in the kitchen. The crime was a major story across the colony, in part because the murderer exhibited complete indifference in the aftermath of the killing. At the crime scene, Mrs Smedley was pronounced dead, having been stabbed numerous times. Mr Smedley came close to joining his wife at the local cemetery because a blacksmith, John Jones, felled the murderer with a couple of large stones he fetched from the roadway. An impromptu, but effective way to catch a killer. The aim of Jones was good and Smedley, now with head wounds, had to be resuscitated before he was handcuffed.[42] The crime was committed in February, with an inquest demanding Smedley head north and stand trial for murder at Tamworth the following April.

The prisoner refused to enter a plea, so the judge entered a plea of not guilty on his behalf. The evidence showed the murder was deliberate and unprovoked. The prisoner was found culpable and sentenced to death, a sentence Smedley received 'with the air of unconcern which had characterised his demeanour throughout the trial'. When the executive council first considered the case in April, it was decided to secure advice to resolve if the prisoner was sane or not, and so Smedley was sent to Sydney for expert assessment. When the matter returned to the council in May, it was agreed that he should hang.[43]

Smedley's last day came. There were no protests for mercy, not even the usual crowd gathered outside the gaol's sandstone walls. The *Herald*, one of Melbourne's earliest newspapers, attributed this 'in some part to the wet weather'. The Darlinghurst Gaol Death Register shows that Smedley was strangled, but public reportage focused on how the hanging was 'most effectual and complete', and readers were told how death was 'painless', the body having fallen 9 feet 6 inches, and that Smedley was left to hang for just a few minutes after the bolt was drawn. Only the post-mortem results revealed Howard's untidiness.[44] Perhaps the rope was not tight enough around the neck, and the error was deemed to be minor. Or, perhaps journalists were more worried about the slaughtered Phoebe Smedley than about the sloppy end of her husband.

The gaol's Death Register specifies that Archer suffered the same cause of death as Smedley: 'Strangulation Executed'. Archer was done for murdering Emma Harrison. Engaged to be married to William Jeater, a newsagent, Harrison was a dressmaker boarding with John and Annie Osbourne on the corner of Burton and Bourke Streets in Woolloomooloo. On 25 March 1893, Mr and Mrs Osbourne went to work at Reid's Assembly Rooms. Returning around midnight, and not seeing anything out of place, they went to bed. When Harrison did not come down for breakfast the next morning, there was some concern. Around lunchtime, Mrs Osbourne investigated and found a crime scene. The room was in disarray, and it was obvious the victim had put up quite a fight as she was raped and strangled.[45]

Indeed, the crime was so disgusting, an anecdote published years afterwards stated that Howard had been talking to a detective just before Archer was arrested. He raised 'his hat as reverently as a bishop', and said, quite uncharacteristically: 'As big an old sinner as I am, I'd hang that – for the love of it'.[46]

Suspicion fell on Jeater. Then, police turned their attention to Archer, an ex-jockey who worked at a local stable, and who boarded with Mr and Mrs Osbourne where he lived in a room with his wife and infant child. This did offer an opportunity to commit an assault as the door to the Archers' room faced the door to Harrison's room. Howard might have believed the prisoner's claim of being struck over the eye by a horse, and that the bloodstains on Archer's shirt and trousers were from his own bleeding nose.[47] With Howard's, supposedly similar, injury unable to be substantiated, the hangman may have just as easily dismissed Archer's story as a simple tale to avoid telling the truth. It did not matter; the police had their man. The accused stood trial for murder in June.

On the fourth day of his trial, Archer gave evidence with a detailed account of his movements on the night that Harrison had been killed. He spoke of his confusion when interrogated by police, and 'he said they perplexed him with so many questions at once that he did not care what he said, and he at last "shut up" altogether'. Refusing to cooperate would have encouraged police to assume guilt, even though 'the right of a suspect or defendant to remain silent' had been entrenched in New South Wales since 1850.[48]

Archer said, perhaps naïvely, that he trusted the jury to acquit him. On the fifth day of what was an unusually long trial, the judge summed up the case. The jury withdrew just after 2:00 pm and returned to the courtroom at 4:00 pm with a verdict that no defendant wants to hear. Archer stated: 'The crime with which I am charged, and on which I have been found guilty, is a horrible one but, although I am not guilty of it, I am not going to ask for mercy'.[49] A sentence of death was issued.

The day before his execution, Archer's wife and baby visited him in his condemned cell. The scene was reported as a farewell 'of a most heartrending description'. The day of the hanging, 11 July 1893, came, and as Howard attended the prisoner, the man being pinioned sent an urgent message to Richard Meagher who, with William Patrick Crick, had defended him, and who had gathered with the other witnesses down in the yard. Archer asked the man who would become the first Labor Lord Mayor of Sydney in 1916 to stay with him so he might 'go to the gallows with a light heart'. He clasped 'Meagher's right hand tightly, and without a tremor or any apparent sign of emotion, walked hand in hand with him to the scaffold'.[50] At the trapdoors, Archer reiterated his innocence. Howard finished his preparations and gave his assistant the signal to draw the bolt:

> The noose had not tightened sufficiently and had been lifted on to the right cheek, just near the nose, and partly under the chin. Then the man kicked his legs about and tried hard to move his arms. Shout after shout came from the man, and fully 10 minutes after the drop the poor fellow fought for his life.[51]

Archer was 5 feet 6 inches tall and weighed 9 stone 11 ounces or just under 127 pounds, dictating a drop of 6 feet 7 inches. Howard sent his client at least 9 feet through the trapdoors. That Archer was strangled, in a 'horrible bungle', indicates Nosey Bob did not fit the rope around the neck properly before giving the signal to his assistant to draw the bolt. The *Evening News* stated that those present 'who had seen numerous executions were loud in their expressions of disgust at what had taken place, and admitted never before witnessing such a frightful end to a man who had suffered the sentence of death'. Such convulsions were, according to Samuel Haughton, an 'unnecessary accompaniment of death by hanging'. Howard knew that being strangled was a painful and an unbearably slow way to die, with *Truth* describing how the hangman wept, 'the tears trickling down the place where his nose used to be'.[52]

It was later reported that Nosey Bob had threatened to quit, and the victim's jewellery was found at the stables where Archer had worked.[53] Was Archer a murderer? Had the real killer just tidied up loose ends? Some criminal cases will always be, if not cold, at least cool.

Howard blamed the number of strangers on the platform that morning for the awful display. The error was more likely Howard's. He described his worry on the day as the prisoner was 'a wild, strong young fellow, who had practised all sorts of rope tricks at the stables'.[54] Whatever the issue, the patient and the executioner both suffered.

CHAPTER 8

A BUSY TIME AT WORK

THE SMALLEST VICTIMS

Howard hanged George Archer in July, but he would hang a very different type of murderer in August. After the scragging of Archer had been so horribly botched, Nosey Bob would have been very anxious about preparations for his next dispatch. There were two causes given for what might have gone wrong when Archer was sent off. The first explanation was that the drop was too short. Indeed, it was claimed that Howard had originally intended to use a drop of 11 feet, similar to the drop he had given to Charles Watson in 1885. The hangman changed his mind, though, and reduced the length of Archer's rope to 9 feet.[1] The new table of drops might have been available in 1892, but it was not being enforced. If the drop was responsible for the bungling, then the mistake was Howard's.

There was also speculation that the error was due to Archer's collapse after his speech on the scaffold. It was plain, to those present, that 'the executioner could see that he was collapsing, and slipping the rope over in a twinkle, and tightening the knot, he lost not a second in giving the warning to his assistant to draw the bolt'. The executioner had rushed. 'Howard either did not, in his haste, on finding the condemned man collapsing, tighten the knot sufficiently, or the noose slipped whilst the body was descending'.[2]

Howard may have blamed other people, but everyone else blamed Howard. The following month, the press issued a firm instruction: do not bungle another hanging. Howard was paying attention. His next scragging, exactly five weeks later, was clinical.

One of the most high-profile and protracted cases in New South Wales in the early 1890s was the case of the baby farmers John and Sarah Makin. In 19th-century Australia, 'while new-born infants were less than 3 per cent of the population, their murder occurred at fifty-five times the rate of the murder of adults'. In a society intolerant of unmarried mothers and their illegitimate newborns, baby farming was common. The industry saw women take in the children of others 'on a sort of reverse hire purchase basis – a lump sum deposit and so much per week – and generally used the profits to help support their own families'.[3] The deaths of babies at the hands of baby farmers, in what were essentially ad hoc and unregulated residential child care homes, were often due to a lack of resources, incompetence or negligence. Some of these deaths were the result of wilful murder.

Two Sydney-based baby farmers were John and Sarah Makin. Both were born in 1845, and they married in 1871. On 24 June 1892, the couple, looking for additional income to support their ten children, saw a notice in the *Evening News* that would change their lives. It was an advertisement for Amber Murray's child: 'WANTED, kindly, motherly person, to adopt fair Baby Boy, 3 weeks, small premium. A.L., Oxford-street P.O.'. The Makins responded to the advertisement under the alias E Hill of George Street, Redfern. The letter was one of three Murray received in response to her advertisement. When deposed in court in December 1892, Murray stated Mrs Makin had been very reassuring. 'If you give me your child I will bring it up as one of my own', she said, while Mr Makin told her he would take £2 10s or £3 for the infant. Murray testified that she was willing to pay £3 if they were 'kind and good to the child'. Mr Makin accepted the full amount and said, 'I will give it a good education. It could not be in better hands than ours'.[4] Mr and Mrs Hill both came across as caring and genuine.

Baby farmers, like the Makins, often used aliases. They also moved around a lot. The Makins packed up and left their home at 25 Burren Street, Macdonaldtown, in August 1892. Only weeks later, on 11 October, two men were employed to lay new drainage pipes in the property's rear yard. A small package was discovered by one of the labourers who, thinking it was a cat, reburied the bundle. The discovery of a second, similar, package the next day revealed a baby and the men alerted police.[5] The constabulary were supplied with information relating to the Makins and their activities by members of the public, initiating a complete excavation of their rear yard at Burren Street on 2 November:

No. 1 found on Wednesday evening about 20 minutes past 5 o'clock: Female child, aged about 14 months, wrapped in a piece of white flannel with a red and blue stripe, and with a napkin pinned around. No. 2 found on Thursday at 9.30 a.m.: Male child, aged about six months, dressed in a coloured shirt, and wrapped in a napkin and a piece of white flannel covered with blood. No. 3 found on Thursday at 10.30 a.m.: Male child, aged about three months, wrapped in white calico, pinned up in several places, and in a white napkin worked with the letter 'F' in black in one corner. No. 4 found on Thursday at 11.30 a.m.: Female child, aged about two months, dressed in a white flannel dress worked in fancy work, and scallops all round, striped pinafore, and striped petticoat. No. 5 found at 2.45 p.m. on Thursday: Female child, aged about two weeks, dressed in flannel wrapper, twisted tightly around the body, and a portion of a thick woollen shawl.[6]

Police found another four babies on 9 November – Babies A, B, C and D – in the yard of 109 George Street, Redfern, where the Makins had lived prior to living in Burren Street. Two more babies were discovered on 13 November at 28 Levey Street, Chippendale, where the Makins had lived the previous year. It was Baby D, little Horace Murray, who sealed the Makins' fate when it was pronounced that Baby D was Amber Murray's baby and that the child had not just died; he had been killed. The mother identified her son by the clothing he was wearing, although a household with so many babies would have had to use one wardrobe for lots of infants. The cause of Baby D's death is also uncertain.

At least some of the babies living with the Makins 'would have died from disease, others from starvation or overdoses of Godfrey's Cordial'.[7] The syrup was used to sedate infants and children so they would not cry even if they were hungry. Godfrey's Cordial contained laudanum and could result in opium poisoning if too much was administered.

In August 1893, the *Sydney Morning Herald* summarised a long investigation, 'followed by an elaborate trial, and the conviction there secured was confirmed as the result of an exhaustive hearing before the Full Court, and subsequently before the Judicial Committee of the Privy Council'.[8] The appeals of the Makins were unsuccessful.

Despite the awfulness of the crimes and the careless ways in which the Makins disposed of infants over and over again, there were actions taken to commute the sentences of death. There was sympathy for 'the petition of relatives for mercy' and there was respect, too, for 'the conscientious convictions of those opposed in principle to capital punishment'. Nevertheless, it was felt by many that 'petitions and convictions cannot be allowed to interfere with the stern course of law or prevent justice from being done'.[9]

In the end, there was a compromise. Mr Makin would hang while Mrs Makin would serve a life sentence, but these outcomes did not impress everyone. An article in the *National Advocate*, a daily newspaper based in Bathurst, raged about how the jury announced both prisoners were guilty but included a rider that the woman should be the subject of mercy. There was no question that crimes had been committed, with 'guilt almost proven by the admission made by the criminals themselves' and, therefore, both should hang. It was even claimed that 'if ever the woman [Louisa] Collins deserved death, the far more barbarous woman Makin deserves it twice over'. When all was said and done, Mrs Makin received mercy twice. She did not meet Nosey Bob, while persistent petitioning resulted in an early release from prison and she was set free in 1911.[10] Mr Makin did not live long enough to see his wife become a free woman again; when she was liberated, he had been dead for nearly eighteen years.

> MORE BUTCHERY – And so Makin is to swing.
> After being postponed for so long, his fate is decided,
> and he will soon follow the innocent little things
> whom he so barbarously put to death. His last hope
> was his appeal to the Privy Council, but it has not
> been entertained, and the date of his execution is to be
> fixed by the Colonial Secretary on the 1st August. For
> goodness sake, Nosey Bob, do the business decently
> this time.[11]

The date was set and Makin was hanged on 15 August 1893. The venue was Darlinghurst Gaol. *Bird O'Freedom* asked: 'Whether the daily papers regard Nosey Bob's bungling with such horror as they pretend?'[12] Some editors were genuinely incensed, others merely wanted to increase circulation. Sure, botched executions were unpleasant, but they were also big business. Nobody was going to complain about a few extra copies of newspapers being sold. For newspaper editors, of all types, there was not much to report when Howard took care of Makin.

When being pinioned, the prisoner 'submitted without a murmur, and walked to the scaffold with a firm step'. The clergyman went as far as the scaffold and then retired, leaving only the sheriff, the executioner and the executioner's assistant by the trapdoors with Australia's most notorious baby farmer. Howard's complaints about crowded platforms had been heard. It was also explained that the sheriff and his deputy had examined the rope prior to the procession. There was, too, a new style of cap deployed over the prisoner's head, with speculation the 'new design of scragging-cap' had been invented by the minister for justice or by Nosey Bob. The cap had been made so that 'all Howard had to do was to pull the front of it over. This he did in an instant. The front of the cap being like a veil, he put the rope under it, instead of over it as had been customary'.[13] The formalities out of the way, the hanging took place:

> The condemned man's face was pale, and as the cap was dropped and the rope fastened round Makin's neck, his lips moved in prayer. When the signal was given and the drop fell, the body went through the trap, and hung almost without a quiver. Not a muscle seemed to move, and death seemed to have been instantaneous.[14]

The murderer 'died as he had lived – a quiet, and apparently indifferent, man'. Makin was 12 stone, or 168 pounds, and his drop 'was 10 feet, 6 inches', well over double the recommendation in the table of drops. Howard, his co-workers and the press were satisfied. The *Weekly Times*, a Melbourne-based newspaper, enthused that 'Howard, the hangman, did his duty satisfactorily', and better than anyone else, for never had an execution been 'more effectively carried out in Darlinghurst Gaol'. The body was left to hang for just seven minutes before it was cut down.[15]

The following month, Howard watched his son Edward marry Mary Ann Stevens. The couple joined hands on Wednesday 20 September 1893 at St Matthias Church in Paddington. The labourer of Waverley and the domestic servant of Paddington offered the parish register signatures that were clear if a little shaky.[16] Howard had given up his work as a labourer and the rector was informed that the groom's father was a civil servant.

TOO LITTLE, TOO LATE

Howard had redeemed himself, after bungling the dispatch of George Archer, with the hanging of John Makin, but it was too little, too late. The label of choker had been firmly affixed by a raucous press corps. Howard had been given a few breaks over the years, but since the hanging of four of the Mount Rennie rapists in 1887, most newspaper editors publicised Nosey Bob's errors without hesitation. Only if there was complete indifference to a felon, as seen when Edward Smedley was dropped for murder in 1893, could Howard botch a job with minimal commentary. Of course, if

Howard neatly dealt with a vile monster, then the hangman's role in cleaning up society was enthusiastically endorsed.

Like many occupations, workers are often only as good as their last, or loudest, review. This meant the man who was out of place in regional New South Wales was also increasingly out of place in Sydney. Howard would have been terribly hurt to have been shunned, not just by cabbies or hoteliers, but by his own employer. When the direct supervisor of the colony's senior executioner celebrated his birthday in September 1893, members of the sheriff's department hosted a weekend picnic in his honour:

> It is stated on authority more or less bad that Mr Robert Howard, the N.S.W. 'public executioner', was a liberal donor to the birthday present to Mr Sheriff Cowper, subscribed by the employés of the Sheriff's department. However, the hangman was not invited to the picnic. The 'line' was drawn at the picnic.[17]

It is not known who might have left Howard off the invitation list, but the rumour of exclusion, then publicised so everyone knew even his own colleagues would not socialise with him, must have cut deeply. The hangman was never accused of being a stingy person, so if a subscription for a gift was arranged, a portrait of the sheriff 'drawn in crayons', he would have undoubtedly contributed.[18] Though the event was gossip for the press, Howard did not have much time to think about picnics. He was busy at work and on the road again within weeks of Charles Cowper's birthday gathering.

In July 1893, Jemmy or Jimmy Hoy murdered a compatriot in Mudgee. The victim was Ah Fook, a shop-keeper, who had been living with Hoy for several months when he was slain. Fook was 'evidently standing before the fire when Jimmy Hoy took an American axe and struck the deceased in the throat, knocking him down'. The wounds to the cheek and neck were long and deep, while the timber back of the axe had been used to strike several blows on Fook's face. 'The body of the deceased lay in a great pool of blood for some hours, and was then dragged by Hoy into another room, where the latter slept'. Napping with a corpse is an odd move, but one that was dismissed by a piece in the *Sydney Morning Herald* that clarified: 'Hoy is a little eccentric'.[19]

Hoy was found guilty of wilful murder at a coroner's court and committed to stand trial at the Mudgee Circuit Court, the week of the sheriff's picnic. There was no obvious motive, and most people in Mudgee had difficulty believing the woodchopper and gardener was capable of violence, but Hoy was deemed responsible for Fook's murder.[20]

So, Howard was back in Mudgee for the first time in fourteen years. This trip was different to when he had headed west to take care of George Pitt for murder in 1876, or to send off Alfred for rape in 1879. This time, there were no controversies around the inequitable application of justice. No mass protests. No reporters at the scene to write up damning appraisals of his face and his skills. When Howard arrived in 1893, nobody 'who saw the fairly well-dressed stranger, minus the best portion of his nasal organ, knew it was the hangman'. Howard even managed a rare chance to mingle with locals at the Paragon Hotel before finding his way to the gaol.[21]

The scaffold used for Pitt and then Alfred had been taken down and put in storage. The *Australian Star* noted: 'All these years since the white ants had performed mischief on some of the portions of the light wood work'. With assistance from the public works department, the scaffold was put together, tested and sections replaced as necessary. On the day of the hanging, Hoy slept well, woke early and ate a solid breakfast. Howard went through his work routine, and his assistant pulled the lever before 'the body fell with a thud'. The neck was broken. 'The hangman and assistant leisurely stepped from the gallows and proceeded to the gaol hospital where they resorted to a pipe to soothe their temperaments'. The *Australian Star* went on to report that Howard described Hoy's hanging, on 24 November 1893, 'as one of the most successful operations he has yet effected'.[22]

Five days later, Howard was in Bathurst for his last job of the year. The tragedy that unfolded at Carcoar, a small town in the central west of New South Wales, is an awful example of senseless violence. At about 2:00 am on 24 September 1893, the town's bank, a branch of the City Bank of Sydney, was broken into. The felon callously murdered the bank manager, John William Phillips, and almost killed his wife, Annie Dorothy Phillips. A guest, Letitia Frances Cavanagh, heard the cries and raced into the dining room where Mr and Mrs Phillips were investigating a noise. Seeing so much blood, Miss Cavanagh 'went and took their baby in her arms', then tried to run. The 'ruffian met her in the dark, and struck her a violent blow with his keen-edged axe, cutting the hand of the child, which was resting on her neck, and half severing her head'. Miss Cavanagh died instantly, while baby Gladys Mary lost an index finger and had two other fingers nearly chopped off (one of which was later amputated).[23]

Mrs Phillips' sister, Susan Jane Stoddart, who was also visiting, tried to help. The two women were confronted by the intruder who demanded the keys to the bank's safe. The keys were with a new manager who was staying at a hotel, and so the murderer fled. In a statement, Mrs Phillips said, 'I am in danger of death and may shortly die', before giving an account of events and identifying Bertie Glasson as the offender. It was noted that Mrs Phillips 'exhibited a degree of pluck rarely found in a man'.[24]

The only physical clues were the theft of a good local horse and a saddle. The animal and his equipment were located in Cowra, south-west of the crime scene, and, 'to the horror of everyone', it was found that the rider was a young man by the name of Edward Hubert Glasson, known as Bertie, who was the son of well-known landowners in the area. He was also positively identified by several witnesses at locations connecting him to the crime. Glasson was found guilty of wilful murder at the coroner's court and ordered to stand trial at the Bathurst Circuit Court on 11 October 1893.[25]

'The prisoner was conveyed', according to the *Goulburn Herald*, to Bathurst in a buggy under the careful charge of police, 'as public opinion was so incensed against him that they were afraid to send him by train'. Those who did travel by rail were Miss Cavanagh and Mr Phillips, whose bodies had been kept in the bank, then transported by mail train to Sydney for burials. The scenes at the stations between Carcoar and Redfern were quite emotional as crowds, hundreds strong, gathered to pay their respects and to place wreaths on the coffins.[26]

The trial was an emotional event for all who attended. The issue of impulsive mania was raised, an attempt to convince the jury that Glasson was not after money. Rather, he did not know what he was doing, even though his financial problems had been proven. The jury was not convinced. They retired just before 4:00 pm, returning less than half an hour later. A death sentence was passed based on the jury's finding and the prisoner immediately instructed his solicitor to petition for a reprieve. The executive council considered the case carefully, and the members commissioned a report from a panel of medical experts. The doctors examined Glasson and found he was of sane mind at the time of assessment and believed he was of the same state of mind when he committed his crimes.[27] There would be no mercy. Glasson would hang.

The new gallows for the Bathurst Gaol were not in a yard as at Darlinghurst Gaol but 'part of an iron platform running across the end of a corridor of cells'. The place already smelled of death as a 'young Scotchman, while laying the final plate of the gallows, fell back upon his head on the hard concrete floor and was killed'. It was Howard's first appearance at Bathurst, and he asked if a low rail could be fixed near the trap to prevent the prisoner from leaping over it, and if a pit could be dug under the trapdoors of 6 feet by 3 feet. These alterations 'were effected with a view to minimising the risk of a "bungle" such as has on more than one occasion occurred with the despatch of condemned criminals in the metropolis'.[28]

Howard's track record was well known, he could not escape it. Neither could the executioner escape the scrutiny of the under-sheriff, the senior witness at an execution in the absence of the sheriff, who had been paying close attention in Mudgee and now in Bathurst to ensure that all went according to plan. There was, on 29 November 1893, nothing to worry about. Howard gave Glasson, the third man he had been ordered to hang on the birthday of his son Edward, a drop of 7 feet. Glasson weighed 10 stone 5 pounds, or 145 pounds, so the drop was longer than necessary, but it was credited for 'the execution being so successfully carried out'.[29] The prisoner's neck was broken.

A HORRIFYING MIX-UP

It was possible that, after a few good hangings in a row, Nosey Bob could have salvaged his tarnished reputation. He could have consolidated his image as a 'gentleman hangman' and discarded the mantle of the 'champion choker'. At the end of 1893, Howard had stood on a scaffold thirty-nine times and sent off forty-three patients. Across seventeen years, well over halfway into his career working for the sheriff, Howard had overseen very few mishaps. There were the near-decapitations of convicted murderers William Liddiard

MR. "CHOKER'S" CARRIAGE.

FIGURE 10 Mr Choker's carriage

SOURCE *Truth*, 20 January 1901, p. 5

in 1886, Louisa Collins in 1889 and Maurice Dalton in 1891, but in Howard's defence, this was a procedural preference. Taking people's heads off is undesirable, but it is a drawn-out strangulation that *really* counts as a bungled hanging.

The throttling of Peter Murdick at Wagga Wagga in 1877, and the issues at Darlinghurst with the scraggings of Thomas Rogan in 1880, Charles Watson and Thomas Williams in 1885, as well as Edward Smedley in 1893, attracted little, if any, comment on the hangman's skills. In sharp contrast, some strangulations resulted in strident public criticism, including the dispatch of Henry Tester at Deniliquin in 1882. Then there were three of the four men hanged for the rape of young Mary Hicks at Darlinghurst in 1887, identified by Old Chum in *Truth* as 'Bob's First Blunder', while the protracted strangling of George Archer, also at Darlinghurst, in 1893, was considered 'an appalling bungle'.[30] Five major scandals out of forty-three jobs, as an assistant and as a principal executioner, or a conspicuous failure rate of about 11 per cent, is not too bad.

Adding in Howard's five early, low-key strangulations and three necks split open give him a bungling rate of 30 per cent at the beginning of 1894. A proud hangman would have wanted a perfect run. Still, botched executions are almost routine regardless of method, with hanging accidents by no means uncommon either in the colony or in other countries. Indeed, despite a colonial-era assumption that hangings were successful in most cases, more recent research has estimated a standard bungling rate of 80–90 per cent with as few as 10–20 per cent of hangings resulting in a hangman's fracture.[31] Based on these statistics Howard's success rate of 70 per cent was, in fact, excellent.

Howard's scorecard as a professional executioner changed slightly when he stepped up to do his second double hanging. It was said that Nosey Bob ended up pulling his 'own strings' because he had been John Henry Want's favourite cabman, and he had pestered the future attorney-general for a safe government position.[32] Howard was given a job in the public service, but probably more responsibility than he was ready for.

A man quick to blame others for errors, Howard was solely responsible for what happened to Charles

Montgomery and Thomas Williams at Darlinghurst in 1894. The scaffold worked well, the ropes had been correctly prepared, the procession from the condemned cell was standard and the executioner's assistant did as he was told. The carnage created in dealing with two men found guilty of attempted murder was entirely the fault of the man known as Nosey Bob.

The events that led to Howard's major bungling on 31 May began in Sydney earlier that year. Three crooks – Montgomery, Williams and a third, never definitively identified man – made an early morning raid on a steamship company's offices in Bridge Street on 2 February 1894.

The building's night watchman noticed something was amiss while on his rounds and was consulting with a policeman when the robbers, unable to break into a safe, left the premises empty-handed. Walking down Bridge Street towards Phillip Street, the felons were confronted by law enforcement officers. The robbers employed their break-and-enter devices, heavy iron jemmy bars of about 2 feet in length, on the constables. Several men were bashed and badly injured. In an impulsive move, one of the robbers pulled out a revolver. A threat to shoot was not carried out, but it facilitated a getaway. The robbers turned and ran up Bent Street where they separated. One man sought refuge in the darkness of the Domain while Montgomery and Williams, both only recent arrivals in Sydney from Melbourne, ran down Phillip Street and, unknowingly, towards the Water Police Station.[33]

A senior constable who was still standing shouted for

reinforcements, with men duly emerging from the very building that the two felons were now running towards. The struggle to subdue Montgomery and Williams was fierce. The *Sydney Morning Herald* reported that the police station 'was the scene of much excitement' and the *Daily Telegraph* stated that the case had sent 'a thrill through the community'. With Montgomery and Williams incarcerated, it was revealed that five members of the constabulary required urgent medical treatment for head injuries and broken bones. Four of the injured were taken by cab to Sydney Hospital on nearby Macquarie Street. Another officer was taken to the hospital the next day when the extent of the internal injuries he had suffered during the affray became apparent.[34]

The inside of a courtroom was not an unfamiliar sight to Montgomery, who was 30, or to Williams, who was 21. The men were career criminals who had served sentences in Pentridge Prison in Melbourne. Montgomery, the more hardened of the two men, had half a dozen aliases. Williams also used several names and was known by detectives in Victoria as Curly. The pair faced court again on 3 April 1894 to answer charges of breaking and entering as well as felonious wounding with intent to murder. The jury left the courtroom at 7:10 pm and returned at 8:00 pm to declare both prisoners guilty. The judge declared Montgomery and Williams to be 'desperate characters' and issued the ultimate penalty, that they shall 'at such time as the Governor shall appoint, ... be hanged by the neck' until their 'bodies are dead'.[35]

In the late 19th century, hanging for attempted murder in New South Wales was rare. Of all Nosey Bob's patients, only five men swung for attempting to kill someone; of those five, four had targeted law enforcement officers. There were calls for the executive council to take a hard line. The incident was also utilised by some to leverage a policy change that would allow police officers to carry firearms as a matter of routine.[36] Alongside public demands for punishment, there were also popular appeals for clemency. The prerogative of mercy remained entrenched in law, but there were new rules around the offering of mercy. For petitioners seeking a remission of the two death sentences by appealing directly to the governor, there was a new barrier:

> It is perhaps not generally known that whereas the prerogative of mercy could formerly be exercised – and has more than once been exercised – by the Governor against the advice of ministers, the latest instructions from the Imperial government have withdrawn this power, and his Excellency now has no actual discretion in the matter.[37]

There were public meetings in the Sydney Town Hall and the Domain. Highlighting the harshness of the penalty, supporters for a reprieve included parliamentarian George Black, Cardinal Patrick Moran and social reformer Rose Scott. A petition, with 50000 signatures, had been signed by eighty members of parliament, all twelve members of the jury that had delivered the guilty verdicts as well as two of the men, constables John Alford and Frederick Bowden, who had been injured in the affray on Bridge Street.[38]

Working desperately hard in the fight to save the lives of

Montgomery and Williams was Richard Meagher, the man who had held Archer's hand on the scaffold in 1893. There was a patent public desire for mercy, but all the legal appeals and the pleas for reprieves were denied.[39] Both men faced the gallows at Darlinghurst Gaol.

Nosey Bob had very sensibly decided to set a short rope for Montgomery as he was the larger of the two men, and to set a longer rope for Williams. When Montgomery fell, his death was instantaneous. Williams, in contrast, became entangled in the rope. Howard's assistant that day, Goldrick, stated that this was because Williams fainted while on the trapdoors. The collapse of Williams was one of two factors that saw the press and the public enraged:[40]

Williams's rope caught under his left arm, and this caused the body to tilt over and kick Montgomery. Williams then fell sideways, the rope passing round his neck and under his arm. The wretched man struggled and kicked violently for two minutes. His struggles were horrible to witness, and it was not till the assistant hangman shook the rope violently that it was released from his arm. Williams was not then dead, but he was gradually suffocated, his struggles and nervous twitchings lasting fully eight minutes.[41]

Much more problematic than Williams being caught up in his own cord, it appeared 'that the men were given the wrong ropes, Montgomery being the tallest man was given a drop of 10 feet and Williams only 8 feet'. These drops were still longer than the planned 6 feet 10 inches for Montgomery and 7 feet 2 inches for Williams. The error was obvious while the reaction was immediate and deafening. 'Our Hangman's Horrible Blunder', cried the *Bird O'Freedom*. The report then asked readers, 'SHOULD HANGING BE ABOLISHED?' before declaring that the executions created 'a tragedy!' Most local headlines were similar. Even other colonies took the opportunity to condemn Howard's hanging abilities with 'A Horrible Bungle' appearing in Queensland, 'Horrible Bungle on the Scaffold' in South Australia and 'Another Bungle' noted for readers in Victoria. The *Bulletin*, naturally, had something to say about capital punishment. This report included a personal attack on Howard: 'And, once again,' it was asked, 'tell us why the State should be so brutal as to confront condamnés in their dying hour with that most hideous of all earthly spectacles, a noseless hangman?'[42]

Despite his best efforts, and his statistical superiority to other hangmen, Howard's work history was seen as a series of bungles.

INTRODUCING SAMUEL GODKIN

Howard paid close attention when he reported for duty on 20 July 1894 at Tamworth Gaol. He was up for another double hanging.

John Cummings and his co-accused Alexander Lee, also known as Joseph Anderson, were charged with robbing the Barraba branch of the Commercial Banking Company of Sydney on 18 April 1894. Both would have just done time if it had been a straightforward case of robbery, but the bank manager was murdered during the hold-up. The case was one of uncertainty and unconfirmed identities. Cummings maintained his innocence until the end, asserting he was not in Barraba, west of Armidale, the day of the robbery. Lee confessed to robbery, but he declared vigorously that he did not murder William Charles McKay and that he did not commit the crime with Cummings but with another man. Like the case of Charles Montgomery and Thomas Williams, there was a third man involved, but he escaped. The idea of a trio of felons was doubted as police had been 'unable to discover any trace of the alleged "third man", and the impression in official minds is that he was a myth conceived by Lee in the desperate hope of obtaining a reprieve for the purpose of identifying anyone who might be arrested'. It was also argued it 'was highly probable that in the scuffle McKay got hold of the pistol and shot himself accidentally'.[43]

Despite appeals and questions about the case unanswered, the first executions planned for the Tamworth Gaol would go ahead as scheduled. It was reported by the *Maitland Daily Mercury*, the colony's oldest regional newspaper, that the 'redoubtable personage known as "Nosey Bob"' went by train to see the law carried out, and that he travelled 'in a closed first-class carriage, but the fact oozed out that he was the unwelcome occupant'. There was no meet and greet and, as usual, he needed to make his own way to town. The man who was listed, by 'his own request, on the electoral roll as a "sheriff's officer"', had to be accommodated in the gaol. The prisoners also dreaded the executioner. 'Cummings maintains a surly demeanour, but Lee has broken down and refuses to rise from his bed'.[44]

The day set for dealing with Cummings and Lee, 20 July 1894, was far more sensational than anyone could have anticipated. At 1:30 am, Cummings 'made a determined attempt to commit suicide in his cell'. The condemned man had managed to smuggle a penknife into the gaol, and he made 'a gash in the left arm that had severed an artery'. Emergency first aid was given to the prisoner who was 'bathed in a pool of blood' and he was stabilised so that he could meet the execution team a few hours later:[45]

> Cummings, who up to a quarter of an hour before the execution had laid in a dead faint, had to be wheeled to the gallows in an invalid's chair, and the spectacle of this almost dead man being carried to his death was a sickening and ghastly one. He was so weak, as much from nervousness as from loss of blood, that it became necessary to almost carry him up the steps of the scaffold, and notwithstanding the fact that several doses of brandy were administered to him he was unable to retain his seat in the chair without support.[46]

Cummings weighed in at 11 stone 9 pounds while Lee came in at 9 stone 5 pounds. The weights were of little consequence to Howard, and he set both men a drop of 8 feet. Nosey Bob's planning paid off and 'their deaths must have been quite instantaneous and entirely painless'. It would soon be discovered that Cummings, 'dipping his finger in the blood which had collected in a pool in his bed, drew three lines on the cell wall to indicate that three men had been concerned in the robbery'. Howard recalled, years afterwards, that while Cummings 'showed the white feather, Lee was as game as a pebble'.[47] For Howard's assistant Goldrick, hanging a man who was almost dead and a man who proclaimed he was innocent of murder must have been too much. It was his last job.

Nosey Bob served as a hangman for twenty-eight years, holding the top spot for over twenty-seven of them. He cared about his craft and quickly settled into a routine for the disposal of felons considered beyond redemption. Even though Howard was able to offer employment stability, he had trouble securing the services of a reliable helper. When Nosey Bob marked his twentieth anniversary at Darlinghurst Gaol in 1896, he said he had supervised seven different assistants.[48] Just like his estimate of the number of people he had hanged, Howard's counting was a little off. As there are missing details relating to the careers of hangmen, the records of their helpers are also incomplete, making a full list difficult to achieve.

It is clear that Howard had an unidentified offsider for the hanging of Thomas Newman in 1877, but he was on his own for the execution of Peter Murdick later the same year. A man named Risby was with him for the hanging of Alfred in 1879 and again for his first double hanging in 1880. Nosey Bob had an experienced man by the name of Reed at his side for the dispatch of Henry Wilkinson in 1881, while Charles Begg was there to help send off William Rice in 1884. A new

and 'evidently nervous' hand helped out with the dispatch
of Robert Hewart in 1888. There was another new man with
Howard when Louisa Collins was hanged in 1889, as the
regular incumbent refused to hang a woman. It was the new
assistant's last shift. In a sign that more and more men were
prepared to take on the job of seeing people dance on air, it
was reported a few days after nearly decapitating Collins that
there had been twenty-three applicants for the new vacancy.
Nosey Bob's assistant when Thomas Reilly was hanged
in November 1889 returned twelve months later for the
hanging of Albert Smidt in November 1890. It is probable
that this man was Jim Goaler, or James Golder, who was also
on hand to help Nosey Bob when Jimmy Tong was sent off
in 1892. Goldrick stood by Howard for the men at the centre
of the Bridge Street affray and again to hang the already half-
dead Cummings and his gaol neighbour Lee in mid-1894.[49]

Some steadiness to the execution team came with the
employment of at least the ninth offsider for Howard, the
30-year-old Samuel Godkin in October 1894. Like Howard,
Godkin is first listed as an assistant executioner, at an annual
salary of £125, in the *New South Wales Government Gazette* in
1896 before he is named in the *Public Service List* of 1897.[50]

There was some sad news for Howard in October 1894
with the passing of a former chief justice of New South Wales
and a one-time supporter of the hangman. Nosey Bob would
have remembered that Alfred Stephen, a major contributor
to the colony's legal system, was prepared to back him after
the awful coverage by the *Evening News* in mid-1879 that
portrayed him as a gorilla.[51] The obituaries for Stephen, who

died of senile decay aged 92, reflected mixed feelings towards the jurist and legislator. His contributions to Australia were remembered, but so too was his failure to consistently emphasise the 'just' in 'justice'. The law, for some, was another arena to reveal the impacts of racism.

A point recalled by many in 1894 was Stephen's refusal in 1879 to grant mercy to a black man, Alfred, for rape while two white men, Alexander Medcalf and Charles Wilkinson, had their sentences for the same type of crime commuted. 'Much public dissatisfaction was occasioned' regarding what was another example of how First Nations men, and men seen as foreigners, were more likely to bear the full brunt of the law than those who looked like they were men of England.[52]

Howard had little time to ruminate. He was ordered to make his first formal appearance with Godkin as his new assistant before the end of the year. The pair, who were workmates until Howard retired, first operated together on Frederick Dennis, also known as Frederick William Paton, at Bathurst.

Dennis, like the Barraba bank robbers Cummings and Lee, had perpetrated a robbery gone wrong. On 6 May 1894, while stealing from Metcalfe's Store in the Parkes area, in the colony's central west, Dennis stole a revolver. With a weapon in hand, he shot John William Hall who, with four other men, tried to stop him at the scene. Hall was taken to the Parkes Hospital where, due to an inability to locate the bullet, his condition was critical. When Hall died from his wound before the month was out, Dennis was charged with 'burglariously entering the store, stealing a revolver, and shooting Hall with intent to murder'.[53] He was tried, found guilty and sentenced to death.

By December, Dennis was 'thoroughly penitent' and kept reiterating how 'he had no idea of shedding blood when he fired the revolver'. This claim, that the shooting was an accident in a fight, would have been some consolation to the victim's daughter, Minnie Hall, who was engaged to marry Dennis at the time of the murder.[54] Most reports on the execution on 11 December 1894 were short. Dennis was calm. His death was instantaneous. One report offered glowing praise for all involved:

> The arrangements for the execution were perfect.
> Howard and his assistant entered the cell at eight
> minutes to 9, pinioned Dennis, and removed his irons.
> From the cell to the drop is a distance of four yards in a
> straight line. At five minutes past 9 the condemned man
> emerged from the cell followed by the hangman. The
> chaplain remaining in the cell reading the burial service.
> In less than a minute it was all over.[55]

The patient was a muscular man of average height and weighed 11 stone 13 pounds. A condemned man of 167 pounds should, according to the 1892 table of drops, fall around 5 feet. Howard, as was his practice, added a bit extra that day and Dennis fell 7 feet to his death. It was good work from Howard and, although several reports credit Goldrick as Nosey Bob's co-worker, it was a good first day for Godkin.[56]

CHAPTER 9

CRIMINALS AS FODDER FOR THE MEDIA

'THE USUAL PRISON FARE'

Criminals have been big news since the emergence of print media in New South Wales. It is logical that the population of a colony overtly founded on crime and crime control would want to keep up to date on the settlement's primary activity. As Sydney Town became a city, as colonists spread north, west and south, as free persons began to outnumber convicts, the interest in crime did not subside. If anything, curiosity about the criminal increased. There was, still, a collective desire to *know* the wrongdoer.

In the colony's first years, crooks were easily identified by chains, uniforms and the scars of punishment. Convicts also wore the effects of harsh work routines and poor hygiene, adding to the visual literature of who was 'bad' and who was 'good'. As homegrown criminals, and a few imports, outnumbered the lawbreakers exported to the colony in bulk, those who might do harm became harder to recognise. Newspaper owners were keen to oblige an ongoing fascination with felons of all types. Their backgrounds, their habits, their breakfasts on the day they faced the fatal drop. No detail was too small.

One reporter was so curious about a prisoner's last meal, he asked Nosey Bob about how the condemned could eat breakfast on the morning of their execution. Howard explained why some of his clients appeared to have strong stomachs:

> I can easily account for that, and also the fact that some of them sleep soundly the night through. Of course, how the ordeal affects each person depends upon their natural nerve. In most cases the unfortunate has, perhaps, been days without eating and nights without sleeping. At last they become thoroughly exhausted, and sleep on the last night in spite of themselves, or in other cases they resign themselves to their fate, knowing that all chance of life is gone. Following a good night's rest an appetite comes also after the days and nights of trouble, though, from the ordeal the person has been in, the appetite may be partly unnatural.[1]

When Thomas Williams, of Wantabadgery bushranger fame, was hanged at Darlinghurst in 1885, he refused a meal on his last morning. Matthew Friske, hanged at Grafton a few months later, did not eat, but 'simply took a drink of tea, which the gaoler's wife sent him'. In 1888, John Creighan also limited himself to a cup of tea at Armidale. A few prisoners needed something stronger. Charles Watson was issued a nip of brandy at Darlinghurst in 1885 to treat his 'very nervous and trembling' state. William Liddiard 'partook of a glass of whiskey' just before his head nearly came off at Grafton in 1886 and John Cummings took several doses of brandy at Tamworth in 1894. Some prisoners managed a little more. Alexander Lee, who was hanged alongside Cummings, had a 'light breakfast' and then 'coolly smoked his pipe until the arrival of the hangman and his assistant'. Thomas Reilly 'ate a light breakfast, consisting of bread and coffee' at Wagga Wagga in 1889, while a few men held down hearty meals, including Thomas Newman at Dubbo in 1877, Albert also at Dubbo in 1880 and Henry Tester at Deniliquin in 1882.[2]

When Alfred Grenon, also known as LaPorte and as Mitchell, was awaiting his execution on the gallows at Darlinghurst Gaol in 1895, details of his incarceration were expected by newspaper readers. 'As usual with all condemned men', it was reported, 'he lost weight at first, but has since picked up and is now about the same weight as when he entered the condemned cell'.[3]

Grenon found himself in his predicament because in 1894 he had shot a nightwatchman, Thomas Harvey, in the chest after committing another crime in the eastern suburbs of Sydney. Harvey survived but, as often happened in cases of attempted murder where the victim was working to keep the community safe, a death sentence was issued after a verdict of guilty was delivered. Grenon was widely considered to be a lost cause – 'even those most opposed to capital punishment did not exert themselves to obtain a reprieve' – and the executive council, after considering the facts and Grenon's previous crimes, decided to let him hang.

The Frenchman continued to eat well until 31 January 1895. When he met Nosey Bob, he weighed 9 stone 4 pounds.[4]

The *Evening News* offered its usual animated reporting, noting Nosey Bob had secured a 'wicker easy chair'. He had a chair on standby for Louisa Collins in 1889, but this one was fitted with a range of gloomy-looking straps. It was Howard's plan, should Grenon struggle or collapse, to properly secure the prisoner to the furniture 'so that when the lever was drawn the man would be hanged in the chair – an uncommon and, to say the least, ludicrous sight'. A more practical, but still peculiar, initiative that day was a hobble strap made fast to each of the prisoner's ankles. This 'new idea of the hangman's, which gave the convict no difficulty in walking to the gallows … would prevent the legs from swinging helplessly when the trap was opened'. The man would not be able to, by accident or design, check his own fall and interfere with the drop that had been set at just over 7 feet.[5]

The chair was not required, but the additional straps combined with the hangman's usual paraphernalia helped complete the execution with the utmost efficiency. In Howard's own words, it was the 'neatest job' he had done in the last five or six years.[6]

As Howard made micro improvements in his workplace, there was agitation for macro change in the legislature. Today, the formal process of changing statute law begins when a bill is introduced into parliament; bills need to win majority votes in the lower and upper houses. Bills introduced by ministers (government bills) support the agenda of the government of the day. Speeches are given. There is some debate. Amendments to the bill might be made. The odd insult is lobbed from one side of a chamber to the other. Voting is usually done along party lines, so government bills are almost guaranteed to succeed. Bills introduced by non-ministerial representatives (private member bills) are much harder to push through as those members still need to secure a majority of votes to see their bill passed into law. In the colonial era, without the big political parties and party discipline that is known today, members had to work hard cajoling and lobbying their colleagues. It could be an overwhelming challenge, especially if the bill was controversial.

After the achievement of self-government, New South Wales saw three distinct periods of parliamentary-based debate to abolish capital punishment in the colony.[7] The leaders against the death penalty came from different backgrounds and were not natural allies, making coordinated progress a negotiator's nightmare.

The first period, 1859–61, was led by Terence Murray. An abolitionist since childhood, Murray, a liberal Roman Catholic who was pro-education and anti-transportation, presented a bill for abolition in 1859. Henry Parkes followed up with similar bills in 1860 and 1861. Samuel William Gray, an Anglican who, like Murray, had been born in Ireland, also offered an abolition bill in 1861.

A second period commenced in 1870, with a bill from William Brookes who also supported the eight-hour day. Without backing, the bill was abandoned but revived the same year. In late 1872 and early 1873, Edward Greville, a newspaper man who was keen on library services, also tried to see a bill become legislation, but he did not succeed. The third period began in 1889 and lasted for over a decade. Thomas Walker, a widely travelled radical, produced a bill that year and another one in 1890. Much like previous efforts, there was only lukewarm support from parliamentarians with different priorities.

The closest New South Wales came to abolition in the colonial era was through the efforts of John Haynes. As staunchly against the gallows in parliament as he was during his days working on newspapers, Haynes proffered bills in 1895, 1896, 1898 and 1899. He presented another bill in 1900, pleading for 'a mastery, so to speak, of the mind over physical vengeance'. Haynes was savvier than many of his elected colleagues and he 'outwardly at least, always appeared willing to compromise on the final outcome of his abolition legislation – perhaps the result could be a simple reduction of the capital code that everyone could agree upon'.[8] Haynes was not, deep down, amenable to compromise and the closest he came to achieving his goal was with his 1896 bill, which also failed. Even if the law had changed, it would have been too late to save Grenon's neck.

Howard might have approved of Haynes' efforts. The sheriff's officer obviously needed an income, but if given a choice between executing people and other duties as required, then tending the gaol yards was much preferred over core business. When rapists Alexander Medcalf and Charles Wilkinson were reprieved in 1879, Howard confessed: 'I cannot tell you how glad I am. I would rather than £50 that the men had got off. I dreaded carrying out the sentence on one so young, for I feared I should never be able to go through with it'.[9] The plethora of bills, over 1859–1900, kept the death penalty at the forefront of debates around punishment in the colony and ensured Nosey Bob stayed in the public eye.

Grenon's last breakfast was 'the usual prison fare'. The death penalty remained on the statue books of New South Wales but, like those who could not face a full breakfast before mounting a scaffold, there were those who could not stomach an execution. After sending off Grenon, Howard had almost twelve months of not needing to worry about hoods or ropes or trapdoors. It meant Howard had more time to be a grandfather when his son Edward and his daughter-in-law Mary had their only child on Tuesday 2 July 1895.[10] Her name was Eunice May.

TWENTY YEARS OF SERVICE

Thomas Meredith Sheridan was hanged for the murder of Jessie Amelia Nicholls on 7 January 1896 in Darlinghurst Gaol. Nicholls had sought Sheridan's abortion services. An underground industry in colonial Australia, Nicholls paid for the procedure in cash and with her life.

Sheridan received some medical training in Paris and had a few years in the workforce behind him. He was not, though, legally qualified to practise medicine in New South Wales, and he was widely seen as an imposter who preyed on the vulnerable. In March 1885, Sheridan had been sentenced to ten years of penal servitude when another woman with an unwanted pregnancy died under his medical supervision. The month that sentence was handed down, Sheridan was given a second term of ten years for another offence of the same type, with half of this term to be served concurrently with his first sentence for a total of fifteen years behind bars. Sheridan was also the subject of three other charges related to performing illegal abortions, but these were not pursued. Good conduct in gaol and poor personal health saw Sheridan released in October 1892.[11] He had been incarcerated for just over seven years. Unable to earn a living as a law-abiding man, he went straight back into his illegal line of work. More death at Sheridan's hands was inevitable.

The death of Nicholls may have been accidental, but there was no question it was negligent. Sheridan's reaction to his mistake was especially heinous. The woman's mutilated body was put in a box and dumped in Woolloomooloo. Mary Ann Nicholls, the victim's mother, had followed her daughter to Sydney from her home near Windsor. She had no knowledge of the purpose of her daughter's trip to the capital, and she certainly did not expect to be called upon to identify the body of her child. Or what was left of it. The shock was so much it was believed that the victim's mother would 'lose her reason'. Mrs Nicholls did not know her daughter was pregnant, but the young woman's fiancé did. Herbert William May, who wanted to marry Nicholls and did not know that she had gone to the city to seek an abortion, had also followed her to Sydney.[12]

Sheridan was told that he was a murderer and was sentenced to death. There were numerous calls for mercy, including a petition signed by nine members of the jury that returned Sheridan's verdict. A jury's recommendation for mercy in a specific case was 'one of the strongest elements' considered by the executive council 'in coming to a decision', but it was not, on this occasion, enough to save the prisoner's neck.[13]

Even the *Sydney Morning Herald* showed some sympathy for the shonky doctor: 'The parting scene between the condemned man and his wife last evening was a very touching one'. It was reported that 'Mrs Sheridan, after the farewell words had been uttered, completely broke down' and was so grief-stricken 'that it was necessary for an official to assist her along the pathway leading from the cells to the gates. She wept piteously, her little child, three or four years of age, walking by her side'. Sheridan wrote an account of his life, penned in prison, in which he stated that he 'had no hope in the mercy of man, it is an unknown quantity in New South Wales'.[14]

A letter to the editor of the *Evening News* made the pertinent observation that 'Sheridan, so far as we know, never solicited the deceased to undergo the operation'. Yes, the felon would be remunerated for his time, but he would also see the woman 'out of her trouble'. The correspondent said, too, that: 'The man that acts thus is to be hanged; the other goes free'.[15] In this case, May wanted to support Nicholls and their child, but there were many examples across the colonies of lesser men who abandoned those they had professed to love at the first sign of the sort of trouble Sheridan worked so industriously to resolve.

When Sheridan's moment came, he made sure that he cooperated fully with the executioner and his assistant. The *Evening News* pointed out that he even made an effort to make sure he was centred on the trapdoors, and he 'remained perfectly motionless while Howard placed the rope around his neck'. It was only when Howard pulled the knot tight that Sheridan's composure began to falter. 'He swayed slightly from side to side. The executioner, holding the rope with one hand, placed the other against Sheridan's back, and nodded to his assistant'. The doctor-turned-patient fell 9 feet 6 inches. Though death was instant and Sheridan's corpse 'was calm and bore no expression of pain', the fact that an execution had taken place inspired at least one damning headline. *Truth* declared: 'SHERIDAN SLAUGHTERED' in a 'Botany Bay Butchery', even though other reports noted that the execution 'was carried out entirely without mistake'.[16]

Shortly afterwards, Howard was interviewed as a '*Sunday Times* Special'. Readers were told that: 'In view of the execution of Sheridan last week, the recurring agitation for a reprieve, and the constant advocacy for the abolition of capital punishment, or its being confined to only the worst cases of deliberate murder, a chat with the public hangman naturally becomes interesting'.[17]

Confirming that Howard's career change took place in 1876, it is specified the hangman was about to mark twenty years in his disreputable position. The interviewer reiterated much of what many across New South Wales already knew about Howard. He kept a neat four-room home, and he took great pride in his garden as well as the animals at his place in Bondi, with its 'splendid view of the Pacific away to the east and south-east'. Howard explained how he was 'always fond of the sea air' and that he has 'enjoyed splendid health' since moving to the coast about nine years before. Nosey Bob bought land in the early 1880s and built his unassuming cottage around 1887, but his living arrangements are unclear. Different newspaper articles give different accounts, including that he lived with one son or with two sons or with a daughter 'who reads everything to him' and 'when required, makes up the fatal white cap'.[18] Households can be places of flux so all these claims could be true.

There is also, in this *Sunday Times* piece, a ready acceptance of Nosey Bob's mantle as the gentleman hangman. Yes, he had made quite a few mistakes and there was no way, at this point in his career, to salvage his record of efficiency. Yet, Howard was much better at his job than many other executioners and it was widely known that he was never deliberately careless when it came to his duties. Even his patients generally tolerated the man who, literally, had the back of Sheridan on the day he was sent through the trapdoors. 'I suppose', Howard mused, 'it is because they fully realise that I am in no way to blame. But it must also be because of the way in which I treat them. I don't go in a bullying, bouncing way, but perform my task as kindly and tenderly as circumstances will permit. What sense is there in being harsh with the poor unfortunates?'[19]

FIGURE 11 **In this cottage … lived Nosey Bob**

SOURCE State Library of Victoria, c. 1914–c. 1941, H22729

Howard is described by his visitor as a 'man past middle age, about medium height, with grey beard, a plentiful crop of hair on his head, and bluish grey eyes that have a good deal of keenness and brightness'. The reporter is most impressed with the hangman's horse, the well-trained steed called upon to fetch Nosey Bob's beer. The animal had been purchased, 'just a bag of bones' and a little wild, at the Woollahra pound for 5s. Now, the beast is 'as fine a hack as anyone would wish to have'.[20]

A few weeks after this interview was published, Howard was at a wedding. His son Sydney, who was now spelling his name Sidney, married Elizabeth Donohue at the Congregational Church on Darlinghurst's Flinders Street on Monday 3 February 1896. The father of the groom is listed as a government servant, while Sidney, who had just turned 26, identifies himself as a gardener. The bride, known as Lizzie, was 21 years old and listed as a domestic servant. Exactly three months later, the couple had the first of their eight children, a daughter they named Florence Emily.[21]

In the world beyond his cottage at Bondi, Howard's job was up for regular discussion as the abolitionists maintained a public debate around the problems of the death penalty while advocating the benefits of other types of punishments. There was a risk that Howard, who once remarked that he 'only does with a rope what judges do with their tongues', would face unemployment that year. John Haynes saw some success with his 1896 bill for abolition. The bill cleared early procedural hurdles, but it fell short of genuine support and was not made law.[22] It was the closest Haynes came to obliterating the gallows. The retentionists had the upper hand, practically if not morally, in the arguments on abolition. The convict stain was considered vile, but so too were the most violent offenders. It was also easier to maintain a system rather than trying to change it, easier to take comfort in knowing how everything worked than to bring about change and the possibility of unexpected consequences.

Then, on 27 April 1896, Henry Parkes died at the age of 80. One of the fathers of colonial politics was known for some policy backflips, including on capital punishment. Howard may have ignored that, instead choosing to remember how Parkes had supported him over the years, including his strong rhetoric that the government, not the hangman, was responsible for death sentences carried out in New South Wales. Howard also found himself with a new boss that year when Sheriff Charles Cowper retired. In July, the under-sheriff CEB Maybury took the position of sheriff and its impressive salary of £750 per annum.[23]

'THE EFFECTS OF HIS GREAT CARE AND KINDNESS'

In the second half of 1896, another interview with the executioner was published. This time, the hangman's comments appeared in the Melbourne-based *Free Lance,* an explicitly classist, misogynist and racist weekly newspaper that only managed a run of six months. The report outlines how, when in Dubbo, and 'contrary to his usual custom –

and "Nosey" thought some hidden influence urged him – he went to have a look at his game during the night'.[24] In what would have been an awkward moment, the executioner was recognised by the condemned man and drawn into a conversation with the legal system's quarry.

'Good Lord, Bob', the prisoner exclaimed, 'what are you doing up here?' 'Oh, nothing much', the hangman replied. 'Are you going to polish me off, Bob?' After a long pause, Howard admitted, 'I came up for that, Jim, but I don't think I will now'. The hangman was told not to be a fool. 'Someone has got to do it'. 'No, I couldn't do it', Howard said. 'Yes, you will, Bob; I won't mind, and you may as well earn the money as anyone else'. Howard goes on to tell his interviewer, Jack Drayton, an experienced journalist later known for his work for the Sydney-based *Smith's Weekly* and fighting for freedom of the press, that he went through with the hanging. He was very sorry about it. 'You see, mister', Howard explains, 'we were mates for years on the diggins, and he wasn't a bad sort'.[25]

If this anecdote is true, who was at the centre of Howard's reminiscence? Howard was not thinking about his most recent trip to Dubbo, the hanging of Harold Mallalieu in 1891. That condemned man was quite young, and he had spent a great deal of his short life at sea. Thomas Newman was Howard's first hanging at Dubbo in 1877, but it is difficult to imagine Howard voluntarily spending time with a man who had raped and murdered a young child. Albert, a First Nations man, hanged at that gaol in 1880, was unlikely to have spent any time on the goldfields. Lars Hansen, hanged at Dubbo in 1891, spoke imperfect English, so such a clear, if casual, catch-up does not make sense. Also, while Hansen had spent time on the diggings, Howard was a cab driver in England and again in Australia, with the only evidence that he tried to earn a living any other way connected to his work as a labourer.[26] This interview is probably a fabrication that says more about a fascination with the New South Wales hangman than it says about Nosey Bob.

The life of Howard must have, for himself at least, felt a little bit more normal in 1896. When Nosey Bob was enjoying a lull between his official gaol engagements, newspapers made the occasional peace offering. For example, the *Australian Star* published a story about a very different type of executioner, one with his sights set on the sea instead of a scaffold. Howard was acknowledged as a fisherman of some skill when he brought in a shark measuring 9 feet 6 inches off Bondi. The animal had first been seen 'flopping about in the surf', the creature disabled as it had been speared with a harpoon. Unable to swim, it was not too difficult to bring the huge beast ashore. 'Once the monster was landed, however, it behaved very differently. Rearing itself up, after the fashion of a kangaroo, it lashed out at its captors, and continued to fight desperately until a gun was procured'. The shark was shot again, this time with a firearm, and its struggling stopped. Credit for the capture of the 'marine monster' was given to Nosey Bob, who was very respectfully described in the report as 'Mr Robert Howard, one of the officials at Darlinghurst Gaol'.[27]

In another snippet, only months before the calendar

ticked over into a new year, it was reported that Mr Robert Howard and his assistant, Mr Samuel Godkin, had become 'regularly graded Civil Servants, the Public Service Board having fixed and gazetted the salary of the former at £156 per annum, and the latter at £125 per annum'. Howard was also singled out from his counterparts in the trade by *Truth* as 'perhaps the only Australian executioner who has held the office for over 20 years, draws an annual salary, lives in his own freehold, and has his name inscribed on the electoral roll of the colony'. There were men who had held the unenviable position in Australia for longer. For example, Solomon Blay, a convict who became an executioner in Van Diemen's Land in 1840 and offered his final resignation in 1891, did around half a century as a scragger. This paragraph in *Truth* is, though, a rare acknowledgment that Howard was not as common as his colleagues.[28]

There was still some haziness around the circumstances of Howard's appointment. In 1880, Howard told a journalist from the *Bulletin* that he took on the role of executioner due to drink.[29] He implies that he just did not think it through. Over fifteen years later, in 1896, he maintained that he did not deliberately seek out the role of hangman. In talking to a reporter from the *Sunday Times*, he offers a slightly different (and much more sober) story to the one he gave JF Archibald, one that more closely aligns with the widely accepted narrative of Nosey Bob:

> I used to drive a cab. I was always amongst horses from a boy, but although I had a good turn-out and was always

well dressed, I found that the public, ladies particularly, objected to engage me owing to this disfigurement, which I had suffered through an accident with a horse. The post of assistant-executioner became vacant and I applied for it and got it. I had no idea then of becoming the principal, but that fell to me in due course.[30]

Like other published accounts of the noseless hangman, the specifics of when, where and how the accident happened are missing. Howard certainly does not volunteer any evidence. His telling of the story sounds almost rehearsed. Perhaps he had just told the same tale too often. Or, if the public were in the market to buy myths about Nosey Bob, then there was nothing to stop Howard from buying those myths too. There were so many stories about the noseless one, that the hangman could pick and choose the chapters he wanted for his own autobiography.

The man from the *Sunday Times* did not push the point but instead connects Howard's facial damage to his situation as an executioner. He is satisfied with the story of a run-in with a horse and suggests: 'All our lives are more or less swayed by accident, and it was the mishap which spoiled Howard's features that caused him to hold the office he does to-day'. Howard was satisfied too. He gave the reporter a tour of his garden, even though it was 'suffering from the dry season'. There were also Howard's companions to inspect, 'the bees, the dogs, magpie, horse and other domestic animals'. For 'Howard is very fond of animals, and he has them all perfectly trained, and showing the effects of his great care and kindness'. The reporter then benefits from Nosey Bob's horse, which he rides to the tram stop to avoid 'trudging over the sandhills', with the 'horse returning home as he is trained to do as soon as dismounted'.[31] Despite a comfortable and quiet home life, Howard was still a hangman and he needed to take care of Charles Hines.

Nosey Bob carried out just one job at the Maitland Gaol, and the governor had to borrow Tamworth Gaol's gallows for the occasion. Hines had been found guilty of assaulting his step-daughter, Mary Emily Hayne, over a period of at least ten years. The prisoner protested his innocence, but the *Evening News* declared he incriminated himself at his trial when he made statements 'showing an almost inconceivable state of depravity'.[32]

Even the prisoner's most vocal supporters believed he had committed the crimes he was accused of, with numerous residents of Maitland signing a petition for a reprieve, which was justified by the idea that 'the unfortunate man is not responsible for his actions, and is classed as a sexual maniac'. John Haynes protested, as was his habit, and based his own plea for clemency 'upon the argument that the mere facts of the case were sufficient proof of the man's insanity'.[33]

The executive council did not budge. Hines was dropped 7 feet 6 inches by Howard with absolute professionalism on 21 May 1897. A local paper, the *Maitland Daily Mercury*, reported that: 'He died firmly and instantaneously. Some of the experienced spectators present – there were twenty altogether – said it was the cleanest thing they had ever witnessed'.[34] Death, when it was classified as instantaneous, was blessedly quick. According to James Barr, an Irish-born medical officer who worked with the prison system in England in the late 1800s, a clean hanging was all over in a fraction of a second:

> It takes a body moving under the influence of gravity
> three-quarters of a second to fall through the space
> of nine feet; and, owing to the velocity acquired
> according to the law of uniformly accelerated motion,
> the time occupied in the last seven inches – during
> which the stretching and tightening of the rope occurs
> – is only .0225 of a second. If to this we add, say, .0275
> for the elasticity of the rope, then the whole time
> during which the shock could be felt is only .05, or
> 1/20 of a second.[35]

The death of Hines was neat, but it also flagged a rarely cited argument against capital punishment: justice for each one of an offender's victims. You can give an offender multiple gaol terms for multiple crimes, to be served concurrently or consecutively, but you can only execute somebody once. Hines had 'two capital charges against him, the second being said by the police to be worse than the first, but being convicted by a jury of his countrymen upon one there was no need to go into the horrible and sickening details of the other'. The victim referred to in this second case was the younger sister of the prosecutrix at the centre of the first case. The crimes were, without doubt, hideous. In handing down a sentence of death, the judge made the shocking assertion that it would have been 'far better for the prisoner, and far better for these children if he had killed them in their infancy. Then their souls would not have been destroyed as he had destroyed them'.[36] The trial was obviously a traumatic process for all of those who were involved. For this criminal, perhaps, one sentence for multiple crimes was a satisfactory result.

'THANK GOD FOR THAT'

The hanging of Thomas Moore on 24 June 1897 in Dubbo Gaol was Nosey Bob's most dramatic piece of work. The damage done to Moore's body was so great that the gaol yard's pit beneath the gallows had to be whitewashed after the execution.

Moore was suspected of having committed at least two murders. The crime that saw him dropped by Howard, in mid-1897, was the murder of Edwin Smith, an elderly man who had been working as a fisherman at Brennan's Bend on the Darling River. The previous November, George Grumley and George McGrath were camped on this bend in the river when they discovered a bag 'out of which a human foot protruded'. Police were notified and able to ascertain that the last man seen with Smith was Moore, the latter now in possession of items that had once belonged to the dead man. Moore also left a trail of Smith's property 'at different people's houses, with the request that they would keep them for him until his return'. In addition, the suspect had benefited from a cheque, for £1 17s, that had been paid to Smith for some of the fish he had caught. Moore was sent south-east to Dubbo to stand trial for a murder that 'was evidently committed with a tomahawk, the skull being fractured and the face being smashed in, so that even if the body had been found in a better state of preservation, the features would have been unrecognisable'.[37]

Had Moore been acquitted of Smith's murder, police were on standby to charge him with the murder of Thomas Andersen. This body had not been covered up on dry land, but instead, it had been 'found floating in the river Namoi enclosed in a sack, and with the head and face smashed in beyond recognition'. Andersen, a Danish man, had some distinctive personal belongings that were found in Moore's possession, while it had been confirmed that Moore was in the area at the time Andersen was killed.[38]

The convicted felon was described as someone who was brooding but holding up, in most of the reports on his incarceration and his imminent demise. He refused breakfast. He never confessed. Moore weighed 11 stone 5 pounds on the day of his execution. For calculating the drop, he weighed 159 pounds and should have fallen around 5 feet 3 inches. Howard dropped him 7 feet 9 inches. The death was certain, but over the top: 'When the bolt was drawn the body shot through the trap, but the head was severed completely from the body, and the body and head fell into separate places in the pit beneath. The body lay in a pool of blood, and the head, capless, lay face skywards'.[39]

The sides of the pit beneath the gallows, with pits often dug to extend the drop, were splashed with blood. Instead of the patient hanging the usual time, or for a length of time deemed appropriate by the medical officer in attendance, the 'body was allowed to remain in the pit for 20 minutes'.[40] The witnesses, undoubtedly, would have been hoping that the pit was porous and that the blood would drain away, like water out of a bathtub. At least it was the middle of winter and there were no inquisitive blowflies to animate the scene.

Harry Tresidder, the gaol's medical officer, tried to argue that the ugly result of the hanging was not Howard's fault. He 'explained that Moore had very thin muscles in the neck, which was composed principally of fat. The bone was very small'. It was shown, too, that all the 'necessary precautions were taken' and that the drop was several inches shorter than Howard had set for 'other men he had executed of the prisoner's size and weight'.[41]

Nosey Bob knew what he was doing. The experienced executioner made an adjustment to the rope, but it was not enough. Moore was 65 years old and so the 'drop was rather too long for such an old man; the small bones of the neck being old and brittle, snapped immediately'. At the inquest, the jury made a simple return: 'death by decapitation'.[42]

Within days of Moore's hanging, there were calls for Howard's dismissal. *Truth*, as vocal as ever, dedicated the first three columns of the paper's front page to the drama at Dubbo:

> It will be well, perhaps, to take a cursory glance at
> 'Nosey Bob's' ghastly, ghoulish, goings-on, during the
> last few years, as a simple record of what a so-called

civilised community, cradled in convictism, fostered by
the flogger, and over-awed by the gallows – kept up as a
fixed and permanent institution – will suffer in the name
of Law and Order, humanity, and public decency.[43]

This story in *Truth* offered an overview of the executioner's
bunglings between 1887 and 1897. The four Mount Rennie
rapists hanged by Howard are mentioned. So, too, are Louisa
Collins, Maurice Dalton and George Archer, as well as
Charles Montgomery and Thomas Williams. The mistakes
are rounded out with 'a fitting ghastly finale to this horrible
list'. The dispatch of Moore, who was 'mangled to death' by
Nosey Bob, made the retention of Howard 'nothing short of
a scandal to the Law and a satire on our civilisation'. Signed
off, not by Old Chum, but the masthead's owner and editor,
this is a plea for abolition based on some of the common
arguments against the death penalty; it is also a plea made
in rage. John Norton, in a chaotic and personal piece that is
written in the style of some of JF Archibald's early articles
against capital punishment, goes on to attack Howard
directly: 'Such is the grim and bloody record of this horrid
ghoul. Yet, year after year he is allowed to add to the horror
attending the hanging of men and women by the exhibition
of his detestable and dreadfully damaged features, and his
clumsy and callous bungling'.[44] Norton then demands
immediate action:

He is entitled to a pension. Let him, for the sake of
our common humanity and public decency, have his

pension and go. Nay, let his pension be doubled if he will but go at once. Failing a decent exit, 'Nosey Bob' must be kicked out with as little ceremony or compunction as he exhibits towards the wretches whom he so cruelly and callously dooms to a double death. Surely less than this public opinion cannot require; and just as surely, less than this Parliament will not dare to exact, and that, too, before 'Nosey Bob' can get a further chance of clumsily 'scragging' another condemned criminal's neck.[45]

There would have been a long list of people unimpressed with Howard's performance in dealing with Moore. The sheriff, the governor of the gaol, his assistant, the witnesses and the cleaners. Still, the authors of the Aberdare Report were correct: a decapitation is preferable to a strangulation. There were complaints, but there was far less coverage of Howard's bloody bungling at Dubbo than when he mixed up the ropes at Darlinghurst for the two men who sparked the Bridge Street affray in 1894. Howard had enjoyed – between the double hanging of Montgomery and Williams, and the hanging of Moore – a clean run of half a dozen men sent into eternity. Six no-fuss dispatches.

Howard would return to Dubbo the next year for the sixth of the seven jobs he would do at that town's gaol. He was reminded by a reporter about 'Moore, whose head and body parted company when Bob last presided at an execution in Dubbo'. Nosey Bob would have remembered the incident all too clearly. 'Well, yes', he said, 'that was a bad case. His neck was as brittle as an egg shell'. The hangman recalled a drop of 7 feet 6 inches, just short of the 7 feet 9 inches that Moore fell. 'I never had such an experience', Howard confessed. 'I can't understand it now'. The interviewer, like several others over the years who had spoken to Howard, knew that the matter was in the past and that whatever had happened with the hanging of Moore could not be changed. There 'was no use continuing the subject'.[46] The condition in which Howard had left the local gaol's number two exercise yard was not raised with the executioner, but it was mentioned in the coverage of Nosey Bob's 1898 return to Dubbo:

> One would think that a person who has been present at so many violent deaths as Bob would be above any trifling superstitious feeling, but like most great men, he has a weak spot. When he arrived in Dubbo the other day, his first inquiry was as to the pit or well, dug underneath the scaffold. When Moore was hanged, his head struck the side, and so did the trunk, and great splashes of blood were on the whitewashed bricks, lining the well. 'Any stains on it', said he in a whisper, and when informed there were not – that all the marks made that day had been whitewashed out, he exclaimed, *ab imo pectore* [from the bottom of my heart], 'Thank God for that'.[47]

Unlike the early years of the settlement, by Howard's day, there was no shortage of people prepared to take on the role of the colony's punisher. It was even rumoured that 'every time "Nosey Bob" Howard, the hangman, is reported to be in ill health, sheafs of applications for the executioner's billet pour in on the governor of Darlinghurst gaol'.[48] There were some hardened individuals who thought they had enough nerve to send off a human being, and believed they would be more reliable than Nosey Bob and so offer a more consistent service to the citizens of New South Wales. Aspiring hangmen would have to wait. Howard was to be on the scaffold for a few more years before he started contemplating retirement.

CHAPTER 10

THE EXECUTIONER'S WORKLOAD EASES

THE 'AL-FRESCO MURDERER'

In mid-1896, a man going by the name of Frank Butler wanted men to join him and head west of Sydney. The plan, advertised by Butler, was to search for gold. The idea of a couple of fellows going on an excursion to try their luck on the goldfields sounds innocent enough. The reality, though, was much more sinister.

The expedition leader had enlisted in, and deserted from, the Royal Navy, the United States Army and the North-West Mounted Police of Canada. The unsettled rogue had seen much of the world when he arrived in Australia in the early 1890s. In and out of prison, on and off the goldfields, the man whose real name was Richard Ashe found himself in New South Wales as Frank Butler Harwood. Having 'failed to make money by theft or fraud', he embarked on a new type of work, and 'with full premeditation and calculated ferocity, the lone wolf was ready to murder for profit'.[1]

Butler, who was described by the *Bulletin* as the 'al-fresco murderer', selected three respondents for his scheme in 1896. Charles Burgess left Sydney with Butler on 13 August, Arthur Preston on 19 October and Lee Weller on 29 October.[2] After luring these hopeful fossickers out west, he told them to start digging for gold. Australia's first recognised serial killer made his victims dig their own graves before they were shot, robbed and buried.

Butler killed at least three people – Burgess, Preston and Weller – and without a doubt murdered others. As the press told of his crimes, he first used the press to attract partners to accompany him in search of gold, just as John and Sarah Makin had answered advertisements to find their infant victims a few years earlier. An example of the press corps unknowingly aiding Butler was one of his last notices, published on 24 October 1896, which was used to lure Weller: 'Prospector wants Mate, young man, experience unnecessary, equal shares. Butler, Metropolitan Hotel, 401 Pitt St'. Nobody missed Burgess, but friends of Preston and Weller raised the alarm in November. Initially, police and all involved in the search thought they were looking for a few men who were just off course in the bush. Suddenly, when dead bodies started turning up, it was realised that everyone was on the hunt for a killer.[3]

The multiple murders discovered in the Blue Mountains sparked a fantastic chase, but Butler was already gone. Sensing his luck was running out in Australia, Butler had made his way to the United States. The killer underestimated the determination of authorities, who caught up with him in California where he was arrested, then extradited back to New South Wales. There were hundreds of articles covering

Butler and his crimes, but one of the most outrageous of these was an interview with the murderer on the final part of his journey from San Francisco to Sydney. His ship, the *Mariposa*, was in Auckland and preparing for departure when he decided to take advantage of his celebrity status and received 'interviewers in a light-brown pyjama suit, and nothing could exceed the coolness of the fellow as he sat on his bunk quietly smoking':[4]

> He had an easy, nonchalant air, and expressed himself as willing to volunteer any information.
>
> 'Well Butler', the reporter said, after the first greeting, which, on his part consisted of a nod and a squint, 'you are charged with several murders, and we understand you have confessed to some'.
>
> 'It is a damned lie', he said savagely, 'that is what I wanted you for. Those 'Frisco reporters made those fakes. I have never confessed to any murders'.[5]

Sitting back on his ship's bunk in 1897, he did not give his real name or age. Butler had been born in England, but he informed reporters that he had been born in Canada and then advised, in perhaps the only truth he told in the interview, that he had arrived in Sydney on 2 August 1896. When questioned about one of the murder victims, Butler declared: 'I won't say anything about it at all'. The pressman recorded that 'the answer was given savagely, and the prisoner's looks presaged storm'.[6] Readers also wanted to know what evil looked like. Could it be easily identified? The *Evening News* obliged reader demand when it carried an adjective-rich article titled 'Butler Described':

> There is a strange mixture of the animal and the man about Frank Butler. His small, cruel, grey-blue eyes, with the small pupils and pale iris, ever restless, suggests the wolf. They are deep-set, with heavy lids, and covered with lowering bushy eyebrows, puckered up towards their meeting point, by two deep seams, which give him, whether laughing or in repose, a perpetual frown, which intensifies to an extraordinary degree when he is put out.[7]

Butler used the press to deny claims he had tried to kill himself, declaring the stories were 'fakes', but he was still placed under close guard in Sydney.[8] The trial commenced on 14 June 1897, with many people going to see the proceedings unfold for themselves:

> The trial of Frank Butler, charged with the murder of Captain Lee Millington Weller at Glenbrook on 31st October last, was commenced at the Central Criminal Court, Darlinghurst yesterday, before the Chief Justice and a special jury. The court was 'crowded' – if such an expression could fairly be used where the arrangements were such that no one was admitted for whom seating accommodation could not be found.[9]

Reportage of the proceedings at Darlinghurst was extensive, with Butler's execution presented as a brief concluding chapter to his lengthy and elaborate story. The death sentence was carried out on 16 July 1897 in Darlinghurst Gaol, exactly one month after he had been sentenced. One newspaper told their readers that it was a small gathering, with just: 'Sixteen persons assembled in the wing of the gaol immediately facing the gallows to witness the end'. Howard was, as usual, on duty that day as a hangman. He was reliable and never missed a hanging. Indeed, it was thought by those at the *Albury Banner and Wodonga Express*, one of the colony's weekly newspapers, that Howard was 'the only honest appointment' the government in New South Wales had ever made, for Nosey Bob 'is the only Government official who does his duty without fear or favor'. Perhaps there was some value in the idea that the 'typical hangman, like the poet, is born and not made'.[10]

The fearless Nosey Bob took the noose and placed it around Butler's neck. The man known for a 'career of gross bungling' was on point. The murderer angrily ordered Nosey Bob to: 'Let go'. The lever was pulled and Butler fell 7 feet and 5 or 6 inches.[11] He died instantly.

The pulling of the bolt is usually the end of the story. Not this time. The extradition of Butler offers an unusual aspect to debates surrounding crime and punishment in colonial Australia. Men were dead, victims of a killer, but this case also realised a high financial cost. John Want, the New South Wales attorney-general, 'and the rest of Australia, were shocked to receive a bill from the American authorities for almost £6,000, or US$28 000, to cover the cost of Butler's incarceration in the States and his lawyers'.[12] This enormous sum would have easily covered Nosey Bob's salary for the twenty-eight years that he held the role of executioner, with enough money left over to keep the hangman on full pay for another decade.

The demand for reimbursement of costs was from 'the solicitors engaged to deal with the case by the British Consul at San Francisco'. The charges on the invoice were considered outrageous, even scandalous. Incompetence was also implied when it was pointed out that on Butler's return to the colony, 'his trial occupied two days and a half from beginning to end … This case in America ought not to have occupied more than one day'. The attorney-general advised the legislative council of New South Wales that if 'in the future, we are to be saddled with bills of this nature, I shall deem it my duty in such cases to advise the Government to allow foreign countries to keep our criminals'. Regarding justice at any cost, the colony paid a reduced claim for Butler's extradition. The amount of £4,418 was approved through the *Act to Appropriate and Apply out of the Consolidated Revenue Fund 1898* (NSW), for the 'Cost of Proceedings in Extradition Case – Frank Butler', and so a serial killer and his victims were reduced to being a budget line in a routine piece of financial legislation.[13]

Eighteen months later, Howard was asked to recall Butler's dispatch. It had been publicised at the time of the hanging, in the *Sydney Morning Herald*, that the murderer had been game on the scaffold and given the impression 'that he was rather desirous of assisting the executioner and his assistants in their work' and not wanting to impede the process in any way. Was it true? Did Butler die game? When Howard was asked if Butler was courageous, 'his eyes sparkled with the pleasure that an old cock fighter shows, when he is reminded of a favorite bird, one that like the Old Guard, died but never surrendered':[14]

> Butler was a brick. He was game, take my word for it. When I went into the cell that morning he says, 'Bob now then, be quick'. He never flinched while I pinioned him, and when I was walking from the cell to the gallows, he leant his head close to mine, and whispered, 'Bob, don't forget, be quick'. Again on the gallows, as I was arranging the rope and cap, he said 'be quick'. I was quick enough for him, and as he dropped, his head hit my knee, and I heard distinctly the words 'Oh Lord', He was a game 'un.[15]

Some people were insatiably curious about the role of the executioner. Others found these types of details uncouth. The press corps pushed on and reported as much as possible, providing numerous opportunities for some people to read about Howard if they were keen, or for others to just skim headlines on the executioner if they were not really interested in the hangman's workday. For Nosey Bob? After so long in the role, he had earned the right to tell a few workplace anecdotes. Just like the rest of us.

SHOWING HIS AGE

The year 1898 began well for the Howards. Sidney and Elizabeth Howard had their second child and their first son, a baby they called Sydney, on Wednesday 19 January.[16] The single parent's brood of grandchildren was growing.

Loss of life was, however, always close by. On 24 August that year, four weeks after the opening of the Queen Victoria Market Buildings, death removed another 'very old colonist' of Sydney. The indefatigable and passionate campaigner for the abolition of capital punishment, Frederick Lee, died at the age of 83 after a short illness. An identity who had been in the colony for over fifty-five years, the successful businessman would be missed by his family, his many friends and all his admirers.[17] The octogenarian had seen great progress in his most noble cause, but he did not live to see the last man hanged in New South Wales. That morning was another forty-one years away.

Lee did, though, live long enough to think that nobody would be hanged in New South Wales in 1898. In February, Frank Adam Benjamin Holmes, who made his living as a tightrope walker, was sentenced to death for wounding his wife with intent to murder her. The penalty was commuted to incarceration and the flamboyant Holmes would serve just twelve months, with hard labour, in gaol. In April, the elderly Samuel Pembroke was given a death sentence for the murder of Frederick Houghton. Tried at Dubbo, the sentence came with a recommendation for mercy, which was granted, and the executive council ordered that he be removed from his condemned cell to spend the rest of his life in prison. In June, Grant Rawethorne Morris was sentenced to death for the rape of 8-year-old Ruby Tucker, but in August it was decided he would be sent to prison for ten years. Lee had died by the time Napoleon Jean Lisson, a tobacconist on Sydney's George Street, was sentenced to death in October for the murder of his sister-in-law Edith Lillian Gorrick. Lisson was given life in prison instead of a few minutes with Nosey Bob.[18]

The abolitionist had passed away before Wong Ming was given a death sentence for murdering Joe Mong Jong in a workers' camp outside of Dubbo. The executive council, after a year of charity, would allow the law to take its course for the 40-year-old Chinese man.

Wong attacked Alice Spong, who apparently kept an opium den in the camp. The two argued and Wong stabbed Spong in the breast and the arm before Jong intervened. Wong then turned on Jong, chasing him with a hunting knife and stabbing him in the abdomen. It was just one thrust, but enough to kill. The prosecution argued in court that Wong returned to the camp and tried to commit suicide by stabbing himself. The prisoner contradicted his accusers and tried to secure an acquittal by arguing that Jong had assaulted him first and he had only stabbed him in self-defence. Wong's trial went for a full day. The jury then found the prisoner guilty of murder and the sentence of death was passed. There were appeals for a reprieve, including petitions signed by seventy-one members of parliament and some of the residents of Dubbo. The Sydney-based businessman, Mei Quong Tart, celebrated for his tea rooms across the city, also lobbied for mercy.[19] All the efforts to save Wong Ming were in vain; the hanging would go ahead.

One evening in early December 1898, a mail train preparing to head west took 'from Redfern two passengers who did not arrive in hansoms, who were not attended by "obliging" porters, and who did not purchase tickets at the ordinary pigeon holes from "obliging" ticket-sellers':

> They crept onto the platform by a side entrance, and
> unostentatiously entered a separate compartment
> with which they appeared to be well acquainted. There
> was no speculation as to these modest passengers; the
> short, stout man might have passed unnoticed, but his
> companion, the tall one with the long arms and the
> iron-grey locks, is easily identified by his terrible facial
> disfigurement. They are Mr Robert Howard, alias 'Nosey
> Bob', Her Most Gracious Majesty's executioner and
> finisher of the law in N.S. Wales and his assistant, *en route*,
> to Dubbo to carry out the last dread sentence of the law.[20]

Howard's first professional visit to Dubbo had been made over twenty years earlier when he went west to deliver the ultimate punishment to Thomas Newman for raping and murdering a 12-year-old girl. Seeing someone change over more than two decades can be startling. Indeed, in a physical reflection of the dawdling death of the policy of capital punishment in New South Wales, it was observed that hangman Howard was also slowly dying.

The difference between the man who hanged Newman in 1877 and who was about to hang Wong on 13 December 1898 was radical. *Truth*, in a piece titled 'Nosey Bob, Our Only Nooseman', described the hangman's decline:

> He was then a well set-up muscular man, with a good head of hair, and except that his face was noseless and consequently his beauty was spoiled, he would pass among the average crowd as nothing out of the common or possessing any of those qualities which for some reason we associate with the gentleman who carries out the last dread sentence of our British law. We have seen him several times since, but on this last occasion – we met him and talked with him a few nights back – it seemed as if he were breaking up fast. His hair is thinner and whiter, and he does not look so active on his legs. We ventured to remark to him that he was fading, and he resented the imputation, for like most of us he does not like to be reminded he is growing old.[21]

The journalist made a remark about the weakness of Nosey Bob's legs. Howard was defensive: 'I showed my leg to the doctor ... he says its water on the knee'. Howard went on to say that he had 'heard of water on the brain, but never of water on the knee'.[22] The damage to his joints and the swelling of his knees was likely the effects of being thrown from the box of Governor Hercules Robinson's carriage back in 1873. If Howard had connected this accident to his physical state, he did not say anything. Just a few months out from his 67th birthday, he would have been feeling that his youth was well and truly behind him.

In a manoeuvre that was out of character for a man known to focus on his life outside of his work, Howard distracted the journalist. 'Now', he asked, turning the attention away from himself, 'did you ever see a prettier bit of rope?' He presented the length of manila that he would use on the scaffold when the time came to send off Wong. 'You say I am getting old,' Howard said, returning to the inescapable subject of ageing, 'well, of course, I ain't getting younger, but there's many a good job in me yet'.[23] There were, to be precise, exactly nine jobs left in Nosey Bob.

The first of these nine dispatches looked a little out of the ordinary because Wong Ming made a request to be hanged in his own culture's traditional dress, which was agreed to by authorities. The prisoner was very pleased when he received his black alpaca coat and tweed trousers as well as a pair of Chinese slippers. The patient slept well and ate a light breakfast before submitting to the hangman and his assistant.[24]

In a shocking epilogue to his story, it was said that Wong was guilty of another murder. The Chinese community in Dubbo took very little interest in Wong's case, believing he had murdered his brother in Queensland years before, and allowed another brother to hang for that crime in the Brisbane Gaol. Cock Tow had been shot and killed in April 1886 over failure to pay back a debt, with Wong Tong hanged for the murder. It was alleged at the time that Wong Ming was the real killer.[25] Wong Ming denied the accusation.

It was not just Wong Ming's own camp community who paid no attention to him or his crime. He was labelled 'a victim of popular apathy' and his end was described as 'about the dullest execution on record in N.S.W.' as nobody appeared interested in his case – even the newsboys declared 'they never sold an extra copy of the evening papers'. The prisoner, as reported by the *Goulburn Evening Penny Post*, remained concerned that his mother, who was 74 years old and 'lived in Canton, China', might find out about his trial and his disgraceful end at the hands of a hangman.[26]

The dispatch was clean. Standing at the scene of Thomas Moore's complete decapitation in 1897, Howard held his nerve. The bolt was drawn without delay, and Wong Ming fell 8 feet 2 inches. Death was instantaneous and not a muscular movement could be seen 'within a second or two after the fall'. Howard's supervisor was certainly impressed. The under-sheriff 'considered the execution one of the most successful conducted during his term of office'.[27] There were few other details given. The amount of time that the body was left to hang was unimportant next to a neck so neatly snapped. The reporter wrapped up the Nosey Bob interview with a comment on his role to service our 'mauvais sujets' [bad subjects]:

> [Howard] has been amongst us, done his work, and
> disappeared as noiselessly as he came. The chief
> executioner of New South Wales is known as 'Nosey
> Bob' among those classes who fear and hate him,
> from probably the instinctive feeling that some day or

another they will be assisted by him in their last toilet, prior to attending that dance upon air which the State provides for the worst of its mauvais sujets.[28]

TO BE SHOT, DROWNED OR HANGED?

For Howard, January 1899 started with the publication of the interview he had given in December 1898. In Dubbo for the dispatch of Wong Ming, a reporter for the *Dubbo Dispatch*, founded in 1865, had taken advantage of the 'rare but not enviable distinction of a visit from the most picturesque figure in connection with our criminal jurisprudence' to spend 'ten minutes with the hangman'. The article was promptly republished in *Truth*. It was also published in the *Cobargo Chronicle*, a masthead dedicated to the interests of the dairying, mining and agricultural industries, despite Howard never having any cause to go to Cobargo, a town over 350 miles from Dubbo.[29] A deeply morbid fascination with the hangman and his clients was widespread.

As 1899 brought newspaper readers more news of the colony's executioner, there were also more stories about crime. One of the biggest stories of the year was about Stuart Wilson Christopher Briggs, who stood trial in February for the murder of Miss Maggie Binud Dutt, aged just 21, and her elderly grandmother, Mrs Margaret Miller.

The crime was, according to the prosecution, premeditated. It was shown at trial that Briggs was jealous of the woman he was courting. In an appalling euphemism for domestic violence, it was stated Briggs had engaged in 'angry words' with Dutt on 11 December 1898. The prisoner had, according to the *Evening News*, hit Dutt across the face so hard he knocked out one of her teeth. More reports detailed how Briggs, on 12 December, deposited his revolver at a gunsmith for repairs, purchased cartridges for the handgun and, on 13 December, penned a letter that outlined his claims of Dutt's unfaithfulness and how he hoped she would prove to be 'a very substantial lesson' to other men.[30]

On 14 December, Briggs went to Dutt's home in Petersham and demanded to see her; Miller resisted, but Dutt indulged the visitor by going downstairs to try and deal with him. In a rage, Briggs shot Dutt and Miller. Kimini Elizabeth Dutt, the only other occupant of the house, was the first witness at the trial. She testified to hearing gunfire and then, running to the balcony, saw Briggs flee and called out: 'Coward'. She went downstairs where she found her sister and her grandmother. Both were dead.[31]

More incriminating than Dutt's testimony was the evidence given by Robert Nelson Swinburne, a private inquiry agent, who stated that he saw the accused run to the Johnston Street Wharf at Annandale and jump off. Swinburne went to assist when Briggs called out: 'I've shot my sweetheart and her grandmother in Douglas-street, Petersham. It was all through jealousy. I just tried to drown myself, but I could not sink. What had I better do now?' Swinburne told Briggs to surrender to police, and he escorted him to the local station. It was also revealed that Briggs had tried to shoot himself after committing the double homicide and before throwing himself into the waters of Rozelle Bay, but he could not do it and instead threw the weapon away. He then said to Swinburne: 'I will hang for this, won't I? but it will be for the one I love.'[32]

The defence team had its own witnesses. Briggs had confessed to murdering Dutt because he believed that she no longer loved him, and also confessed to murdering Miller for interfering in his relationship with Dutt. Despite his detailed confession, Briggs pled not guilty to both shootings by reason of insanity. Several people came forward to swear that Briggs had been acting strangely and that he had been suffering from insomnia before the murders were perpetrated. The members of the jury were unmoved by the case made for Briggs and, after deliberating for just thirty minutes, they shared their finding of guilty.[33]

In lobbying for clemency, John Haynes argued against capital punishment but also against the integrity of the trial. Haynes proposed that the prosecution offered as 'fact' the belief that Briggs 'immediately took his revolver and had it put in good working order' after he argued with Dutt. Haynes complained that this 'fact' had been 'relied upon as undoubted proof that the murder was premeditated'. Haynes asserted the revolver had been taken for repair on 10 December, the day before Briggs argued with Dutt, and that this proved there was no premeditation in the commission of the crime. Haynes also criticised his former colleagues in the press, accusing them of repeating the misinformation about when the revolver had been taken to the gunsmith.[34]

There was, too, the deployment of one of the abolitionist's favourite tools: the petition. Over 2000 signatures were secured asking for clemency for a death sentence that was handed down without a recommendation for mercy.[35]

Haynes was applauded, even by those who disagreed with him, for it was acknowledged that he was 'actuated by high motives, indeed it is well-known that he is entirely opposed to capital punishment altogether'. The question was, though, for the men and women seeking punishment: 'Are all our sympathies to be reserved for murderers and are we to have no compassion for those who are hurried into eternity at a moment's notice?' It was noted that there were 'strong arguments in favour of the abolition of capital punishment' and that offering Briggs mercy could be the end of this policy. It was suggested that if Briggs were given a commutation, then the colony could give up on the death penalty altogether because 'it will be difficult to find an excuse for hanging anybody unless it is such an atrocious fiend as [Frank] BUTLER who made a business of murder'.[36]

The executive council did assemble a panel of medical experts to examine the prisoner and support a review of the death sentence given to Briggs. It was found that Briggs was sane when Miss Dutt was killed from 'two bullet wounds one within an inch of the other. Both bullets had passed through the skull' and when 'Mrs Miller was killed by one bullet, which went through the temple and remained embedded in the brain'. His claims of insanity, made by himself or by others, should not be the cause of 'any interference with the sentence imposed'.[37]

Those who had been following the case also knew that Briggs was coherent at the moment of the crime, and in its immediate aftermath, as seen in how he made sure he had achieved his goal. The arresting constable, in consoling the prisoner at the station shortly after the murderer had given himself up, said: 'I don't know; they might not be dead'. To which Briggs, who was just 25 years old, offered an emphatic response: 'Oh, yes! I moved them about. I know they are dead'.[38]

The man who had tried to shoot himself, then drown himself, would be hanged. Understandably, some anxiety circulated around the dispatch. Despite growing concern about the death penalty, many people still supported the concept of the ultimate punishment. Theory is one thing while reality could be quite another, and most people were revolted by the scenes that unfolded when an execution was botched. The routine 'bungling of the execution procedure, both major and minor, distracted from the example of the punishment'.[39] There was no need for anyone to be concerned about a mishap on 5 April 1899.

Briggs woke up at the usual time, 'ate a good breakfast' and complied with the directions of legal and religious authorities. Nosey Bob, on his home gallows at Darlinghurst Gaol, had a good start to the day. Except for a slight pendulum-like movement, 'the body hung motionless after the drop. There was an absence even of the muscular contraction which frequently follows an execution by hanging'. Briggs weighed 14 stone and was given a drop of 7 feet 6 inches. Not quite double the length of the rope recommended in the table of drops, which stipulates that a person of 196 pounds should drop close to 4 feet 3 inches. Nosey Bob was, again, erring on the side of decapitation. The year before, after Nosey Bob hanged Wong Ming, the executioner was told by one of the gentleman witnesses: 'Well, Howard, that was clean work'. Nosey Bob offered a salute and replied: 'Yes, sir, very good job indeed'.[40] The executioner could have repeated that exchange with a witness at Darlinghurst, word for word, when he saw off Briggs.

Howard had a few months off after giving his regrets to Briggs. He kept going to Darlinghurst Gaol – a collection of buildings that included cell blocks, a morgue, a chapel and workshops – as a regular civil servant and tended to the grounds. He was also known to roam the adjacent complex, the Darlinghurst Court House. The main entrance of the courts faced Oxford Street, but like the gaol it had flanks on Forbes Street and Darlinghurst Road while the two sites were connected by underground tunnels. Howard was a familiar face across the two companion institutions. Even when not hanging people, he always tried to be worthy of his designation as the gentleman hangman. He was a man who was generally amiable and always wanted to be helpful:

Wilfred Blacket, the [King's Counsel] is a frail man.
Some years ago, in the gloom of a winter's evening,
he was trying to fumble into his overcoat after the
conclusion of a case at Darlinghurst. 'Nosey' Bob, the
historic hangman, was a frequenter of the corridors, and
noticed this. Coming up from behind, he adjusted the

counsel's coat. His hands lingered lovingly round the collar, as he said, appraisingly: 'You've got a bee-utiful thin neck, Mr. Blacket'.[41]

Howard's appraisal skills were well known, with it stated that he had 'just the same eye for the neck that a painter has for a pretty scene'.[42] It would be interesting to know how Blacket felt after his chance encounter and if he rejected future offers of assistance, preferring to struggle into his own coat and keep his neck free from the warmth of the hangman's breath.

A MAN WHO IS NOT ASHAMED

Howard once told JF Archibald that he took the position of executioner knowing not everyone would approve. 'I don't care', he said, maybe too forcefully, 'I'm not ashamed of it'. It is possible that Howard was not ashamed of his work, but he was ashamed of something else. The story about how Nosey Bob was the victim of a vicious horse, sometime between driving a colonial governor and his family to the circus in 1873 and starting on a regional gaol's scaffold three years later, has rarely been questioned. A few other theories have been put forward over the decades, but nothing has been able to threaten the official narrative of the making of Nosey Bob. It is, on the surface, an easy tale to believe. Horses can be dangerous. That horses regularly kicked people in the face is undisputed.[43] Yet, such assaults usually resulted in a suite of injuries. Eye sockets. Cheekbones. Jawbones. Teeth. All were in line to receive a disgruntled horse's hoof. To suffer the very specific damage that Nosey Bob suffered, because of a horse, is unrealistic.

There are no photographs of the noseless hangman. There are, though, multiple illustrations that depict the executioner. All these pictures, many showing a side profile of the hangman, portray Howard with a saddle nose. That is, a type of nose where the bridge has collapsed. The rest of the once good-looking cabbie's face is still all in one piece. Even the callous caricatures drawn by Phil May, illustrations that appeared in the *Bulletin*, which presented the hangman as bald, nearly toothless and without his famous beard, show a face without any other obvious injuries. May, a talented English artist who spent three years in Australia, ignored the hangman and focused instead on the death associated with him. Nosey Bob, a figure of decay, is unrecognisable, and the caricatures only make sense because of their captions.[44]

In some cases of saddle nose, the bridge collapses completely and leaves a person with no nose at all. A saddle nose can be associated with trauma. In the 19th century, it was also closely associated with disease, particularly leprosy and syphilis.

Adopting a story already believed by almost everyone would have been an easy way to avoid the embarrassment associated with having a sexually transmitted infection. Until the discovery of penicillin in 1928, there was no effective treatment for syphilis and the great pox spread unchecked. Syphilis might also explain why Howard did not seek a reconstruction. There were primitive surgical options to repair damaged noses available in Howard's day.

GOOD NOOSE.

FIGURE 12 Good noose

SOURCE *Bulletin*, 31 March 1888, p. 9

Doctors would, though, be reluctant to perform these high-risk procedures after an accident and would be even more hesitant if disease meant the nose might deteriorate further.[45] Or, Howard did not explore surgery because he had simply accepted his fate. He never covered his face, and he did not wear a crude prosthetic. If Howard did have syphilis, it is strange that no newsman speculated his deformity had been caused by disease. Calling Nosey Bob a sinner would have been an easy score against the much-hated hangman.

Howard may have been able to tolerate more bad press and absorb the shame associated with syphilis as he absorbed bad headlines documenting bungled hangings. He was, without doubt, more resilient than other finishers of the law. There was the odd run-in with authorities, but nothing serious. There was, too, the rare scuffle with those who took a strong objection to him. He drank, but not more than the average colonial bloke, and never on the day of a job, and he was not, despite some rumours, a raging alcoholic like other Sydney-based hangmen.[46] He suffered numerous indignities because of his position, but it was never suggested he be institutionalised like some of the hangmen before him.

He was insulted, but he gave as good as he received. His name, too, was an insult. Acute offence was taken, for example, in the New South Wales parliament when William P Crick called George F Hutchison 'Nosey Bob' in 1889. A quarrel ensued and the chairman was forced to call 'upon the hon. member to withdraw the offensive expression "Nosey Bob" which he applied to the hon. Member for Canterbury, and to apologise'.[47]

He was, sadly, without his wife, a son and a daughter, but he still had family and friends. As his children married and started their own families, there were also grandchildren to fuss over and to teach. There were even casual acquaintances, happy to be congenial, including a Bondi neighbour who did not 'mind him leaning on the fence and yarning', though he felt 'invitations to afternoon tea' were too much. In 1895, gossip columns revealed how a 'certain very ugly Australian finisher of the law now drives through the principal streets in a dog-cart, accompanied by a lady!' The sightings continued with another report in 1897 telling of how Howard drives 'his trap, occasionally with a lady in it'.[48] He was also a homeowner with extra-curricular interests. Howard was, in most ways, an ordinary worker: loyal, reliable and as efficient as the vagaries of his trade allowed.

Howard had come to the job with competencies that lent themselves to a career in law and order. He was an immigrant, so he had a bit of pluck. He was good at manual labour. He was good with a rope. He could sign his own name, and so was slightly better educated than some of the hangmen snatched from the ranks of convicts. As a man who had run his own cab business, he was organised and self-directed. As evidenced by the pride he took in his gardens, he was a dedicated and persistent problem solver who could learn from his mistakes and make improvements each season. In striking contrast to some executioners, who were little better than con artists and thieves, he had a value system entrenched through caring for others. His wife, his children and, despite the sadness of several deaths, his many grandchildren.

Howard also brought something quite unique to the role of the sheriff's most controversial officer: he had no olfactory organ. If it was syphilis or, if it was, as one newspaper suggested, because his nose had been bitten off by a convict, life was already rough for the man who still sneezed but could not smell.[49] For Howard, there were no scents to enrich the basics that most people take for granted. The aromas of beer, food, flowers, perfume, even the smell of himself, were all absent. One plus, maybe, was that he could not smell death either. He was a man for whom every breath was uncomfortable because without a nose acting as a humidifier, air was not at a regulated temperature when it reached his lungs. His lungs also had to accommodate constant intrusions because grit and smaller particles could not be filtered. The cabbie-turned-scragger was already an outsider. He had lived with startled looks, hushed whispers and avoidance since he was disfigured. The infamy of being the hangman accentuated his experiences, but having to deal with stigma was nothing new. When it came to being ostracised, Howard had heard it, seen it and felt it all before.

For Nosey Bob, simple tasks like shopping were events that needed to be endured. A trip to the butcher near where he worked would see children 'run away in mock terror'. Earning extra money was not straightforward either, as his pigs were sold for less at the market because 'pork fattened by the hangman' was considered 'unpalatable'. There were also the boycotts, even as he sought to discharge his professional duty, that resulted in country cabmen refusing 'to cart him and rope', while he had to sleep within the confines of gaols, placing him uncomfortably close to his patients.[50]

In his early years as an executioner, publicans did not want much to do with him either. At one establishment in Waverley, 'the landlord always broke the glass after the hangman had finished his drink. As "Nosey" was a constant customer this practice became expensive, and the publican had a cupboard constructed in which were kept a special set of measures' for the exclusive use of Nosey Bob.[51] His well-trained horse solved that problem.

Howard was never *just* the hangman; he was always the *noseless* hangman. He did, though, manage to remain the gentleman hangman. He was the executioner who wore a good black coat, turned up on time, did his best, and was, feasibly, a very distant relative of the Duke of Norfolk. At least according to Howard after a couple of drinks. This idea of lineage was entertained, surely humorously, by those who thought of Nosey Bob as a good man, one with standards, even as 'a kind of aristocrat, for he would not soil his hands by flogging larrikins'.[52]

Nosey Bob was a merry chap, despite having to bear the weight of his terrible profession. Even in his later years, when he was a pensioner, there were those who lined up to raise a glass to Mr Howard's health and success, especially if Bob was picking up the tab:

> Nosey Bob is a jolly good fellow,
> With humor both genial and mellow;
> One you'd greet when you meet
> In a pub or the street
> With a clap on the back and a "hellow!"[53]

Nosey Bob's sense of humour might have been genial, but it could also be dark. When he asked mates over for a drink, he would eye them up and down 'before asking 'em to have a "drop".[54] Howard needed that sense of humour. As the calendar recognised a new century, the government of New South Wales still recognised the right to hang those who had committed the worst crimes.

CHAPTER 11

A GOLDEN JUBILEE

ON THE EVE OF FEDERATION

By 1900, Nosey Bob had hanged prisoners in twelve towns and cities across New South Wales. It was a lot of ground to cover by cab, rail and coach, with the final leg of many journeys to a regional centre often made on foot. Howard had, in the name of the law, travelled thousands of miles. He was about to head to Goulburn for his fifty-sixth job.

The focus of Nosey Bob's attention in Goulburn was John Sleigh, also known as Frank Ward and Frank Quinlan, who murdered Francis Curran on 25 August 1900. The men, working as rural labourers, had been arguing when Sleigh became 'wildly exasperated, and taking up his rifle shot Curran, killing him instantly'. Like some other colonial-era killers, Sleigh thought he could just cover up his crime by burning the body. He succeeded in burning Curran's legs off and charring the body to the extent that the features of his victim were completely unrecognisable, but the corpse of Curran remained. Having failed to destroy the evidence, Sleigh went to the homestead on the Cambalong Station to tell the Wolfe family what had happened.[1]

FIGURE 13 The places where Nosey Bob worked

SOURCE John Frith, Flat Earth Mapping, 2021

The confession to Mrs Jane Wolfe was chilling: 'He won't come back, I have done for him. I met him in a paddock; gave him two bullets, and knocked his brains out'. Sleigh then attempted to intimidate all four members of the Wolfe family, demanding they keep silent about him and his crime. Miss Rose Wolfe managed to coax Sleigh's rifle from him, while her brother, Master Henry Wolfe, managed to make it to the nearby town of Bombala, around 20 miles from the Victorian border, to alert police. When the constabulary arrived, Sleigh had gone into the bush, but Mr Michael George Wolfe, who was head of the selection and Curran's step-brother, was able to entreat him to come back to the house where the adaptable and svelte Sergeant Sim was hiding under a sofa. Sim emerged and, after a violent struggle, Sleigh was subdued and arrested.[2]

New South Wales in 1900 was almost unrecognisable from New South Wales in 1788, but there had not been enough change to save Sleigh's neck from the hangman's noose. The number of executions carried out in Australia, from first colonisation, 'steadily declined in proportion to a growing population'. On the eve of Federation, hanging 'was a punishment used mostly as a last resort – there only to check crimes of the severest type'.[3] In the colony that sprawled out from Sydney, murderers were obvious candidates for a handshake with the hangman. This was also seen across the continent as capital crimes on the books of the various colonies were drastically reduced. In the final days of the 19th century, the dream of becoming a more civilised society had not been fully realised, but nightmares about the early embrace of state-sanctioned violence became fewer and fewer. Agreement on abolition did not necessarily mean agreement on other issues. Differences of opinion, of every conceivable type, fed political conflict and factions. Also, most abolitionists were men with full agendas.

John Haynes had his own problems with three wives, eight children and numerous creditors who, between 1873 and 1907, brought a total of fourteen bankruptcy petitions against him. Thomas Walker, a man with many passions, fought for women's rights in advocating for birth control and easier divorce. In 1889, Walker's past caught up with him with an inquiry into how he had been accused of murder, in 1874, in the Canadian city of Toronto. As a teenager earning a living as a spiritualist, he performed a stunt with phosphorus that went tragically wrong and resulted in the death of John Saunders. Walker was lucky when the Canadians decided not to pursue him. Then, in 1892, he accidentally shot and wounded, admittedly while drunk, the Reverend David Laseron while the two were travelling in a railway carriage on a suburban line in Sydney. Doctors struggled to find the bullet in Laseron's shoulder, and it was eventually removed in 1899.[4] Walker served just over seven years in the legislative assembly of New South Wales, but he moved to Western Australia in the late 1890s, living and working there for the rest of his life.

Another abolitionist, Richard Meagher, had his own regrettable run-in with the law when he defended George Dean for attempting to poison his wife in 1895. Dean was found guilty and Meagher lobbied hard for a reprieve. Controversially, a pardon was given even though the solicitor knew his client had committed the crime. Meagher was struck from the roll of solicitors, and it was years before he made a full professional recovery. Frederick Lee and Terence Murray did charity work, while William Brookes was concerned for workers' rights. It was hardly a united and singularly focused team.

Compensating for slow progress of the abolitionist cause was the increased application of the prerogative of mercy. A commutation of a death sentence 'did not, by letter of the law, reverse the verdict like a modern court of appeal might', but the men and women reprieved were not necessarily complaining.[5] Prison terms allocated in lieu of an appointment with the hangman were typically long and usually included a term in irons or doing hard labour. Most prisoners would settle into their new routines, but some would never adjust to the strict surroundings, and the committing of crimes in gaols across the colony was common. In Nosey Bob's time as hangman, he dispatched Charles Cunningham for attempted murder in Berrima Gaol in 1882 and Thomas Williams for attempted murder in Parramatta Gaol in 1885. Howard also took care of Robert Hewart for committing murder during a short stay in the Sydney Police Cells in 1888. The men who reoffended while incarcerated, like career crooks, would always have a hard time arguing they were worthy of mercy.

The noose really had become an accessory for the unredeemable, the worst of the worst. So infrequent was the need to carefully stretch a length of manila rope that Nosey Bob started to be seen as belonging to an old and outdated world. Those who believed the death penalty was the only genuine deterrent to the foulest crimes clung to the concept of the hangman and his tools. Those who wanted the promises of nationhood to be delivered were keen to see the end of the executioner. In the lead-up to Federation, Howard was asked: 'Have you ever felt any compunction about carrying out the execution in particular cases?' The chief scragger's response was explicit:

> No; if I had I would not have done it. I don't concern myself about that aspect of it. I just think that it is my duty to do a certain thing, and when called upon I go and do it to the best of my ability. The law says the individual has to suffer, and the judge and jury have settled the rights and wrongs of the case before my duty begins.[6]

While the law was as it was, Howard would do what he was told to do. If he was told to hang Sleigh, he would turn up and fit the cap and noose, say 'no one regrets this more than I do' and then give the signal for the bolt to be drawn.

When Sleigh turned up to be tried for murder in October, just weeks after the death of Curran, his defence team had manufactured an elaborate tale that retold a case of murder as one of simple misadventure. At trial, Sleigh stated that had gone to a paddock where Curran was working, with Master Wolfe, to say it was time for dinner. Sleigh was carrying a rifle, fully cocked as he usually did, with the weapon pointing towards Curran when it went off accidentally. 'I'm shot Jack', Curran cried, 'I thought that rifle would shoot somebody'. The young Wolfe ran home and could not be stopped. Sleigh then tried to carry Curran, on his own, back to the homestead, when he realised that his co-worker was dead. The lifeless body was too heavy, so the prisoner left Curran and went to tell Mrs Wolfe that there had been an accident. 'He told her that a man with his character stood in a bad position' and said that he had no choice but to go to the police. The story continued: 'He would either have to do that or put a bullet through himself'. Mrs Wolfe had testified at the inquest that Sleigh did threaten suicide. At trial, the court was told that Mrs and Miss Wolfe began to cry when Sleigh confessed and begged him to just 'do away with the body'. After some convincing, Sleigh consented and early the 'next morning he left for the purpose of burning the body'. As a contingency, if the re-imagined story of what had happened to Curran was not taken seriously, the defence claimed that 'Sleigh committed the deed under an epileptic homicidal seizure and was not responsible for the act'.[7]

Well, the jury did not buy either of the stories the defence team was selling. The verdict was guilty, and the sentence was death. On reflection, claiming to have had a seizure was not unreasonable. That defence had worked for Sleigh sixteen years earlier. On 26 June 1884, while doing time for highway robbery under arms in Darlinghurst Gaol, Sleigh seriously wounded a warder. The weapon, that time, was a pipe that Sleigh deployed with so much force it broke the third time he struck Alexander Elliott's head. There was conflicting evidence on Sleigh's seizures and if they were authentic or an act. At the 1884 trial, Sleigh was given a death sentence, but it was not carried out. He was in prison, but he was released after serving just seven years, prompting a piece in *Truth* to ask, in relation to Curran's death: 'Who is really responsible?' The journalist also demanded that the officer who authorised Sleigh's release 'should be known'.[8]

Again, mercy in the form of early release from gaol could be as problematic as the commutation of a death sentence.

The *Sydney Morning Herald* informed readers that Sleigh's last night alive was spent sleeping well, and that he woke and ate his breakfast. Sleigh made a speech on the gallows on 5 December 1900 in which he complained, unreasonably, about his treatment. Once Howard placed the cap over his head, he said: 'Good-bye, gentlemen, God bless you all'. Then, to everyone's relief, the lever was pulled 'and there was not a visible tremor, death appearing to be instantaneous'. Nosey Bob had dropped his patient 7 feet 9 inches.[9]

A STORY OF LOVE AND DEATH

With the colonies of Australia having voted for Federation, some rules changed in 1901. The new Commonwealth took broad powers of defence, immigration and postal services, while the former colonies, now states, held fast to social, cultural, administrative and legal differences, including the number of crimes punishable by death. South Australia, a piece of real estate which at that time stretched from Adelaide to Darwin, was the most progressive of the new states, with only two capital crimes on the books. Queensland and Western Australia each listed five capital offences, Tasmania listed eight and Victoria listed nine.[10]

In New South Wales there were eleven crimes that could set someone up for a date with the executioner. Nine of these were listed in the *Criminal Law Amendment Act*

1883 (NSW). The crimes were murder, attempted murder, acts done to property with intent to murder, and burglary with intent to murder or to cause grievous bodily harm. Rape remained a capital crime, as did carnally knowing a girl under the age of 10. Arson was also treated as a capital crime if it involved setting fire to a church or dwelling when it was known that a person was inside. Setting fire to or destroying a ship or vessel carrying people would see a death sentence issued, as would exhibiting a false light or signal with intent to bring a vessel into danger. In addition, New South Wales listed treason and arson in royal dockyards under applicable Imperial laws.[11]

Only three death sentences were carried out in New South Wales in 1901. The first two were carried over from convictions made in 1900, and the third was the only death sentence, of eight handed down across the first year of the federated era, that saw the law take its course. For Nosey Bob, the roster required one trip to Dubbo and two hangings in Darlinghurst Gaol, which was considered the senior correctional facility in New South Wales, with 'the governor of that establishment hold[ing] the first position among gaolers.'[12]

On 10 December 1898, Jimmy Governor married Ethel Mary Jane Page at the Church of England rectory in the small southern town of Gulgong. Ethel was 16 and already five months pregnant with their first child, a son they called Sidney. The couple had a second child, a daughter, but Jimmy did not live long enough to see Thelma born. The marriage was put under immense strain because so many people did not approve of an Aboriginal man being with a white woman.

In 1900, Governor was living with his small family on a selection in Breelong, a town not far from Gilgandra in the state's central west. He was a member of a fencing crew for Mr John Mawbey while his wife was a housekeeper, in exchange for rations, for Mrs Sarah Mawbey. Slavery had been abolished the previous century, but it continued in Australia as seen in the way First Nations workers were underpaid, not paid agreed amounts or given only basic rations and cheap goods in return for their labour.[13]

Soon, a place that few people had heard of became famous as the site of the Breelong Massacre. The young Mrs Governor was taunted for her choice of husband, with people saying 'rough and nasty things of her'. Her mother was also criticised for encouraging the Governor and Page union. 'One naturally wonders', pondered the *Daily Telegraph*, 'what manner of woman the mother was who insisted on uniting her daughter for life to a low-bred savage [A]boriginal'.[14] The women at the Mawbey household were also irrationally disgusted by Mrs Governor's private life.

The males in the Mawbey family were staying at an older house on the property, having toiled late on 20 July 1900. Mr Governor took the opportunity to go and confront Mrs Mawbey and Miss Helen Josephine Kerz, the local teacher who lived with the Mawbeys, about their comments to his wife. He went to the homestead with at least one other Aboriginal man, probably his friend and a member of the fencing team, Jacky Underwood. Miss Elsie Clarke, Mrs Mawbey's younger sister and seven children were also at the main homestead that night. Conflict erupted and Governor was enraged. Mrs Mawbey and Miss Kerz were killed with clubs and a tomahawk, as were three of the Mawbey children, Grace aged 16, Percival aged 14 and Hilda aged 11. Elsie, aged 18, was seriously injured. Albert went and alerted his father while a cousin, George, hid under a bed. Two infants slept through it all. Mr Mawbey claimed he was on good terms with the fencers, and that he had never 'chaffed Governor's wife about living with a blackfellow'. He said he did not think the women of the house did either, 'but that they may have'.[15]

After the murders at the Mawbey property, Jimmy Governor went on the run with Underwood, his brother Joe Governor, and Jack Porter and Jacky, who were also from the camp. He took his wife and baby as well.[16]

Jimmy soon told Ethel to take their child to her parents in Dubbo, while Jack and Jacky also split from the group. Underwood, with a lame leg, could not keep up with the able-bodied bushrangers, and he was caught and charged in July while Ethel Governor and Jacky Porter were also taken into custody. Accounts of who was at the Mawbey home while the murders were committed changed over the months that followed, but three men would pay an extreme price for the crimes in Breelong. Jimmy and Joe stayed on the run, committing around eighty crimes, including another four murders. It was the biggest manhunt in Australian history, with hundreds of police and volunteers tracking the pair across 2000 miles. The Governors evaded authorities for months, thanks in part to Jimmy's previous employment as a police tracker, but lucrative rewards of £1,000 for each man were incentives that made capture assured. Jimmy was taken in an ambush on 27 October, while Joe escaped only to be shot and killed on 31 October. Joe Governor was buried just outside of Singleton in the Upper Hunter.[17]

October saw the trial of Underwood, also known as Charles Brown, at Dubbo. He had trouble comprehending the English-based legal processes, but 'after some difficulty had been experienced in making the accused understand, he pleaded not guilty'. The prosecution opened with an argument that 'even if it could not be proved that the prisoner actually struck the fatal blow or blows' which caused death, if 'he were present at the murder and actively participating, he was fully responsible at law'. The testimonies of the survivors were confused. Albert Mawbey, aged 9, said he 'saw a blackfellow in the sitting-room hitting Percy with a tomahawk or rifle or stick – didn't know which', while Albert and another child, 13-year-old George, both swore that they did not see the prisoner in the house the night of the murders. Mrs Governor told the court 'the prisoner admitted to her that he killed Percy'. Underwood confessed to hitting 'one girl' who did 'not die'. The jury took only an hour to be 'able to come to an opinion as to the prisoner's guilt, but they could not come to a decision as to who struck the fatal blows on Percy Mawbey'.[18]

Underwood was hanged on 14 January 1901 in Dubbo Gaol. He was, at the end, pitifully alone. As Underwood faced death, he only had the company of gaol officers and official witnesses. There was, too, the obligatory if culturally inappropriate religious support for a First Nations man, with the prisoner asking if he would 'be in heaven in time for dinner'. On the scaffold, 'Howard, the hangman from Sydney, adjusted the rope and the white cap'. The drop was 'lengthy' and death was instantaneous. He was left to hang for twenty minutes before he was cut down. It was shown that Howard's preparations, for his last paid appearance outside Sydney, were excellent and 'there had been a perfect dislocation of the cervical vertebrae'.[19] But there was no time for reflection. Nosey Bob was needed at Darlinghurst Gaol.

Jimmy Governor could have been shot, just like his brother Joe, as an outlaw. Instead, he went on trial in November. Governor said he challenged Mrs Mawbey and Miss Kerz as he wanted to know if they had mistreated his wife. The pair laughed at him. The schoolteacher was especially indignant: 'Pooh, you black rubbish, you want shooting for marrying a white woman'. The jury retired at 12:15 pm, returning ten minutes later with a 'verdict of guilty on a charge of murder'.[20]

There were rumours Governor's execution had been put off 'until the authorities', recovering from festivities to celebrate Federation, had 'sobered up sufficiently to enjoy the hanging'. Even with a delay, it was still a modest turnout on 18 January 1901. There were only a few officials, four members of the press and five private citizens, including 'Mr G Mawbey of Surry Hills, a brother of the settler whose family was so brutally butchered at Breelong' in attendance. Pinioned, Governor still managed to smoke a cigarette as he emerged as the most important member of the execution parade. 'Howard appeared in a correctly cut suit of black, minus the coat; his assistant wore a uniform resembling that of a warder'. The drops set for First Nations men were rarely reported, but Governor was so famous, it was noted he fell 7 feet 6 inches. Death was instant:[21]

> The last chapter in the unhappy history of the Breelong blacks closed with the execution of their leader, Jimmy Governor, last week. Thus Nemesis, if comparatively slow, has overtaken each of the gang that so unaccountably broke out in murderous outrage at Breelong. Joe Governor shot by a pursuer, Jacky Underwood and Jimmy Governor hanged – that constitutes the tale. The adaptability and bushmanship of the men enabled them for months to defy capture; but capture came. The days when it was possible for the bushranger to roam at large for years in Australia have passed away.[22]

When Jimmy Governor was cut down from the scaffold at Darlinghurst, twelve people had died since the first murder at the Mawbey property in Breelong.

WORK AND LEISURE

Joseph Francis Aloysius Campbell was the last man to be hanged for the crime of rape in New South Wales. Campbell had sexually assaulted a 9-year-old girl, Violet Evelyn Oldfield, terrifying her and her two young companions. The crimes took place in the Queanbeyan area, not far from where the city of Canberra would be established as the capital of the newly federated nation.

On 24 October 1901, Oldfield was playing on the edges of the bush with two of her friends, May Ward, who was aged 9, and May's sister, Maudie Ward, who was aged 7. Campbell boldly approached the trio. At first, he asked the girls to mind his swag for him while he went to the post office. Then, he asked them to follow him on a promise to help them find bird nests. The girls, wanting to see magpies, were curious and tagged along with the stranger. Then, 'Oldfield was cruelly abused and her younger companions subjected to foul treatment by a brute in human form'. As Campbell was a stranger in the area, one who was accurately and quickly described to police by his victims, it did not take long to locate the child molester and to bring him into custody.[23]

Local authorities heard the charges against Campbell at the Queanbeyan Police Court on 1 November 1901. There was physical evidence. There was medical evidence. There was also some of the most stunning witness testimony ever given in New South Wales. Oldfield detailed what had happened, even though she was so small she had to sit in a chair on a table so that all the officers of the court could see and hear her. In cross-examination, Campbell asked 'whether the man that assaulted her was like him'. The victim was articulate and certain. The *Queanbeyan Observer*, a local newspaper that covered the crime and its aftermath in detail, paraphrased Oldfield's statement: 'It was not a man like you; it was you, and that the boots worn then were those he had on in the court'. The older of the two Ward sisters also testified. She talked about Oldfield's rape and then the indecent assaults on her and on Maudie Ward. 'He told us not to tell, and we promised not to tell. He then gave Violet 3d'. Campbell paying one of his traumatised victims threepence was not the only transaction that morning. The children also gave their attacker some food they had in exchange for being allowed to live. May Ward also endured extensive questioning by the prisoner 'as to the details of the crime, but she did not vary from her evidence-in-chief'.[24]

The idea of a man accused of a sex crime interrogating a complainant, especially a child, is abhorrent. It was an accepted and, for some, a barely tolerated practice. It would be more than a century after the Campbell case before the rules in New South Wales changed with the passing of the *Criminal Procedure Amendment (Sexual Offence Evidence) Act 2003* (NSW). The new legislation stipulated that an accused will not question the accuser, with complainants to be 'examined instead by a person appointed by the court'. Less confronting than cross-examining two of his victims, Campbell brought his own witness. Richard Stanley Symonds was called to testify that, the day before the assaults, he had been with Campbell and had seen him fall from a log while fishing, and that the fall had caused him to be covered in blood. Symonds met Campbell's story halfway. He remembered the fall but 'nothing about the alleged bleeding, and as a matter of fact he saw no blood on the prisoner'. Campbell was formally committed to be tried in Sydney. The prisoner requested bail, which was promptly denied.[25]

The trial was held on 20 November 1901. The evidence presented was 'similar to that given at the lower court'. At 9:20 pm, the jury went to consider the evidence. The twelve men returned to the court at 9:30 pm to say the prisoner was guilty. The judge stated that: 'It is simply intolerable that little children can't go about without being assaulted by filthy, disgusting brutes like you, who lie in wait for them and treat them like this'. The sentence of death was then passed in the usual way.[26]

There was no public outcry demanding mercy for Campbell, the felon who was 'unquestionably a monstrosity'. When the executive council met to look at his case, they must have felt that their decision was straightforward. There was, too, the matter of a similar assault committed on 8-year-old Stella Haddon at Ramsay's Bush in the Sydney suburb of Haberfield, near Leichhardt, on 1 October 1901. A crime for which police had a strong case against Campbell. The charges for this crime were withdrawn by police on 26 November as Campbell was already sitting under a sentence of death.[27]

It was also suggested that the members of the council were influenced by the fact, not previously made public, 'that Campbell had been several times previously charged with offences of a somewhat similar, though less serious character'. Campbell, a man in his mid-twenties, had also been found guilty of 'an indecent assault on a girl under 14', and sentenced to suffer three years of penal servitude on 31 January 1899. Yet, he was released in July 1901, only two years and six months from his sentencing date.[28] On the dates that the little girls in Ramsay's Bush and Queanbeyan were sexually assaulted, Campbell should have still been in gaol.

The prisoner woke early on 20 December 1901. He had slept well and was focused on paying attention to his religious advisor for the few minutes he had left. Campbell had, before his time came, admitted that the statements made against him at trial were true and that his own story was a lie. He 'unreservedly confessed to having committed not only the outrage at Queanbeyan, but also a similar outrage at Ramsay's Bush'. He asked for forgiveness from the victims and attributed the rapes to his 'neglect' of his 'religious duties'.[29]

A small crowd gathered for the hanging in the execution yard of Darlinghurst Gaol. The *Maitland Daily Mercury* let readers know that at least one man present, a member of the New South Wales legislature, was not registered in the official paperwork that day. 'Don't put my name in', the additional witness told a clerk at the gaol, 'it's nothing I would like advertised'. Some people were still ardent supporters of capital punishment, but the great social swell against the death penalty meant that a clutch at the noose was not always the proud public statement that it once was. The *Sydney Morning Herald* remarked on Howard's efficiency, and how 'the executioner adjusted the rope and placed a white cap over the man's face. These preparations were carried out expeditiously, only occupying a few seconds'. Howard did not even wait for Campbell to finish his prayer before he gave the signal to draw the bolt. The prisoner, who weighed 154 pounds, fell 7 feet 9 inches.[30]

As 1901 drew to a close, nobody, not even Nosey Bob, could have predicted how quiet 1902 would be. It was the first year since Howard launched his career on a scaffold in 1876 without a judicial execution in New South Wales. Charles Henry Lukins murdered Rachel Baikie in April, and Thomas Nicholas Birch murdered his brother-in-law Augustine Lawrence the same month. Both men had their death sentences commuted. Both prisoners were told that, instead of receiving Howard's regrets, they would be lifelong residents in one of the New South Wales sheriff's lodging places.[31]

Violet Oldfield, Campbell's small but incredibly feisty victim, went on with her life. She grew up and, almost nine years to the day after her assault, married Edward John Francis Cartwright. 'The bride's dress was of white embroidery trimmed with valenciennes lace and insertion. A wreath and veil were also worn'.[32]

The reprieves issued after Howard's work on Campbell gave the hangman a year off from his supreme duty. There were the Darlinghurst Gaol gardens to attend to. There were also his gardens at home that required attention. At Paddington, he grew cabbages and grapes and flowers.[33] At Bondi, doing battle with salty air and strong winds, he also grew produce because it was practical or just because it was decorative. Industrious at work and at home, Howard was, at the beginning of 1902, a man who was about to turn 70. So, how does a state executioner, one who had seen so much loss of life, spend his leisure time? The *Truth* reported on one of Howard's favourite hobbies:

He is a fisherman, but does not spend his time like most professors of the gentle art in hooking schnapper, whiting, and such harmless members of the finny tribe. As on the land, where his main work is in choking the thugs and human tigers who commit crimes so deep-dyed that they cry to heaven for vengeance, so on the water he concentrates his efforts to dealing with the savage tigers of the deep.[34]

Howard's garden at Bondi defied contemporary expectations when it came to his choice of ornaments to supplement his displays of greenery. The average gardener might be content with a birdbath, a few gnomes or some wide paths between attractive blooms and tasty vegetables. Not Nosey Bob. The garden grown by 'a great lover of flowers' showcased rare specimens of the remains of the 'marine man-eaters which infest our coast', with the jaws of sharks surrounding his cottage. 'When I hook a particularly big chap', Howard had explained, 'a fellow that is too big for me single-handed, I make fast the line, and get the old horse to pull him out'. Beneath his tall Norfolk Island pines, shark bones, of all sorts and sizes, could be seen. Llewellyn Jones, a solicitor and one-time member of parliament, took several curios with him on a visit to England, which included 'the jaws of a mammoth shark, which Bob had captured'.[35]

The scaffold was not going anywhere, and Howard would be back on the gallows at Darlinghurst Gaol in 1903. He would stand on the platform shortly after his 71st birthday.

'AN EXCEPTIONALLY
CLEAN BIT OF WORK'

Nosey Bob would have appreciated some respite. Yes, he was still the executioner and his name was a frequent feature in newspapers and magazines, but without a greased and stretched rope in his hands, he was not at any risk of being the subject of headlines for stories detailing decapitations or strangulations. Howard was, across 1902, able to enjoy the status of being an everyday city worker. He continued in his thoughtful, unassuming ways and remained ready to 'do a good deed for any of his fellow creatures'. John Longford, the keeper of the imposing Darlinghurst Gaol gates, told a representative of *Freeman's Journal* about 'many a case of distress which Howard would relieve', while some of Howard's colleagues told *Truth* of his generosity 'with long beers and whisky' while observing how the hangman was often addressed at quiet gatherings as Mr Howard.[36] For an entire year, the executioner went to work, earned a salary and did not have to kill anyone.

There were no regional-based rejections that year as the only need for Howard's services was in the local gaol yards to do some gardening and some maintenance. Like most workers across the city, the sheriff's officer commuted from his own abode to his employer's place of business, and he continued to be the 'gentleman who almost every day takes his seat among ladies in the Paddington tram, passes their fares, and gives them change, and otherwise makes himself most agreeable'.[37]

There were those who discriminated against him,

either taking offence at his facial disfigurement or his job title, but Howard kept his sense of humour. When one of the Waverley trams pulled into Darlinghurst one evening, the cars were heaving with people, leaving only standing room opportunities for the most determined commuters. 'However, a distinguished passenger, the famous finisher of the law, wanted to get in; but a passenger objected, saying there was no room'. The rejection of Howard was probably not calculated, but simply the words of someone who wanted to go home after a long day. Indeed, 'the passenger evidently did not know the important official, and a row ensued'. Howard had some advice: 'Perhaps you'll have to stand yourself some day!'[38] Nosey Bob might have had to wait for the next tram, but at least he had the last word in that evening's verbal volleying.

Howard was on light duties that year; an informal preview of what retirement might look like. When he was back doing the heavy work that his role demanded, after almost sixteen months off, it might have felt like he had not had a break at all because Howard's next patient had an eerie connection to the last man that he had seen off. This new crime was murder, not rape, but the offences committed – the murder of a young girl by Thomas Moore in 1902 and one of the sexual assaults of several young girls by Joseph Campbell in 1901 – unfolded in the same place: Ramsay's Bush in Sydney.

Moore, an Aboriginal man, killed Janie Irene Smith on 23 December 1902 while the girl had been out gathering flowers. At trial, on 25 February 1903, it was revealed that

Smith had left home in the morning and had been discovered in an unconscious state just before 11:00 am. 'The little one was lying in the bush, bathed in blood, which had flowed from injuries to her head. Her dress was disarranged, and one of her garments had been torn'. She had not been sexually assaulted, but she had awful head injuries and was suffering from blood loss. Nothing could be done to save her, and she died the same day at Lewisham Hospital. Several witnesses identified Moore in the area, and he was quickly picked up by police and questioned about the crime. Moore did not confess, but he did say: 'I will have to suffer for it now. I am sure to get the rope round my neck for this'. He also said, 'I only came out of the Parramatta Gaol on the 16th, and have been drinking ever since'. The court was told that Moore did, eventually, confess to having killed Smith. 'He said he hit her three times on the head with the same stone'.[39]

Mental health issues were poorly understood during the colonial period and into the new era of Federation, and there was a pattern of using insanity as a defence of last resort. Nosey Bob had certainly fitted nooses around the necks of men who had asserted that they had been insane at the time of committing the crimes that brought them to stand before him on a scaffold. Some, like Henry Tester in 1882, were obviously pretending to be unwell. Others had more genuine claims. Moore, a Queenslander who was around 33 years of age at the time of the attack, had a record for drunkenness and larceny. There was, though, no mention of aggression before he killed Smith.[40]

At trial, Moore's own statement in the dock was

compelling in comparison to Tester's simple refusal to talk. Moore said: 'When I picked up the stone and hit the girl, I was mad, and didn't know what I was doing. When I hit the girl, I thought there was a lot of people all around me, and I didn't know how to get away'. Was Moore mentally unstable? The jury did not think so. It took only half an hour to come back to the courtroom with a verdict of guilty. The judge issued the customary sentence and committed Moore to the care of those men who would decide if the punishment would be carried out or not.[41]

The executive council decided that the law should take its course, and Smith's murderer would be hanged on 14 April 1903. In a calm response to the news, Moore expressed 'a desire that the sentence should not be commuted, because he says he could not tolerate gaol life for any length of time'.[42] This attitude fell into line with one of the arguments of the abolitionists. Amidst cries demanding a more refined society, and the need to take the high moral ground, were suggestions that imprisonment was a punishment much worse than death. This argument assumed that a life of incarceration and reflection, with each day only ever being a bleak replay of the day before, was a greater deterrent than the privacy of a condemned cell, some religious company and a quick end:

> Deprived of liberty, obliged to submit to strict
> discipline, debarred from the indulgence in spirituous
> liquors, compelled to labor, and at the close of each
> day's work, locked up like a wild beast in his den for

twelve weary hours in a dark cell, a prey to his gloomy thoughts, not permitted to indulge in obscene language, cut off from all his vicious associates, and all his most deeply cherished gratifications disallowed.[43]

There was little interest in Moore's last hours. The usual 'gathering of the morbidly curious' crowds of fifty or even 100 people lurking around Darlinghurst Gaol's main entrance on Forbes Street hoping to hear the gallows, or to see who was attending the execution, was completely absent. This overall lack of concern was reiterated by the small number of witnesses who came together to see a murderer's end. The under-sheriff and the medical officer were there, as were a few officials on the gaol's staff and four members of the press corps.[44] It was almost as if such a long period of time between hangings had made people realise that they could live without their perverse inquisitiveness about capital punishment.

In a subtle foreshadowing that Nosey Bob's time with the team at Darlinghurst Gaol was coming to an end, the *Evening News* reported on changes behind Sydney's most famous sandstone walls. The gaol yard 'presented a very different appearance to-day to that on the morning of the last execution' because 'formerly a small grass plot, with a flower or two, occupied the centre of the gravelled enclosure. This has been changed, and a low brick wall separates the space into two asphalted exercise yards'. Howard's gardens were being pulled up. The yards were, naturally, quiet, as all the inmates were locked in their cells where they would remain until after the hanged man's body had been cut down and carted to the dead house, as was standard practice. Prayers were offered, Howard pinioned the prisoner, and the usual procession from the condemned man's cell to the scaffold took place. Moore's hands were clenched, but otherwise he 'wore a look of indifference':[45]

> There was a rattle of falling doors, as the floor beneath the prisoner's feet collapsed, released by the assistant-hangman's lever. The body shot downwards until about 8ft 10in of slack rope had been exhausted, and then, after a few seconds' oscillation, and a half-turn, due to the slight twist in the rope, it hung motionless. Death had been instantaneous.[46]

Despite the public inertia towards Moore, the *Evening News* had specified his drop. Meanwhile, *Truth* published a half-generous report on the executioner: 'Sometimes he has blundered, but, as a rule, Bob has done his work well. The "passing" of Tom Moore, on Tuesday morning, was an exceptionally clean bit of work'.[47] Moore was Howard's sixtieth patient, and it was a solid performance for the hangman's golden jubilee. Nosey Bob did not know his special services would only be called on one more time. Before the year was out, Howard was required to step up and facilitate another double hanging, his fifth go at dispatching multiple men at once. His last appointment on the scaffold would not be classified as a clean bit of work.

CHAPTER 12

LAID TO REST

A GRAND MISCARRIAGE OF JUSTICE

Howard spent time in numerous towns and cities as a hangman, travelling to scaffolds across New South Wales. There was some speculation that he also did public services in other jurisdictions within Australia, but other sheriffs had their own officers for special duties as required. Tasmania, for example, had an executioner from the very early 1800s, but took the position off their books in 1868, as the long-serving 'hangman was worn out in the service and had retired on a pension, and it was intended only to obtain the services of an officer of that description when required'. Solomon Blay, who had been appointed in 1840, resigned and went back to England in 1868. Shunned at home, he and his wife returned to Hobart in 1870. Blay was promptly given his old post back, hanging around until 1891.[1]

One rumour had Nosey Bob in Brisbane. In a letter to the *Bulletin* in 1888, an outraged reader asked: 'Could not the noseless one be compelled to adorn himself in the old crape [sic] mask face-gear? Anything would be better than the repulsive hideousness ushered upon criminals in their

last moments by this intercolonial launcher-into-eternity'.
It is certainly not impossible, but there is no proof that
Howard ever returned to the birthplace of his youngest
daughter, Fanny, as a courtesy to authorities in Brisbane. If
Howard had been a hangman before Queensland separated
from New South Wales in 1859, this tale would be more
plausible. There was, though, no need for government
men in Queensland to request the services of a consultant
executioner in the late 1880s. William Ware, who did not
'care a "hang" whether his name [was] made public or not'
and who was known to have favoured 'the "long drop"
system', was the hangman at Brisbane Gaol on Boggo Road
at the time. Ware had been appointed in 1886, and he held
onto the post until his death, aged 57, in 1899.[2] Howard
might have enjoyed some warm weather, but his expertise
was not required so far north.

Melbourne's *Punch*, an illustrated weekly, published
another rumour that the man who hanged Frances Knorr
for infanticide on 15 January 1894 in Melbourne, a man
identified as Roberts, was none other than Nosey Bob. It
was more likely that a 'comparatively inexperienced' man
had taken care of Knorr as the regular executioner was
unavailable. Thomas Perrins, who was usually referred to in
the press as Jones, killed himself the week before Knorr was
scheduled to be hanged. Jones had made his way calmly to
his workroom at the Melbourne Gaol and cut his own throat
'with a strong, keen razor'. For Jones, suicide was preferable
to hanging a woman.[3] A baby farmer who did not operate on

the same scale as John and Sarah Makin but one who still shocked Australia, the 25-year-old Knorr admitted her guilt not long before she stood on the trapdoors:

> I now desire to state that upon the two charges known in evidence as No. 1 and 2 babies, I confess to be guilty. Placed as I am now within a few hours of my death, I express a strong desire that this statement be made public, with the hope that my fall will not only be a warning to others, but also act as a deterrent to those who are perhaps carrying on the same practice.[4]

Penitence was not enough to see Knorr offered mercy and her hanging went ahead. This meant that somebody had to fit the noose around her neck. Nosey Bob had no official duties scheduled that January, which led to speculation that he was the hangman:

> The impression that 'Roberts', who engineered the hanging of Mrs. Knorr, is 'Nosey Bob' is not yet dispelled. Anyhow, he came from Sydney. If he is 'Nosey Bob' the action of the New South Wales Government in lending Victoria their hangman shows a sisterly feeling and a desire to please that we did not expect from the older colony. When the provinces lend each other their hangman – as good neighbours in certain quarters lend each other the frying-pan – we may be certain that Federation is in the air.[5]

Another report asserted that Roberts, having come from a respectable family in Scotland, 'inherited money and spent his fortune like the biblical prodigal in "riotous living"'. In need of a regular pay day, the young man took on a sheriff's most dreadful work. It was noted that Roberts 'lived in Sydney, drawing his salary of 5s a day from the Victorian Government and attending at executions when wanted'. Another article supported this scenario: 'The executioner having killed himself, it remains to be seen whether Jones's under-study – who is now in Sydney, and has been communicated with – will entertain any scruples'.[6] This would explain how it was widely thought that a man named Roberts, of a Sydney residence, attended the gallows in Melbourne. The Roberts in this article, though, was not Robert Howard.

A more substantial rumour circulated around the double hanging of John Caffrey and Henry Albert Penn in New Zealand. A couple of newspapers in regional New South Wales printed stories about Nosey Bob 'and his mate' going abroad 'to hang Caffrey and Penn, the Great Barrier murderers'. The duo had been done for killing Robert Taylor in 1886 and were sent off on 21 February 1887 at Mount Eden Prison, Auckland. The *Otago Witness*, a newspaper in the country's South Island, carried a story in 1920 about how Nosey Bob supplied his services as a favour because the government had been 'unable to get a man to draw the lever at the execution' and *Smith's Weekly* picked up the story in 1937.[7] It was not impossible. Nosey Bob would have been available for the job. He had just bungled a quadruple hanging in January 1887 and there were no calls on him to hang anyone else at home for the rest of the year.

Howard taking a set of his dreaded lengths of rope overseas, so soon after hanging some of the Mount Rennie rapists, would have been a big story in all the city newspapers. Also, Mary Hicks, the victim of the most publicised and talked about sexual assault in the history of New South Wales, was sent to New Zealand as funds had been raised to help her escape Australia and her past.[8] That the man who had just bungled the hanging of four rapists then followed their victim across the Tasman Sea went unnoticed by Sydney-based journalists, who were so keen to report on all of Howard's scraggings, makes this story a bit far-fetched.

Howard was definitely in Sydney in 1903 when Digby Grand and Henry Jones were charged with the felonious and malicious murder of Constable Samuel William Long. The men broke into the Royal Hotel in the Sydney suburb of Auburn just before 2:00 am on 19 January 1903.[9]

Grand had gained access to the hotel through a trapdoor 'which opened out onto the footpath and then disappeared into the cellar'. After breaking in, he opened the front door of the premises to admit Jones. Neither of the thieves thought to stop and lock the pub's main door. Long, who was doing his rounds of the area, tried the door. Finding that it was unfastened, he did what any police officer would do: he went inside to investigate. There was gunfire, a single shot. The sound woke the licensee, Theodore Charles Trautwein, who was then spurred into action on hearing 'heavy groans, proceeding from the direction of the bar, which is semi-detached from the main building'. When Trautwein made it to the bar, he 'stumbled over the prostrate body of Constable Long' and immediately sent for help. With a couple of others, he tried to assist the dying policeman, but it was no use. Long was dead before he reached a hospital. Meanwhile, Grand and Jones had made off with some cigarettes and escaped in a sulky that was parked nearby.[10]

Grand and Jones left no clues at the crime scene, and so a reward of £200 for information was offered. Before the end of the month, a tip-off led to several arrests. Grand, a 32-year-old bootmaker, also known as Newbold, Stevens and Ward, was arrested for murder. His associates John Thomas Woolford and Alfred Yeomans were both done for related charges. Jones, a 37-year-old mechanic, also known as John McGuire and Baker, was another person of interest and the public were asked to look out for a man who was stooped and with a 'determined facial expression'. Just weeks after the murder, the charge against Yeomans was withdrawn while Woolford was discharged after making a deal to become a witness for the prosecution. Grand remained in custody and Jones was arrested 'in a house at Pyrmont' where he was found 'at a table playing cards'.[11]

The trial of Grand and Jones, after a couple of delays, commenced on 6 April at the Darlinghurst Court House. It was quite the event, as eager spectators rushed to secure a seat. 'In a second or two all the available accommodation was taken up, and dozens of people were turned away disconsolate and disappointed'.[12]

Some of the excitement was because Long had been

shot in the back of the head. This was not just a murder; it was an execution. Grand and Jones pleaded not guilty. The trial proceeded, but the prosecution had some difficulty with their main witness. 'Woolford, who had given much evidence at the inquest, showed peculiar mannerisms, and hung his head while he gave evidence', indicating he did not understand the questions being asked. The judge, AJ Rogers, was miffed and asked Woolford directly: 'Have you been drinking or are you in a bad state of health?' The witness said his head felt poorly, but he 'had only one drink'. He was given permission to stand down until he felt better. It was the opinion of a medical officer that Woolford was quite sane, 'but he was in a nervous condition. The man was frightened and had not slept well for some time'. The prosecution argued that without Woolford's testimony, 'on which the case absolutely turns', the trial could not proceed. Rogers considered the matter and then discharged the jury.[13]

A second trial commenced on 11 May. Rogers was back at the bench, his overt siding with the prosecution seeing him described as 'the thirteenth juror'. Woolford, having spent a short stint in the Lunatic Reception House in Darlinghurst, appeared capable of being examined and cross-examined. His testimony, in addition to proof that the round in Long's head was a match for a revolver found on Grand, was enough to secure findings of guilty against both men. According to the *Daily Telegraph*, the jury's foreman made a recommendation to mercy, 'on the grounds that there is no evidence who fired the shot, and there was a possibility of a third person being present'.[14]

There was an appeal, but the full court upheld the sentence. There were also protests based on the Christian principle that, even if the old laws demanded 'an eye for an eye, and a tooth for a tooth, they could not justly demand two eyes for one eye, and two teeth for one tooth'. When what is commonly referred to as the *Crimes Act 1900* (NSW) was first passed, the word 'accomplice' occurred just once: under the definition of murder, to cover all those engaged in the commission of this type of crime. Like those who were present in the committing of the murders of the Breelong Massacre, all were culpable. In this case, according to the law, it did not matter which man pulled the trigger and killed Long.[15] The executive council were comfortable with this and saw no reason to offer mercy, and the pair would swing.

Howard's fourth double hanging, on 7 July 1903, generated a mixed result. The *Wellington Times*, a masthead founded to support the labour movement, reported that: 'In the case of Grand, the cause of death was strangulation by hanging, and injuries to the great blood vessels of the neck, and in the case of Jones the cause of death was dislocation of the cervical vertebrae and injury to the spinal cord'. Grand was dropped 9 feet 6 inches, a full foot longer than the drop of 8 feet 6 inches set for Jones. Both deaths should have been clean, but the vagaries of execution by hanging meant that a neat result was never guaranteed. On this occasion, Grand struggled for several minutes after he fell. The bodies of the two men were cut down after 'waiting the requisite 20 minutes' and then the usual inquests were held.[16]

There were multiple comparisons of this double send-off to Howard's bungling of Charles Montgomery and Thomas Williams on the same gallows back in May 1894, when Montgomery was given an instant death and Williams was slowly strangled. When the hanging of Grand and Jones was covered by *Truth*, it was the final instalment in the 'Howard's Holocaust' series. Old Chum had written his last piece in this run of stories about death at Darlinghurst in February 1898, with updates on Howard's hanging record being published anonymously from December that year. Despite the bungled hanging of Grand, *Truth* claimed that: 'From long experience the NOSELESS ONE performs his work like a well-oiled machine, and on Tuesday morning the "machine" worked without a hitch'.[17] It might have been a polite farewell, motivated by an instinct that Howard's days as a hangman were nearly over.

On 20 June 1908, the *Newsletter*, promoted as an Australian paper for Australians and edited by Charles Haynes, son of abolitionist John Haynes, printed a new statement from the frightened witness Woolford. The prosecution's most important witness perjured himself at trial in 1903, or in print five years later, with a shocking claim:

1. Make oath and say that in May, in the year 1903, at Darlinghurst Court House, in Sydney, that I was forced under punishment and threats with life in gaol to commit murder in the form of swearing the lives of two men, Grand and Jones, to the gallows for the Auburn murder.

2. That I was sent to gaol for some considerable time on a false charge, and there threatened with life in gaol if I did not give evidence to hang the said Grand and Jones.

That I was paid by the Government before and after trial of the said two men; that I had received the sum of £100 for swearing their lives away; that I was liberated after the execution of Grand and Jones, which took place on the 7th July, 1903.[18]

The *Newsletter* ran an aggressive campaign, demanding the case be revisited. Alfred Jackson, who also gave testimony against Grand and Jones in 1903, was offended by the implication that he, too, had perjured himself, and he sued. The *Newsletter* was ordered to pay Jackson £350 in damages.[19] Was Woolford a liar? Yes. Was the trial fair? No. Did Howard hang two innocent men? Maybe.

OUT WITH THE OLD, IN WITH THE NEW

Howard retired in May 1904, after sending off sixty-one men and one woman. He was an assistant for three of those hangings and the senior scragger for fifty-nine. Forty-six patients were taken care of without any obvious hitches. Not everyone was lucky. There were seven high-profile strangulations, five less-dramatic chokings, three throats cut and one decapitation. *Truth* asserted his 'troubles' were not caused by nervousness, 'as Bob Howard had no nerves'.[20]

More mistakes were made on gallows in New South Wales, but they would not be Howard's fault. The pain and suffering of Nosey Bob were over. There was, however, enough energy at the office of the *Critic*, an Adelaide-based weekly newspaper, to muster up a couple of last snide comments. Nosey Bob was reminded that he was, essentially, illiterate and that, despite being on the sheriff's team for the bulk of his adult life, the executioner was still an outsider:

> Robert Howard ('Nosey Bob'), N.S. Wales retiring hangman, is thinking of writing a book of his life. Howard is a well-known figure in Sydney, the nose deformity making him conspicuous on the street. He thinks that the Prison Department should present him on his retirement with some mark of esteem for his long and faithful services. A humorous warder in Darlinghurst gaol has started a collection for a miniature gold scaffold for Bob's watch chain, but threepence is the highest single subscription yet received.[21]

Howard was still a hangman. His retirement merely earned him the honorific of 'ex': the 'ex-finisher of the law'. Nosey Bob's imminent departure solved a problem of negative publicity, but it created another issue: a vacancy. On 27 April 1904, the *Sydney Morning Herald* invited, on behalf of the sheriff, applications for the position of executioner. In a surprise, Samuel Godkin, who had worked with Nosey Bob for almost ten years, was overlooked and George Russell was made the finisher of the law for New South Wales. Russell took Howard's salary and quickly earned an additional £2 10s in travel allowance to go to Dubbo Gaol and meet a murderer.[22]

In the Peak Hill district south of Dubbo, Ah Chick or Check was ringbarking trees when he argued with his employer, William Skewes Tregaskis, on 17 February 1904. Aggrieved by Tregaskis, the Chinese man hacked him to death with an axe. Pleas for mercy were ignored and it was confirmed the dispatch of Chick 'will be the first job which will engage the attention of Mr "Nosey" Howard's successor'.[23]

The hanging was ghastly. The death on 28 June 1904 was instantaneous, but 'as the body fell the carotid artery was severed, and blood poured out'. Despite a rough start, Russell held on long enough to deal with five murderers, but he could not outdo Howard's length of service. Russell tossed in his job; his resignation was effective 4 March 1908. The sheriff decided enough was enough, and the *Public Service List* of 1908 notes: 'Executioner ... Permanent Position Abolished'.[24]

There was, though, one more man who was a long-term feature on the books at the New South Wales Department of Justice. James Golder, probably the Jim Goaler who served as an assistant to Nosey Bob in the late 1880s and early '90s, was on a hangman's retainer. Not publicly listed as an executioner, it was reported that, in contrast to the £156 in salary paid to Howard and his immediate successor Russell, with some allowances paid, Golder was paid £100 per annum and £10 per hanging. With mercy the norm, rather than the exception, there was nobody to hang, and the role was not proving very lucrative. Golder resigned in 1911.[25]

It may not just have been boredom on the job, or a lack of bonus payments, that precipitated Golder's departure from Darlinghurst Gaol. Within weeks of giving up his post, a warrant was issued for Golder's arrest, with the 52-year-old charged with wife desertion. The hangman had married the widowed Emily Mary Raybould in late 1909, but he had not been entirely upfront about how he earned a living. The marriage certificate showcased that old hangman's ploy, and stated he worked as a labourer. Only four months after the wedding, details of Mr Golder's work life 'leaked out, and the news had an injurious effect upon the home'. Mrs Golder left her husband and sued for maintenance, with a magistrate granting an order that she would be paid '7s 6d per week'.[26]

THE DEATH OF ROBERT RICE HOWARD

Nosey Bob saw his youngest child, William, who was working as a porter, marry Lily May Coote, a waitress from Dungog north of Newcastle, on Tuesday 29 November 1904. William was 32 years old that day, making him much older than any of his siblings had been when they were married. Perhaps he had waited until his dad was no longer an executioner before starting his own family. The 23-year-old bride's own father was a carpenter, while her new father-in-law was simply identified as a 'Government Servant (Retired)'.[27]

Howard did not, though, live long enough to see the departure of his successor, George Russell. On Saturday

3 February 1906, the tenth wedding anniversary of Sidney and Elizabeth Howard, the ex-finisher of the law passed away aged 74. He was survived by five of his seven children. The uncommon hangman, identified upon his death as a retired civil servant, died of endocarditis and senile decay, or what would now be referred to as dementia. Endocarditis, an inflammation of the heart's inner lining, can be caused by an infection. It is also a condition that, like dementia, has been associated with syphilis.[28] An invitation to join family members in celebrating the life of Nosey Bob appeared in the *Sydney Morning Herald*:

> The Friends of the late ROBERT RICE HOWARD
> are kindly invited to attend his Funeral; to leave his
> late residence, Bondi Beach, Bondi, THIS (Monday)
> AFTERNOON, at 3 o'clock, for Waverley Cemetery.[29]

Howard was wrapped in a lawn shroud and placed in a black casket. Four horses and two carriages took him to his resting place in a Church of England section of Waverley Cemetery. Nosey Bob's funeral cost £10 18s 6d, a small price to be reunited with his wife Jane and his daughter Emily. Howard also joined a grandchild at Waverley. Jane, a child of Sidney and Elizabeth, had died of extreme gastritis on Friday 1 January 1904, aged 19 months.[30]

Right to the end, Howard's priorities were clear. He left each of his three sons – Edward, Sidney and William – a block of land in Bondi, having purchased lots 9, 10 and 11 in section six of the Queenscliff Estate. He also left his two surviving daughters – Mary and Fanny – blocks of land in Florence Street in the Richmond Park Estate at Richmond. Any monies held at his death were to be equally distributed among the five children. To Sidney, his primary carer, he also bequeathed his 'clothing, watch and chain and jewellery, furniture, horse or horses, harness or harnesses, vehicle or vehicles, dogs and poultry, all my personal effects'.[31]

Obituaries, from short snippets to lengthy overviews, appeared in dozens of newspapers. Some of the facts and figures in these printed tributes are wrong, with Nosey Bob's length of service and the number of times he undertook his supreme duty routinely exaggerated. Most, though, remembered the hangman's kindnesses and how *different* he was to most of the other men who had held the same role:

> Robert Howard ... At the time of his death he was
> 74 years of age and though occupying the most
> degrading position in the land he was said to have been
> of a sober, steady, and charitable disposition. When
> John Langdon was gatekeeper at Darlinghurst, he had
> instructions from Howard to let him know of any cases
> of real distress occurring through the incarceration
> of the breadwinner in gaol. It is said that Howard
> possessed a considerable amount of property.[32]

The *Australian Star*, a newspaper that had reported on much of Howard's work, acknowledged that some biographical details on the noseless executioner were out of reach:

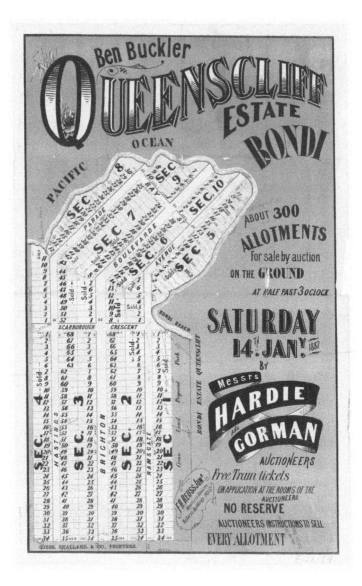

FIGURE 14 **Bondi, Queenscliff, Ben Buckler Estate**

SOURCE State Library of NSW, 1882, 064 – Z/SP/B23/64

DEATH OF THE HANGMAN.

ROBERT HOWARD PASSES AWAY.

After ailing for some weeks Robert Howard, the public
hangman of New South Wales until 1904, passed
peacefully away on Saturday, at a cottage occupied by
him for the last twenty years at Bondi.

Howard was appointed to the position in June, 1876,
and retained it for close on thirty years, when, it is
understood, his advancing years made it necessary for
the Government to retire him. Subsequently Howard
lived in strict retirement up to the time of his death.
It is stated that, before receiving his appointment, the
deceased official drove a cab in the streets of Sydney.
Although for so long the public executioner of New
South Wales, and for so long a time drawing a salary or
allowance, his name never appeared on the 'estimates',
though it appeared in the Public Service Annual for a
year or two. The exact number of doomed persons who
passed through Howard's hands cannot be stated exactly
at the present moment, but they may be estimated at
something over 70.

The deceased was familiarly termed 'Nosey Bob' by his
friends and acquaintances – not because he possessed
too great a protuberance, but because he had hardly

any at all. He took the sobriquet quite contentedly, and seemed to enjoy life in his own way.

Now he has gone on the same dark journey to which he despatched so many during his long reign as executioner. The deceased was over 70 years of age when he joined the majority.[33]

It may have surprised Howard that there was so much sadness at his death. Even those at the *Bulletin* had, over time, softened. The magazine's treatment of Howard had begun as a vexatious campaign that eased off into habitual thoughtlessness and ended, finally, in recognition. A couple of years after Howard's passing, in 1908, the *Bulletin*'s readers saw a suggestion that the Department of Justice 'must look back with a certain sorrow to the steady, deep-rooted times of Nosey Bob, who was N.S.W.'s reliable executioner for something like 30 years.'[34]

In 1919, months before his own death and interment at Waverley Cemetery, JF Archibald spoke of Howard almost affectionately, recalling how he had once helped the hangman. The journalist was waiting at Darlinghurst Gaol to meet Walton Lockyer Merewether. Archibald pointed out that 'daylight was failing fast, and the gas was unlit' when he heard shuffling footsteps. 'Mister Merewether', the voice said, 'will you kindly write another letter for me?' Archibald recognises Howard and, instead of complaining about how the hangman had no memory for faces or voices, he explains how the misidentification was easily made. 'There I was, sitting in Merewether's seat, with Merewether's very visible dog bearing me company; besides, the barrister and I were both bespectacled and bearded, of similar complexion and height, and similarly dressed.' The would-be-secretary-to-the-executioner did not turn around; instead, he took up a piece of paper as Merewether, a long-serving prosecutor, had obviously done before. 'Well, Mr Merewether', Howard said, 'it's the same old thing. I'm to be pitied for not having been taught to read and write. Thank God, I've had my children well learned.'[35] Howard started dictating a letter to his youngest son William, who was still single at the time:

My dear son, – I got your kind letter weeks ago, but couldn't answer it, you know why. When you were at home, after your poor mother died, you was always a good boy, and never gave me a bit of trouble, but now you're away, I sometimes think that you might get on the wrong track. So, my dear son, let me advise you again. Beware of bad women and strong drink. Them's the roads to the gallows. I've stood alongside lots of men on the gallows, and they was all afraid when it come to the pinch. The women and the drink had gone, and there they was, left alone with me, the finishin' schoolmaster. No more at present, from your loving father.[36]

Archibald signed the letter 'Mr Robert Howard' and promised to find an envelope and a stamp. Howard's shock, when Merewether promptly rounded the corner, was enough to make him swear 'I'll take no more gin with my beer'.[37]

Stories around Howard's life and employment swirled. He was, for some, the successful cab proprietor, a man who jobbed for vice-regal and regal passengers, but who lost his business when he lost his nose. A life turned upside down because of one accident. With limited options, 'his forbidding features fitted in well with the ominous work' of the executioner. A scragger from 1876 until 1904, he was proud to say he 'dressed in decent black clothes, so's you can 'ardly tell me from the parson'. He was slighted, insulted, boycotted and even assaulted.[38] Demonised by the press corps. Recast as a caricature of all that was wrong with an uncivilised system of punishment. Turned into an ape or a gorilla, something less than human. The noseless hangman was, for many, just one more villain in Darlinghurst Gaol. Despite Howard's insistence that he was never ashamed of what he did, it would have been an incredibly long twenty-eight years.

The myths around Nosey Bob continued to form and the press started to openly doubt its own reportage. *Freeman's Journal*, having covered the hangman and his work for decades, published an obituary after Howard's funeral that included a story they 'would not vouch for'. Apparently, on a bitter morning in the state's west, Howard was affixing the cap and the noose 'when the condemned man began to shiver on the scaffold. It was very cold, and a few flakes of snow fell on the neck of the condemned, who said to "Bob", "Hurry up; I'm cold", "Never mind", was the reply, "you'll be warm enough presently"'. This might be a reference to Albert, dispatched at Dubbo for murder in the winter of

1880, when the 'snowy air of the morning caused him to shiver in his white duck trousers'.[39]

The man who had done the worst job in New South Wales was routinely subjected to profiles written up by those more interested in selling newspapers than in unpacking the life of the executioner. In between evaluations of his work on scaffolds are snippets, rumours and repackaged anecdotes. These stories are supplemented by interviews with Howard, allowing the hangman's own voice, snuffly and with remnants of an English accent, to be heard long after his death. Somewhere among the facts, fictions and occasional interjections by Howard is the real story of Nosey Bob. The *real story* had been told by Howard often over the years. He was, as he said, a man who took pride in everything he did, who was good with animals, who kept an excellent garden and who found pleasure in sitting down, over a beer and a smoke, to talk about his children.

FINALLY, THE END

William Blackstone's *Commentaries on the Laws of England*, a four-volume epic published between 1765 and 1769, could be found in the luggage of David Collins, marine and judge advocate, when he boarded the *Sirius* in May 1787 as a member of the First Fleet. Blackstone had consolidated a 'mass of disparate material into a coherent order' to make common law more accessible to more people by offering 'a clear expression of familiar rules'. Yet, the colony of New South Wales was anything but familiar and the *Commentaries* are unsuited for 'tricky or developing areas of law'.[40] Still, as the settlement's fledgling legal system was populated by men forced into positions of legal authority by circumstance rather than by training, a text suggested for law students was probably not a bad choice.

The *Commentaries* outlined three species of punishment: those punitive measures that sought to reform individual offenders, those that were leveraged as examples to deter others, and those that totally prevented any further criminal activity.[41] Transportation may have reformed some and deterred others, but for the total prevention of reoffending, the noose was deployed with barbaric regularity in Sydney's youth. The executioner's burden was alleviated as New South Wales matured, but capital punishment remained a blight on the statute books.

Reasons for abolishing the death penalty were recited in parliament, at public meetings and protests, as well as in letters, newspapers, books and pamphlets. There were also fights for mercy for specific cases. We should not need a personal connection to a prisoner to feel empathy, but an individual's backstory, their circumstances and their possible innocence were more compelling claims than general pleas for legislative change. One of the greatest arguments for abolition was, of course, a botched execution. The blood. The strained gasps for air. The excruciating waits for deaths to be confirmed.

Almost twenty-eight years after John Trevor Kelly, sent off for murder at Long Bay Gaol in 1939, became the last man hanged in New South Wales, Ronald Joseph Ryan became the last man hanged in Australia. Ryan was serving a sentence in Melbourne's Pentridge Prison for his role in the robbery of a butcher shop when an escape plan went horribly wrong and a guard, George Hodson, died. He was convicted of murder, despite great doubt circulating around his guilt. The prisoner was wary of sedatives but, like some of the men who had swung before him, he had a nip of brandy before walking onto the trapdoors. Ryan's last words were to the hangman: 'God bless you. Please make it quick.'[42] The hangman obliged, and Ryan was killed instantly on 3 February 1967, sixty-one years to the day that the noseless hangman of New South Wales died in Bondi.

Most crimes were made non-capital offences in New South Wales in 1955. For another three decades, hanging remained an option for people convicted of treason, arson in naval dockyards and piracy with intent to murder. These offences were only made non-capital in 1985. The first colony to hang a man under English law was the last state to give up the old punishment. Queensland was the first Australian state to eradicate executions in 1922, followed by Tasmania in 1968, the Australian Capital Territory and Northern Territory in 1973, Victoria in 1975, South Australia in 1976 and Western Australia in 1984. The *Death Penalty Abolition Act 1973* (Cth) abolished capital punishment under federal law. This was followed by the *Crimes Legislation Amendment (Torture Prohibition and Death Penalty Abolition) Act 2010* (Cth), which prohibits the reintroduction of capital punishment in any Australian state or territory.[43]

A society that judicially executes its own citizens needs

an executioner. Most of the Sydney-based hangmen went slowly insane, turned to drink or just disappeared. Perhaps Howard had an unbreakable faith in God. Perhaps he had honed the ability to accept whatever life threw at him and had the type of natural nerve that he lamented was lacking in others. It is possible he thought of himself as a military man: a common foot soldier in the government's war on crime. Or, he had perfected the concept of compartmentalisation. Whatever the source of Nosey Bob's strength, it made him a New South Wales hangman like no other. He might not have broken the record for the number of patients attended to, but he did stick it out longer than those who went before him, or the man who followed. Even with details on the resumés of some hangmen missing Nosey Bob, with his twenty-eight years at the gallows, holds the title as the longest-serving full-time scragger for Australia's first colony-turned-state.

Howard was also, despite his profession, an ordinary man. He raised his family and held down a government job. Howard's temper was seen a few times over the years, and he had a reputation for swearing, but there is no record of him being violent off a scaffold, except in self-defence. He drank and smoked, but he did not live in a state of constant inebriation. He died at home and not within the confines of an asylum. If not for his profession, Howard might even be considered boring. Had he managed to keep his job as a cab driver, he would have faded into obscurity instead of becoming an icon of popular culture.

Like the famous English hangmen 'Bull' and 'Jack Ketch', 'Nosey Bob' became a byword for an executioner for years.

In an overview of hangmen of Melbourne, *Smith's Weekly* referred to 'The Most Worshipful Company of Hangmen Victoria's Platoon of "Nosey Bobs"'. Howard's nickname was even a threat to do someone harm: 'If you move a muscle I'll rob Nosey Bob of the job'. The hangman's label was also used to describe an aggressive greyhound, one who did 'not want much encouragement, because his powers having been reserved for the coursing field, he had become a perfect "Nosey Bob" among the cats, and was prepared to kill all and sundry if only given liberty'. Shortly before Howard died, one author wisecracked, 'I'm that thirsty I'd drink with Nosey Bob', a phrase that became an Australian colloquialism. When it was rumoured that the retired politician and judge William C Windeyer was writing a book of poetry, there was a public request for 'the volume to open with an apostrophe to the gallows, and to conclude with a sonnet to "Nosey Bob"'.[44]

Newspapers made countless contributions to debates around the death penalty, particularly 'about execution and mercy' and on adopting a 'more civilised approach to maintaining social order'. Press coverage of hangmen, good and bad, kept these conversations going even before the science of hanging was well understood. When John Franks volunteered to assist Joseph Bull in late 1871, before doing his first job as principal in 1873, the benefits of the long drop implemented by William Marwood in England were clear. As an assistant executioner, Franks had been involved in some terribly botched hangings, but as the man in charge, he had a clean run of the rope with ten fuss-free dispatches before he died in 1876. His assistant-turned-successor, William Tucker, managed a hat trick as principal before he resigned.[45] Maybe the fashionable finisher finally understood the alcoholic teacher he had openly scorned. Howard did not achieve the perfect success rate of the drunk or the dandy, but as the senior hangman, he supervised forty-nine more hangings than Franks and fifty-six more hangings than Tucker. He had made a total of sixteen errors over his career, giving him a final bungling rate of about 25 per cent. Nosey Bob's unfortunate occurrences, over such a long tenure, were inevitable. Even after hangings were codified with tables of drops, the executioners of Empire still made mistakes.

As abolition was implemented, reports on hangings faded from newspapers, and so did stories of the hangmen. The lawyers, judges, juries and crooks who once attracted the attention of the executioner continue to obsess reporters, but the most significant difference between the 19th century and the 21st century is that executioners have been replaced by gaolers. The men who stretched ropes, pinioned and sent felons into eternity are relics of the past. Their work sites have been taken down, modified or turned into curiosities.

Hangmen occupy an uneasy space in our history. They do not qualify for traditional biographies that tell stories of the grand or the great, the influencers or the inspirational. They were ordered to rid the world of wickedness, but they are not heroes. They served their governments without question, but they are not celebrated for their loyalty. As hired killers, they took care of problems that people who claimed to be good and decent wanted solved. Revealing the stories of these men is a challenging undertaking. Basic facts remain out of reach as they were shunned by record keepers, administrators, colleagues and employers, as well as by the press and the public. They were shunned, too, in most cases, by neighbours, families and those who were once friends. The evidence of their lives has been scattered, destroyed or simply lost. Many wanted the hangman's job done, but only a few cared about the hangman. Executioners were, in lots of ways, shameful. Careless. Drunkards. Fraudsters. Violent. Mad.

Howard was different to all his peers, but even the uncommon hangman resists having his story told. The pragmatic finisher of the law who loved animals and people, but who could slaughter a pig and dispatch a wrongdoer, is elusive. He left no personal archive of diaries and letters. The official records are incomplete. There are no personnel files. No induction records or annual performance reviews. No leave forms or payslips. Newspapers present a few facts and a lot of innuendo, with broadsheets and tabloids often serving as paper boxing rings for conflicting stories on the noseless executioner to fight it out. There are fragments of this hangman's life that survive, but the specifics of what, where and when are scarce.

And so, I have listened for the truths, among all the myths, to tell the story of a man who was once a household name. A man who, like his scaffold, is now silent. This is an unusual biography because it is without schoolyard tales or details of a romantic first outing with a future wife. Instead, this is a biography that has explored how one life was lived through sixty-two deaths. Howard was neither grand nor great, but he tells us much about the story of Australia, about who we were and who we wanted to be. A man who was, despite assumptions that executioners are inherently monstrous, human. The bloke known as Nosey Bob is gone, as is the smell of his pipe, but his mark on our shared history remains. It is indelible. Robert Rice Howard has only ever been cast as an extra in someone else's play. Here, for the first time, he took the lead. I hope you heard his voice, one that was cranky, generous, indignant and often darkly funny.

THE FIRST AND LAST MEN

THOMAS BARRETT

Of all the privileges that the colonisers of New South Wales took for granted and systematically abused, it was the cutting down of trees that left the most obvious scars on the ancient place now known as Sydney. The timber getters had an immediate, and extremely negative, impact upon a landscape that had been carefully managed for millennia by First Nations peoples.

The members of the First Fleet had been encased in timber for months. Eleven ships left Portsmouth, England on 13 May 1787, with the monotony of the long journey out to the Great South Land only broken three times. A short stop was made at Santa Cruz at Tenerife, off the north-west African coast, in June. A second and more substantial stop was made in South America at Rio de Janeiro in August. Finally, there was another brief stop in Africa at Cape Town in October. For some, the luxury of dry land offered respite. These places were sites of amusements, exploration, fresh food and drink, as well as supplies of all kinds. For those who ventured beyond the bustling activities of the ports, there were patches of unsalted air. Freedom was, however, only for the few. Most of the convicts remained confined. Their timber surrounds served as a constant reminder of their status. The smell of it. The sound of it. For some, the fear of it.

The floating village arrived in Botany Bay between 18 and 20 January the following year. Acts of survival and symbolism merged seamlessly with the tenets of capitalism. Timber meant that fires could be lit and temporary shelters could be propped up. Timber also made possible the ceremony where Governor Arthur Phillip staked a claim to the eastern side of the continent for His Majesty King George III. Having decided that Botany Bay was not a suitable location for the settlement, Phillip moved the fleet north and, on the edge of Sydney Cove, a small group gathered to supervise the raising of the Union Jack, on a modest flagpole, on 26 January 1788. A few years later, in 1791, samples of some local timbers were sent back to England where men in meeting rooms assessed the perceived value of the natural resources against the costs of their exploitation.[1]

Timber was also just as easily wielded for death. Makeshift gallows – a ladder against a sturdy tree – were set within weeks of the fleet's arrival in the deep waters of Port Jackson. Life was tenuous in the new settlement, and those individuals who threatened the survival of the group would be brutally, and publicly, punished. Just one month and one day after Phillip took possession of an enormous swathe of property marked out on British maps as New South Wales, Thomas Barrett was put to death. Barrett's motivation to steal critical food supplies is unclear. Perhaps he was hungry, perhaps he saw an opportunity to establish the colony's first black market. His fellow thieves were spared, but Barrett paid for his crime with his life. The convict was hanged on 27 February 1788, on an unremarkable patch of land between the men's and women's camps. The execution site is now the modern-day intersection of Essex and Harrington Streets, just one block back from George Street, which serves as a major thoroughfare for the city of Sydney.[2]

Today, the area known as The Rocks is usually crowded with residents, workers and tourists. The only crowds gathered there on a warm but wet day in February 1788 were convicts, marines, seamen and a few officials. Within this strange group of lawbreakers and law enforcers were the first men to protest the policy of capital punishment on Australian soil.

Barrett, a man in his mid-30s, had a long criminal record of forgery, mutiny and theft. With three others, he had been convicted of 'stealing butter, pease and pork' provisions merely hours before he was hanged. Justice was harsh in Sydney Town, and it was incredibly fast. Ralph Clark, a lieutenant in the Royal Marines, wrote in his diary that the charges against the four who had stolen food supplies were clearly proven. Barrett, Henry Lovell and Joseph Hall were sentenced to death, and John Ryan was sentenced to 300 lashes. Clark described the scene, and how at 'a Quarter after 5, the Unhappy men wair [sic] brought to the place Where the[y] were to Suffer'.[3]

The surgeon Arthur Bowes Smyth also documented the

event and noted that it was not just the marines who were called as witnesses, but that 'all the Convicts were summon'd to see the deserved end of their Companions'. Lovell and Hall were both given reprieves and told their lives would be spared, but Barrett would hang if a key obstacle to the process could be overcome. Indeed, it was 'some time before the man (a Convict who had undertaken the Office of hangman,) cd. be prevail'd upon to execute his office nor wd. he at last have comply'd if he had not been severely threaten'd … by … orders to the Marines to shoot him'.[4]

The unlikeliness of this open disobedience in a militarised penal settlement is difficult for most of us, as modern-day readers, to comprehend. It is a statement on the social position of the office of executioner and how, in a strictly hierarchical setting, the hangman was destined to sit beneath the worst members of society. Even the most notorious convicts would have greater cachet than the man tasked with carrying out the most extreme sentence of the law. Nobody was volunteering to do the deed. Nobody was volunteering to watch the deed get done, either.

At a time when, in England and many other countries, watching a hanging was usually seen as just another form of entertainment, all the witnesses on this occasion had to be coerced, and the executioner threatened with violence. This minor rebellion can be seen as more than a reluctance to take on a reviled occupation, or as a general aversion to watching an execution. In the context of the sanctions that could be issued to individuals for disobeying an order, and how defiance as a group could be seen as mutinous, this was dissent. Small, spontaneous and without banners or slogans, it was an early and important protest against the death penalty in the country that would become Australia.

Phillip, charged with establishing and running the new colony, had no enthusiasm for the noose. He would have understood, if not endorsed, the reluctance to carry out the order. Generally considered to be a decent man, he is often remembered as methodical and moral, a perfectionist compromised by some of his associates and his situation. Phillip's efforts to exert control over a community of military men, misfits and a miscellany of others saw him give up his general disapproval of the death penalty – for all crimes except murder and sodomy – and he quickly sanctioned the most terrible punishment for theft. Even the supervisor of the military police, Henry Brewer, was a reluctant participant in the administration of harsh justice when he was 'under the disagreeable Necessity of mounting the Ladder Himself, in order to fix the halter' on Barrett.[5]

The unwilling executioner is not named in the archives, but without anybody lining up for the job, it is often assumed that Ryan, who escaped the lash when his sentence was forgiven, was the man forced at gunpoint to remove the ladder and carry out the hanging of his one-time collaborator. This could have been the precedent for pardoning James Freeman after he had been caught stealing flour two days later. Freeman received the first pardon issued in New South Wales, having been spared the death penalty for theft on condition that he become the executioner for a term equivalent to his original seven-year sentence of transportation for highway robbery.[6] Ryan, and then Freeman, were the first men in a line of criminals that swapped their own punishments for the position of the Sydney-based hangman.

Barrett approached the makeshift scaffold and climbed the ladder against the tree. Brewer affixed the noose, and it is entirely likely that Ryan saw him launched into eternity. Like most professions, a hangman requires skill and quality equipment. Unfortunately, neither was available on this occasion. The first man hanged in the colony, after Phillip and all his charges began the long process of colonisation, was denied a quick death. Barrett's body was 'hung an hour & was then buried in a grave dug very near the Gallows'.[7] His death was a message that, in a foreign environment with limited supplies, infractions by an individual threatening the wellbeing of everyone would not be tolerated.

JOHN KELLY

John Kelly was the last man hanged in New South Wales. A mechanic working on a property named Hillcrest near Tenterfield in the state's north, Kelly murdered Marjorie Constance Sommerlad, aged 35, and tried to kill her brother, Eric Alfred Sommerlad, aged 25, on 4 February 1939. Kelly, who was only 24 years old, assaulted Miss Sommerlad, striking her so hard with an axe that she died instantly. Kelly later told police he had fought with her brother over his drinking, and that he first attacked Mr Sommerlad, asleep on a verandah he used as a bedroom, making at least three blows to the head. The gruesome scenes were discovered by a sister of the victims, Miss Dulcie Emma Sommerlad, who had come to visit for a holiday. When she received no greeting, then no answer, she entered the house and found her sister and brother covered in blood. She also 'found a bloodstained axe in a back room'. The injuries were so awful that the trained nurse assumed that both were dead before she realised her brother was still alive and ran to a neighbour's house to raise the alarm.[8]

Kelly was nowhere to be seen. After committing the two crimes, he stole Miss Sommerlad's diamond solitaire ring and Mr Sommerlad's distinctive green Studebaker utility truck and fled over the border into Queensland. At a hotel in Toowoomba, he asked the licensee, Nita Eileen Aitken, to keep the ring for safekeeping, and said he was going to Brisbane. He wanted company for the drive, so Aitken decided to take her son and travel with Kelly so she could visit a sick relative. Once in Brisbane, the truck was easily found by police, with Kelly nearby. Later, Aitken's testimony and the identification of Miss Sommerlad's ring, stolen at the scene of her murder, would be important evidence in proving Kelly's guilt.[9]

At Armidale, on 3 May 1939, Kelly was found guilty and sentenced to death for the murder of Miss Sommerlad. Mr Sommerlad had, miraculously, recovered. Kelly appealed to the Court of Criminal Appeal. When that was unsuccessful, he appealed to the High Court, where he was also dismissed. There were loud protests, petitions, even a hunger strike, followed by aggressive debates in parliament, including an assertion that Kelly was allocated inexperienced counsel.

The executive council could not be swayed. Many believed that the denial of mercy was purely political. The murder victim was the niece of Ernest Christian Sommerlad, a conservative member of the legislative council, while a neighbour of the Sommerlads, Michael Frederick Bruxner, was the leader of the Country Party.[10] There were always those more prepared to sacrifice a man's life on a scaffold than votes at a ballot box, but this was also a very personal crime for people in positions of power.

Kelly spent his last days in the State Penitentiary Long Bay. Darlinghurst Gaol, operational in 1841, closed in 1914 with the State Reformatory for Women at Long Bay opened in 1909, followed by the State Penitentiary for Men in 1913. On 79 acres, the new facility, in Sydney's south-east, was almost sixteen times the size of Darlinghurst, but there was no space set aside in the yards for gallows. Nosey Bob would not have recognised the contraption that was hidden away inside a cell block at the end of Four Wing, although he had used an indoor gallows at Bathurst Gaol in the 1890s. Kelly, like other men condemned to swing at Long Bay, slept just feet away from where he would meet the hangman.[11]

The execution took place at 8:00 am on 24 August 1939, with the basic ceremony witnessed by eleven men, including 'the sheriff, gaol officials and pressmen'. Pinioned and with his head covered by a hood, 'Kelly came from the small cell near the gallows and was executed within 15 seconds'. The timber beam of the gallows at Long Bay took a man's weight for the last time, and within minutes of the drop the gaol surgeon 'examined the body, and certified that Kelly had died instantly'.[12] It was a job Nosey Bob would have been pleased with.

The hangman's tree had done its work, with the beam central to facilitating the dispatch of Kelly, reiterating a long-standing reliance on timber in New South Wales. Darlinghurst is known for its impressive sandstone walls, and Long Bay for its brick, concrete and lengths of razor wire. Both sites used a piece of hardy timber to execute those sentenced to death, while the country's earliest gaols were totally dependent upon timber for their construction. In 1796, in a strange example of taxation, colonists were required to offer timber to build the colony's first gaols: one in Sydney and one in Parramatta. Settlers on small land holdings were required to provide ten logs each week. The system was indexed and those on larger land holdings were required to provide twenty logs each week. Logs were to be '9 feet long, not under nor over 7 inches diameter' and they were to be 'quite straight'. Deliveries were to be made until sufficient supplies had been received, with receipts issued by colonial authorities. Unlike most taxes, there were no complaints. Indeed, settlers were so eager to offer logs for the control of crime and the carrying out of punishments that these timber taxes were paid faster than the carpenters building the gaols could work. Not everyone was enthusiastic about the new facilities, and both gaols were destroyed by arson soon after they were completed.[13]

Between the hangings of Thomas Barrett in February 1788 and John Kelly in August 1939, hundreds of men and women were dealt with on gallows across New South Wales.

Nosey Bob helped to send off three of those condemned souls, and he was directly responsible for dispatching another fifty-nine. At Darlinghurst Gaol, now the National Art School, a knowledgeable guide can show you the outline of where the gallows were. The remnants of the scaffold at what is now the Long Bay Correctional Complex are more obvious. The bolt is no longer there and the trapdoors have been welded shut, but the heavy timber beam is still in place.[14] The beam is a reminder of how timber supported the survival of the first colonisers, flagged the potential for profit, helped incarcerate repeat offenders and was vital in carrying out the ultimate punishment.

APPENDIX A

EXECUTIONERS OF NEW SOUTH WALES

Not all the names of executioners, or their assistants, are readily available in the historical records. Some names and dates in this list are missing, and details provided here occasionally conflict with established narratives of Australian hangmen.[1] Those who are apocryphal have been excluded. For example, John Fitzgibbon and Henry Stain are both identified in secondary records, but no primary sources have been found to confirm the appointment of either man to the position of executioner.[2]

It should be noted that some assistant executioners identified here may have worked before and/or after their confirmed public appearances.

John Ryan?, February 1788[3]
Assisted by Henry Brewer, February 1788[4]

James Freeman, February 1788 – March 1791[5]

John (or William) Johnson, early 1790s – early 1800s[6]

Thomas Hughes, January 1811 – January 1834[7]
> Assisted by Thomas Worrall, 1822 – January 1834[8]

Alexander Green, February 1834 – May 1855[9]
> Assisted by Thomas Worrall, February 1834 – July 1846[10]
> Operated without an assistant, August 1846 – May 1855[11]

Robert Elliott, May 1855 – May 1863[12]

Joseph Bull, May 1863 – April 1873[13]
> Assisted by Robert Elliott, May 1863 – May 1871[14]
> Assisted by John Franks, December 1871 – April 1873[15]

John Franks, April 1873 – April 1876[16]
> Assisted by Ernest Dowling, April 1873 – September 1874[17]
> Assisted by a Warder from Darlinghurst Gaol, December 1875[18]
> Assisted by William Tucker, ? – April 1876[19]

William Tucker, May 1876 – July 1876[20]
> Assisted by Robert Howard, June 1876 – July 1876[21]

Robert Howard, August 1876 – May 1904[22]
> Assisted by an unidentified man, May 1877[23]
> Operated without an assistant, December 1877[24]

Assisted by Risby, June 1879 – January 1880[25]
Assisted by Reed, June 1881[26]
Assisted by a new man (first and last job), September 1888[27]
Assisted by a new man (first and last job), January 1889[28]
Assisted by James Goaler (or Golder), November 1889 – December 1892[29]
Assisted by Charles Begg, April 1884[30]
Assisted by Goldrick, May – September 1894[31]
Assisted by Samuel Godkin, October 1894 – May 1904[32]

George Russell, June 1904 – March 1908[33]
Assisted by Samuel Godkin, June 1904[34]

Executioner's position permanently abolished, 1908[35]

James Golder (or Goaler), May 1908 – April 1911[36]

Assistant executioner's position publicly listed for last time, 1917[37]
Casual executioners until last execution in New South Wales, March 1908 – August 1939[38]
Capital punishment abolished in New South Wales, 1985[39]

APPENDIX B

THE PATIENTS OF ROBERT 'NOSEY BOB' HOWARD

SCENE OF THE EXECUTION, SKETCHED ON THE SPOT.

FIGURE 15 Nosey Bob deals with Frank Butler

SOURCE *Truth*, 18 July 1897, p. 5

Not all drop lengths were reported in the coverage of executions. Inclusion of this detail became more common after the release of the first table of drops in 1888. In a reflection of the racism of the day, the drops for First Nations men and Chinese men were not always reported.

Patients identified here as being strangled were those who did not suffer an instant death, but their additional suffering attracted little, if any, attention in newspapers. Patients identified as being slowly strangled were the ones who generated public outrage.

	Patient	Crime	Hanged	Gaol	Drop	Death
	Nosey Bob as Assistant Executioner					
1	George Pitt	Murder	21.6.1876	Mudgee	---	Instant
2	Michael Connolly	Murder	28.6.1876	Tamworth	7 feet	Instant
3	Daniel Boon	Murder	19.7.1876	Wagga Wagga	'sufficient'	Instant
	Nosey Bob as Principal Executioner					
4	Thomas Newman	Murder	29.5.1877	Dubbo	---	Instant
5	Peter Murdick	Murder	18.12.1877	Wagga Wagga	8 feet	Strangled
6	In Chee	Murder	28.5.1878	Goulburn	---	Instant
7	Alfred	Rape	10.6.1879	Mudgee	---	Instant
8	Thomas Rogan	Murder	20.1.1880	Darlinghurst	6 or 7 feet	Strangled
9	Andrew G Scott	Murder	20.1.1880	Darlinghurst	6 or 7 feet	Instant
10	Albert	Murder	26.5.1880	Dubbo	---	Instant
11	Dan King	Murder	11.6.1880	Tamworth	---	Instant
12	William Brown	Rape	29.3.1881	Darlinghurst	6 feet	Instant

	Patient	Crime	Hanged	Gaol	Drop	Death
13	Henry Wilkinson	Murder	1.6.1881	Albury	---	Instant
14	John McGuan	Murder	22.11.1882	Armidale	8 or 9 feet	Instant
15	Charles Cunningham	Attempted murder	29.11.1882	Goulburn	---	Instant
16	Henry Tester	Murder	7.12.1882	Deniliquin	'not sufficiently great'	Slowly strangled
17	George Rugsborne	Murder	23.5.1883	Armidale	10 feet	Instant
18	William Rice	Murder	23.4.1884	Darlinghurst	10 feet	Instant
19	Joseph Gordon	Murder	13.6.1884	Deniliquin	8 feet	Instant
20	Charles Watson	Murder	14.4.1885	Darlinghurst	11 or 12 feet	Strangled
21	Thomas Williams	Attempted murder	14.7.1885	Darlinghurst	---	Strangled
22	Matthew Friske	Murder	10.12.1885	Grafton	---	Instant
23	William Liddiard	Murder	8.6.1886	Grafton	---	Almost decapitated
24	Alfred Reynolds	Murder	8.10.1886	Darlinghurst	6 feet	Instant
25	George Duffy	Rape	7.1.1887	Darlinghurst	8 feet 6 inches	Instant
26	Joseph Martin	Rape	7.1.1887	Darlinghurst	8 feet 6 inches	Slowly strangled
27	William Boyce	Rape	7.1.1887	Darlinghurst	8 feet 6 inches	Slowly Strangled
28	Robert Read	Rape	7.1.1887	Darlinghurst	8 feet 6 inches	Slowly strangled
29	John Creighan	Murder	29.5.1888	Armidale	7 feet	Instant
30	Robert Hewart	Murder	11.9.1888	Darlinghurst	8 feet	Instant
31	Louisa Collins	Murder	8.1.1889	Darlinghurst	5 feet 6 inches	Almost decapitated
32	James Morrison	Murder	20.8.1889	Darlinghurst	12 feet	Instant

	Patient	Crime	Hanged	Gaol	Drop	Death
33	Thomas Reilly	Murder	6.11.1889	Wagga Wagga	9 feet	Instant
34	Albert Smidt	Murder	18.11.1890	Wagga Wagga	6 feet 6 inches	Instant
35	Lars P Hansen	Murder	2.6.1891	Dubbo	8 feet	Instant
36	Maurice Dalton	Murder	17.11.1891	Darlinghurst	6 feet	Almost decapitated
37	Harold D Mallalieu	Murder	26.11.1891	Dubbo	9 feet	Instant
38	Jimmy Tong	Murder	29.11.1892	Armidale	'the required distance'	Instant
39	Edward Smedley	Murder	13.6.1893	Darlinghurst	9 feet 6 inches	Strangled
40	George MW Archer	Murder	11.7.1893	Darlinghurst	9 feet	Slowly strangled
41	John Makin	Murder	15.8.1893	Darlinghurst	10 feet 6 inches	Instant
42	Jemmy Hoy	Murder	24.11.1893	Mudgee	---	Instant
43	Edwin H Glasson	Murder	29.11.1893	Bathurst	7 feet	Instant
44	Charles Montgomery	Attempted murder	31.5.1894	Darlinghurst	10 feet	Instant
45	Thomas Williams	Attempted murder	31.5.1894	Darlinghurst	8 feet	Slowly strangled
46	John Cummings	Murder	20.7.1894	Tamworth	8 feet	Instant
47	Alexander Lee	Murder	20.7.1894	Tamworth	8 feet	Instant
48	Frederick Dennis	Murder	11.12.1894	Bathurst	7 feet	Instant
49	Alfred Grenon	Attempted murder	31.1.1895	Darlinghurst	7 feet	Instant
50	Thomas M Sheridan	Murder	7.1.1896	Darlinghurst	9 feet 6 inches	Instant

	Patient	Crime	Hanged	Gaol	Drop	Death
51	Charles Hines	Rape	21.5.1897	Maitland	7 feet 6 inches	Instant
52	Thomas Moore	Murder	24.6.1897	Dubbo	7 feet 9 inches	Decapitated
53	Frank Butler	Murder	16.7.1897	Darlinghurst	7 feet 5 or 6 inches	Instant
54	Wong Ming	Murder	13.12.1898	Dubbo	8 feet 2 inches	Instant
55	Stuart WC Briggs	Murder	5.4.1899	Darlinghurst	7 feet 6 inches	Instant
56	John Sleigh	Murder	5.12.1900	Goulburn	7 feet 9 inches	Instant
57	Jacky Underwood	Murder	14.1.1901	Dubbo	'lengthy'	Instant
58	Jimmy Governor	Murder	18.1.1901	Darlinghurst	7 feet 6 inches	Instant
59	Joseph FA Campbell	Rape	20.12.1901	Darlinghurst	7 feet 9 inches	Instant
60	Thomas Moore	Murder	14.4.1903	Darlinghurst	8 feet 10 inches	Instant
61	Digby Grand	Murder	7.7.1903	Darlinghurst	9 feet 6 inches	Slowly strangled
62	Henry Jones	Murder	7.7.1903	Darlinghurst	8 feet 6 inches	Instant

FIGURE 16 **Autograph of Robert Howard**

SOURCE State Library of NSW, no date, DLDOC 2

SELECT BIBLIOGRAPHY

ARTICLES AND BOOKS

Allen, JA, *Sex and Secrets: Crimes Involving Australian Women since 1880*, Oxford University Press, Oxford, 1990.

Anderson, S, *A History of Capital Punishment in the Australian Colonies, 1788–1900*, Palgrave Macmillan, London, 2020.

Arasse, D, *The Guillotine and the Terror*, C Miller (trans), Penguin Books, London, [1987]1989.

Azize, J, 'The prerogative of mercy in NSW', *Public Space: The Journal of Law and Social Justice*, vol. 1, art. 6, 2007, pp. 1–36.

Bagnall, K, 'Rewriting the history of Chinese families in nineteenth-century Australia', *Australian Historical Studies*, vol. 42, no. 1, 2011, pp. 62–77.

Barr, J, 'Judicial hanging', *Lancet*, vol. 123, no. 3171, 1884, pp. 1023–25.

Beattie, JM, 'Scales of justice: Defense counsel and the English criminal trial in the eighteenth and nineteenth centuries', *Law and History Review*, vol. 9, no. 2, 1991, pp. 221–67.

Beck, D, *Hope in Hell: A History of the Darlinghurst Gaol and the National Art School*, Allen & Unwin, Sydney, 2005.

Beckett, R & R Beckett, *Hangman: The Life and Times of Alexander Green, Public Executioner to the Colony of New South Wales*, Thomas Nelson, Melbourne, 1980.

Bedford, R, *The Snare of Strength*, William Heinemann, London, 1905.

Bennett, M, *Pathfinders: A History of Aboriginal Trackers in NSW*, NewSouth, Sydney, 2020.

Berry, J, *My Experiences as an Executioner*, Percy Lund & Co, London, 1892.

Blackstone, W, *Commentaries on the Laws of England* [IV volumes], Clarendon Press, Oxford, 1765–69.

Bladen, FM (ed.), *Historical Records of New South Wales* [VII volumes], Government Printer, Sydney, 1892–1901.

Borg, MJ & ML Radelet, 'On botched executions', P Hodgkinson & WA Schabas (eds), *Capital Punishment*, Cambridge University Press, Cambridge, [2004]2009, pp. 143–68.

Brennan, A, 'The thirteenth juror', *The Incredible Saint*, Frank Johnson, Sydney, c. 1954–55, pp. 62–95.

Castle, T, 'Constructing death: Newspaper reports of executions in colonial New South Wales, 1826–1837', *Journal of Australian Colonial History*, vol. 9, 2007, pp. 51–68.

——, 'Watching them hang: Capital punishment and public support in colonial New South Wales', *History Australia*, vol. 5, no. 2, 2008, pp. 43.1–43.15.

Cobley, J, *Sydney Cove*, vol. I (1788) [V volumes], Angus & Robertson, Sydney, [1962]1980.

Collins, D, *An Account of the English Colony in New South Wales: With Remarks on the Dispositions, Customs, Manners, &c. of the Native Inhabitants of that Country* [II volumes], Cadell & Davies, London, 1798 & 1802.

Cossins, A, *The Baby Farmers: A Chilling Tale of Missing Babies, Shameful Secrets and Murder in 19th Century Australia*, Allen & Unwin, Sydney, 2013.

Creed, JM, *My Recollections of Australia and Elsewhere, 1842–1914*, H Jenkins, London, 1916.

Crofton Croker, T (ed.), *Memoirs of Joseph Holt: General of the Irish Rebels in 1798*, vol. II [II volumes], Henry Colburn, London, 1838.

Cunneen, C, *William John McKell: Boilermaker, Premier, Governor-General*, UNSW Press, Sydney, 2000.

Currey, J, *David Collins: A Colonial Life*, Melbourne University Press, Melbourne, 2000.

Cushing, N, 'Woman as murderer: The defence of Louisa Collins', *Journal of Interdisciplinary Gender Studies*, vol. 1, no. 2, 1996, pp. 147–57.

Dawson, C, *No Ordinary Run of Men: The Queensland Executioners*, Inside History, Brisbane, 2010.

Duff, C, *A Handbook on Hanging: Being a Short Introduction to the Fine Art of Execution*, Nonsuch Publishing, Gloucestershire, [1928]2006.

Field, D, *Crimes that Shaped the Law*, LexisNexis Butterworths, Sydney, 2015.

Finnane, M, *Punishment in Australian Society*, Oxford University Press, Oxford, 1997.

Foster, JK, *The Dark Man: Australia's First Serial Killer*, Big Sky Publishing, Sydney, 2013.

Foucault, M, *Discipline and Punish: The Birth of the Prison*, A Sheridan (trans), Penguin Books, London, [1977]1991.

Frost, A, *Arthur Phillip 1738–1814*, Oxford University Press, Oxford, 1987.

——, *Botany Bay and the First Fleet: The Real Story*, Black Inc, Melbourne, [2011]2019.

Furphy, J, *Such is Life: Being Certain Extracts from the Diary of Tom Collins*, Bulletin Newspaper Co, Sydney, 1903.

Gascoigne, J, *The Enlightenment and the Origins of European Australia*, Cambridge University Press, Cambridge, 2002.

Gatrell, VAC, *The Hanging Tree: Execution and the English People 1770–1868*, Oxford University Press, Oxford, 1994.

Ghanem, KG, S Ram & PA Rice, 'The modern epidemic of syphilis', *New England Journal of Medicine*, vol. 382, no. 9, 2020, pp. 845–54.

Gilchrist, C, *Murder, Misadventure and Miserable Ends*, HarperCollins, Sydney, 2019.

Gleeson, K, 'From centenary to the Olympics, gang rape in Sydney', *Current Issues in Criminal Justice*, vol. 16, no. 2, 2004, pp. 183–201.

Godfrey, B & P Lawrence, *Crime and Justice since 1750*, 2nd ed., Routledge, Oxford, 2015.

Grabosky, PN, *Sydney in Ferment: Crime, Dissent and Official Reaction, 1788 to 1973*, Australian National University Press, Canberra, 1977.

Gregory, J, *Victorians Against the Gallows: Capital Punishment and the Abolitionist Movement in Nineteenth Century Britain*, Bloomsbury, London, [2012]2020.

Griffen-Foley, B (ed.), *A Companion to the Australian Media*, Australian Scholarly Publishing, Melbourne, 2014.

Haggerty, EK, *Path to Abolition* [Exhibition Catalogue], Sir Harry Gibbs Legal Heritage Centre, Brisbane, June, 2014.

Handbook, Department of Justice New South Wales, Government Printer, Sydney, 1892–1896.

Harris, S, *Solomon's Noose: The True Story of Her Majesty's Hangman of Hobart*, Melbourne Books, Melbourne, 2015.

Harrison, P, 'The life of Alexander Green revisited: Did he really hang 490 criminals in the colony of New South Wales?', *Journal of the Royal Australian Historical Society*, vol. 103, no. 2, 2017, pp. 181–200.

Haughton, S, 'On hanging considered from a mechanical and physiological point of view', *London, Edinburgh and Dublin Philosophical Magazine and Journal of Science*, vol. 32, no. 213, 1866, pp. 23–34.

Heaton, JH, *Australian Dictionary of Dates and Men of the Time*, George Robertson, Sydney, 1879.

Hijikata, S, I Hongo, S Nakayama, T Yamaguchi, Y Sekikawa, T Nozato & T Ashikaga, 'Infective endocarditis due to *Treponema pallidum*: A case diagnosed using polymerase chain reaction analysis of aortic valve', *Canadian Journal of Cardiology*, vol. 35, 2019, pp. 104.e9–104.e11.

Howard, A, *Rope: A History of the Hanged*, New Holland, London, 2016.

Isaacs, V & R Kirkpatrick, *Two Hundred Years of Sydney Newspapers: A Short History*, Rural Press, Sydney, 2003.

James, R & R Nasmyth-Jones, 'The occurrence of cervical fractures in victims of judicial hanging', *Forensic Science International*, vol. 54, 1992, pp. 81–91.

Johns, R, *Trial by Jury: Recent Developments*, NSW Parliamentary Library Research Service, Sydney, 2005.

Johnson, S, M Quinlisk, R Mills & C Morris, *Long Bay Correctional Complex Conservation Management Plan*, Clive Lucas Stapleton & Partners, Sydney, 2004.

Jones, B (ed.), *The Penalty is Death*, Sun Books, Melbourne, 1968.

Kaladelfos, A, 'The "condemned criminals": Sexual violence, race and manliness in colonial Australia', *Women's History Review*, vol. 21, no. 5, 2012, pp. 697–714.

Karskens, G, *The Colony: A History of Early Sydney*, Allen & Unwin, Sydney, [2009]2010.

——, *People of the River: Lost Worlds of Early Australia*, Allen & Unwin, Sydney, 2020.

Keneally, T, *The Commonwealth of Thieves: The Sydney Experiment*, Random House, Sydney, [2005]2006.

Kercher, B, 'Recovering and reporting Australia's early colonial case law: the Macquarie Project', *Law and History Review*, vol. 18, no. 3, 2000, pp. 659–65.

——, *An Unruly Child: A History of Law in Australia*, Routledge, Oxford, [1995]2020.

Lawson, H, *The Rising of the Court and Other Sketches in Prose and Verse*, Angus & Robertson, Sydney, 1910.

Lawson, S, *Archibald's Paradox: A Strange Case of Authorship*, Miegunyah Press, Melbourne, [1983]2006.

Lee, F, *Abolition of Capital Punishment: A Lecture*, Hanson and Bennet Printers, Sydney, 1864.

Lennan, J & G Williams, 'The death penalty in Australian law', *Sydney Law Review*, vol. 34, 2012, pp. 659–94.

The Life of John Knatchbull: Executed at Darlinghurst, Sydney, on Tuesday, February 13, 1844, for the Horrid Murder of Mrs Jamieson, H Evers, Sydney, 1844.

Linnell, G, *Moonlite: The Tragic Love Story of Captain Moonlite and the Bloody End of the Bushrangers*, Michael Joseph, Sydney, 2020.

Lobban, M, 'Rationalising the common law: Blackstone and his predecessors', A Page & W Prest (eds), *Blackstone and His Critics*, Hart, Oxford, 2018, pp. 1–22.

Lydon, J & L Ryan (eds), *Remembering the Myall Creek Massacre*, NewSouth, Sydney, 2018.

McConville, S, *English Local Prisons, 1860–1900: Next Only to Death*, Routledge, Oxford, [1995]2018.

McCulloch, JES, 'Baby-farming and benevolence in Brisbane, 1885–1915', *Hecate*, vol. 36, no. 1/2, 2010, pp. 42–56.

McLeod, H, 'God and the gallows: Christianity and capital punishment in the nineteenth and twentieth centuries', *Studies in Church History*, vol. 40, 2004, pp. 330–56.

McNab, D, *Waterfront: Graft, Corruption and Violence – Australia's Crime Frontier from 1788 to Now*, Hachette, Sydney, 2015.

Main, J, *Hanged*, Bas Publishing, Melbourne, 2007.

Melbourne, ACV, *Early Constitutional Development in Australia, New South Wales 1788–1856*, Oxford University Press, London, 1934.

Morgan, K, *The Particulars of Executions 1894–1967: The Hidden Truth about*

Capital Punishment at the Old Melbourne Gaol & Pentridge Prison, Old Melbourne Gaol, Melbourne, 2004.

Murray, L, *Sydney Cemeteries: A Field Guide*, NewSouth, Sydney, 2016.

O'Donohue, J, 'The short life of First Fleeter Thomas Barrett', *Founders*, vol. 50, no. 5, 2019.

Oldfield, J, *The Penalty of Death, or, the Problem of Capital Punishment*, G Bell & Sons, London, 1901.

Overington, C, *Last Woman Hanged: The Terrible, True Story of Louisa Collins*, HarperCollins, Sydney, 2014.

Pembroke, M, *Arthur Phillip: Sailor, Mercenary, Governor, Spy*, Hardie Grant Books, Melbourne, [2013]2014.

Phelps, J, *Australian Heist: The Incredible True Story of Australia's Biggest Steal*, HarperCollins, Sydney, 2018.

Plater, D & S Milne, '"The quality of mercy is not strained": The Norfolk Island mutineers and the exercise of the death penalty in colonial Australia 1824–1860', *Australia and New Zealand Law and History Journal*, vol. 1, 2012, pp. 1–43.

Potas, I & J Walker, 'No. 3: Capital punishment', *Trends and Issues in Crime and Criminal Justice*, Australian Institute of Criminology, Canberra, 1987, pp. 1–6.

Potter, H, *Hanging in Judgment: Religion and the Death Penalty in England*, Continuum, New York, 1993.

Public Service List, NSW Government Printing Office, Sydney, 1897–1917.

Ramsland, J, *With Just but Relentless Discipline: A Social History of Corrective Services in New South Wales*, Kangaroo Press, Sydney, 1996.

Rayes, M, M Mittal, SM Rengachary & S Mittal, 'Hangman's fracture: A historical and biomechanical perspective', *Journal of Neurosurgery: Spine*, vol. 14, February, 2011, pp. 198–208.

Report of the Committee Appointed to Inquire into the Existing Practice as to carrying out Sentences of Death, and the Causes which in several recent Cases have led either to failure or to unseemly occurrences [Aberdare Report], Eyre & Spottiswoode, London, 1888.

Richards, M, *The Hanged Man: The Life and Death of Ronald Ryan*, Scribe, Melbourne, 2002.

Robert 'Nosey Bob' Howard (1832–1906), WLLSC, Sydney, 2009.

Robin, GD, 'The executioner: His place in English society', *British Journal of Sociology*, vol. 15, no. 3, 1964, pp. 234–53.

Rothman, DJ, *The Discovery of the Asylum: Social Order and Disorder in the New Republic*, rev. ed., Routledge, Oxford, [2002]2017.

Sands Sydney, Suburban and Country Commercial Directory, John Sands Ltd, Sydney, [1858–1933, but not published in 1872, 1874, 1878 & 1881] 1871, 1873, 1875–77, 1879–80, 1882–1901.

Schneebaum G & SJ Lavi, 'The riddle of *sub-judice* and the modern law of contempt', *Critical Analysis of Law*, vol. 2, no. 1, 2015, pp. 173–98.

Schofield-Georgeson, E, *By What Authority? Criminal Law in Colonial New South Wales 1788–1861*, Australian Scholarly Publishing, Melbourne, 2018.

Shaw, AGL, *Convicts and the Colonies: A Study of Penal Transportation from Great Britain and Ireland to Australia and other parts of the British Empire*, Melbourne University Press, Melbourne, [1966]1981.

Spierenburg, P, *A History of Murder: Personal Violence in Europe from the Middle Ages to the Present*, Polity Press, Cambridge, 2008.

Sturma, M, 'Death and ritual on the gallows: Public executions in the Australian penal colonies', *Omega*, vol. 17, no. 1, 1986-87, pp. 89–100.

Taylor, AJ, *Capital Punishment: Reasons Why the Death Penalty should be Abolished, with Suggestions for an Efficient Substitute*, Davies Bros, Hobart, 1877.

Thomas, DJ, 'Hospital reports, Melbourne Hospital [operation on John Cooke]', *The Australian Medical Journal*, January, 1871, pp. 12–14.

Travers, R, *Murder in the Blue Mountains: Being the True Story of Frank Butler One of Australia's Most Notorious Criminals*, Hutchinson Australia, Melbourne, 1972.

Twomey, A, *The Constitution of New South Wales*, Federation Press, Sydney, 2004.

Walker, RB, *The Newspaper Press in New South Wales, 1803–1920*, Sydney University Press, Sydney, 1976.

Ward, R, *The Office of the Sheriff: A Millennium of Tradition*, Department of Courts Administration, Sydney, 1992.

Wardley, E, *The Abolition of Capital Punishment Considered by 'Fiat Justitia'*, Gibbs, Shallard, & Co, Sydney, 1869.

Watson, F (ed.), *Historical Records of Australia*, ser. I [XXVI volumes], Library Committee of the Commonwealth Parliament, Canberra, 1914–25.

——, *Historical Records of Australia*, ser. IV [I volume], Library Committee of the Commonwealth Parliament, Canberra, 1922.

Waverley Council, *Draft Waverley Council Heritage Assessment*, vol. I [II volumes], Waverley Council, Sydney, 2020.

Whitman, JQ, *The Origins of Reasonable Doubt: Theological Roots of the Criminal Trial*, Yale University Press, New Haven, 2008.

Wilkes, GA, *A Dictionary of Australian Colloquialisms*, new ed., Sydney University Press in association with Oxford University Press, Sydney and Oxford, 1990.

Woods, GD, *A History of Criminal Law in New South Wales 1788–1900*, Federation Press, Sydney, 2002.

——, *A History of Criminal Law in New South Wales 1901–1955*, Federation Press, Sydney, 2018.

Young, S, *Paper Emperors: The Rise of Australia's Newspaper Empires*, UNSW
Press, Sydney, 2019.

ARCHIVAL COLLECTIONS AND UNPUBLISHED MATERIALS

Bondi, Queenscliff, Ben Buckler Estate, 1882, SLNSW, 064-Z/SP/
B23/641882.

Borough of Waverley, Bondi Ward, Rate Books, 1884–1923, WLLSC.

Certificates of Execution, 1873–96, NSWSA, NRS-13240.

Clark, R, 'A Journal [First Fleet]', c. 1790, SLNSW, SAFE 1/27a.

Collectors' Books, Census, 1891, NSWSA, NRS-683.

Collectors' Books, Census, 1901, NSWSA, NRS-685.

Colonial Secretary's Papers, 1788–1826, NSWSA, NRS-897.

Colonial Secretary's Papers, 1826–1982, NSWSA, NRS-905.

Colonial Secretary's Papers, Special Bundles, 1874–1900, NSWSA, NRS-906.

Condemned Prisoners' Daily Record [Darlinghurst Gaol], 1892–1903,
NSWSA, NRS-2163.

Convict Indents, First Fleet, Second Fleet and Ships to 1801, 1788–1801,
NSWSA, NRS-1150.

Convicts Embarked, New South Wales, 1787, TNA, HO 10.

Copies of Letters Sent [Sheriff], 1831–1923, NSWSA, NRS-13210.

Copies of Letters Sent by Gaoler and Visiting Justice [Maitland Gaol],
1849–1877, NSWSA, NRS-2316.

Copies of Letters Sent to the Colonial Secretary, 1851–1879, NSWSA,
NRS-1825.

Copies of Miscellaneous Returns [Sheriff], 1894–1910, NSWSA, NRS-13230.

Copy of Letter Received [Comptroller General of Prisons], 1876, CSNSW
Museum.

Darlinghurst Gaol Death Register, 1867–1914 [transcript], in Norrie, P, 'An
analysis of the causes of death in Darlinghurst Gaol 1867–1914, and
the fate of the homeless in nineteenth-century Sydney', MA Thesis,
University of Sydney, 2007.

Darlinghurst Gaol Ground Plan, 1890, WL Vernon, Government Printing
Office, SLNSW, 89/457.

Entrance to Darlinghurst Gaol, 1887, photographer unknown, Government
Printing Office, SLNSW, SPF/169.

Franks, R, 'Documenting our most heinous sins: True crime and the conscience
collective in colonial Australia', PhD Thesis, University of Sydney, 2020.

Funeral Register, 1906, Walter Carter Funerals.

Gallows at Darlinghurst Gaol, from the Keep Yard, before 1914, creator
unknown, SLNSW, SSVl/Gao/Darh/2.

Governor's Diary [Darlinghurst Gaol], 1873–99, NSWSA, NRS-2162.

Grave 82/83, Church of England Ordinary, Section 2, Waverley Cemetery.

Howard, R, 'Autograph of Robert Howard, the New South Wales hangman', n.d., SLNSW, DLDOC 2.

Howard, Robert: Probate Packet, 1880–1939, NSWSA, NRS-13660-5-SC001531 in series 4_36697.

Howard, Robert [vertical file]: 'Nosey Bob' the Hangman, 1832–1906, WLLSC, VF HOWA.

In this cottage at North Bondi, Sydney, lived Nosey Bob, the famous hangman, c. 1914–c. 1941, AC Dreier Postcard Collection, SLV, H22729.

Jacobson, FJ, 'Correspondence concerning an improved gallows', 1893, NAA, A4618 4544.

John Feltham Archibald and John Haynes, journalists of *The Bulletin*, in Darlinghurst Gaol, c. 1882, photographer unknown, SLNSW, P1/58.

Judge Advocate, Pardons, 1788–1803, NSWSA, NRS-5601.

Ledger – Stores [Darlinghurst Gaol], 1887–88, NSWSA, NRS-2180.

Map of Sydney in 1802, updated in 1873, 1802 & 1873, Norman Selfe after Charles A Lesueur, SLNSW, Z M2 811.17 1802 2.

Minutes of Executive Council Meetings, 1875–1901, NSWSA, NRS-4232.

Miscellaneous Notes Relating to Gaols, 1876–92, NSWSA, NRS-13223.

Plan de la ville de Sydney, capitale des colonies anglaises aux terres australes 1802 [detail], 1824, Arthus Bertrand, Paris, SLNSW, Ce 82/2.

Plan of Darlinghurst Gaol, 1891, Henry Louis Bertrand, SLNSW, SV1/Gao/Darh/3.

Prison Commission and Home Office Prison Department, 'Execution procedures: Table of drops', 1904–06, TNA, PCOM 8/212.

Prison Commission and Home Office Prison Department, 'Execution procedures: Table of drops', 1912–14, TNA, PCOM 8/213.

Punishment Books [Darlinghurst Gaol], 1867–1914, NSWSA, NRS-2182.

Rauch, E, 'Hanging by a thread: The 1848 conviction and execution of Patrick Bryan for the murder of Mrs Eliza Neilson', BA(Hons) Thesis, Southern Cross University, 2021.

Record of Officers' Services [Darlinghurst Gaol], 1862–1914, NSWSA, NRS-2177.

Record of Prison Staff, 1843–1931, NSWSA, NRS-1837.

Registers of Immigrant Ships' Arrivals, 1848–1912, QSA, S13086.

Register of Inquests and Inquiries [Sydney City Coroner], 1862–1941, NSWSA, NRS-1783.

Richmond Park, Richmond, Government Road … through to Maud Street, 1882–1937, SLNSW, 003-Z/SP/R8/3 & 007-Z/SP/R8/9.

Royal Navy Registers of Seamen's Services [Samuel Joseph Godkin, Service No. 107188], 1848–1939, TNA, ADM 188.

Secretary of State for the Colonies, 'Circulars on capital punishment', 27 June & 28 December 1880, QSA, ITM17282.

Sheridan, TM, 'Epitome de ma vie [Abridgement of my life]', 1896, SLNSW, MLMSS 6526.

Sheriff's Letter Book, June 1875–June 1887, NSWSA, NUA-588 [10].

Sheriff's Office, SCV, 'Particulars of executions book: Table of drops', 1894–1967, PROV, VPRS 14526.

Sheriff's Private Letter Book, 1889, NSWSA, NUA-588 [9].

Sheriff's Staff Register, 1900–44, NSWSA, NRS-13234.

Smyth, AB, 'A Journal [First Fleet]', c. 1790, SLNSW, SAFE 1/15.

Worgan, GB, 'A Journal [First Fleet]', 1788, SLNSW, SAFE 1/114.

WEB RESOURCES

Ancestry, Ancestry LLC, Lehi, <www.ancestry.com.au>.

AIATSIS, Australian Institute for Aboriginal and Torres Strait Islander Studies, Canberra, <aiatsis.gov.au>.

AustLII, Australasian Legal Information Institute, Sydney, <www.austlii.edu.au>.

AustLit, Resource for Australian Literary, Print, and Narrative Cultures, University of Queensland, Brisbane, <www.austlit.edu.au>.

Australian Dictionary of Biography, Australian National University, Canberra, <adb.anu.edu.au>.

Australian Medical Pioneers Index, State Library of Victoria, Melbourne, <www.medicalpioneers.com>.

Colonial Case Law, Macquarie Law School, Sydney, <www.law.mq.edu.au/research/colonial_case_law/>.

Criminal Indictments Index, 1836–1919, NSWSA, Sydney, <www.records.nsw.gov.au/archives/collections-and-research/guides-and-indexes/node/10885171/browse>.

Dictionary of Sydney, State Library of NSW, Sydney, <home.dictionaryofsydney.org>.

Documenting a Democracy, Museum of Australian Democracy, Canberra, <www.foundingdocs.gov.au/area-aid-3.html>.

Family History, Births, Deaths and Marriages NSW, Sydney, <familyhistory.bdm.nsw.gov.au/lifelink/familyhistory/search?0>.

Family History Research Service, Births, Deaths and Marriages Queensland, Brisbane, <www.familyhistory.bdm.qld.gov.au>.

Former Members, Parliament of NSW, Sydney, <www.parliament.nsw.gov.au/members/formermembers/pages/former-members-index.aspx>.

General Register Office, Her Majesty's Passport Office, London, <www.gov.uk/order-copy-birth-death-marriage-certificate>.

Gaol Inmates and Prisoners Photos Index, 1870–1930, NSWSA, Sydney, <www.records.nsw.gov.au/archives/collections-and-research/guides-and-indexes/node/1566/browse>.

Hansard and House Papers, Parliament of NSW, Sydney, <www.parliament.nsw. gov.au/hansard/Pages/hansard-house-paper-overview.aspx>.

Judicial Commission of NSW, Judicial Commission of NSW, Sydney, <www.judcom.nsw.gov.au>.

NSW Capital Convictions Database, 1788–1954, Francis Forbes Society for Australian Legal History, Sydney, <research.forbessociety.org.au>.

NSW Law Almanacs, NSW Bar Association, Sydney, <lawalmanacs.info>.

NSW Legislation, Parliamentary Counsel's Office, Sydney, <www.legislation. nsw.gov.au>.

Trove, National Library of Australia, Canberra, <trove.nla.gov.au>.

ACKNOWLEDGMENTS

The transformation of an idea into a published work began with a conversation I had with Phillipa McGuinness and Andrew Tink. Thank you. Of course, this work would not have been possible without the wonderful team at NewSouth, especially Kathy Bail, Elspeth Menzies, Sophia Oravecz, Josephine Pajor-Markus and Gabriella Sterio. For indexing, I was fortunate to have the services of Neil Radford.

It meant a lot to have the warm support of Sharen Rees, Robert Howard's great-great-granddaughter.

I offer my thanks to John Frith of Flat Earth Mapping, Ingrid Grace at Waverley Library, Donna Newton at the Royal Australian Historical Society, as well as to Laura Signorelli, who was of assistance in the early days of this project. I am appreciative of the efforts of specialist staff at City of Sydney Archives, Corrective Services NSW, Liquorland at World Square, National Archives of Australia, NSW State Archives, Public Record Office Victoria, Queensland State Archives, State Library of NSW, Supreme Court of Victoria, Sydney Living Museums, The National Archives of the United Kingdom and Walter Carter Funerals.

I am, as always, grateful to my colleagues and friends for generous encouragement, patience, random acts of kindness, timely advice and the occasional glass of gin: Lynne Billington, Jillene Bydder, Darby Carr, Rodney

Cavalier, David Coombe, Patricia Curthoys, Nancy Cushing, Mark Dunn, Laila Ellmoos, Ellen Forsyth, Rosie Handley, Peter Hobbins, Wendy Holz, Joy Lai, Carol Liston, Jaidae McLachlan, Susan Mercer, Lisa Murray, Richard Neville, Sabrina Organo, Maggie Patton, Cathy Perkins, Anne Reddacliff, Alexandra Roginski, Philippa Scarf, Therese Scott, Kathi Spinks, John Vallance, Sean Volke, Rebekah Ward, Bonnie Wildie and Sally Young.

Edith Ho spent many hours patiently researching Chinese-language newspapers in Australia, looking for details of executions, while Kate Bagnall provided advice and information to help me better understand the histories of Chinese families in New South Wales. Melissa Jackson – Bundjalung woman, librarian and friend – helped me navigate stories of crime involving First Nations peoples.

Pamela Harrison was indispensable when it came to investigating Nosey Bob's predecessors. The assistance of Deborah Beck and Philip Norrie, who shared with me their knowledge of Darlinghurst Gaol during the days of Nosey Bob, was invaluable. Katherine Biber freely shared with me her time and expertise on law, order and Jimmy Governor.

Robert Clancy and Norman Olbourne offered critical medical insights. Robert Phiddian and Richard Scully made useful comments on cartoons depicting Nosey Bob. Gregory D Woods and John Dowd were of assistance in explaining some key points of colonial law. Kathy Bowrey spent much time teaching me about the law and its many challenges, for which I am very grateful.

For making me a better writer, I am indebted to Paula Hamilton, Peter Kirkpatrick, Craig Munro, Alistair Rolls and Elizabeth Webby.

Thanks, of course, go to Linda Brainwood for believing in this project from the very beginning, Bridget Griffen-Foley for checking in and Kim D Weinert for always being there. Simon Dwyer supplied expert project support services, including the provision of extraordinary amounts of caffeine.

DARLINGHURST
GAOL

Scale of Feet

1890.

GROUND PLAN

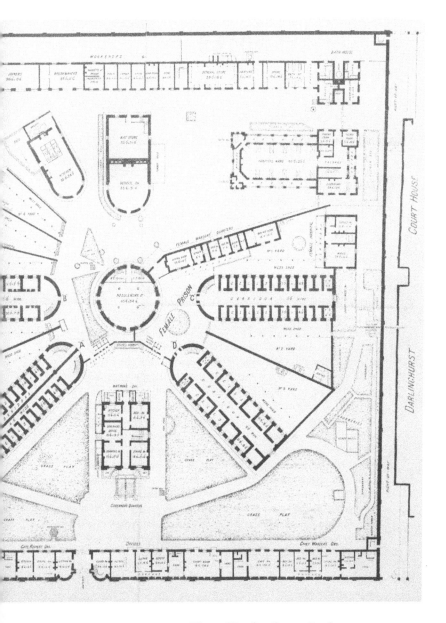

FIGURE 17 Plan of Darlinghurst Gaol

SOURCE Darlinghurst Gaol Ground Plan, 1890, WL Vernon,
Government Printing Office, State Library of NSW, 89/457

NOTES

INTRODUCTION: LOOKING FOR A NOSELESS HANGMAN
1   *Freeman's Journal*, 17 February 1906, p. 16.

1 LEARNING ON THE JOB
1   *Australian Star*, 16 August 1894, p. 5.
2   In this cottage at North Bondi, Sydney, lived Nosey Bob, the famous hangman, c. 1914–c. 1941, AC Dreier Postcard Collection, SLV, H22729.
3   There are no birth certificates in England or Wales before July 1837, forcing a reliance on baptism records. The Parish Register of the Holy Trinity Church, County of Norfolk lists Robert Rice Howard's baptism as 14 March 1832, line 525. A second entry lists the baptism as 12 March 1832: 'This child was privately baptized during my absence, and the Parents, neglected to give notice or to see it registered at the time. Arthur Browne, Vicar of Marham. Witness Mary Anne Howard, the mother of the child, her X mark', line 653. Both entries list Howard's parents as Henry and Mary Ann, but his record of death lists his parents as Henry and Mary Elsie. Robert Rice Howard: Death, 3 February 1906, NSWBDM, 3518/1906; Robert Rice Howard and Jane Townsend: Marriage, 26 October 1858, GROEW, MXH 826435; Mary Ann Howard: Baptism, 19 February 1860 [date of birth, 19 November 1859, in margin], Parish Register of the Christ Church Bermondsey, County of Surrey, line 203; Emily Jane Howard: Birth, 20 May 1862, Superintendent Registrar's District Tetbury, Counties of Gloucester and Wells, line 282; Edward Charles Howard: Birth, 29 November 1864, Superintendent Registrar's District Hendon, County of Middlesex, line 451; Registers of Immigrant Ships' Arrivals, 1848–1912, 27 February 1866, QSA, S13086; Fanny Howard: Birth, 13 June 1867, RBDB, line 7155; Sydney Howard: Birth, 5 November 1869, NSWBDM, 16207/1869; William George Howard: Birth, 30 June 1872, NSWBDM, 1660/1872.
4   *Mudgee Guardian and North-Western Representative*, 25 February 1915, p. 6.
5   *Truth*, 18 July 1897, pp. 5, 7; *Truth*, 20 January 1901, p. 5; *Kiama Reporter and Illawarra Journal*, 23 February 1901, p. 4; *Truth*, 22 May 1904, p. 3; *Truth*, 14 November 1915, p. 16; *Worker*, 3 August 1932, p. 5; *Sydney Morning Herald*, 13 March 1868, p. 2.

6   *Sands Sydney, Suburban and Country Commercial Directory*, John Sands
Ltd, Sydney, 1876–77; Fanny Howard's birth record (1867) has a
Brisbane address and Sydney Howard's birth record (1869) has a
Prospect address, although his marriage record (1896) states he was
born in Gosford. As an adult, Sydney started spelling his name Sidney.
Fanny Howard: Birth, 13 June 1867, RBDB, line 7155; Sydney Howard:
Birth, 5 November 1869, NSWBDM, 16207/1869; Sidney Howard and
Elizabeth Donohue: Marriage, 3 February 1896, NSWBDM, 332/1896.

7   *Sydney Morning Herald*, 15 July 1873, p. 4.

8   *Truth*, 18 July 1897, p. 7; *Mudgee Guardian and North-Western
Representative*, 25 February 1915, p. 6; *Table Talk*, 20 August 1897, p. 2.

9   *Bird O'Freedom*, 16 November 1895, p. 4; *Sunday Times*, 12 January 1896,
p. 2; *Bulletin*, 15 February 1896, p. 25.

10   *Truth*, 8 August 1915, p. 13; *Truth*, 27 June 1897, p. 1.

11   *Sands Sydney, Suburban and Country Commercial Directory*, John Sands
Ltd, Sydney, 1873 & 1875–77.

12   *Sydney Morning Herald*, 7 May 1874, p. 2; *Sydney Morning Herald*,
22 August 1874, p. 8.

13   Alexander Green was appointed hangman in 1834, replacing Thomas
Hughes, but his starting year is often listed as 1828, replacing Henry
Stain. Green was replaced by Robert Elliott, who was followed by Joseph
Bull. Bull's last job before being committed to the Benevolent Asylum
in Liverpool was the hanging of George Nichols and Alfred Lester for
the murder of William Percy Walker on 18 June 1872. Bull's health had
been in obvious decline since at least 1871. The next executioner was
John Franks (who is no relation to the author). Franks started as an
assistant, and his first job as principal was the double hanging of William
McCrow and Thomas Scource, both executed for murder, on 8 April
1873. His last job was Ah Chong, for murder, on 18 April 1876. Franks
was replaced by William Tucker. Pamela Harrison, 'The life of Alexander
Green revisited', *Journal of the Royal Australian Historical Society*, vol. 103,
no. 2, 2017, p. 188; Ray Beckett & Richard Beckett, *Hangman*, Thomas
Nelson, Melbourne, 1980, pp. 66–67, 187; *Evening News*, 18 June 1872,
p. 2; Copies of Letters Sent [Sheriff], 1831–1923, 16 June 1871, NSWSA,
NRS-13210; Copies of Letters Sent [Sheriff], 1831–1923, 5 December
1871, NSWSA, NRS-13210; *Northern Argus*, 15 April 1873, p. 3; *Evening
News*, 18 April 1876, p. 2; *Australian Town and Country Journal*, 24 June
1876, p. 9; *New South Wales Government Gazette*, 17 June 1896, p. 4182;
Public Service List, NSW Government Printing Office, Sydney, 1897,
p. 80; *Truth*, 22 May 1904, p. 3.

14   The lack of recordkeeping around criminal matters during the colonial
era has created gaps in the historical narratives of law and order. Even

essential records of courts were not kept, resulting in 'a great paucity of law reporting in colonial Australia'. Towards the end of the 19th century, James Gordon Legge compiled a set of reports based on newspaper accounts that documented selected cases in New South Wales from 1830 to 1862 [II volumes]. Following Legge's efforts is a series known as *Reports of Cases Argued and Determined in the Supreme Court of New South Wales*, which, also based on newspaper accounts, documents cases in the colony between 1863 and 1879 [XIII volumes]. Law reporting, as we know it today, did not commence until 1879 with the *New South Wales Law Reports*. Bruce Kercher, 'Recovering and reporting Australia's early colonial case law', *Law and History Review*, vol. 18, no. 3, 2000, pp. 660–61; Michel Foucault, *Discipline and Punish*, A Sheridan (trans), Penguin Books, London, [1977]1991, p. 9.

15   *Armidale Express and New England General Advertiser*, 29 September 1876, p. 2.

16   *Evening News*, 11 August 1875, p. 3; *Newcastle Chronicle*, 16 September 1875, p. 2.

17   *Evening News*, 17 April 1875, p. 5.

18   *Newcastle Chronicle*, 11 December 1875, p. 6.

19   *Sydney Morning Herald*, 19 April 1876, p. 5.

20   *Burrangong Argus and Burrowa, Murrumburrah, and Marengo General Advertiser*, 22 April 1876, p. 2.

21   *Evening News*, 18 April 1876, p. 2; *Newcastle Morning Herald and Miners' Advocate*, 20 April 1876, p. 3.

22   Deborah Beck, *Hope in Hell*, Allen & Unwin, Sydney, 2005, p. 137.

23   *Maitland Mercury and Hunter River General Advertiser*, 15 May 1873, p. 3; *Molong Argus*, 25 March 1898, p. 1; *Mudgee Guardian and North-Western Representative*, 20 June 1904, p. 2; Copies of Letters Sent [Sheriff], 1831–1923, 2 December 1873, NSWSA, NRS-13210.

24   Sheriff's Letter Book, 1875–1887, 1 June 1876, NSWSA, NUA-588 [10].

25   Copies of Letters Sent [Sheriff], 1831–1923, 21 November & 5 December 1871, NSWSA, NRS-13210; *Newcastle Morning Herald and Miners' Advocate*, 29 April 1876, p. 2; *Empire*, 27 November 1873, p. 2; *Empire*, 30 April 1874, p. 3; John Franks: Death, 27 April 1876, NSWBDM, 991/1876.

26   Copy of Letter Received [Comptroller General of Prisons], 2 May 1876, CSNSW Museum; *Sydney Morning Herald*, 26 May 1875, p. 6; *New South Wales Government Gazette*, 17 June 1896, p. 4182; *Public Service List*, NSW Government Printing Office, Sydney, 1897, p. 80.

27   The term 'Noose South Wales' was used by the *Bulletin* in the mid-1880s and picked up by several newspapers including *Australian Star* and *World's News*. Steven Anderson, *A History of Capital Punishment in the Australian*

Colonies, 1788–1900, Palgrave Macmillan, London, 2020, p. xiii; Ivan Potas & John Walker, 'No. 3: Capital punishment', *Trends and Issues in Crime and Criminal Justice*, Australian Institute of Criminology, Canberra, 1987, pp. 1–6; Jo Lennan & George Williams, 'The death penalty in Australian law', *Sydney Law Review*, vol. 34, 2012, p. 660.

28   *Colonial Times*, 12 June 1838 p. 7; *Maitland Mercury and Hunter River General Advertiser*, 16 March 1850, p. 2; *Brisbane Courier*, 25 October 1892, p. 2.

29   Harrison 2017, p. 182.

30   Eugenia Rauch, 'Hanging by a thread', BA(Hons) Thesis, Southern Cross University, 2021.

31   *Sydney Morning Herald*, 21 October 1848, p. 2.

32   James Berry, *My Experiences as an Executioner*, Percy Lund & Co, London, 1892, pp. 30–31; Samuel Haughton, 'On hanging considered from a mechanical and physiological point of view', *London, Edinburgh and Dublin Philosophical Magazine and Journal of Science*, vol. 32, no. 213, 1866, pp. 23–34; *Report of the Committee Appointed to Inquire into the Existing Practice as to carrying out Sentences of Death* [Aberdare Report], Eyre & Spottiswoode, London, 1888.

33   Josiah Oldfield, *The Penalty of Death*, G Bell & Sons, London, 1901, p. 161.

34   *Truth*, 27 June 1897, p. 1.

35   *Truth*, 18 July 1897, p. 7; *Molong Argus*, 3 February 1899, p. 8; *Yass Evening Tribune*, 16 February 1899, p.1; *Crookwell Gazette*, 21 February 1899, p. 4; *Voice*, 2 May 1936, p. 1.

36   *Australian Town and Country Journal*, 24 June 1876, p. 9; *Illawarra Mercury*, 3 August 1866, p. 4; *Sunday Times*, 12 January 1896, p. 2.

37   *Australian Town and Country Journal*, 24 June 1876, p. 9.

38   *Evening News*, 21 June 1876, p. 2.

39   *Evening News*, 12 April 1876, p. 3.

40   *Evening News*, 12 April 1876, p. 3.

41   *Evening News*, 12 April 1876, p. 3.

42   The *Imperial Acts Adoption Act 1837*, 8 Will.IV no. 2 (NSW) adopted several pieces of Imperial law including the *Act to prevent the Fact of a previous Conviction being given in Evidence to the Jury on the case before them except when Evidence to Character is given 1836*, 6 & 7 Will.IV c.111 (UK); *Queanbeyan Age*, 19 April 1876, p. 2.

43   *Naracoorte Herald*, 25 April 1876, p. 4; *Evening News*, 12 April 1876, p. 3.

44   *Maitland Mercury and Hunter River General Advertiser*, 29 June 1876, p. 4.

45   James Q Whitman, *The Origins of Reasonable Doubt*, Yale University Press, New Haven, 2008, p. 35. The Church of England was a vital supporter of the death penalty across the Empire. When the position of the Church

changed in the mid-20th century, abolition was inevitable. Harry Potter, *Hanging in Judgment*, Continuum, New York, 1993.

46   Anderson 2020, p. 98.

47   *Herald*, 8 July 1876, p. 2; *Manaro Mercury and Cooma and Bombala Advertiser*, 15 July 1876, p. 4.

48   Galia Schneebaum & Shai J Lavi, 'The riddle of sub-judice and the modern law of contempt', *Critical Analysis of Law*, vol. 2, no. 1, 2015, pp. 173–98; *Evening News*, 3 July 1876, p. 3.

49   Hugh McLeod, 'God and the gallows', *Studies in Church History*, vol. 40, 2004, p. 330.

2 ALLOWING THE LAW TO TAKE ITS COURSE

1   R v Howe [1826] NSWKR 2; [1826] NSWSupC 64; *The Monitor*, 27 October 1826, p. 3; *Sydney Gazette and New South Wales Advertiser*, 4 November 1826, p. 2.

2   *Judgment of Death Act 1823*, 4 Geo.IV c.48 (UK); GD Woods, *A History of Criminal Law in New South Wales 1788–1900*, Federation Press, Sydney, 2002, pp. 115–16; David Plater & Sue Milne, 'The quality of mercy is not strained', *Australia and New Zealand Law and History Journal*, vol. 1, 2012, p. 13; Bruce Kercher, *An Unruly Child*, Routledge, Oxford, [1995]2020, p. 22. When William Blackstone confessed to his role in the Bank of Australia robbery in 1828, giving up his fellow robbers, his evidence was tainted because he had previously been issued a death sentence that was then commuted. R v Farrell, Dingle and Woodward [1831] NSWSupC 44; (1831) NSWSelCas (Dowling) 136 (28 June 1831).

3   Frederick Watson (ed.), *Historical Records of Australia*, ser. IV, vol. I, Library Committee of the Commonwealth Parliament, Canberra, 1922, p. ix; AGL Shaw, *Convicts and the Colonies*, Melbourne University Press, Melbourne, [1966]1981, p. 21.

4   *New South Wales Act 1823*, 4 Geo.IV c.96 (UK); *Constitution [Conferral] Act 1855*, 18 & 19 Vict. c.54 (UK); Woods 2002, pp. 168, 285–91; Frederick Watson (ed.), *Historical Records of Australia*, ser. I, vol. XXII, Library Committee of the Commonwealth Parliament, Canberra, 1924, pp. 122–23, 178–79; Joseph Azize, 'The prerogative of mercy in NSW', *Public Space: The Journal of Law and Social Justice*, vol. 1, art. 6, 2007, pp. 4–5.

5   James Phelps, *Australian Heist*, HarperCollins, Sydney, 2018; *Sydney Mail*, 31 January 1863, p. 10; *Empire*, 26 February 1863, p. 5; *Sydney Morning Herald*, 21 April 1863, p. 5.

6   Phelps 2018; Colonial Secretary's Papers, 1826–1982, 1863, NSWSA, NRS-905 [63/1795] & [63/2215]; *Freeman's Journal*, 4 April 1863, p. 4.

7   Woods 2002, pp. 194–203.

8   *Manaro Mercury and Cooma and Bombala Advertiser*, 25 September 1875, p. 4; *Evening News*, 16 November 1875, p. 4.

9   *Evening News*, 13 April 1876, p. 2; *Freeman's Journal*, 3 June 1876, p. 15; *Australian Town and Country Journal*, 8 July 1876, p. 27.

10   *Evening News*, 24 July 1876, p. 3; *Evening News*, 18 January 1876, p. 2; *Wagga Wagga Advertiser*, 19 January 1876, p. 2.

11   *Sydney Morning Herald*, 14 April 1876, p. 3; *Sydney Mail and New South Wales Advertiser*, 15 April 1876, p. 498; *Sydney Morning Herald*, 12 June 1876, p. 2.

12   *Gundagai Times and Tumut, Adelong and Murrumbidgee District Advertiser*, 21 July 1876, p. 2; *Manaro Mercury and Cooma and Bombala Advertiser*, 29 July 1876, p. 3; *Australian Town and Country Journal*, 29 July 1876, p. 28. One account claimed that William Tucker was 'exquisitely dressed', but he was also so drunk he assaulted a police officer. *Burrangong Argus*, 22 July 1876, p. 3.

13   *Australian Town and Country Journal*, 29 July 1876, p. 28.

14   *Manaro Mercury*, 29 July 1876, p. 4; *Wagga Wagga Advertiser*, 22 July 1876, p. 2; *Burrangong Argus*, 26 July 1876, p. 3.

15   *Armidale Express and New England General Advertiser*, 28 July 1876, p. 2.

16   *Sydney Mail and New South Wales Advertiser*, 3 March 1877, p. 264; *Australian Town and Country Journal*, 24 February 1877, p. 6; *Freeman's Journal*, 14 April 1877, p. 2.

17   *Sydney Mail and New South Wales Advertiser*, 3 March 1877, p. 264.

18   *Sydney Mail and New South Wales Advertiser*, 14 April 1877, p. 463.

19   *Sydney Mail and New South Wales Advertiser*, 14 April 1877, p. 463.

20   *Freeman's Journal*, 14 April 1877, p. 2; *Maitland Mercury and Hunter River General Advertiser*, 10 April 1877, p. 3.

21   *Sydney Morning Herald*, 6 March 1877, p. 3.

22   *Kyneton Guardian*, 6 June 1877, p. 3; *Glen Innes Examiner and General Advertiser*, 13 June 1877, p. 5.

23   *Glen Innes Examiner and General Advertiser*, 13 June 1877, p. 5; *Freeman's Journal*, 2 June 1877, p. 9.

24   *Smith's Weekly*, 8 March 1919, p. 2; Robert Howard, 'Autograph of Robert Howard, the New South Wales hangman', n.d., SLNSW, DLDOC 2; *Truth*, 8 January 1899, p. 8.

25   *Albury Banner and Wodonga Express*, 13 October 1877, p. 13.

26   *Sydney Morning Herald*, 11 October 1877, p. 3; *Evening News*, 26 March 1877, p. 3; *Australian Town and Country Journal*, 6 October 1877, p. 9; JM Beattie, 'Scales of justice', *Law and History Review*, vol. 9, no. 2, 1991, p. 222; *Prisoners' Counsel Act 1836*, 6 & 7 Will.IV, c.114 (UK); *Defence on Trials for Felony Act 1840*, 4 Vict. no. 27 (NSW).

27   *Wagga Wagga Advertiser*, 19 December 1877, p. 2.

28   *Australian Town and Country Journal*, 22 December 1877, p. 40.

29   *Australian Town and Country Journal*, 22 December 1877, p. 40.

30   *Sydney Mail and New South Wales Advertiser*, 22 December 1877, p. 782.

31   GD Woods, *A History of Criminal Law in New South Wales 1901–1955*, Federation Press, Sydney, 2018, pp. 25–26.

32   *Truth*, 3 October 1897, p. 2; *Mudgee Guardian and North-Western Representative*, 25 February 1915, p. 6.

33   *Truth*, 3 October 1897, p. 2; Sheriff's Letter Book, 1875–1887, 1 June 1876, NSWSA, NUA-588 [10].

34   *New South Wales Government Gazette*, 17 June 1896, p. 4182; *Public Service List*, NSW Government Printing Office, Sydney, 1897, p. 80; Copies of Miscellaneous Returns [Sheriff], 1894–1910, NSWSA, NRS-13230; *Public Service List* 1903, p. 64; James Berry, *My Experiences as an Executioner*, Percy Lund & Co, London, 1892, pp. 117–23; Chris Dawson, *No Ordinary Run of Men*, Inside History, Brisbane, 2010, pp. 42–44; *Public Service List* 1917, p. 57.

35   *Truth*, 5 June 1904, p. 7.

36   *Truth*, 12 July 1903, p. 5; *Bulletin*, 15 February 1896, p. 25.

37   Garry Linnell, *Moonlite*, Michael Joseph, Sydney, 2020, pp. 6–8.

38   *Bulletin*, 15 February 1896, p. 25; *Truth*, 8 January 1899, p. 8.

39   Ray Beckett & Richard Beckett, *Hangman*, Thomas Nelson, Melbourne, 1980, pp. 185, 97; Pamela Harrison, 'The life of Alexander Green revisited', *Journal of the Royal Australian Historical Society*, vol. 103, no. 2, 2017, p. 186.

40   *Goulburn Herald and Chronicle*, 13 April 1878, p. 2.

41   *Goulburn Herald and Chronicle*, 13 April 1878, pp. 2–3.

42   *Goulburn Herald and Chronicle*, 29 May 1878, p. 2.

43   Robert 'Nosey Bob' Howard (*1832–1906*), WLLSC, Sydney, 2009, p. 2; Jane Howard: Death, 22 August 1878, NSWBDM, 3220/1878.

44   Robert 'Nosey Bob' Howard (*1832–1906*) 2009, p. 2.

45   Edward Hawkins and Mary Ann Howard: Marriage, 20 May 1879, NSWBDM, 1847/1879; *Empire*, 27 November 1873, p. 2.

46   *Evening News*, 19 February 1879, p. 2; *Family History: Indigenous Names*, Australian Institute of Aboriginal and Torres Strait Islander Studies, Canberra, <aiatsis.gov.au/family-history/you-start/indigenous-names>; Andy Kaladelfos, 'The "condemned criminals"', *Women's History Review*, vol. 21, no. 5, 2012, p. 703.

47   There were fifty-two people hanged in 1829. Out of 111 sentences handed down that year, forty-six people were hanged in addition to six executions carried over from 1828. Peter N Grabosky, *Sydney in Ferment*, Australian National University Press, Canberra, 1977, p. 11; *NSW Capital Convictions Database, 1788–1954*, Francis Forbes Society for Australian Legal History, Sydney, <research.forbessociety.org.au>.

48 *Sydney Morning Herald*, 5 July 1879, p. 3.

49 *Sydney Gazette and New South Wales Advertiser*, 15 December 1840, p. 2.

50 Colonial Secretary's Papers, Special Bundles [Petitions: An Aboriginal named Alfred, Alexander Metcalf and Charles E Wilkinson], 1874–1900, 1879, NSWSA, NRS-906 [4/6029]; Kaladelfos 2012, pp. 703–10; *Evening News*, 7 June 1879, p. 4; *Sydney Morning Herald*, 5 July 1879, p. 3.

51 Sylvia Lawson, *Archibald's Paradox*, Miegunyah Press, Melbourne, [1983]2006, pp. 64–65.

52 Lawson [1983]2006, p. 68; *Gundagai Times and Tumut, Adelong and Murrumbidgee District Advertiser*, 13 June 1879, p. 3; *Sydney Mail and New South Wales Advertiser*, 14 June 1879, p. 950.

53 *Evening News*, 10 June 1879, p. 3.

54 *Sydney Mail and New South Wales Advertiser*, 14 June 1879, p. 950.

55 Archibald Family Papers [JF Archibald, Notebooks], 1872–1919, 1879, SLNSW, A 2256, vol. 7, p. 123.

56 *Daily Telegraph*, 8 July 1879, p. 2; *Evening News*, 7 July 1879, p. 2.

57 Alexander Green: Death, 31 August 1879, NSWBDM, 8129/1879; *Freeman's Journal*, 18 August 1877, p. 17; Harrison 2017, pp. 191–94; Copies of Letters Sent [Sheriff], 1831–1923, 4 April 1867, NSWSA, NRS-13210; Robert Elliott: Death, 24 May 1871, NSWBDM, 551/1871; Beckett & Beckett 1980, p. 187; *Evening News*, 26 May 1871, p. 2; *Evening News*, 12 May 1873, p. 2; John [Joseph] Bull: Death, 9 May 1873, NSWBDM, 4752/1873.

3 IN THE SWING OF THINGS

1 Garry Linnell, *Moonlite*, Michael Joseph, Sydney, 2020, pp. 255–65; *Sydney Morning Herald*, 12 December 1879, p. 8.

2 *Sydney Morning Herald*, 1 January 1880, p. 3; *Freeman's Journal*, 3 January 1880, p. 16; *Sydney Morning Herald*, 31 December 1879, p. 7.

3 *Bulletin*, 31 January 1880, pp. 4–5.

4 *Bulletin*, 31 January 1880, p. 5.

5 *Sands Sydney, Suburban and Country Commercial Directory*, John Sands Ltd, Sydney, 1876–79; Robert Rice Howard: Birth, 14 March & 12 March 1832, Parish Register of the Holy Trinity Church, County of Norfolk, lines 525, 653 [father a labourer]; Robert Rice Howard and Jane Townsend: Marriage, 26 October 1858, GROEW, MXH 826435 [father a coachman]; Robert Rice Howard: Death, 3 February 1906, NSWBDM, 3518/1906 [father a gardener]; *Burrangong Argus*, 26 July 1876, p. 3; *Evening News*, 10 June 1879, p. 3; *Mudgee Guardian and North-Western Representative*, 25 February 1915, p. 6.

6 *Bulletin*, 31 January 1880, p. 5.

7 *Bulletin*, 31 January 1880, p. 5.

8 *Bulletin*, 31 January 1880, p. 5.

9   *Evening News*, 20 January 1880, p. 3; *Bulletin*, 31 January 1880, pp. 4–6; Darlinghurst Gaol Death Register, 1867–1914 [transcript].

10   *Bulletin*, 31 January 1880, pp. 6.

11   *Armidale Express and New England General Advertiser*, 4 June 1880, p. 3; R v Murrell and Bummaree [1836] NSWSupC 35 (5 February 1836).

12   *Maitland Mercury and Hunter River General Advertiser*, 10 April 1880, p. 6.

13   *Burrowa News*, 7 May 1880, p. 2; *Freeman's Journal*, 22 May 1880, p. 16; *Sydney Morning Herald*, 15 May 1880, p. 5.

14   *Armidale Express and New England General Advertiser*, 4 June 1880, p. 3.

15   *Armidale Express and New England General Advertiser*, 9 January 1880, p. 3; *Daily Telegraph*, 1 January 1880, p. 3.

16   *Armidale Express and New England General Advertiser*, 9 January 1880, p. 3; Kate Bagnall, 'Rewriting the history of Chinese families in nineteenth-century Australia', *Australian Historical Studies*, vol. 42, no. 1, 2011, pp. 66, 68.

17   *Sydney Gazette and New South Wales Advertiser*, 14 September 1811, p. 2; *Family Law Act 1975* (Cth), *Sydney Morning Herald*, 6 March 1862, p. 2; *Sydney Morning Herald*, 14 December 1887, p. 7.

18   *Maitland Mercury and Hunter River General Advertiser*, 8 April 1880, p. 6; *Armidale Express and New England General Advertiser*, 9 January 1880, p. 3.

19   *Armidale Express and New England General Advertiser*, 18 June 1880, p. 6.

20   *Bulletin*, 31 January 1880, p. 5.

21   Michel Foucault, *Discipline and Punish*, A Sheridan (trans), Penguin Books, London, [1977]1991, p. 10.

22   Secretary of State for the Colonies, 'Circulars on capital punishment', 27 June 1880, QSA, ITM17282.

23   Secretary of State for the Colonies 27 June 1880, ITM17282.

24   Secretary of State for the Colonies 27 June & 28 December 1880, ITM17282.

25   Charles Edward Hawkins: Death, 28 March 1880, NSWBDM, 3798/1880; William Sidney Hawkins: Birth, 24 June 1881, NSWBDM, 8732/1881; Ulric Edward Hawkins: Birth, 24 May 1884, NSWBDM, 15989/1884; Ulric Edward Hawkins: Death, 12 November 1884, NSWBDM, 7513/1884; Jane Mary Hawkins: Birth, 2 August 1886, NSWBDM, 17316/1886; Victor Thomas Albert Hawkins: Birth, 22 November 1889, NSWBDM, 30537/1890; Reginald Malcolm Lyle Hawkins: Birth, 21 September 1894, NSWBDM, 29654/1894.

26   Robert Howard's occupation, on his daughter's death certificate, is freeholder. The certificate also states that Emily Howard spent eighteen months in Victoria, but this is likely an error as there is no reference to the time spent in Queensland upon her arrival in Australia. A son of Robert

and Jane Howard, deceased, is listed on the birth records of Fanny, Sydney and William Howard. Emily Jane Howard: Death, 20 December 1880, NSWBDM, 3998/1880; Fanny Howard: Birth, 13 June 1867, RBDB, line 7155; Sydney Howard: Birth, 5 November 1869, NSWBDM, 16207/1869; William George Howard: Birth, 30 June 1872, NSWBDM, 1660/1872.

27   Bruce Kercher, *An Unruly Child*, Routledge, Oxford, [1995]2020, p. xi; David Collins, *An Account of the English Colony in New South Wales*, vol. I, Cadell & Davies, London, 1798, p. 11.

28   An example of David Collins setting legal precedent is his acknowledgment that convicts, under felony attaint, had property rights. Collins ordered Duncan Sinclair, Master of the *Alexander*, to pay £15 to Henry and Susannah Cable in compensation for their lost baggage. Cable v Sinclair [1788] NSWSupC 7; [1788] NSWKR 7 (1 July 1788); FM Bladen (ed.), *Historical Records of New South Wales, Hunter, 1796–1799*, vol. III, Government Printer, Sydney, 1895, p. 597.

29   Collins 1798, p. 11.

30   David J Rothman, *The Discovery of the Asylum*, rev. ed., Routledge, Oxford, [2002]2017, p. xxiv; Pieter Spierenburg, *A History of Murder*, Polity Press, Cambridge, 2008, p. 173; Daniel Arasse, *The Guillotine and the Terror*, C Miller (trans), Penguin Books, London, [1987]1989, p. 124.

31   *Act to Regulate the Execution of Criminals 1855*, 17 Vict. no. 40 (NSW); Steven Anderson, *A History of Capital Punishment in the Australian Colonies, 1788–1900*, Palgrave Macmillan, London, 2020, p. 146; James Gregory, *Victorians Against the Gallows*, Bloomsbury, London, [2012]2020, p. 41.

32   Anderson 2020, p. 135.

33   *Substitution of Punishments of Death Act 1841*, 4 & 5 Vict. c.56 (UK); Anderson 2020, pp. 24–25.

34   Anderson 2020, p. 30; Henry Carey Dangar, in *NSW Parliamentary Hansard*, Legislative Assembly, 14 September 1882, p. 412.

35   *Sydney Morning Herald*, 29 March 1881, p. 5; *Evening News*, 29 March 1881, p. 2.

36   *Evening News*, 22 February 1881, p. 2; *Sydney Morning Herald*, 22 February 1881, p. 7.

37   *Evening News*, 22 February 1881, p. 2; *Evening News*, 29 March 1881, p. 2; *Act to Regulate the Execution of Criminals 1855*, 17 Vict. no. 40 (NSW), s. 2.

38   *Sydney Mail and New South Wales Advertiser*, 16 April 1881, p. 629.

39   *Wagga Wagga Advertiser*, 4 June 1881, p. 2; *Ovens and Murray Advertiser*, 2 June 1881, p. 3.

40   *Bulletin*, 8 January 1881, p. 1.

41 *Bulletin*, 15 January 1881, p. 2; *Freeman's Journal*, 21 May 1881, p. 16.

42 *Australian Town and Country Journal*, 11 March 1882, p. 8.

43 *Mudgee Guardian and North-Western Representative*, 25 February 1915, p. 6; *Truth*, 5 June 1904, p. 7; *Cobargo Chronicle*, 20 January 1899, p. 4; *Truth*, 14 November 1915, p. 16.

44 *Robert 'Nosey Bob' Howard (1832–1906)*, WLLSC, Sydney, 2009, p. 2; *Arrow*, 27 May 1899, p. 5.

45 *Daily Telegraph*, 16 March 1882, p. 3.

46 *Daily Telegraph*, 5 April 1882, p. 4.

47 *Daily Telegraph*, 5 April 1882, p. 4.

48 *Maitland Mercury and Hunter River General Advertiser*, 29 November 1873, p. 3.

49 *Evening News*, 21 April 1882, p. 2.

50 *Armidale Express and New England General Advertiser*, 24 November 1882, p. 8; *Wagga Wagga Advertiser*, 27 April 1882, p. 2.

51 *Queanbeyan Age*, 20 October 1882, p. 2.

52 *Armidale Express and New England General Advertiser*, 24 November 1882, p. 8; *Manaro Mercury and Cooma and Bombala Advertiser*, 25 November 1882, p. 3.

53 *Armidale Express and New England General Advertiser*, 24 November 1882, p. 8.

4 KEEPING COUNT

1 *Peak Hill Express*, 16 February 1906, p. 17.

2 *Sunday Times*, 12 January 1896, p. 2.

3 *Bulletin*, 31 January 1880, p. 5.

4 *Australian Town and Country Journal*, 24 June 1876, p. 9; *Australian Town and Country Journal*, 8 July 1876, p. 27; *Wagga Wagga Advertiser*, 22 July 1876, p. 2; *Glen Innes Examiner and General Advertiser*, 13 June 1877, p. 5.

5 *Wagga Wagga Advertiser*, 19 December 1877, p. 2.

6 *Sydney Morning Herald*, 1 December 1882, p. 9; *Daily Telegraph*, 8 September 1882, p. 3.

7 *Daily Telegraph*, 8 September 1882, p. 3; *Goulburn Evening Penny Post*, 12 October 1882, p. 4.

8 *Daily Telegraph*, 13 October 1882, p. 3.

9 *Queanbeyan Age*, 29 November 1882, p. 2; *Goulburn Herald*, 30 November 1882, p. 2.

10 *Sunday Times*, 12 January 1896, p. 2.

11 *Manaro Mercury and Cooma and Bombala Advertiser*, 2 December 1882, p. 3.

12 *Riverine Herald*, 20 July 1882, p. 3.

13 *Riverine Herald*, 20 July 1882, p. 3.

14   *Sydney Morning Herald*, 21 October 1882, p. 12; *Sydney Morning Herald*, 23 October 1882, p. 8.

15   *Sydney Mail and New South Wales Advertiser*, 4 November 1882, p. 800; *Goulburn Evening Penny Post*, 26 October 1882, p. 4.

16   *Sydney Morning Herald*, 23 October 1882, p. 8; *Sydney Morning Herald*, 16 October 1882, p. 5; *Newcastle Morning Herald and Miners' Advocate*, 8 November 1882, p. 2; *Armidale Express and New England General Advertiser*, 24 November 1882, p. 3.

17   *Albury Banner and Wodonga Express*, 3 November 1882, p. 15.

18   *Sydney Mail and New South Wales Advertiser*, 18 November 1882, p. 895.

19   *Armidale Express and New England General Advertiser*, 15 December 1882, p. 4.

20   *Truth*, 18 July 1897, p. 7; *Molong Argus*, 3 February 1899, p. 8; *Yass Evening Tribune*, 16 February 1899, p. 1; *Crookwell Gazette*, 21 February 1899, p. 4; *Voice*, 2 May 1936, p. 1.

21   Mahmoud Rayes et al., 'Hangman's fracture', *Journal of Neurosurgery*, vol. 14, February, 2011, pp. 198–208.

22   Kevin Morgan, *The Particulars of Executions 1894–1967*, Old Melbourne Gaol, Melbourne, 2004, pp. 10–15.

23   *Goulburn Herald*, 12 December 1882, p. 2.

24   *Goulburn Herald*, 12 December 1882, p. 2; *Albury Banner and Wodonga Express*, 15 December 1882, p. 15; *Armidale Express and New England General Advertiser*, 15 December 1882, p. 4.

25   *Evening News*, 17 March 1883, p. 4.

26   *Evening News*, 17 March 1883, p. 4.

27   *Daily Telegraph*, 20 March 1883, p. 3.

28   *Goulburn Evening Penny Post*, 20 March 1883, p. 2; *Southern Argus*, 22 March 1883, p. 3; *Armidale Express and New England General Advertiser*, 23 March 1883, p. 6.

29   *Maitland Mercury and Hunter River General Advertiser*, 24 March 1883, p. 8; *Evening News*, 31 March 1883, p. 3.

30   *Sydney Morning Herald*, 14 April 1883, p. 12.

31   *Queanbeyan Age*, 17 April 1883, p. 2.

32   *North-Eastern Ensign*, 27 April 1883, p. 2.

33   *Sunday Times*, 12 January 1896, p. 2.

34   *Truth*, 18 July 1897, p. 7.

35   *Sunday Times*, 12 January 1896, p. 2.

36   *Cobargo Chronicle*, 20 January 1899, p. 4.

37   *Bega Gazette and Eden District or Southern Coast Advertiser*, 2 June 1883, p. 2; *Newcastle Morning Herald and Miners' Advocate*, 24 May 1883, p. 2; *Clarence and Richmond Examiner and New England Advertiser*, 26 May 1883, p. 5; *Armidale Express and New England General Advertiser*, 25 May 1883, p. 8.

38 *Australian Town and Country Journal*, 26 May 1883, p. 11.

39 *Truth*, 30 September 1900, p. 7.

40 JH Heaton, *Australian Dictionary of Dates and Men of the Time*, George Robertson, Sydney, 1879, p. 90; *Sydney Gazette and New South Wales Advertiser*, 22 October 1828, p. 2.

41 *Maitland Mercury and Hunter River General Advertiser*, 29 June 1853, p. 4; *Gympie Times and Mary River Mining Gazette*, 25 February 1874, p. 3.

42 *Arrow*, 25 February 1899, p. 6.

43 *Maitland Weekly Mercury*, 21 July 1894, p. 16.

44 *Evening News*, 29 February 1884, p. 3.

45 *Evening News*, 23 April 1884, p. 5.

46 *Evening News*, 23 April 1884, p. 5.

47 *Daily Telegraph*, 19 April 1884, p. 5; *Evening News*, 14 May 1884, p. 8.

48 *Daily Telegraph*, 7 May 1884, p. 5; *Daily Telegraph*, 12 June 1884, p. 8; *Evening News*, 14 May 1884, p. 8.

49 *Newcastle Morning Herald and Miners' Advocate*, 14 June 1884, p. 4; *Goulburn Evening Penny Post*, 14 June 1884, p. 4; *Bendigo Advertiser*, 19 March 1889, p. 1.

5 THE HORROR OF BOTCHED HANGINGS

1   Harry Bullenthorpe and Fanny Howard: Marriage, 4 April 1885, Parish Register of the Church of St Peter, County of Cumberland, line 570; Maria Frances Bullenthorpe: Death, 13 April 1885, NSWBDM, 5026/1885.

2   *Sydney Morning Herald*, 14 April 1885, p. 14; *Evening News*, 14 April 1885, p. 5.

3   *Evening News*, 14 April 1885, p. 5.

4   *Evening News*, 14 April 1885, p. 5; *Singleton Argus*, 15 April 1885, p. 2; *Burrowa News*, 24 April 1885, p. 2.

5   *Act to Regulate the Execution of Criminals 1855*, 17 Vict. no. 40 (NSW); *Criminal Law Amendment Act 1883*, 46 Vict. no. 17 (NSW), s. 391.

6   *Daily Telegraph*, 24 April 1884, p. 6; *Newcastle Morning Herald and Miners' Advocate*, 14 June 1884, p. 4; *Evening News*, 15 April 1885, p. 3.

7   *Gundagai Times and Tumut, Adelong and Murrumbidgee District Advertiser*, 9 June 1885, p. 4.

8   *Gundagai Times and Tumut, Adelong and Murrumbidgee District Advertiser*, 9 June 1885, p. 4.

9   *Gundagai Times and Tumut, Adelong and Murrumbidgee District Advertiser*, 9 June 1885, p. 4; *Sydney Morning Herald*, 14 July 1885, p. 5.

10 *Sydney Morning Herald*, 15 July 1885, p. 6; Darlinghurst Gaol Death Register, 1867–1914 [transcript].

11 *Daily Telegraph*, 8 August 1885, p. 5; *Daily Telegraph*, 12 August 1885, p. 5.

12   *Sydney Mail and New South Wales Advertiser*, 5 December 1885, p. 1212.
13   *Evening News*, 11 December 1885, p. 6.
14   *Bathurst Free Press and Mining Journal*, 12 March 1853, p. 3; *Sydney Morning Herald*, 8 March 1853, p. 2.
15   *Bell's Life in Sydney and Sporting Reviewer*, 19 March 1853, p. 2.
16   *Bathurst Free Press and Mining Journal*, 16 April 1853, p. 2.
17   *Bathurst Free Press and Mining Journal*, 16 April 1853, p. 2.
18   *Bathurst Free Press and Mining Journal*, 16 April 1853, p. 2.
19   *Freeman's Journal*, 23 April 1853, p. 3; Pamela Harrison, 'The life of Alexander Green revisited', *Journal of the Royal Australian Historical Society*, vol. 103, no. 2, 2017, p. 191; Ray Beckett & Richard Beckett, *Hangman*, Thomas Nelson, Melbourne, 1980, p. 180.
20   *Northern Star*, 16 June 1886, p. 3; *Evening News*, 21 April 1886, p. 6; *Sydney Morning Herald*, 20 April 1886, p. 8; *Clarence and Richmond Examiner and New England Advertiser*, 13 February 1886, p. 4.
21   *Goulburn Evening Penny Post*, 30 March 1886, p. 2; *Burrowa News*, 23 April 1886, p. 3.
22   *Northern Star*, 16 June 1886, p. 3; *Sydney Morning Herald*, 21 April 1886, p. 12.
23   *Northern Star*, 16 June 1886, p. 3.
24   *Clarence and Richmond Examiner and New England Advertiser*, 3 July 1886, p. 4.
25   *Sydney Morning Herald*, 21 July 1853, p. 2; *South Australian Advertiser*, 8 October 1858, p. 2.
26   *Australian*, 15 February 1844, p. 3; *Bell's Life in Sydney and Sporting Reviewer*, 25 September 1852, p. 2.
27   *Bell's Life in Sydney and Sporting Reviewer*, 9 November 1850, p. 1.
28   Steven Anderson, *A History of Capital Punishment in the Australian Colonies, 1788–1900*, Palgrave Macmillan, London, 2020, p. 140.
29   *Sydney Morning Herald*, 21 July 1853, p. 2.
30   *Sydney Morning Herald*, 21 July 1853, p. 2; Jane Lydon & Lyndall Ryan, 'Introduction', J Lydon & L Ryan (eds), *Remembering the Myall Creek Massacre*, NewSouth, Sydney, 2018, pp. 3–4; *Freeman's Journal*, 23 July 1853, p. 7.
31   *Act to Regulate the Execution of Criminals 1855*, 17 Vict. no. 40 (NSW), ss. 1–2.
32   *Act to Regulate the Execution of Criminals 1855*, 17 Vict. no. 40 (NSW), s. 4.
33   Anderson 2020, p. 101.
34   *Queanbeyan Age*, 1 June 1878, p. 1; *Armidale Express and New England General Advertiser*, 4 June 1880, p. 3.
35   *Sydney Morning Herald*, 1 September 1886, p. 7.
36   *Evening News*, 8 October 1886, p. 5.
37   *Evening News*, 8 October 1886, p. 5.

38   *Singleton Argus*, 11 September 1886, p. 2; Kate Gleeson, 'From centenary to the Olympics, gang rape in Sydney', *Current Issues in Criminal Justice*, vol. 16, no. 2, 2004, p. 189; *Glen Innes Examiner and General Advertiser*, 7 December 1886, p. 4; *South Australian Advertiser*, 17 December 1886, p. 5; *Macleay Argus*, 18 December 1886, p. 2; *Daily Telegraph*, 7 January 1887, p. 5; *Gaol Inmates and Prisoners Photos Index*, 1870–1930, SARNSW, <www.records.nsw.gov.au/archives/collections-and-research/guides-and-indexes/node/1566/browse>; Register of Inquests and Inquiries [Sydney City Coroner], 1862–1941, 7 January 1887, NSWSA, NRS-1783.

39   *Sydney Morning Herald*, 17 March 1841, p. 2.

40   *Bell's Life in Sydney and Sporting Reviewer*, 25 September 1852, p. 2; *New South Wales Government Gazette*, 14 January 1887, p. 330; *Sydney Morning Herald*, 8 January 1887, p. 8; *Clarence and Richmond Examiner and New England Advertiser*, 15 January 1887, p. 4.

41   *Sydney Morning Herald*, 8 January 1887, p. 8; *Clarence and Richmond Examiner and New England Advertiser*, 15 January 1887, p. 4; *Goulburn Evening Penny Post*, 8 January 1887, p. 4.

42   *Clarence and Richmond Examiner and New England Advertiser*, 15 January 1887, p. 4.

43   *Australasian*, 8 January 1887, p. 28; *Sydney Mail and New South Wales Advertiser*, 15 January 1887, p. 128; *Maffra Spectator*, 10 January 1887, p. 3.

44   *Clarence and Richmond Examiner and New England Advertiser*, 15 January 1887, p. 4; *Sydney Mail and New South Wales Advertiser*, 15 January 1887, p. 128.

45   *Goulburn Evening Penny Post*, 8 January 1887, p. 4; Darlinghurst Gaol Death Register, 1867–1914 [transcript]; *Sydney Mail and New South Wales Advertiser*, 15 January 1887, p. 128; *Freeman's Journal*, 15 January 1887, p. 18.

46   *Argus*, 8 January 1887, p. 10.

47   *Goulburn Evening Penny Post*, 8 January 1887, p. 4.

48   *Wagga Wagga Advertiser*, 8 January 1887, p. 2; *Maffra Spectator*, 10 January 1887, p. 3; Secretary of State for the Colonies, 'Circulars on capital punishment', 28 December 1880, QSA, ITM17282; *Goulburn Evening Penny Post*, 8 January 1887, p. 4.

49   *Sunday Times*, 12 January 1896, p. 2.

50   Waverley Council, *Draft Waverley Council Heritage Assessment*, vol. 1, Waverley Council, Sydney, 2020, p. 25; *Evening News*, 17 November 1887, p. 5.

51   *Evening News*, 17 November 1887, p. 5.

52   *Bulletin*, 7 April 1888, p. 9; *Sunday Times*, 12 January 1896, p. 2; *Table Talk*, 20 August 1897, p. 2; *Punch*, 26 August 1897, p. 4.

6 A CRUEL EQUALITY

1   *Queensland Figaro and Punch*, 18 February 1888, p. 15.
2   Steven Anderson, *A History of Capital Punishment in the Australian Colonies, 1788–1900*, Palgrave Macmillan, London, 2020, p. 192; *Hebrew Standard of Australasia*, 26 August 1898, p. 8; Frederick Lee, *Abolition of Capital Punishment*, Hanson and Bennett, Sydney, 1864, p. 44.
3   Lee 1864, pp. 25–29, 4.
4   *Freeman's Journal*, 30 November 1867, p. 9; Anderson 2020, pp. 44–45; R v Bacon [1806] NSWSupC 2; [1806] NSWKR 2 (29 August 1806).
5   Lee 1864, pp. 30–31.
6   James Gregory, *Victorians Against the Gallows*, Bloomsbury, London, [2012]2020, p. 42; *Sydney Morning Herald*, 24 December 1867, p. 5; *Sydney Morning Herald*, 25 February 1868, p. 3.
7   *Armidale Express and New England General Advertiser*, 1 June 1888, p. 3; *Goulburn Evening Penny Post*, 31 May 1888, p. 4.
8   *Armidale Express and New England General Advertiser*, 1 June 1888, p. 3; *Wagga Wagga Advertiser*, 31 May 1888, p. 3.
9   *Sydney Morning Herald*, 19 April 1884, p. 8; *Sydney Morning Herald*, 16 December 1886, p. 3.
10 The available records imply that Henry Bullenthorpe abandoned Fanny Howard soon after the death of their daughter. James Pamment and Fanny Howard: Marriage, 31 July 1888, NSWBDM, 2096/1888. James Joseph Pamment: Birth, 21 November 1888, NSWBDM, 4506/1889; Ethel May Pamment: Birth, 7 February 1891, NSWBDM, 25339/1891; Winifred Jane Pamment: Birth, 13 November 1893, NSWBDM, 27037/1893. James Pamment drowned, with three other men, in a boating tragedy at Botany Heads on 28 March 1895. His wife was 'prostrated with grief' and said he 'never went out boating before' and he only went 'for a day's pleasure'. The community rallied and a concert was held at the Waterloo Town Hall, raising £31 0s 3d for the widow and her children. After the death of her second husband, Fanny had two more children, who were given the surname Pamment. *Evening News*, 29 March 1895, p. 6; *Evening News*, 21 May 1895, p. 6; Dorothy Vera Pamment: Birth, 23 April 1903, NSWBDM, 9452/1903; Walter Maurice Pamment: Birth, 23 December 1905, NSWBDM, 311/1906.
11 *Sydney Morning Herald*, 10 September 1888, p. 4; *Daily Telegraph*, 12 September 1888, p. 2; *Daily Telegraph*, 6 June 1888, p. 3.
12 *Protestant Standard*, 15 September 1888, p. 7; Lee 1864, pp. 14–16; *The Life of John Knatchbull*, H Evers, Sydney, 1844; *Evening News*, 22 August 1888, p. 6.
13 *Australian Star*, 12 September 1888, p. 2; *Evening News*, 11 September 1888, p. 5; *Daily Telegraph*, 12 September 1888, p. 4.
14 *North Australian*, 18 July 1884, p. 5.

15   *Truth*, 18 July 1897, p. 7; *Molong Argus*, 3 February 1899, p. 8; *Yass Evening Tribune*, 16 February 1899, p. 1; *Crookwell Gazette*, 21 February 1899, p. 4; *Voice*, 2 May 1936, p. 1.
16   Caroline Overington, *Last Woman Hanged*, HarperCollins, Sydney, 2014, pp. 8–26.
17   *Evening News*, 13 July 1888, p. 6.
18   *Evening News*, 13 July 1888, p. 6; *Evening News*, 27 December 1888, p. 6.
19   Overington 2014, pp. 81–148.
20   *Evening News*, 10 December 1888, p. 4.
21   *Australian Star*, 4 January 1889, p. 4.
22   *Australian Star*, 4 January 1889, p. 4; *Bowral Free Press and Berrima District Intelligencer*, 22 December 1888, p. 1; *Sydney Morning Herald*, 4 January 1889, p. 4.
23   *Goulburn Evening Penny Post*, 3 January 1889, p. 2.
24   *Daily Telegraph*, 4 January 1889, p. 6; Colonial Secretary's Papers, Special Bundles [Petitions: Louisa Collins], 1874–1900, 1889, NSWSA, NRS-906 [4/895.1 part].
25   *Sydney Morning Herald*, 9 January 1889, p. 7; *Australian Star*, 8 January 1889, p. 5.
26   *Maitland Mercury*, 14 January 1899, p. 14.
27   Overington 2014, p. 236.
28   *Sydney Morning Herald*, 9 January 1889, p. 7; *Evening News*, 8 January 1889, p. 4.
29   *Australian Star*, 8 January 1889, p. 5.
30   *Sunday Times*, 12 January 1896, p. 2; *Goulburn Herald*, 10 January 1889, p. 2.
31   *Evening News*, 2 January 1872, p. 2.
32   *Evening News*, 2 January 1872, p. 2; *Truth*, 2 August 1896, p. 5.
33   *Truth*, 2 August 1896, p. 5.
34   *Evening News*, 2 January 1872, p. 2.
35   *Sydney Morning Herald*, 5 June 1872, p. 5; *Evening News*, 18 June 1872, p. 2; *Evening News*, 15 September 1875, p. 2; Ray Beckett & Richard Beckett, *Hangman*, Thomas Nelson, Melbourne, 1980, p. 187; John [Joseph] Bull: Death, 9 May 1873, NSWBDM, 4752/1873.
36   Tim Castle, 'Watching them hang', *History Australia*, vol. 5, no. 2, 2008, p. 43.4.
37   *Freeman's Journal*, 6 January 1872, p. 7; *Goulburn Herald and Chronicle*, 6 January 1872, p. 5.
38   *Bathurst Free Press and Mining Journal*, 22 August 1889, p. 2; *Daily Telegraph*, 9 June 1886, p. 5; *Australian Star*, 8 January 1889, p. 5; *Report of the Committee Appointed to Inquire into the Existing Practice as to carrying out Sentences of Death* [Aberdare Report], Eyre & Spottiswoode, London,

1888, n.p.; *Maryborough Chronicle, Wide Bay and Burnett Advertiser*, 21 August 1889, p. 2.

39 *Queanbeyan Age*, 24 August 1889, p. 4.

40 *Freeman's Journal*, 6 November 1941, p. 28.

41 GD Woods, *A History of Criminal Law in New South Wales 1788–1900*, Federation Press, Sydney, 2002, pp. 170–73; *Evidence Law Act 1858*, 22 Vict. no. 7 (NSW) s. 11; *Criminal Law Amendment Act 1883*, 46 Vict. no. 17 (NSW) s. 357; *Act to consolidate the Statutes relating to Criminal Law 1900*, no. 40 (NSW), s. 410; *Evidence Act 1995* (NSW), ss. 84, 85.

42 *Sydney Morning Herald*, 19 September 1889, p. 8.

43 *Sydney Morning Herald*, 28 September 1889, p. 12; *Sydney Morning Herald*, 19 September 1889, p. 8.

44 *Newcastle Morning Herald*, 9 October 1886, p. 5; *Cootamundra Herald*, 9 November 1889, p. 5; Lee 1864, pp. 20–21.

45 *Sydney Morning Herald*, 6 November 1889, p. 5.

46 *Daily Telegraph*, 25 November 1889, p. 6.

47 *Burnley Express and Clitheroe Division Advertiser*, 1 January 1890, p. 2.

48 *Albury Banner and Wodonga Express*, 1 December 1882, p. 16; *Illawarra Mercury*, 12 July 1884, p. 4; *North Australian*, 18 July 1884, p. 5.

49 Miscellaneous Notes Relating to Gaols, 1876–92, NSWSA, NRS-13223; *Herald*, 2 November 1889, p. 1; James Barr, 'Judicial hanging', *Lancet*, vol. 123, no. 3171, 1884, p. 1025; *Herald*, 24 June 1879, p. 2.

50 *Australian Star*, 6 November 1889, p. 5.

51 *Sydney Morning Herald*, 7 November 1889, pp. 6, 8; *Australian Star*, 6 November 1889, p. 6; *Australian Star*, 7 November 1889, p. 5.

52 *Goulburn Evening Penny Post*, 7 November 1889, p. 2.

53 *Goulburn Evening Penny Post*, 7 November 1889, p. 2.

7 SHORT AND LONG DROPS

1 *Goulburn Herald and County of Argyle Advertiser*, 13 October 1855, p. 2; *Empire*, 16 May 1857, p. 4.

2 Colonial Secretary's Papers, 1863, NSWSA, NRS-905 [63/1795]; *Sydney Morning Herald*, 1 May 1868, p. 2; *Truth*, 18 July 1897, p. 7.

3 *Manaro Mercury and Cooma and Bombala Advertiser*, 15 July 1876, p. 4; *Queanbeyan Age*, 1 June 1878, p. 1. Henry Lawson wrote his poem 'One Hundred and Three' while he was an inmate in Darlinghurst Gaol (the title of the poem was his prisoner number). Henry Lawson, *The Rising of the Court and Other Sketches in Prose and Verse*, Angus & Robertson, Sydney, 1910, p. 111.

4 *Arrow*, 1 April 1899, p. 5.

5 *Arrow*, 1 April 1899, p. 5.

6 *Arrow*, 1 April 1899, p. 5.

7   Mark Finnane, *Punishment in Australian Society*, Oxford University Press, Melbourne, 1997, p. 126; *Sydney Morning Herald*, 25 July 1914, p. 23.

8   *Sydney Morning Herald*, 25 July 1914, p. 23; Finnane 1997, p. 126; *Sydney Morning Herald*, 28 July 1914, p. 7.

9   *Wagga Wagga Advertiser*, 1 May 1890, p. 3.

10   *Daily Telegraph*, 1 May 1890, p. 3; *Newcastle Morning Herald and Miners' Advocate*, 30 April 1890, p. 5.

11   *Daily Telegraph*, 1 May 1890, p. 3.

12   *Evening News*, 20 October 1888, p. 5; *Wagga Wagga Advertiser*, 15 May 1890, p. 2; *Argus*, 17 May 1890, p. 10.

13   *Australian Town and Country Journal*, 22 November 1890, p. 13.

14   *Bird O'Freedom*, 16 November 1895, p. 4.

15   *Truth*, 18 July 1897, p. 7.

16   James Berry, *My Experiences as an Executioner*, Percy Lund & Co, London, 1892, p. 18; Secretary of State for the Colonies, 'Circulars on capital punishment', 27 June 1880, QSA, ITM17282; *Goulburn Herald*, 27 November 1883, p. 4.

17   *Hillston Spectator and Lachlan River Advertiser*, 4 March 1904, p. 2; *Bulletin*, 1 January 1887, p. 5; *World's News*, 7 July 1937, p. 20. Daniel Frederick Jacobson, of Hurstville in Sydney, designed an improved gallows and secured provisional protection for his invention in 1893, but the protection lapsed and so the device was not patented. FJ Jacobson, 'Correspondence concerning an improved gallows', 1893, NAA, A4618 4544.

18   *Australian Town and Country Journal*, 6 June 1891, p. 41; *Evening News*, 2 June 1891, p. 5.

19   *Australian Star*, 2 June 1891, p. 5; *Macleay Argus*, 8 October 1890, p. 3; *Bathurst Free Press and Mining Journal*, 22 January 1891, p. 2.

20   *Freeman's Journal*, 11 October 1890, p. 16.

21   *Bowral Free Press and Berrima District Intelligencer*, 6 June 1891, p. 2; *Evening News*, 2 June 1891, p. 5.

22   *National Advocate*, 18 November 1891, p. 2; *Wagga Wagga Advertiser*, 19 November 1891, p. 3.

23   *Bathurst Free Press and Mining Journal*, 15 April 1891, p. 3; *Wagga Wagga Advertiser*, 19 November 1891, p. 3.

24   *National Advocate*, 6 October 1891, p. 3; *Wagga Wagga Advertiser*, 19 November 1891, p. 3.

25   *Burrangong Argus*, 18 November 1891, p. 3; *Kiama Independent and Shoalhaven Advertiser*, 20 November 1891, p. 4.

26   *Wagga Wagga Advertiser*, 19 November 1891, p. 3; *Kiama Independent and Shoalhaven Advertiser*, 20 November 1891, p. 4.

27   *Australian Town and Country Journal*, 11 April 1891, p. 11; *Burrowa News*, 27 November 1891, p. 3; *Bathurst Free Press and Mining Journal*, 13 October 1891, p. 3.

28 *Bathurst Free Press and Mining Journal*, 13 October 1891, p. 3; *Riverine Herald*, 8 April 1891, p. 2.

29 *Yass Courier*, 27 November 1891, p. 2; *Burrowa News*, 27 November 1891, p. 3.

30 *Report of the Committee Appointed to Inquire into the Existing Practice as to carrying out Sentences of Death* [Aberdare Report], Eyre & Spottiswoode, London, 1888, cover.

31 *Report of the Committee* 1888, n.p.

32 GD Robin, 'The executioner', *British Journal of Sociology*, vol. 15, no. 3, 1964, p. 250; Samuel Haughton, 'On hanging considered from a mechanical and physiological point of view', *London, Edinburgh and Dublin Philosophical Magazine and Journal of Science*, vol. 32, no. 213, 1866, pp. 23–34; Berry 1892, pp. 30, 34; Charles Duff, *A Handbook on Hanging*, Nonsuch Publishing, Gloucestershire, [1928]2006, appendix.

33 Haughton 1866, pp. 23–34; *Report of the Committee* 1888, n.p.; *Evening News*, 14 April 1885, p. 5; *Singleton Argus*, 15 April 1885, p. 2.

34 Sheriff's Office, SCV, 'Particulars of executions book: Table of drops', 1894–1967, PROV, VPRS 14526, inside cover; Prison Commission and Home Office Prison Department, 'Execution procedures: Table of drops', 1904–06, TNA, PCOM 8/212; Prison Commission and Home Office Prison Department, 'Execution procedures: Table of drops', 1913–14, TNA, PCOM 8/213.

35 Grace Karskens, *People of the River*, Allen & Unwin, Sydney, 2020, p. 465; the *Imperial Acts Adoption Act 1837*, 8 Will.IV no. 2 (NSW) adopted several pieces of Imperial law including the *Act to abolish the practice of hanging the Bodies of Criminals in Chains 1834*, 4 & 5 Will.IV c.26 (UK).

36 Berry 1892, p. 46.

37 *New South Wales Government Gazette*, 6 December 1892, p. 9637.

38 *Evening News*, 10 November 1891, p. 4; *Australian Star*, 10 November 1891, p. 5; *Australian Star*, 17 November 1891, p. 5.

39 *Australian Star*, 21 April 1892, p. 5.

40 *Evening News*, 13 October 1892, p. 6; *Daily Telegraph*, 14 October 1892, p. 5; *Daily Telegraph*, 30 November 1892, p. 5; *Armidale Express and New England General Advertiser*, 2 December 1892, p. 7; *Evening News*, 30 November 1892, p. 6.

41 Prison Commission and Home Office Prison Department, 'Execution procedures: Table of drops', 1904–06, TNA, PCOM 8/212; Prison Commission and Home Office Prison Department, 'Execution procedures: Table of drops', 1913–14, TNA, PCOM 8/213.

42 *Evening News*, 21 February 1893, p. 6; *Australian Star*, 21 February 1893, p. 5.

43 *Daily Telegraph*, 13 April 1893, p. 5; *Sydney Morning Herald*, 27 April

1893, p. 5; *Australian Town and Country Journal*, 20 May 1893, p. 14; *Sydney Morning Herald*, 27 May 1893, p. 9.

44   *Herald*, 13 June 1893, p. 1; Darlinghurst Gaol Death Register, 1867–1914 [transcript]; *Australian Star*, 13 June 1893, p. 5; *Evening News*, 13 June 1893, p. 4.

45   Darlinghurst Gaol Death Register, 1867–1914 [transcript]; *Australian Star*, 27 March 1893, p. 5; *Daily Telegraph*, 27 March 1893, p. 5.

46   *Bulletin*, 27 October 1910, p. 14.

47   *National Advocate*, 13 July 1893, p. 2; *Daily Telegraph*, 6 April 1893, p. 3.

48   *Evening News*, 10 June 1893, p. 6; GD Woods, *A History of Criminal Law in New South Wales 1788–1900*, Federation Press, Sydney, 2002, pp. 172–73.

49   *Evening News*, 10 June 1893, p. 6; *Sydney Morning Herald*, 12 June 1893, p. 8.

50   *Evening News*, 11 July 1893, p. 5.

51   *Evening News*, 11 July 1893, p. 5.

52   *Evening News*, 11 July 1893, p. 5; Haughton 1866, p. 29; *Truth*, 9 January 1898, p. 7.

53   *Macleay Argus*, 16 August 1893, p. 3; *Truth*, 9 January 1898, p. 7.

54   *Truth*, 9 January 1898, p. 7; *Sunday Times*, 12 January 1896, p. 2.

8 A BUSY TIME AT WORK

1   *Australian Star*, 12 July 1893, p. 6.

2   *Australian Star*, 12 July 1893, p. 6.

3   Judith A Allen, *Sex and Secrets*, Oxford University Press, Oxford, 1990, p. 31; John ES McCulloch, 'Baby-farming and benevolence in Brisbane, 1885–1915', *Hecate*, vol. 36, no. 1/2, 2010, p. 48.

4   *Evening News*, 24 June 1892, p. 1; Annie Cossins, *The Baby Farmers*, Allen & Unwin, Sydney, 2013, pp. 173–74; *Evening News*, 20 December 1892, p. 4.

5   Cossins 2013, pp. 70–71.

6   *Sydney Morning Herald*, 5 November 1892, p. 10.

7   *Sydney Morning Herald*, 10 November 1892, p. 4; *Sydney Morning Herald*, 14 November 1892, p. 4; Cossins 2013, pp. 186, 228–229.

8   *Sydney Morning Herald*, 15 August 1893, p. 4.

9   *Sydney Morning Herald*, 15 August 1893, p. 4.

10   *National Advocate*, 10 March 1893, p. 3; Cossins 2013, p. 253.

11   *Nepean Times*, 29 July 1893, p. 4.

12   *Bird O'Freedom*, 15 July 1893, p. 1.

13   *Sydney Mail and New South Wales Advertiser*, 19 August 1893, p. 388; *Bird O'Freedom*, 19 August 1893, p. 1; *Weekly Times*, 19 August 1893, p. 15.

14   *Sydney Mail and New South Wales Advertiser*, 19 August 1893, p. 388.
15   *Weekly Times*, 19 August 1893, p. 15.
16   Edward Charles Howard and Mary Stevens: Marriage, 20 September 1893, Parish Register of the Church of St Matthias, County of Cumberland, line 20.
17   *Bulletin*, 14 October 1893, p. 15.
18   *Sydney Mail and New South Wales Advertiser*, 7 October 1893, p. 743.
19   *Sydney Morning Herald*, 6 July 1893, p. 5.
20   *Daily Telegraph*, 7 July 1893, p. 4; *Australian Star*, 24 November 1893, p. 5.
21   *Australian Star*, 24 November 1893, p. 5.
22   *Australian Star*, 24 November 1893, p. 5.
23   *Northern Star*, 30 September 1893, p. 8; *Barrier Miner*, 30 September 1893, p. 2.
24   *Northern Star*, 30 September 1893, p. 8.
25   *Barrier Miner*, 25 September 1893, p. 4; *Northern Star*, 30 September 1893, p. 8; *Bathurst Free Press*, 29 September 1893, p. 2.
26   *Goulburn Herald*, 2 October 1893, p. 2; *Australian Star*, 27 September 1893, p. 5.
27   *Goulburn Herald*, 23 October 1893, p. 2; *Goulburn Herald*, 8 November 1893, p. 2.
28   *Bowral Free Press and Berrima District Intelligencer*, 22 November 1893, p. 4; *Australian Star*, 29 November 1893, p. 5.
29   *Kiama Independent and Shoalhaven Advertiser*, 2 December 1893, p. 2.
30   *Truth*, 28 November 1897, p. 7; *Australian Star*, 11 July 1893, p. 5.
31   Marian J Borg & Michael L Radelet, 'On botched executions', P Hodgkinson & WA Schabas (eds), *Capital Punishment*, Cambridge University Press, Cambridge, [2004]2009, pp. 156–57; Colonial Secretary's Papers, 1826–1982, 1863, NSWSA, NRS-905 [63/1795]; Josiah Oldfield, *The Penalty of Death*, G Bell & Sons, London, 1901, p. 162; Amanda Howard, *Rope*, New Holland, London, 2016, p. 27; Ryk James & Rachel Nasmyth-Jones, 'The occurrence of cervical fractures in victims of judicial hanging', *Forensic Science International*, vol. 54, 1992, pp. 81–91.
32   *Smith's Weekly*, 3 January 1920, p. 22.
33   *Sydney Morning Herald*, 3 February 1894, p. 9.
34   *Sydney Morning Herald*, 2 February 1894, p. 5; *Daily Telegraph*, 3 February 1894, p. 5; *Sydney Morning Herald*, 5 February 1894, p. 5.
35   *Evening News*, 2 February 1894, p. 4; *Evening News*, 5 February 1894, p. 4; *Evening News*, 4 April 1894, p. 4.
36   *Evening News*, 3 May 1894, p. 4.
37   *Goulburn Herald*, 1 June 1894, p. 2.
38   *Sydney Morning Herald*, 26 May 1894, p. 12; *Sydney Morning Herald*,

28 May 1894, p. 5; *Australian Star*, 31 May 1894, p. 3; *Daily Telegraph*, 22 May 1894, p. 6; *Evening News*, 12 May 1923, p. 6.

39 *Sydney Morning Herald*, 28 May 1894, p. 5.

40 *Sydney Morning Herald*, 1 June 1894, p. 5; *Evening News*, 1 June 1894, p. 5.

41 *Bathurst Free Press and Mining Journal*, 31 May 1894, p. 3.

42 *Bathurst Free Press and Mining Journal*, 31 May 1894, p. 3; *Evening News*, 1 June 1894, p. 5; *Bird O'Freedom*, 2 June 1894, p. 4; *Maryborough Chronicle, Wide Bay and Burnett Advertiser*, 1 June 1894, p. 2; *Naracoorte Herald*, 1 June 1894, p. 3; *Age*, 1 June 1894, p. 5; *Bulletin*, 9 June 1894, p. 14.

43 *Richmond River Herald and Northern Districts Advertiser*, 29 June 1894, p. 4; *Maitland Daily Mercury*, 18 July 1894, p. 3; *Daily Telegraph*, 23 June 1894, p. 5.

44 *Evening News*, 20 July 1894, p. 5; *Maitland Daily Mercury*, 16 July 1894, p. 3; *Newcastle Morning Herald and Miners' Advocate*, 19 July 1894, p. 4.

45 *Evening News*, 20 July 1894, p. 6.

46 *Australian Town and Country Journal*, 28 July 1894, p. 13.

47 *Evening News*, 20 July 1894, p. 6; *Armidale Express and New England Advertiser*, 24 July 1894, p. 4; *Cobargo Chronicle*, 20 January 1899, p. 4.

48 *Sunday Times*, 12 January 1896, p. 2.

49 *Freeman's Journal*, 2 June 1877, p. 9; *Australian Town and Country Journal*, 22 December 1877, p. 40; Archibald Family Papers [JF Archibald, Notebooks], 1872–1919, 1879, SLNSW, A 2256, vol. 7, p. 123; *Bulletin*, 31 January 1880, p. 4; *Ovens and Murray Advertiser*, 2 June 1881, p. 3; *Evening News*, 23 April 1884, p. 5; *Evening News*, 11 September 1888, p. 5; Caroline Overington, *Last Woman Hanged*, HarperCollins, Sydney, 2014, p. 236; *Armidale Express and New England General Advertiser*, 22 January 1889, p. 8; *Australian Star*, 15 November 1890, p. 6; *Armidale Express and England General Advertiser*, 2 December 1892, p. 7; *Evening News*, 1 June 1894, p. 5; *Australian Town and Country Journal*, 28 July 1894, p. 13.

50 *New South Wales Government Gazette*, 17 June 1896, p. 4182; *Public Service List*, NSW Government Printing Office, Sydney, 1897, p. 80.

51 *Evening News*, 10 June 1879, p. 3; *Bulletin*, 31 January 1880, p. 5.

52 *Daily Telegraph*, 16 October 1894, p. 5.

53 *Australian Star*, 10 May 1894, p. 5; *Evening News*, 29 May 1894, p. 6.

54 *Richmond River Herald and Northern Districts Advertiser*, 21 December 1894, p. 4; *Burrangong Argus*, 15 December 1894, p. 2.

55 *Burrangong Argus*, 15 December 1894, p. 2.

56 *Evening News*, 11 December 1894, p. 6; *Burrangong Argus*, 15 December 1894, p. 2; *Maitland Weekly Mercury*, 15 December 1894, p. 7.

9 CRIMINALS AS FODDER FOR THE MEDIA

1 *Sunday Times*, 12 January 1896, p. 2.

2 *Goulburn Herald*, 16 July 1885, p. 4; *Sydney Mail and New South Wales Advertiser*, 12 December 1885, p. 1257; *Armidale Express and New England General Advertiser*, 1 June 1888, p. 3; *Singleton Argus*, 15 April 1885, p. 2; *Northern Star*, 16 June 1886, p. 3; *Evening News*, 20 July 1894, p. 6; *Australian Town and Country Journal*, 28 July 1894, p. 13; *Goulburn Evening Penny Post*, 7 November 1889, p. 2; *Glen Innes Examiner and General Advertiser*, 13 June 1877, p. 5; *Evening News*, 27 May 1880, p. 3; *Armidale Express and New England General Advertiser*, 15 December 1882, p. 4.

3 *Newcastle Morning Herald and Miners' Advocate*, 30 August 1890, p. 5; *Australian Star*, 10 January 1895, p. 5.

4 *Richmond River Herald and Northern Districts Advertiser*, 18 January 1895, p. 8; *Barrier Miner*, 4 February 1895, p. 2; *Evening News*, 31 January 1895, p. 6.

5 *Evening News*, 31 January 1895, p. 6.

6 *Evening News*, 31 January 1895, p. 6.

7 Steven Anderson, *A History of Capital Punishment in the Australian Colonies, 1788-1900*, Palgrave Macmillan, London, 2020, pp. 208-20.

8 John Haynes, in *NSW Parliamentary Hansard*, Legislative Assembly, 24 July 1900, p. 1218; Anderson 2020, pp. 212-13.

9 *Herald*, 24 June 1879, p. 2.

10 *Evening News*, 31 January 1895, p. 6; Eunice May Howard: Birth, 2 July 1895, NSWBDM, 28113/1895.

11 Catie Gilchrist, *Murder, Misadventure and Miserable Ends*, HarperCollins, Sydney, 2019, pp. 304-17; *Australian Star*, 9 December 1895, p. 7.

12 *Armidale Express and New England General Advertiser*, 6 September 1895, p. 5; *Evening News*, 18 September 1895, p. 4.

13 *Australian Star*, 3 January 1896, p. 3; Anderson 2020, p. 45; Albert John Gould, in *NSW Parliamentary Hansard*, Legislative Assembly, 7 July 1896, p. 1357.

14 *Sydney Morning Herald*, 7 January 1896, p. 6; Thomas Meredith Sheridan, 'Epitome de ma vie [Abridgement of my life]', 1896, SLNSW, MLMSS 6526, p. 44.

15 *Evening News*, 4 January 1896, p. 3.

16 *Evening News*, 7 January 1896, p. 6; *Armidale Express and New England General Advertiser*, 10 January 1896, p. 4; *Truth*, 12 January 1896, p. 5; *Glen Innes Examiner and General Advertiser*, 10 January 1896, p. 2.

17 *Sunday Times*, 12 January 1896, p. 2.

18 *Sunday Times*, 12 January 1896, p. 2; Howard, Robert [vertical file]: 'Nosey Bob' the Hangman, 1832-1906, WLLSC, VF HOWA; Borough of

Waverley, Bondi Ward, Rate Books, 1884–1923, WLLSC; *Truth*, 18 July 1897, p. 7; *Critic*, 18 May 1904, p. 7; *Wagga Wagga Advertiser*, 19 April 1884, p. 2.

19   *Sunday Times*, 12 January 1896, p. 2.

20   *Sunday Times*, 12 January 1896, p. 2.

21   Sidney Howard and Elizabeth Donohue: Marriage, 3 February 1896, NSWBDM, 332/1896; Florence Emily Howard: Birth, 3 May 1896, NSWBDM, 9970/1896; Sydney Howard [Junior]: Birth, 19 January 1898, NSWBDM, 363/1898; Elsie May Howard: Birth, 10 September 1900, NSWBDM, 28323/1900; Ruby Howard: Birth, 28 May 1902, NSWBDM, 27605/1902; Jane Howard: Birth, 28 May 1902,NSWBDM, 27606/1902; Vera Howard: Birth, 16 October 1906, NSWBDM, 40486/1906; Edith Howard: Birth, 12 March 1909, NSWBDM, 20404/1909; Doris Howard: Birth, 27 September 1912, NSWBDM, 36805/1912.

22   *Critic*, 18 May 1904, p. 7; Anderson 2020, p. 189.

23   *Supplement to the New South Wales Government Gazette*, 17 June 1896, p. 4155.

24   *Free Lance*, 19 September 1896, p. 10.

25   *Free Lance*, 19 September 1896, p. 10.

26   *Goulburn Evening Penny Post*, 28 November 1891, p. 4; *Evening News*, 30 May 1877, p. 3; *Armidale Express and New England General Advertiser*, 4 June 1880, p. 3; *Leader*, 6 June 1891, p. 23.

27   *Australian Star*, 6 August 1896, p. 6.

28   *Truth*, 2 August 1896, p. 5; Steve Harris, *Solomon's Noose*, Melbourne Books, Melbourne, 2015, pp. 83, 302.

29   *Bulletin*, 31 January 1880, p. 5.

30   *Sunday Times*, 12 January 1896, p. 2.

31   *Sunday Times*, 12 January 1896, p. 2.

32   *Evening News*, 21 May 1897, p. 6.

33   *Singleton Argus*, 19 May 1897, p. 4; *Evening News*, 21 May 1897, p. 6.

34   *Maitland Daily Mercury*, 21 May 1897, p. 2.

35   James Barr, 'Judicial hanging', *Lancet*, vol. 123, no. 3171, 1884, p. 1025.

36   *Maitland Daily Mercury*, 21 May 1897, p. 2; *Evening News*, 21 May 1897, p. 6.

37   *Dubbo Liberal and Macquarie Advocate*, 26 June 1897, p. 2.

38   *Dubbo Liberal and Macquarie Advocate*, 26 June 1897, p. 2.

39   *Sydney Mail and New South Wales Advertiser*, 3 July 1897, p. 46.

40   *Dubbo Liberal and Macquarie Advocate*, 26 June 1897, p. 2.

41   *Sydney Mail and New South Wales Advertiser*, 3 July 1897, p. 46; *Albury Banner and Wodonga Express*, 2 July 1897, p. 31.

42   *Clarence and Richmond Examiner*, 26 June 1897, p. 5; *Sydney Mail and New South Wales Advertiser*, 3 July 1897, p. 46.

43   *Truth*, 27 June 1897, p. 1.
44   *Truth*, 27 June 1897, p. 1.
45   *Truth*, 27 June 1897, p. 1.
46   *Truth*, 8 January 1899, p. 8.
47   *Truth*, 8 January 1899, p. 8.
48   *Molong Argus*, 25 March 1898, p. 1.

10 THE EXECUTIONER'S WORKLOAD EASES

1   Robert Travers, *Murder in the Blue Mountains*, Hutchinson Australia, Melbourne, 1972, p. 10.
2   *Bulletin*, 23 January 1897, p. 13; Travers 1972, pp. 13, 23, 33; *West Australian*, 9 February 1897, p. 3.
3   *Daily Telegraph*, 24 October 1896, p. 16; *Cumberland Free Press*, 12 December 1896, p. 9.
4   R v Butler [1897] NSWLawRp 53; (1897) 18 LR (NSW) 146 (23 June 1897); *Australian Town and Country Journal*, 1 May 1897, p. 32.
5   *Kalgoorlie Miner*, 24 April 1897, p. 5.
6   *Kalgoorlie Miner*, 24 April 1897, p. 5.
7   *Evening News*, 28 April 1897, p. 2.
8   *Evening News*, 23 April 1897, p. 5.
9   *Sydney Morning Herald*, 15 June 1897, p. 5.
10   *Sydney Morning Herald*, 17 June 1897, p. 3; *Sydney Mail and New South Wales Advertiser*, 24 July 1897, p. 203; *Albury Banner and Wodonga Express*, 16 December 1887, p. 16; *Bulletin*, 20 June 1928, p. 55.
11   *Bird O'Freedom*, 15 July 1893, p. 1; *Sydney Mail and New South Wales Advertiser*, 24 July 1897, p. 203.
12   Jason K Foster, *The Dark Man*, Big Sky Publishing, Sydney, 2013, p. 308.
13   *Sydney Morning Herald*, 5 August 1897, p. 5; Foster 2013, p. 308; *Act to appropriate and apply out of the Consolidated Revenue Fund 1898*, no. 35 (NSW), s. III(118).
14   *Sydney Morning Herald*, 17 July 1897, p. 9; *Truth*, 8 January 1899, p. 8.
15   *Truth*, 8 January 1899, p. 8.
16   Sydney Howard [Junior]: Birth, 19 January 1898, NSWBDM, 363/1898.
17   *Evening News*, 25 August 1898, p. 5; *Hebrew Standard of Australasia*, 26 August 1898, p. 8.
18   *Daily Telegraph*, 16 March 1898, p. 6; *Sydney Morning Herald*, 20 April 1898, p. 7; *Evening News*, 10 May 1898, p. 5; *Armidale Chronicle*, 11 June 1898, p. 3; *Newcastle Morning Herald and Miners' Advocate*, 10 August 1898, p. 5; *Northern Star*, 10 September 1898, p. 4; *Sydney Mail and New South Wales Advertiser*, 12 November 1898, p. 1166.
19   *Kalgoorlie Miner*, 24 December 1898, p. 7; *Sydney Morning Herald*, 7 October 1898, p. 7; *Dubbo Liberal and Macquarie Advocate*, 14 December 1898, p. 3.

20   *Truth*, 18 December 1898, p. 5.

21   *Truth*, 8 January 1899, p. 8.

22   *Truth*, 8 January 1899, p. 8.

23   *Truth*, 8 January 1899, p. 8.

24   *Sydney Morning Herald*, 14 December 1898, p. 7.

25   *Burrowa News*, 16 December 1898, p. 2; *Brisbane Courier*, 13 May 1886, p. 3.

26   *Hay Standard and Advertiser*, 24 December 1898, p. 4; *Goulburn Evening Penny Post*, 15 December 1898, p. 4.

27   An article in a Chinese-language newspaper, printed in Australia, suggests that the gallows were 8 feet 2 inches high and that Wong Ming fell 'a few feet'. Yet, gallows frames were generally much higher, not including the pit beneath. For example, the gallows for George Pitt's dispatch in Mudgee Gaol in 1876 was 16 feet high, with a 5-foot deep pit. Also, 3-foot drops were phased out from the 1860s. It is probable that the fall and not the gallows frame was 8 feet 2 inches, especially as this length of rope is so close to Nosey Bob's favourite drop. *Guang yi hua bao* [*Chinese Australian Herald*], 16 December 1898, p. 5; *Australian Town and Country Journal*, 24 June 1876, p. 9; *Dubbo Liberal and Macquarie Advocate*, 14 December 1898, p. 3.

28   *Truth*, 8 January 1899, p. 8.

29   *Truth*, 8 January 1899, p. 8; *Cobargo Chronicle*, 20 January 1899, p. 4.

30   *Daily Telegraph*, 17 February 1899, p. 3; *Evening News*, 20 December 1898, p. 4; *Australian Star*, 16 February 1899, p. 5; *Daily Telegraph*, 21 December 1898, p. 8.

31   *Evening News*, 20 December 1898, p. 5; *Daily Telegraph*, 17 February 1899, p. 3.

32   *Daily Telegraph*, 17 February 1899, p. 3.

33   *Daily Telegraph*, 17 February 1899, p. 3; *Evening News*, 17 February 1899, p. 4; *Queanbeyan Age*, 22 February 1899, p. 3.

34   *Evening News*, 4 April 1899, p. 5.

35   *Evening News*, 5 April 1899, p. 6.

36   *Leader*, 5 April 1899, p. 2.

37   *Evening News*, 5 April 1899, p. 6.

38   *Daily Telegraph*, 17 February 1889, p. 3.

39   Steven Anderson, *A History of Capital Punishment in the Australian Colonies, 1788–1900*, Palgrave Macmillan, London, 2020, p. 7.

40   *Australian Town and Country Journal*, 15 April 1899, p. 57; *Cobargo Chronicle*, 20 January 1889, p. 4.

41   *Smith's Weekly*, 29 March 1919, p. 11.

42   *Truth*, 8 January 1899, p. 8.

43   *Bulletin*, 31 January 1880, p. 5. A horse kicked an omnibus driver in the face in stables at Ultimo. The kick 'fractured his lower jaw in a frightful

manner, and literally smashed in his mouth'. A horse kicked an 8-year-old boy in the face in Woodhouselee, the 'head and face were most frightfully bruised and swollen, the nose broken, the upper and lower jaws fractured, and that the teeth had been driven in'. A horse kicked an older man in the face in Alstonville; he died the following day. A horse kicked a farmworker in the face in the Mornington District. He lost his nose 'and every bone of the face was found to be broken'. A horse kicked a 7-year-old boy in the face in Cootamundra; he lost his nose and died soon after the accident. Famously, a horse kicked Johanna Jorgensen when she was a teenager in the late 1850s, breaking, but not slicing off, her nose and damaging her face. The disfigured Jorgensen decided to dress and live as a man and was subsequently immortalised as 'Nosey Alf' in Joseph Furphy's *Such is Life* (1903). *Sydney Mail and New South Wales Advertiser*, 17 January 1874, p. 89; *Evening News*, 15 February 1877, p. 2; *Daily Telegraph*, 26 April 1895, p. 5; *Age*, 24 March 1898, p. 6; *Sunday Times*, 11 April 1920, p. 2; *Bendigo Independent*, 8 September 1893, pp. 2–3; Joseph Furphy, *Such is Life*, Bulletin Newspaper Co, Sydney, 1903.

44   *Bulletin*, 31 March 1888, p. 9.

45   A horse kicked a man in the face in the Melbourne area in 1870. He lost his nose and the 'adjoining right side of his cheek'. Using a piece of pasteboard and taking skin from the patient's forehead, a new nose was made. The procedure was risky, painful and required multiple surgeries. The doctor was reluctant to perform the reconstruction, but the patient was engaged to be married and insistent a repair be made. DJ Thomas, 'Hospital reports, Melbourne Hospital [operation on John Cooke]', *The Australian Medical Journal*, January, 1871, pp. 12–14.

46   One article claimed that: 'For three weeks prior to an execution Bob is confined in Darlinghurst to keep him sober'. *Wagga Wagga Advertiser*, 19 April 1884, p. 2. This is easily contradicted by looking at Howard's arrivals in regional centres and how he usually only had a day or two to prepare. Also, some jobs were listed on a tight schedule. For example, George Pitt was hanged on 21 June 1876 in Mudgee Gaol and Michael Connolly was hanged on 28 June 1876 in Tamworth Gaol, while John McGuan was hanged on 22 November 1882 in Armidale Gaol and Charles Cunningham on 29 November 1882 in Goulburn Gaol.

47   William Patrick Crick and George Fairhurst Hutchison, in *NSW Parliamentary Hansard*, Legislative Assembly, 13 August 1889, p. 4011.

48   John Mildred Creed, *My Recollections of Australia and Elsewhere, 1842–1914*, H Jenkins, London, 1916, pp. 287–88; *Bulletin*, 1 June 1895, p. 10; *Truth*, 18 July 1897, p. 7.

49   *Smith's Weekly*, 23 February 1929, p. 17.

50   The Oxford Street butchery near Darlinghurst Gaol belonged to Robert McKell. One of the children was Robert's son, William McKell, who

would go on to be premier of NSW and then governor-general of Australia. Chris Cunneen, *William John McKell*, UNSW Press, Sydney, 2000, p. 10; *Truth*, 18 July 1897, p. 7; *Hamilton Spectator*, 5 November 1889, p. 2.

51 *Truth*, 18 July 1897, p. 7.

52 *Week*, 14 February 1885, p. 13.

53 *Sydney Sportsman*, 5 April 1905, p. 3.

54 *Truth*, 16 December 1900, p. 1.

11 A GOLDEN JUBILEE

1 *Daily Telegraph*, 27 August 1900, p. 4.

2 *Wagga Wagga Advertiser*, 28 August 1900, p. 2; *Delegate Argus and Border Post*, 1 September 1900, p. 4.

3 Steven Anderson, *A History of Capital Punishment in the Australian Colonies, 1788–1900*, Palgrave Macmillan, London, 2020, pp. 4–6.

4 RB Walker, *The Newspaper Press in New South Wales, 1803–1920*, Sydney University Press, Sydney, 1976, p. 110; Colonial Secretary's Papers, Special Bundles [Thomas Walker MP, Spiritualist: Canadian Verdict of Murder against for Death of John Saunders, in 1874], 1874–1900, 1889, NSWSA, NRS-906 [4/895.2]; *Bathurst Free Press and Mining Journal*, 6 June 1892, p. 2; *Clare's Weekly*, 15 April 1899, p. 6.

5 Anderson 2020, p. 42.

6 *Sunday Times*, 12 January 1896, p. 2.

7 *Bombala Times and Manaro and Coast Districts General Advertiser*, 12 October 1900, p. 2; *Delegate Argus and Border Post*, 1 September 1900, p. 4.

8 *Sydney Mail and New South Wales Advertiser*, 22 November 1884, p. 1039; *Clarence and Richmond Examiner*, 1 September 1900, p. 4; *Truth*, 14 October 1900, p. 7.

9 *Sydney Morning Herald*, 6 December 1900, p. 5.

10 Queensland: treason, piracy, attempted piracy with personal violence, murder and wilful murder. South Australia: murder (including petit treason), piracy and attempt to murder. Tasmania: murder (including petit treason), attempts to murder by administering poison or wounding, destroying or damaging a building with gunpowder, setting fire to or casting away a ship, attempting to administer poison, shooting or attempting to shoot, attempting to drown with attempt to murder, attempted murder by any other means, sodomy and piracy with attempted murder. Victoria: murder (including petit treason), attempted murder by poisoning or wounding, attempted murder by setting fire to or destroying ships, rape, carnally knowing and abusing a girl under the age of 10, buggery (on a person under the age of 14, or with violence, or without consent), robbery with wounding, burglary with wounding

and setting fire to a house with anyone in it. Western Australia: murder, attempted murder by administering poison or wounding, rape, burglary with violence and treason. Jo Lennan & George Williams, 'The death penalty in Australian law', *Sydney Law Review*, vol. 34, 2012, pp. 667–68.

11   *Criminal Law Amendment Act 1883*, 46 Vict. no. 17 (NSW), ss. 9, 16–17, 39, 41, 103, 177, 212, 215; Lennan & Williams 2012, p. 668.

12   *Australian Town and Country Journal*, 20 April 1889, p. 28.

13   *Slave Trade Act 1807*, 47 Geo.III sess.1 c.36 (UK); *Slavery Abolition Act 1833*, 3 & 4 Will.IV c.73 (UK).

14   *Daily Telegraph*, 24 July 1900, p. 7.

15   *Daily Telegraph*, 24 July 1900, p. 7.

16   Michael Bennett, *Pathfinders*, NewSouth, Sydney, 2020, pp. 99–100.

17   Bennett 2020, p. 101; *Advertiser*, 23 July 1900, p. 6; *Bathurst Free Press and Mining Journal*, 26 July 1900, p. 3; *New South Wales Police Gazette and Weekly Record of Crime*, 10 October 1900, p. 367; *Queenslander*, 10 November 1900, p. 987.

18   *Dubbo Liberal and Macquarie Advocate*, 6 October 1900, p. 3.

19   *Australian Star*, 14 January 1901, p. 5.

20   *New South Wales Government Gazette*, 5 October 1900, p. 7832; *Felons Apprehension Act 1899*, no. 26 (NSW); *Sydney Morning Herald*, 24 November 1900, p. 11.

21   *Sydney Sportsman*, 26 December 1900, p. 7; *Australian Star*, 18 January 1901, p. 5; *Clarence River Advocate*, 22 January 1901, p. 3.

22   *Sydney Mail and New South Wales Advertiser*, 26 January 1901, p. 202.

23   *Queanbeyan Observer*, 5 November 1901, pp. 2–3.

24   *Mudgee Guardian and North-Western Representative*, 4 November 1901, p. 2; *Queanbeyan Observer*, 5 November 1901, pp. 2–3.

25   *Criminal Procedure Act 1986* (NSW) s. 294, inserting *Criminal Procedure Amendment (Sexual Offence Evidence) Act 2003* (NSW) s. 294A; *Queanbeyan Observer*, 5 November 1901, p. 3.

26   *Advertiser*, 21 November 1901, p. 5; *Australian Star*, 21 November 1901, p. 3; *Australian Town and Country Journal*, 30 November 1901, p. 26.

27   *Dungog Chronicle, Durham and Gloucester Advertiser*, 10 December 1901, p. 2; *Mudgee Guardian and North-Western Representative*, 4 November 1901, p. 2; *Maitland Mercury*, 30 November 1901, p. 10.

28   *Evening News*, 5 December 1901, p. 3; *New South Wales Police Gazette and Weekly Record of Crime*, 17 July 1901, p. 277.

29   *Maitland Daily Mercury*, 20 December 1901, p. 3.

30   *Maitland Daily Mercury*, 20 December 1901, p. 3; *Sydney Morning Herald*, 21 December 1901, p. 10.

31   *National Advocate*, 20 May 1902, p. 3; *North Western Advocate and the Emu Bay Times*, 27 June 1902, p. 3.

32   *Queanbeyan Age*, 25 October 1910, p. 2.

33 *Bulletin*, 31 January 1880, p. 5.

34 *Truth*, 8 January 1899, p. 8.

35 *Maitland Weekly Mercury*, 10 February 1906, p. 10; *Truth*, 8 January 1899, p. 8.

36 *Sunday Times*, 12 January 1896, p. 2; *Freeman's Journal*, 17 February 1906, p. 16; *Truth*, 18 July 1897, p. 7.

37 *North Australian*, 18 July 1884, p. 5.

38 *Evening News*, 24 March 1891, p. 5.

39 *Daily Telegraph*, 26 February 1903, p. 8.

40 *Bombala Times and Manaro and Coast Districts General Advertiser*, 17 April 1903, p. 3.

41 *Daily Telegraph*, 26 February 1903, p. 8.

42 *Mudgee Guardian and North-Western Representative*, 26 March 1903, p. 12.

43 Frederick Lee, *Abolition of Capital Punishment*, Hanson and Bennett, Sydney, 1864, p. 23.

44 *Evening News*, 14 April 1903, p. 4.

45 *Evening News*, 14 April 1903, p. 4; *Sydney Morning Herald*, 15 April 1903, p. 8.

46 *Evening News*, 14 April 1903, p. 4.

47 *Truth*, 26 April 1903, p. 3.

12 LAID TO REST

1 *Mercury*, 13 August 1868, p. 3; Steve Harris, *Solomon's Noose*, Melbourne Books, Melbourne, 2015, pp. 244, 247, 302.

2 *Bulletin*, 15 December 1888, p. 18; Eleanor Kiefel Haggerty, *Path to Abolition* [Exhibition Catalogue], Sir Harry Gibbs Legal Heritage Centre, Brisbane, June, 2014, p. 8; *Maryborough Chronicle, Wide Bay and Burnett Advertiser*, 31 May 1886, p. 2; *The Week*, 17 November 1899, p. 28.

3 *Punch*, 25 January 1894, p. 4; *Age*, 16 January 1894, p. 5; *Sydney Morning Herald*, 8 January 1894, p. 6; *Herald*, 15 January 1894, p. 2; *Camperdown Chronicle*, 9 January 1894, p. 3.

4 *Age*, 16 January 1894, p. 5.

5 *Punch*, 25 January 1894, p. 4.

6 *Gippsland Farmers' Journal*, 2 February 1894, p. 3; *Camperdown Chronicle*, 9 January 1894, p. 3.

7 *Armidale Express and New England General Advertiser*, 25 February 1887, p. 3; *Richmond River Herald and Northern Districts Advertiser*, 4 March 1887, p. 2; *Otago Witness*, 4 May 1920, p. 42; *Smith's Weekly*, 11 September 1937, p. 6.

8 *Sydney Morning Herald*, 27 November 1896, p. 5.

9 *Daily Telegraph*, 19 January 1903, p. 5.

10 *Daily Telegraph*, 19 January 1903, p. 5; *Daily Telegraph*, 7 April 1903, p. 7.

11 *Sydney Morning Herald*, 20 January 1903, p. 5; *Maitland Daily Mercury*, 26 January 1903, p. 3; *Australian Star*, 6 February 1903, p. 5; *Evening News*, 20 May 1903, p. 2; *Bligh Watchman and Coonabarabran Gazette*, 10 February 1903, p. 2; *Singleton Argus*, 3 February 1903, p. 2; *Wagga Wagga Express*, 4 June 1903, p. 2; *Scone Advocate*, 10 February 1903, p. 2.

12 *Daily Telegraph*, 7 April 1903, p. 7.

13 *Sydney Morning Herald*, 7 April 1903, p. 3; *Daily Telegraph*, 8 April 1903, p. 10; *Evening News*, 8 April 1903, p. 4.

14 A Brennan, 'The thirteenth juror', *The Incredible Saint*, Frank Johnson, Sydney, c. 1954–55, pp. 62–95; *Evening News*, 12 May 1903, p. 6; *Daily Telegraph*, 7 April 1903, p. 7; *Daily Telegraph*, 20 May 1903, p. 6.

15 *Goulburn Evening Penny Post*, 11 June 1903, p. 4; R v Grand and Jones [1903] NSWStRp 60; (1903) 3 SR (NSW) 216 (9 June 1903); *Mudgee Guardian and North-Western Representative*, 2 July 1903, p. 7; *Act to consolidate the Statutes relating to Criminal Law 1900*, no. 40 (NSW), s. 18(1)(a).

16 *Wellington Times*, 9 July 1903, p. 6; *Goulburn Evening Penny Post*, 9 July 1903, p. 3.

17 *Truth*, 12 July 1903, p. 5.

18 *Newsletter*, 20 June 1908, p. 4.

19 *Sydney Morning Herald*, 17 December 1908, p. 7.

20 *Truth*, 5 June 1904, p. 7.

21 Robert Howard was considered an adult when he turned 21 in 1853. This meant that he spent twenty-three years as a male of full age before he became an executioner, and then spent twenty-eight years on the scaffolds. Howard would spend a little over eighteen months in retirement. *Critic*, 8 June 1904, p. 9.

22 *Sydney Morning Herald*, 27 April 1904, p. 16; *Truth*, 22 May 1904, p. 3; *Government Gazette of the State of New South Wales*, 10 June 1904, p. 4721; Copies of Miscellaneous Returns [Sheriff], 1894–1910, SARNSW, NRS-13230.

23 *Australian Star*, 18 May 1904, p. 6; *Mudgee Guardian and North-Western Representative*, 6 June 1904, p. 2.

24 *Sydney Morning Herald*, 29 June 1904, p. 8; *Supplement to the Government Gazette of the State of New South Wales*, 1 April 1908, p. 1894; *Public Service List*, NSW Government Printing Office, Sydney, 1908, p. xv. The last mention of an assistant executioner appears in the list of 1917. *Public Service List* 1917, p. 57.

25 *Leader*, 1 June 1911, p. 2; *Evening News*, 31 May 1911, p. 8.

26 *New South Wales Police Gazette and Weekly Record of Crime*, 3 May 1911, p. 168; James Golder and Emily Mary Raybould: Marriage, 2 November 1909, NSWBDM, 9990/1909; *Bulletin*, 7 April 1910, p. 6; *Evening News*, 31 March 1910, p. 3.

27   William Howard's death notice advises that he and Lily Coote had a son
      named Bill. William George Howard and Lily May Coote: Marriage,
      29 November 1904, NSWBDM, 9724/1904; *Sydney Morning Herald*,
      4 October 1943, p. 8.

28   Robert Rice Howard: Death, 3 February 1906, NSWBDM, 3518/1906;
      S Hijikata et al., 'Infective endocarditis due to *Treponema pallidum*',
      Canadian Journal of Cardiology, vol. 35, 2019, pp. 104.e9–104.e11;
      KG Ghanem et al., 'The modern epidemic of syphilis', *New England
      Journal of Medicine*, vol. 382, no. 9, 2020, pp. 845–54.

29   *Sydney Morning Herald*, 5 February 1906, p. 10.

30   Funeral Register, Walter Carter Funerals, Sydney, 1906; Grave 82/83,
      Church of England Ordinary, Section 2, Waverley Cemetery; Jane
      Howard: Death, 1 January 1904, NSWBDM, 3667/1904.

31   Nosey Bob's estate at probate was valued at £377 16s 7d. Howard,
      Robert: Probate Packet, 1880–1939, 1906, NSWSA, NRS-13660-
      5-SC001531 in Series 4_36697. Sidney Howard and his family lived
      next door to his father at Bondi while Nosey Bob's other children were
      scattered.

32   *Wyalong Star and Temora and Barmedman Advertiser*, 13 February 1906,
      p. 3.

33   *Australian Star*, 6 February 1906, p. 7.

34   *Bulletin*, 9 April 1908, p. 18.

35   *Smith's Weekly*, 8 March 1919, p. 2.

36   *Smith's Weekly*, 8 March 1919, p. 2.

37   *Smith's Weekly*, 8 March 1919, p. 2.

38   *Sun*, 30 August 1930, p.7; *Sun*, 12 July 1914, p. 11.

39   *Freeman's Journal*, 17 February 1906, p. 16; *Armidale Express and New
      England General Advertiser*, 4 June 1880, p. 3.

40   William Blackstone's work was one of several texts in a small law library
      arranged for David Collins by the Home Office of the United Kingdom.
      FM Bladen (ed.), *Historical Records of New South Wales, Grose and
      Paterson, 1793–1795*, vol. II, Government Printer, Sydney, 1893, pp. 339–
      40; John Currey, *David Collins, A Colonial Life*, Melbourne University
      Press, Melbourne, 2000, pp. 54, 325; Michael Lobban, 'Rationalising the
      common law', A Page & W Prest (eds), *Blackstone and His Critics*, Hart,
      Oxford, 2018, p. 22.

41   William Blackstone, *Commentaries on the Laws of England*, vol. IV,
      Clarendon Press, Oxford, 1769, pp. 11–12.

42   Ronald Ryan had asked for a nip of whisky, but he was given brandy.
      Mike Richards, *The Hanged Man*, Scribe, Melbourne, 2002, pp. 371, 468.

43   Jo Lennan & George Williams, 'The death penalty in Australian law',
      Sydney Law Review, vol. 34, 2012, p. 680; *Commonwealth Death Penalty*

Abolition Act 1973, no. 100 (Cth); *Crimes Legislation Amendment (Torture Prohibition and Death Penalty Abolition) Act 2010*, no. 37 (Cth).

44 *Smith's Weekly*, 19 May 1923, p. 2; *Australian Star*, 9 April 1892, p. 7; *Freeman's Journal*, 21 October 1893, p. 22; Randolph Bedford, *The Snare of Strength*, William Heinemann, London, 1905, p. 294; GA Wilkes, *A Dictionary of Australian Colloquialisms*, Sydney University Press with Oxford University Press, Sydney & Oxford, 1990, p. 129; *Truth*, 6 December 1896, p. 1.

45 Tim Castle, 'Watching them hang', *History Australia*, vol. 5, no. 2, 2008, p. 43.11; *Evening News*, 8 April 1873, p. 2; *Sydney Morning Herald*, 12 July 1873, p. 6; *Illawarra Mercury*, 26 December 1873, p. 2; *Freeman's Journal*, 23 May 1874, p. 2; *Border Watch*, 11 July 1874, p. 4; Darlinghurst Gaol Death Register 1867–1914 [transcript]; *Newcastle Chronicle*, 11 December 1875, p. 6; *Evening News*, 18 April 1876, p. 2; *Evening News*, 21 June 1876, p. 2; *Manaro Mercury and Cooma and Bombala Advertiser*, 15 July 1876, p. 4; *Wagga Wagga Advertiser*, 22 July 1876, p. 2.

EPILOGUE: THE FIRST AND LAST MEN

1 JF Watson (ed.), *Historical Records of Australia*, ser. I, vol. I, Library Committee of the Commonwealth Parliament, Canberra, 1914, p. 304.

2 John Cobley, *Sydney Cove*, vol. I (1788), Angus & Robertson, Sydney, [1962]1980, pp. 87–88.

3 Pease is a 'porridge of compacted peas'. Tom Keneally, *The Commonwealth of Thieves*, Random House, Sydney, [2005]2006, p. 8; Ralph Clark, 'A Journal [First Fleet]', c. 1790, SLNSW, SAFE 1/27a, p. 130.

4 Arthur Bowes Smyth, 'A Journal [First Fleet]', c. 1790, SLNSW, SAFE 1/15, p. 107.

5 George Worgan, 'A Journal [First Fleet]', 1788, SLNSW, SAFE 1/114, p. 26.

6 Duncan McNab, *Waterfront*, Hachette, Sydney, 2015, pp. 11–12; Judith O'Donohue, 'The short life of First Fleeter Thomas Barrett', *Founders*, vol. 50, no. 5, 2019, p. 7; Cobley [1962]1980, p. 91; Convicts Embarked, New South Wales, 1787, TNA, HO 10, piece 6, p. 12; Convict Indents, First Fleet, Second Fleet and Ships to 1801 [James Freeman], 1788–1801, NSWSA, NRS-1150, INX-77-12376; Judge Advocate, Pardons [James Freeman], 1788–1803, 29 February 1788, NSWSA, NRS-5601.

7 Smyth c. 1790, p. 107.

8 *Newcastle Sun*, 7 March 1939, p. 7; *Newcastle Morning Herald and Miners' Advocate*, 8 March 1939, p. 7; *Daily News*, 6 February 1939, p. 1.

9 *Sun*, 7 March 1939, p. 3; *Morning Bulletin*, 9 March 1939, p. 7; *Newcastle Morning Herald and Miners' Advocate*, 8 March 1939, p. 7; *Daily News*, 8 March 1939, p. 2.

10   *Sydney Morning Herald*, 10 August 1939, p. 9; GD Woods, *A History of Criminal Law in New South Wales 1901–1955*, Federation Press, Sydney, 2018, pp. 823–25; Clive Raleigh Evatt, in *NSW Parliamentary Hansard*, Legislative Assembly, 22 August 1939, p. 5758.

11   Sean Johnson et al., *Long Bay Correctional Complex Conservation Management Plan*, Clive Lucas Stapleton & Partners, Sydney, 2004, p. 138.

12   *Government Gazette of the State of New South Wales*, 25 August 1939, p. 4275; *Goulburn Evening Penny Post*, 24 August 1939, p. 5; *Daily Examiner*, 25 August 1939, p. 4.

13   Johnson et al., 2004, pp. 96, 105; Watson 1914, pp. 698–99; JF Watson (ed.), *Historical Records of Australia*, ser. I, vol. II, Library Committee of the Commonwealth Parliament, Canberra, 1915, pp. 355, 434.

14   Johnson et al., 2004, p. 138.

APPENDIX A: EXECUTIONERS OF NEW SOUTH WALES

1   Much of the detail presented in this list is the work of Pamela Harrison, who generously shared her extensive research as well as her time to help craft this chronology of the executioners for New South Wales. Bonnie Wildie, from NSW State Archives, was also of great assistance in completing this work.

2   JHM Abbott, *Bulletin*, 20 June 1928, pp. 55, 57; Ray Beckett & Richard Beckett, *Hangman*, Thomas Nelson, Melbourne, 1980, pp. 36–37, 67.

3   John Ryan was found guilty of stealing food from the colony's food stores with Thomas Barrett, Henry Lovell and Joseph Hall. Barrett, Lovell and Hall were sentenced to death while Ryan was sentenced to 300 lashes. Lovell, Hall and Ryan were reprieved, but Barrett was hanged. There are no primary sources to support the claim that Ryan hanged Barrett on 27 February 1788, but good arguments in secondary sources have been made for Ryan as the man forced at gunpoint to dispatch Barrett, his one-time co-conspirator. John Cobley, *Sydney Cove*, vol. I (1788), Angus & Robertson, Sydney, [1962]1980, pp. 87–88; Duncan McNab, *Waterfront*, Hachette, Sydney, 2015, pp. 11–12; Judith O'Donohue, 'The short life of First Fleeter Thomas Barrett', *Founders*, vol. 50, no. 5, 2019, p. 7.

4   Henry Brewer, the colony's provost-marshal, was the man who fixed the noose around the neck of Thomas Barrett on 27 February 1788. George Worgan, 'A Journal [First Fleet]', 1788, SLNSW, SAFE 1/114, p. 26.

5   James Freeman was found guilty of stealing flour with William Shearman. Freeman was 'pardoned on condition of being the common executioner', while Shearman was reprieved. Freeman received the first official pardon issued in the colony and became the colony's first official executioner. He had to keep the role until he had served his sentence of transportation, for seven years, for highway robbery. Cobley [1962]1980, p. 91; Convicts

Embarked, New South Wales, 1787, TNA, HO 10, piece 6, p. 12; Convict Indents, First Fleet, Second Fleet and Ships to 1801 [James Freeman], 1788–1801, NSWSA, NRS-1150, INX-77-12376; Judge Advocate, Pardons [James Freeman], 1788–1803, 29 February 1788, NSWSA, NRS-5601.

6   John (or William) Johnson appears in several primary and secondary sources, but his dates of service as an executioner are unclear. Several convicts by the name of John Johnson or William Johnson arrived in Sydney in 1788, 1790 and 1791. R v Nicholls [1799] NSWKR 3; [1799] NSWSupC 3; FM Bladen (ed.), *Historical Records of New South Wales, Hunter, 1796–1799*, vol. III, Government Printer, Sydney, 1895, p. 597; Entry for John Johnson [Executioner], Bench of Magistrates Index, 1788–1820, July 1799, NSWSA, INX-11-570; T Crofton Croker (ed.), *Memoirs of Joseph Holt: General of the Irish Rebels in 1798*, vol. II, Henry Colburn, London, 1838, p. 119.

7   Pamela Harrison, 'The life of Alexander Green revisited', *Journal of the Royal Australian Historical Society*, vol. 103, no. 2, 2017, p. 185; Colonial Secretary's Papers, Letters, 1788–1826, 23 January, 29 January & 31 January 1811, NSWSA, NRS-897; *Sydney Monitor*, 21 February 1834, p. 2.

8   Harrison 2017, p. 185.

9   Alexander Green was appointed principal executioner in 1834 replacing Thomas Hughes, but his starting year is often listed as 1828, replacing Henry Stain. Green served as the principal executioner until 1855. Harrison 2017, p. 188; Beckett & Beckett 1980, pp. 66–67.

10   Harrison 2017, p. 191; NSW Death Registration: 513/1846 V1846513 31B.

11   Harrison 2017, p. 191.

12   Robert Elliott was appointed principal executioner in 1855. After his high-profile bungling of the hanging of Henry Manns in March 1863, there was an investigation and Elliott was demoted to the position of assistant executioner. Elliott, despite his reduced standing, still referred to himself as the senior man on the scaffold until shortly before his death in May 1871. Copies of Letters Sent by Gaoler and Visiting Justice [Maitland Gaol], 1849–1877, 16 April & 20 April 1855, NSWSA, NRS 2316; Colonial Secretary's Papers, 1863, NSWSA, NRS-905 [63/1795]; Beckett & Beckett 1980, pp. 186–87; Harrison 2017, pp. 191–93.

13   Joseph Bull was appointed principal executioner in May 1863, a position he held until shortly before his death in May 1873. Colonial Secretary's Papers, 1826–1982, 2 May & 5 May 1863, NSWSA, NRS-905; John [Joseph] Bull: Death, 9 May 1873, NSWBDM, 4752/1873.

14   Robert Elliott: Death, 24 May 1871, NSWBDM, 551/1871.

15 John Franks was appointed assistant executioner in December 1871. Copies of Letters Sent [Sheriff], 1831–1923, 21 November & 5 December 1871, NSWSA, NRS-13210.

16 John Franks was promoted to principal executioner in April 1873, a position he held until his death in April 1876. An obituary on Franks noted he 'had held office for about five years', which neatly covers his service for the sheriff from 1871–76. Copies of Letters Sent [Sheriff], 1831–1923, 21 November & 5 December 1871, NSWSA, NRS-13210; *Evening News*, 8 April 1873, p. 2; *Evening News*, 18 April 1876, p. 2; John Franks: Death, 27 April 1876, NSWBDM, 991/1876; *Albury Banner and Wodonga Express*, 6 May 1876, p. 16.

17 Ernest Henry, or Henry Ernest, Dowling was appointed assistant executioner in April 1873 after he was sentenced to spend twelve months in Darlinghurst Gaol, with hard labour, for burglary in March 1873. After signing on to work for the sheriff, Dowling appeared in court for failure to pay wife maintenance. Copies of Letters Sent to the Colonial Secretary, 1851–1879, 1 April 1873, NSWSA, NRS-1825; *Australian Town and Country Journal*, 8 March 1873, p. 5; *Maitland Mercury and Hunter River General Advertiser*, 29 November 1873, p. 3; *Manaro Mercury and Cooma Bombala Advertiser*, 23 May 1874, p. 2.

18 *Australian Town and Country Journal*, 11 December 1875, p. 28.

19 *Evening News*, 18 April 1876, p. 2.

20 *Australian Town and Country Journal*, 24 June 1876, p. 9; *Armidale Express and New England General Advertiser*, 28 July 1876, p. 2.

21 Robert Howard was appointed assistant executioner in June 1876 and was quickly promoted. *New South Wales Government Gazette*, 17 June 1896, p. 4182; *Public Service List*, NSW Government Printing Office, Sydney, 1897, p. 80.

22 Robert Howard's first job as an assistant executioner was George Pitt in June 1876. His first job as the principal executioner was Thomas Newman in May 1877, with his last job being the double dispatch of Digby Grand and Henry Jones in July 1903. *Australian Town and Country Journal*, 24 June 1876, p. 9; *Glen Innes Examiner and General Advertiser*, 13 June 1877, p. 5; *Wellington Times*, 9 July 1903, p. 6.

23 *Glen Innes Examiner and General Advertiser*, 13 June 1877, p. 5.

24 *Wagga Wagga Advertiser*, 19 December 1877, p. 2.

25 Archibald Family Papers [JF Archibald, Notebooks], 1872–1919, 1879, SLNSW, A 2256, vol. 7, p. 123; *Bulletin*, 31 January 1880, p. 4.

26 *Ovens and Murray Advertiser*, 2 June 1881, p. 3.

27 *Evening News*, 11 September 1888, p. 5.

28 Caroline Overington, *Last Woman Hanged*, HarperCollins, Sydney, 2014, p. 236; *Armidale Express and New England General Advertiser*, 22 January 1889, p. 8.

29   James, or Jim, Goaler is identified by name as assisting Robert Howard at
      the execution of Jimmy Tong in November 1892. It is likely that he also
      assisted Howard at the earlier executions of Thomas Reilly in November
      1889 and Albert Smidt in November 1890. *Armidale Express and New
      England General Advertiser*, 2 December 1892, p. 7; *Australian Star*,
      15 November 1890, p. 6.
30   *Evening News*, 23 April 1884, p. 5.
31   *Evening News*, 1 June 1894, p. 5; *Australian Town and Country Journal*,
      28 July 1894, p. 13.
32   Samuel Godkin was born in Ireland in 1863. He served in the Anglo-
      Zulu War in 1879 and was at the Bombardment of Alexandria in 1882.
      After twelve years in the Royal Navy, and having also worked as a shop
      assistant, page boy and groom, Godkin became the assistant executioner
      in New South Wales. It was noted that after his military engagements,
      he 'had a strong desire for a quiet life', which he found in 1894 'at
      Darlinghurst' working for long-serving hangman Robert Howard and
      then Howard's replacement George Russell. Shortly after Russell's
      appointment as executioner in 1904, Godkin took up a position as a
      cleaner at Darlinghurst Court House before becoming a Court Keeper
      in 1921. Godkin retired in July 1929, after thirty-five years at Sydney's
      great centre of crime and punishment. The battle-weary Godkin also had
      a full personal life. He married Elizabeth Jacklin at St David's Church
      in Surry Hills on 16 May 1892 and had three sons. In retirement, he
      was Vice President of the United Imperial Navy and Army Veterans'
      Association and was appointed a Commission of the Peace in 1940.
      Unlike his former supervisor, Howard, who was regularly snubbed when
      it came to social events, Godkin mingled easily with others and was even
      seen at garden parties at Government House. He died at his home in
      Watson Street, Bondi (an easy walk from Howard's cottage on Brighton
      Boulevard, North Bondi) in 1946. He was 83 years old. *The Sun*, 5 March
      1929, p. 16; Royal Navy Registers of Seamen's Services [Samuel Joseph
      Godkin, Service No. 107188], 1848–1939, TNA, ADM 188, piece 129;
      Daily Telegraph, 12 April 1937, p. 6; *New South Wales Government Gazette*,
      17 June 1896, p. 4182; *Public Service List*, NSW Government Printing
      Office, Sydney, 1897, p. 80; *Government Gazette of the State of New South
      Wales*, 10 June 1904, p. 4721; Copies of Miscellaneous Returns [Sheriff],
      1894–1910, NSWSA, NRS-13230; *Special Gazette for the Government
      Gazette of the State of New South Wales*, 16 December 1921, p. 7280;
      Supplement to the Government Gazette of the State of New South Wales,
      13 April 1922, p. 2317; *Government Gazette of the State of New South
      Wales*, 26 July 1929, p. 3283; *Daily Telegraph*, 6 March 1929, p. 3; Samuel
      Joseph Godkin and Elizabeth Jacklin: Marriage, 16 May 1892, Parish
      Register of St David's Church, Surry Hills, County of Cumberland, line

796; *Supplement to the Government Gazette of the State of New South Wales*, 11 December 1940, p. 4867; *Bulletin*, 14 October 1893, p. 15; *Daily Telegraph*, 8 May 1935, p. 9; *Sydney Morning Herald*, 9 September 1946, p. 14.

33 George Russell was appointed principal executioner in June 1904 and resigned his position in April 1908. *Government Gazette of the State of New South Wales*, 10 June 1904, p. 4721; *Supplement to the Government Gazette of the State of New South Wales*, 1 April 1908, p. 1894.

34 Samuel Godkin worked with George Russell at least once. Copies of Miscellaneous Returns [Sheriff], 1894–1910, NSWSA, NRS-13230.

35 *Public Service List*, NSW Government Printing Office, Sydney, 1908, p. xv.

36 James Golder (or Goaler) was not publicly listed as a salaried executioner, but he was on a government retainer. It was reported that, in contrast to the salary of £156, plus allowances, paid to Robert Howard and then George Russell, Golder was paid £100 per annum and then £10 per hanging. Without anybody to hang, the role was not proving very lucrative and Golder, who is probably the Jim Goaler noted as an assistant to Howard in the late 1880s and early '90s, resigned in 1911. Like Ernest Dowling, Golder was pursued for wife maintenance. *Leader*, 1 June 1911, p. 2; *Evening News*, 31 May 1911, p. 8; *Evening News*, 31 March 1910, p. 3; *New South Wales Police Gazette and Weekly Record of Crime*, 3 May 1911, p. 168.

37 *Public Service List*, NSW Government Printing Office, Sydney, 1917, p. 57.

38 No executioners or assistant executioners are listed by name in the *Public Service List* from 1908, when the permanent position of executioner was abolished. Neither of these positions are listed after 1917.

39 Jo Lennan & George Williams, 'The death penalty in Australian law', *Sydney Law Review*, vol. 34, 2012, p. 660.

INDEX

Notes: A year in brackets after a person's name is the year of their execution.

Page numbers in bold refer to an illustration.

Chinese people in colonial newspapers were often given the prefix 'Ah'. The names for Chinese people, where the surname is unclear, have been listed as published in the *New South Wales Government Gazette*.

Victims, sometimes anonymised in stories of crime, are listed here where their names are known, but the family members of victims and the witnesses that appeared at various inquests and trials are not.

INDEX

NOSEY BOB'S JOB'S DONE.

FIGURE 18 Nosey Bob's job's done

SOURCE *Truth*, 18 July 1897, p. 5

Lightning Source UK Ltd.
Milton Keynes UK
UKHW011054100522
402721UK00001B/31